LET'S BEGIN READING RIGHT

A Developmental Approach to Emergent Literacy

FIFTH EDITION

MARJORIE V. FIELDS
University of Alaska

LOIS A. GROTH
George Mason University

KATHERINE L. SPANGLER
University of Alaska

PEARSON

Merrill
Prentice Hall

Upper Saddle River, New Jersey
Columbus, Ohio

Library of Congress Cataloging-in-Publication Data

Fields, Marjorie Vannoy.
  Let's begin reading right : development approach to emergent literacy / Marjorie V.
Fields, Lois A. Groth, Katherine L. Spangler.—5th ed.
    p. cm.
  Includes bibliographical references and index.
  ISBN 0-13-049491-7
  1. Reading (Primary) 2. Child development. 3. Children—language. 4. Reading—Language experience
approach. I. Groth, Lois A. II. Spangler, Katherine.
III. Title.

LB1525.F43 2004
372.4—dc21

2003042033

Vice President and Executive Publisher: Jeffrey W. Johnston
Assistant Vice President and Publisher: Kevin M. Davis
Editorial Assistant: Autumn Crisp
Production Editor: Sheryl Glicker Langner
Production Coordination: Lea Baranowski, Carlisle Publishers Services
Design Coordinator: Diane C. Lorenzo
Cover Designer: Ali Mohrman
Cover Photo: Corbis
Production Manager: Laura Messerly
Director of Marketing: Ann Castel Davis
Marketing Manager: Amy June
Marketing Coordinator: Tyra Poole

This book was set in Newtext Book by Carlisle Communications, Ltd. It was printed and bound by
R.R. Donnelley & Sons Company. The cover was printed by Phoenix Color Corp.

Photo credits: Marjorie V. Fields, pp. 2, 9, 17, 19, 51, 54, 58, 60, 65, 74, 78, 91, 103, 110, 115, 117, 124, 129, 144, 149,
155, 157, 167, 172, 183, 193, 196, 210, 229, 232, 238, 258, 292, 303, 307, 309, 311, 314, 321, 346, 353, 356, 361, 366, 367,
380, 382, 386, 388; Lois Groth, pp. 6, 12, 24, 44, 88, 93, 128, 132, 134, 136, 162, 180, 185, 206, 214, 220, 224, 235, 240, 263,
275, 283, 290, 306, 363, 372, 377; Tom Priest Photography, p. 14; Bruce Johnson/Merrill, p. 49; Jean-Claude Lejeune,
p. 56; Gail Fleming, pp. 70, 71; Richard Crisci, pp. 81, 85, 121, 152, 242, 339, 343, 384; David Gelotte, pp. 102, 165;
Katherine L. Spangler, pp. 269, 272, 273, 278, 280, 296, 350, 374; Mary Kancewick, p. 285.

Pearson Education Ltd.
Pearson Education Singapore Pte. Ltd.
Pearson Education Canada, Ltd.
Pearson Education—Japan

Pearson Education Australia Pty. Limited
Pearson Education North Asia Ltd.
Pearson Educación de Mexico, S.A. de C.V.
Pearson Education Malaysia Pte. Ltd.

10 9 8 7 6 5 4 3 2 1
ISBN: 0-13-049491-7

*For young children and their teachers everywhere.
In support of meaningful teaching,
meaningful learning,
and meaningful reading and writing.*

EDUCATOR LEARNING CENTER: AN INVALUABLE ONLINE RESOURCE

Merrill Education and the Association for Supervision and Curriculum Development (ASCD) invite you to take advantage of a new online resource, one that provides access to the top research and proven strategies associated with ASCD and Merrill—the Educator Learning Center. At www.EducatorLearningCenter.com you will find resources that will enhance your students' understanding of course topics and of current educational issues, in addition to being invaluable for further research.

How the Educator Learning Center will Help your Students Become Better Teachers

With the combined resources of Merrill Education and ASCD, you and your students will find a wealth of tools and materials to better prepare them for the classroom.

Research

- More than 600 articles from the ASCD journal Educational Leadership discuss everyday issues faced by practicing teachers.
- A direct link on the site to Research Navigator™ gives students access to many of the leading education journals, as well as extensive content detailing the research process.
- Excerpts from Merrill Education texts give your students insights on important topics of instructional methods, diverse populations, assessment, classroom management, technology, and refining classroom practice.

Classroom Practice

- Hundreds of lesson plans and teaching strategies are categorized by content area and age range.
- Case studies and classroom video footage provide virtual field experience for student reflection.
- Computer simulations and other electronic tools keep your students abreast of today's classrooms and current technologies.

Look into the value of Educator Learning Center yourself

Preview the value of this educational environment by visiting www.EducatorLearningCenter.com and clicking on "Demo." For a free 4-month subscription to the Educator Learning Center in conjunction with this text, simply contact your Merrill/Prentice Hall sales representative.

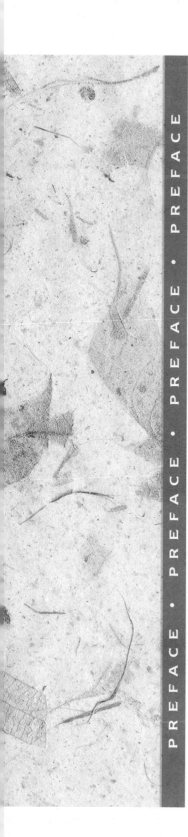

PREFACE

In June 2002, International Reading Association President-elect Lesley Mandel Morrow convened a group of early childhood educators to discuss how the International Reading Association can have an impact on U.S. early childhood programs. "It is expected that early childhood literacy will become a key issue for IRA as the Association seeks to expand its relationships with professionals who are working with young children." The links between early childhood and literacy are strengthening and becoming public knowledge. Politics and policies have embraced early reading, thereby making it the focus of discussion at all levels—national, state, and local—and involving all parties, researchers, practitioners, and parents. Concurrently, professional organizations are becoming increasingly public in their cry for improved practices. What a thrilling time to be working in the field of early literacy!

However, we must be especially cautious, as this burgeoning interest in early literacy is not without its risks. Increased emphasis on accountability correlates with intense pressure to raise children's assessment scores. Many of these high-stakes assessments are inappropriate for young children. We fear that teachers will return to didactic instructional methods that have been discouraged for years. These methods are also inappropriate for young literacy learners.

Now more than ever, we need to remain firm in our commitment to link what we know about how children learn and our teaching practices. Since its first edition, *Let's Begin Reading Right* has focused on how young children construct literacy and the experiences that support its development. We recognize there are naysayers whose voices are many and whose volume is loud. This fifth edition is our response. With it, we continue to spread the word about developmentally appropriate practice.

We start by briefly describing children's learning process in general; then we give some detail on how the learning process works with oral language acquisition. We build from that to explain how youngsters come to understand and use written language. This theory base provides the foundation for all our subsequent teaching descriptions and recommendations. We include numerous examples of children's writing as evidence of children's thinking and hypotheses as they progress in their knowledge of written language. Children in preschool through the primary grades are our main focus, though we briefly address the literacy development of infants and toddlers.

PREFACE

This book is also designed to help the teacher of young children to understand and validate the importance of play in the child's literacy development. We describe how oral language proficiency and meaningful interaction with print are linked to play. We have made a special point of describing print-rich environments that encourage children to explore functional writing. Developmentally appropriate early childhood education practices are further encouraged through recommendations for providing a variety of experiences and oral language opportunities as part of helping children learn to read and write. Teaching examples illustrate the importance of an authentically integrated curriculum for meaningful involvement in literacy events.

In an attempt to dispel the pervasive misconception that isolated drill in skills is better than learning skills in a meaningful context, we carefully explain the development of reading and writing skills within authentic literacy events. Answers to the inevitable questions about teaching phonemic awareness, phonics, and spelling assure the fearful that children are being helped to learn phonemic awareness, phonics, and spelling in the most effective ways. Discussions of reading skills emphasize the necessity of helping youngsters balance their attention to graphophonemic, semantic, and syntactic information when reading. We try to show that this balance is essential for maintaining a focus on meaning while reading. We also explain how writing skills—from learning to form letters of the alphabet to using punctuation effectively—are best learned through authentic reading and writing activities. In addition, we offer a chapter that focuses entirely on selecting instructional materials for reading and writing.

We make sure to discuss assessment procedures that are congruent with comprehensive, holistic approaches to literacy, and we give detailed examples of how effective teaching and assessment occur simultaneously. Chapter 8 explains performance-based assessment, documenting acquisition of literacy skills during children's meaningful involvement with print. The chapter also explains current assessment recommendations in terms of developmentally appropriate practice. As we try to dispel some confusion about performance-based assessment, we also outline the problems inherent in high-stakes, standardized testing. Detailed scenarios of reading and writing instructional conferences in Chapters 6 and 7 as well as Chapter 8 help in visualizing assessment as part of a child-centered approach to teaching.

As in previous editions, our recommendations for teaching literacy combine developmentally appropriate early-childhood practice with research-based views of emergent literacy and holistic literacy. In addition, we link recommendations arising from the latest research on early childhood, emergent literacy, and comprehensive literacy with constructivist learning theory. *Let's Begin Reading Right* continues to remind readers of how young children learn, challenging teachers to use that understanding as the bases for teaching decisions.

CHANGES IN THE FIFTH EDITION

As we worked on this revision, we were again amazed at how much classrooms had changed in the four years since we wrote the previous edition. These changes include modifications in the materials teachers use to teach, the ever increasing level of diversity in the classrooms, and the current "hot" issues. Once again, the most significant change is in the political climate, with direct impact on the classroom. There has been resurgence in the use of skills-based classroom literacy activities, especially in the area of phonemic awareness, phonics, vocabulary, and spelling. We continue to outline authentic learning opportunities in all areas, showing better ways of accomplishing the goals shared by both proponents of isolated skills drill and by those who are convinced that skills are best learned in a meaningful context.

Changes to this edition specifically address phonemic awareness and vocabulary development as well as phonics and spelling. Assessment is another political hotbed. We reaffirm our position against high-stakes testing during early childhood and offer additional options for holistic assessment.

We added to the writing chapters to more fully explain shared and interactive writing. The emergent-writing chapter now mirrors the emergent-reading chapter in its outline of levels of assistance during instruction. Reading to, with, and by students complements writing to, with, and by students and vice versa. Providing the right help at the right time is emphasized for all children regardless of ability or special needs or language or diversity.

As we updated references and materials, we were reminded that technology continues to gain influence in education. We added Internet sources where appropriate and provide an outline for evaluating the utility of computer as well as traditional texts. Teachers need to know more about technology than ever before. We have enjoyed our journey of growth and change as we worked to keep this book current. We are pleased to be able to offer a new edition that reflects our process as well as our purpose, beginning reading right!

ACKNOWLEDGMENTS

Marjorie Fields

I wish to thank my past and present mentors in my quest to better understand how young children learn and become literate: Constance Kamii and Dorris Lee have been extremely influential in my learning. In addition, I have been inspired by all the wonderful teachers who have given me access to their classrooms and let me observe their teaching. Among them are Kathy Hanna, Chris Thomas, Jennifer Thompson, Vivian Montoya, Debbie Fagnant, and Debbie Hillstead. I also want to thank my graduate students who regularly share their classrooms and teaching challenges with me, keeping me grounded in the real world of children, families, and schools. I also appreciate the questions and suggestions from teachers and prospective teachers who have used previous editions of this text. A new source of inspiration and learning is my granddaughter Sarah, who constantly reminds me of the joy of discovering literature with a young child.

I thank my new coauthor Lois Groth for joining the team and making an outstanding contribution to the book. I continue to appreciate coauthor Katy Spangler, who has been my partner through several previous editions.

Lois Groth

I wish to thank Marjorie Fields and Katy Spangler for giving me the opportunity to work on this project. A special thanks goes to Joan Isenberg for her networking and vote of confidence. I am indebted to Greta Fein, who provides endless inspiration. The Annandale Terrace Elementary School community, led by Mary Ann Ryan, has been a model of exemplary education. A special thank you to Michelle Kem, Charlene O'Brien, Cathy Owens, and Tuyen Vu for sharing their practices and their students who are pictured throughout this edition. A tremendous thanks to my children, Kyle, Jennifer, and Sara, for providing me with inspiration as well as daily models of emerging literacy. Finally, it would all be impossible for me without the support and humor provided by my husband, John.

Katy Spangler

I wish to thank the many colleagues, teachers, and loved ones who have made this project possible. The inspiration provided for me early in my career by Joy Lucas, Nancy Hansen-Krening, Dianne Monson, Sam Sebesta, and Phillip Gonzales still guides me. Janice Summers has been a model of extraordinary teaching and has provided exemplary experiences both for me and for my children in her classroom at Eagle River Elementary School. Julia Gibeault provided valuable research assistance when I most needed it. My colleague Marjorie Fields and my husband, Mike McCormick, are models and inspirations to me in their passion for upholding the educational rights of children. My children, Patrick and Mary McCormick, have grown up with this book and are now literate teenagers. Their continued idiosyncratic, unique, and sometimes magical developments in literacy have validated the philosophy of learning that is the basis of our book.

We would also like to thank the reviewers for our manuscript for their feedback and comments: Lisa L. Borden-King, Minot State University; Marcia Broughton, University of Northern Colorado; Adrienne Herrell, California State University, Fresno; Beth N. Quick, Tennessee State University; and Maurine V. Richardson, University of South Dakota.

DISCOVER THE COMPANION WEBSITE ACCOMPANYING THIS BOOK

The Prentice Hall Companion Website: A Virtual Learning Environment

Technology is a constantly growing and changing aspect of our field that is creating a need for content and resources. To address this emerging need, Prentice Hall has developed an online learning environment for students and professors alike—Companion Websites—to support our textbooks.

In creating a Companion Website, our goal is to build on and enhance what the textbook already offers. For this reason, the content for each user-friendly website is organized by topic and provides the professor and student with a variety of meaningful resources. Common features of a Companion Website include:

For the Professor

Every Companion Website integrates **Syllabus Manager**™, an online syllabus creation and management utility.

- **Syllabus Manager**™ provides you, the instructor, with an easy, step-by-step process to create and revise syllabi, with direct links into Companion Website and other online content without having to learn HTML.

- Students may log on to your syllabus during any study session. All they need to know is the web address for the Companion Website and the password you've assigned to your syllabus.

- After you have created a syllabus using **Syllabus Manager**™, students may enter the syllabus for their course section from any point in the Companion Website.

- Clicking on a date, the student is shown the list of activities for the assignment. The activities for each assignment are linked directly to actual content, saving time for students.

- Adding assignments consists of clicking on the desired due date, then filling in the details of the assignment—name of the assignment, instructions, and whether or not it is a one-time or repeating assignment.

- In addition, links to other activities can be created easily. If the activity is online, a URL can be entered in the space provided, and it will be linked automatically in the final syllabus.

- Your completed syllabus is hosted on our servers, allowing convenient updates from any computer on the Internet. Changes you make to your syllabus are immediately available to your students at their next logon.

For the Student

- **Introduction**—General information about the topic and how it will be covered in the website.
- **Web Links**—A variety of websites related to topic areas.
- **Timely Articles**—Links to online articles that enable you to become more aware of important issues in early childhood.
- **Learn by Doing**—Put concepts into action, participate in activities, examine strategies, and more.
- **Visit a School**—Visit a school's website to see concepts, theories, and strategies in action.
- **For Teachers/Practitioners**—Access information you will need to know as an educator, including information on materials, activities, and lessons.
- **Current Policies and Standards**—Find out the latest early childhood policies from the government and various organizations, view state, federal, and curriculum standards.
- **Resources and Organizations**—Discover tools to help you plan your classroom or center and organizations to provide current information and standards for each topic.
- **Electronic Bluebook**—Paperless method of completing homework or essays assigned by a professor. Finished work can be sent to the professor via email.
- **Message Board**—Virtual bulletin board to post and respond to questions and comments from a national audience.

To take advantage of these and other resources, please visit the *Let's Begin Reading Right: A Developmental Approach to Emergent Literacy*, Fifth Edition, Companion Website at

www.prenhall.com/fields

ABOUT THE AUTHORS

Marjorie V. Fields

Marjorie V. Fields is Professor Emeritus of early childhood education at the University of Alaska Southeast. She coordinated early childhood graduate teacher education programs throughout the state of Alaska for many years. A former kindergarten and first grade teacher, she has studied how children become literate for several decades. She has published several articles in professional journals and chapters in edited books on the topic of emergent literacy and has also written the book *Your Child Learns to Read and Write* for parents on that topic (Olney, MD: Association for Childhood Education International, 1998). She has been active in early childhood professional associations, having served as vice president of the National Association of Early Childhood Teacher Educators and also having been on the Governing Board of the National Association for the Education of Young Children. Her proudest accomplishments relate to raising two sons: Michael, an employment law attorney, and David, a structural engineer. Her new focus is her granddaughters Sarah and Caroline, who will be closely documented during their emergent literacy process.

Lois A. Groth

Lois A. Groth is an assistant professor in the Graduate School of Education at George Mason University. A former elementary teacher, she now teaches literacy courses in the elementary education and literacy programs. Lois does staff development in early literacy, most recently with the Fairfax County, Virginia, Office for Children, to develop an Early Literacy Institute for early childhood practitioners. She has three young children, Kyle, Jennifer, and Sara, who help her practice reading and writing right.

Katherine L. (Katy) Spangler

Katherine L. (Katy) Spangler is a professor of education at the University of Alaska Southeast, where she coordinates and teaches in an elementary teacher credential program for students in small, rural communities in Alaska. A former bilingual elementary teacher, she now teaches courses in reading and writing methods and children's literature. She has a special interest in literature for children from Alaska and the North. Katy is the Alaska editor of *Exploring Our United States: The Pacific States* (Oryx, 1994) and frequently gives workshops in Alaskan children's literature. Her two children, Patrick and Mary McCormick, grew up with *Let's Begin Reading Right* and are now in high school and middle school.

BRIEF CONTENTS

CONTENTS

CONTENTS

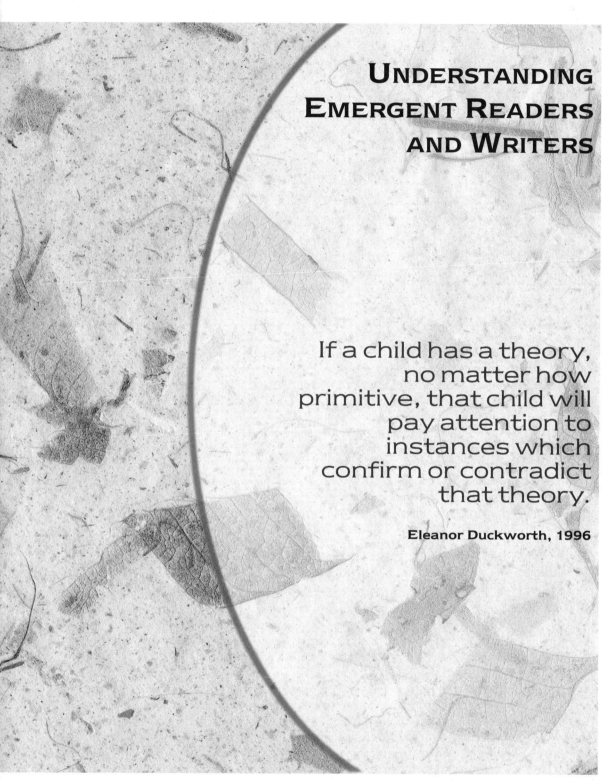

UNDERSTANDING EMERGENT READERS AND WRITERS

If a child has a theory,
no matter how
primitive, that child will
pay attention to
instances which
confirm or contradict
that theory.

Eleanor Duckworth, 1996

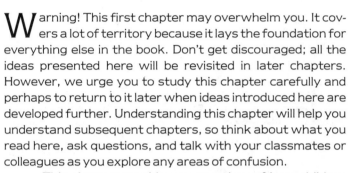

Throughout this book you will see names and dates in parentheses. Do you know what they are and how to use them?

They give you the author and publication date of a book or article that tells more about the topic in that sentence. If you want to know more about an idea presented in this book, look to see if such sources of more information are listed. Once you have the author's name and the publication date, you can find the title and publisher by looking in the reference section at the back of the book. Once you have all the publication data, you can get a copy of that book or article and read further on the subject.

Warning! This first chapter may overwhelm you. It covers a lot of territory because it lays the foundation for everything else in the book. Don't get discouraged; all the ideas presented here will be revisited in later chapters. However, we urge you to study this chapter carefully and perhaps to return to it later when ideas introduced here are developed further. Understanding this chapter will help you understand subsequent chapters, so think about what you read here, ask questions, and talk with your classmates or colleagues as you explore any areas of confusion.

This chapter provides an overview of how children learn, how they learn language, and how they learn written language—a lot to cover. We are convinced that the necessary first step in considering how to help young children become literate is learning about children themselves. We will describe children who are just beginning to read and write, from preschool through primary grades. These are generally accepted as the crucial years for becoming a reader. This chapter discusses how youngsters in these early childhood years learn and think differently from adults and older children. These children are not only physically smaller and less competent than older kids but also different intellectually. Young children perceive the world, its people, and print in a unique fashion. Their views may surprise you.

Examining these differences is helpful in tailoring learning experiences to the needs of young children. Unless we make this effort, we run the risk of schools becoming a place where children are fitted into teacher-made tasks rather than a place where children are helped to refine their views of the world and to come to a greater understanding of it and of themselves. Our goal as teachers is to foster this understanding, not merely to train children to give answers that are correct but that they may not understand.

Preschool, kindergarten, and grades 1 through 3 represent the early childhood years. Teachers with a background in early childhood education emphasize all aspects of child development. They realize that they must nurture the growth of the "whole child" rather than focus only on intellectual development. Even though we are discussing the language arts curriculum here, it is impossible to ignore the child's total development. We know that reading and writing involve the child's social and emotional self, and we know that physical development works together with intellectual development in learning.

Because physical development is observable, adults accept and understand its nature more easily than they do intellectual or emotional development. No one questions that children sit before they stand, stand before they walk, or walk before they run. We see children's gradual progress in specific skills, such as jumping and throwing. Our acceptance of immature efforts at physical prowess can be our guide in acceptance of immature intellectual and emotional responses. Adults are less likely to expect youngsters to perform physical feats beyond their capacity than they are to expect youngsters to master advanced academic or social skills. For instance, no one tries to teach a baby to walk before she can sit up; however, plenty of people try to teach children the names and sounds of letters long before they can even distinguish a letter from other kinds of marks (Ferreiro, 1978).

HOW CHILDREN LEARN

Understanding how children learn is essential to effective teaching, yet schooling practices have long been based on an incomplete and superficial view of the learner. Old teaching methods considered the student as a passive recipient of the teacher's knowledge. However, research has demonstrated that learning actually is an active process in which each learner must construct personal understanding (Ferreiro, 1986; Kamii & Ewing, 1996; Piaget & Garcia, 1991).

We reject the view of learning as merely memorizing and repeating. This book presents the view of learning as thinking, experimenting, and interpreting. Teachers around the world have come to value educational practices that encourage thought, support experimentation, and assist interpretation processes (see Armington, 1997; Reese & Shortland-Jones, 1994; Strickland, 1994). This approach requires teaching in ways that may be very different from those you experienced as a child. It is a more demanding process for both teachers and students, but most people consider it worth the effort. The goal is not merely to teach children what their teachers have learned but rather to create learners and decision makers for an unknown future.

Thinking

Children work hard at making sense of their world. They are constantly thinking: making connections, comparisons, and contrasts. Thinking is the most important part of learning. In the process of trying to figure out how things work, children come up with some amazing theories. These "wrong" answers are proof that children are producing their own knowledge because no adult would have told them such things (Kamii, 1991).

For instance, we asked Andrew what makes waves. Andrew explained that waves are sometimes made from wind and sometimes made from the ocean. This thinking sounds fairly reasonable to an adult until we look past the surface to what those words mean to the child. When pressed for further details, Andrew revealed that the things that live in the ocean, "like fish and whales and seals," make waves when they swim. He claimed that fish make little waves, whales make big waves, and seals make middle-sized waves. This explanation demonstrates Andrew's reasoning ability and his active involvement in trying to understand his experiences and observations. He has made waves himself by splashing in a swimming pool, and he apparently was using that experience to explain the surf he plays in at the beach. Clearly, Andrew constructed his own theory on the basis of his experiences.

In the process of trying to figure out how reading and writing work, children come up with some amazing theories.

Questions

Adults often have a hard time letting such false impressions go uncorrected. They want to give children their adult understanding but end up giving them only their words. For instance, Andrew can give the "correct" explanation when asked where rain comes from, citing the clouds holding water and the sea as the source. Hearing this answer, we might believe that Andrew has learned about rain. But if we delve deeper into Andrew's knowledge, we find that he has merely learned the right words; he really has no idea what they mean. This is evident from Andrew's answer when he is asked where clouds come from; Andrew apparently forgets what he has just said about rain coming from clouds that come from the ocean. Instead, he uses his own observation of a local paper mill and says that clouds come from "the mill paper thing; it stinks. It makes clouds go higher and higher, and they stay there."

As long as Andrew keeps thinking, he will keep learning. Adult explanations tend to stop the thinking and learning by making youngsters mistrust their own reasoning. The best approach to teaching often requires asking questions instead of giving information. Questions that cause a child to look at a situation differently or that create an intellectual conflict encourage deeper thought. For example, we might point out that there are no paper mills where Grandpa lives and ask why there are clouds there. Such questioning requires sensitivity to the child, however, so as not to be disrespectful or discouraging. We must accept children's thinking in order to help them develop confidence in themselves as thinkers (Bredekamp & Rosegrant, 1995). It is all too easy to destroy that confidence by insisting on adult views of correct thinking. Without confidence in their own thinking, children cease their efforts to understand and thus limit their intellectual development by merely repeating what they are told.

Exchange of Viewpoints

Differences of opinion among peers is often the best impetus to get children to rethink their current ideas. Youngsters working together as a team are likely to learn much more than when working alone as individuals. Children learn better when they can debate their ideas with other children.

If Sukey disagrees with Chantel, they will both explain and defend their ideas. The argument will cause each girl to think more about what she believes. One may persuade the other, or they may continue to disagree; either way, the debate process is part of the learning process. Therefore, effective learning environments include many chances for children to interact and discuss their views (Vygotsky, 1978). The teacher's opinion is not the only one that counts, nor is the teacher's voice the only one that can be heard. Effective teaching encourages youngsters to exchange viewpoints.

Experiences

Youngsters can perceive flaws in their reasoning not only through adult questioning and peer debates but also as a result of their own questions about their observations. Therefore, effective teaching provides many opportunities for observation through firsthand experiences. Experiences provide essential fuel for thought.

In fact, experiences tend to be the basis for the initial explanations children create for themselves. Tanya's description of tidal action demonstrates the role of experience in a child's understandings. She surprised her teacher by talking about when the sea "drains." When Ms. Montoya asked Tanya what she meant, Tanya said, "When it goes away; like in the shower." As she pondered Tanya's words, Ms. Montoya realized that Tanya's perception was based on a limited view of tides. Their community is at the head of a huge bay; when the tide goes out, it leaves behind only mudflats. It would be reasonable to think that the water had "drained."

Different experiences of tides, not adult explanations, are needed to alter Tanya's understanding. However, seeing a different result of tidal action won't change her theory immediately. It is typical for youngsters (and adult learners) to try to keep their original ideas and to create a subsystem or additional explanation for new phenomena. Eventually, more encompassing theories are created as more and more variations are included. Learning seems to be driven by a search for coherence, or consistency (Siegrist & Sinclair, 1991).

Having an idea, or hypothesis, will help Tanya continue learning the subject. As Eleanor Duckworth (1996) has told us, it is through the exploration of their own theories that children learn and become more aware of evidence that either fits their current views or indicates the need for a different theory. Teachers who encourage children to formulate any ideas—right or wrong—generate thought and activate the learning process. Teachers who give children adult answers, by contrast, close thought.

Information

We don't mean to say that teachers should never tell children anything. Though children must construct their own understanding of complex ideas, there is much factual information that someone needs to tell them. Much of this information consists of names given to things in their language. Young children constantly ask to have things named for them as they learn to talk. The names we use for letters, numbers, shapes, and colors also are part of the information adults can and do give to children. However, the meaning behind the names and the relationships among items named cannot be given to anyone; everyone has to make sense of those in his or her own way. We sometimes see teachers who focus on teaching the names for things and who seem to forget that there is much more involved in learning.

There are also many things children can learn from observing adult models. Therefore, observing someone more competent can be a valuable way to learn. Children can learn a lot about interpersonal skills, athletic skills, oral language, and even reading and writing just by watching and listening to people. It can be amusing to watch young children at play who are imitating older children or adults. However, this behavior is much more than cute; it is also serious practice.

The Teacher's Role

We have just discussed thinking, exploring, and gaining information from others as three ways of learning. The type of thing to be learned determines the most appropriate way of learning, and each way of learning requires a different way of teaching. Constructivist learning theorists refer to knowledge gained through thinking as "logical-mathematical knowledge." The term "physical knowledge" describes knowledge gained by exploring and experimenting. Information that cannot be independently figured out or discovered is called "social/arbitrary knowledge" because it must be transmitted from one person to another and because it varies from one situation or culture to another.

Though teachers certainly must give some of that arbitrary information to children, true teaching is much more complex than just providing information. Effective teaching involves encouraging reflective thinking, providing meaningful experiences, and also offering relevant information. Encouraging thinking includes making time for reflection, asking questions, and stimulating the exchange of viewpoints among peers. The goal is to keep children examining and improving their theories. Unfortunately, in the past children had to do most of their thinking

Children learn not only from adults giving them information and from their experiences, but also from thinking. They must make personal sense of information and experiences in order to understand them.

outside of school because their school days were taken up with busywork to please their teachers. With more informed teachers, schools can support more of children's learning processes.

HOW CHILDREN LEARN LANGUAGE

Studies of language development show that children do much more than imitate others as they learn to talk (Gallas et al., 1996; Piaget & Inhelder, 1969; Weaver, 1996). In fact, while learning to talk, children provide some of the best examples of how they construct all knowledge. If you have been around young children, you have heard evidence that they do more than mimic adult talk; rather, they create their own theories about language. They definitely use the ideas gained from more competent speakers but obviously analyze them in an effort to understand how it all fits together. When Betsy says, "He falled me," she clearly is constructing her own understanding of language as she practices it, trying out her current theories about how to put words together.

Children have a lot to learn in the process of becoming verbal. Early in life, most babies start to figure out that the sounds people make are a means of communicating with other human beings—a way of expressing their desires, sharing their feelings, and explaining their experiences. Then, babies start to work on the complexities of accurate communication. When they are only about six months old, youngsters who can hear talk will usually imitate speech intonations so that it sounds as if they are saying something understandable. At this point youngsters still have to work on the specific sounds involved. Before their first year is over, most babies have narrowed their utterances from all the possible sounds to those significant in their environment. Babies in Mexico will trill the r sound, babies in Germany will practice the guttural sounds they hear, and babies in English-speaking countries will learn neither. Before long, typically developing children begin to make the sounds of their language in combinations that mean something specific. As soon as they acquire this ability to communicate with words, they begin to string them together for even greater results.

As they begin to use words in combination, children generally put them together in ways matching the grammatical rules of their language (*syntax*). English-speaking children put the subject before the verb and, when they become more sophisticated, the object after the verb. However, they also clearly demonstrate their learning process as they reinvent grammar rules, for instance, adding an *s* to make a plural in *foots* and *mouses* and adding *ed* for the past tense in *runned* and *digged*. Young children also are motivated to increase their vocabulary, and so they incessantly ask the names of things.

By the time teachers see them in preschool, most children seem to be proficient with language. They generally are able to make themselves understood to others and are fairly good at understanding what others say to them. How did they learn so much in such a short time? They did not learn it by being drilled in the sounds and grammar of their language. They learned by being immersed in language—by using it in their everyday lives.

The Child's Process

An old joke says that if we taught children to talk the way we teach them to read, there would be a lot of nontalkers. Yet few people seem to turn the joke around and suggest that if we taught children to read the way we teach them to talk, we wouldn't have many nonreaders. Teaching children to read the way we teach them to talk is precisely what much current research is suggesting that teachers do (International Reading Association [IRA] and National Association for the Education of Young Children [NAEYC], 1998; Neuman, Copple, & Bredekamp, 2000).

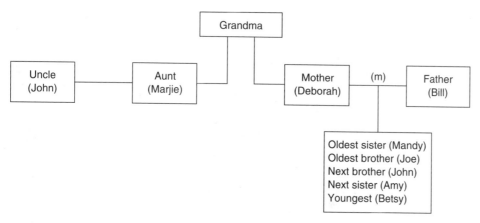

FIGURE 1.1
Meet Betsy and her family.

Therefore, let's look carefully at how a child learns to talk. Watch the neighbors' new baby, Betsy, when her parents bring her home from the hospital (see Figure 1.1). Already there is communication between Betsy and her parents. Mostly, she makes random noises and cries to express her discomfort; however, her communications bring responses from her parents, sisters, and brothers. People babble to her in imitation of the sounds she makes, or someone feeds or changes her in response to her cries. She discovers the power of communication. Halliday (1982) said that youngsters "learn to mean" before they learn the forms for expressing their meanings. We see this same sequence as children learn to write.

The social contexts of language give it meaning. When Betsy's dad bathes her, he talks to her about how warm the water is, how slippery the soap feels, and what cute little toes she has. When her mother dresses her, Betsy hears about her dry diaper, the snaps on her jumpsuit, and her sweet smile. When her big brother Johnny plays with Betsy, he shows her all his toys and tells her what is happening as he drives his toy trucks around her baby seat. Johnny makes her laugh.

Betsy hears lots of talk, both directed to her and surrounding her as her family goes about its daily life. She likes to participate in conversations, and her progress with the forms of language is seen as she utters strings of sounds that make the others in her family stop and listen. These sounds are much like "real" language, but close attention reveals that there are no words in Betsy's sentence. She has mastered some general sounds of language but not the specifics; she seems to have picked up the intonations, such as those of questioning or scolding, that go with different meanings. Betsy scolded her mom roundly when she saw her mom standing on the counter one day to reach something. She didn't need words to do it; her tone of voice said it all.

More and more, the sounds Betsy makes are the sounds she hears. One day she makes a "da" sound, and her dad suddenly pays attention and bends over

An old joke says, "If we taught children to talk the same way we teach them to read, we'd have a lot of nontalkers." Let's turn the joke around: Let's teach children to read the way we teach them to talk. Then there won't be so many nonreaders.

her and repeats, "Da-da." Betsy makes the sound again, and her dad responds with attention and an expression of pleasure. When Betsy is about a year old, she is able to make several sounds that get a specific response from her family. She may make the same sound to mean different things, which she indicates by her tone, facial expression, pointing gestures, or other nonverbal clues. Her language is contextual. Mostly, the members of her family understand her intent according to the situation. For instance, "Ma-ma" can mean "Where is Mama?" or "I want my Mama!" or "There is my Mama." Soon Betsy begins to add action words to nouns, allowing her to communicate in two-word sentences. Again, these two-word "telegraph" sentences can mean different things, depending on the context in which they occur. Already Betsy knows that the meaning is inherent not in the words alone but also in the mutual understanding between speaker and listener. This interpersonal aspect of communication remains true even after Betsy has mastered adult-sounding sentences.

The Home Environment

As Betsy's knowledge of words and her ability to create sentences grow, her previously "good" grammar seems to deteriorate. Her big sister Mandy is concerned because Betsy says, "I goed to the store." Mandy patiently corrects her and says, "No, you *went* to the store." "That's right," says Betsy happily as she wanders off. Their mother comforts Mandy by explaining that Betsy will talk correctly before long and that she makes mistakes because she is trying to make sense of grammar right now. Obviously, Betsy is not imitating adult language here. Her errors are clear evidence of her active efforts at making sense of language (Tabors, 1997). Betsy's mistake is an overgeneralization of the rule for the past-tense form. Mandy's mom asks her not to correct Betsy for fear of discouraging Betsy from practicing language.

When she is three years old, Betsy still finds it hard to make all the sounds in her language. She still can't make *l*, *r*, or *s* sounds because they take more coordination than she has yet mastered. But, although she may say *tore* instead of *store*, she gets upset if someone else says the words incorrectly. Betsy's mother knows that the baby talk will disappear by itself if others talk to Betsy in adult language rather than imitate her baby talk. Correcting her actually could slow down the learning process because it could create a fear of failure and reluctance to talk. Reluctance to talk gets in the way of practice important to learning.

As Betsy becomes more proficient with language, she has much she wants to say, and she speaks eagerly. Betsy sometimes trips over her words in her rush to speak. Her uncle thinks she is stuttering, so he says, "Slow down, Betsy. Start again and say it slowly." Although this advice may appear sound, Betsy's mother asks him not to interrupt Betsy or call attention to the problem. Uncle John gets a valuable lecture on *normal nonfluency*—how it isn't stuttering but can become stuttering if a child is made nervous about it (Swan, 1993). Betsy's mother tells him that the best help he can give Betsy is his undivided attention so she won't feel rushed.

As the members of Betsy's family help her learn their language, they don't have to be told about most of the important things they do to help her learn. Talking to her and paying attention to her when she talks are the most helpful, especially given their serious efforts to understand her early attempts to communicate. Her brothers and sisters sometimes point to various things when they don't understand Betsy, saying, "Is this what you mean?" People around her help her communicate beyond what she can do on her own (Dixon-Krauss, 1996; Otto, 2002).

Members of her family also naturally assist Betsy's language attempts by adjusting how they speak to her according to her changing ability to understand. Apparently, an unconscious accommodation to a child's emerging language ability guides the length and complexity of adult speech to children (Fields, 1998).

Families teach language to their children by being language models and by trying to understand when youngsters try to communicate.

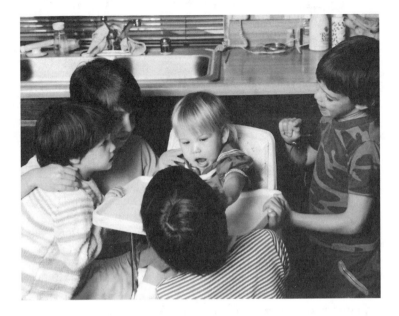

Therefore, adults automatically tend to simplify their grammar, limit their vocabulary, repeat words often, and enunciate slowly and clearly to young children.

Betsy's parents, like many other parents, respond to her speech by adding to what she says and extending her immature sentences. At Betsy's first birthday, when she says, "Mama!" her mother answers, "You want Mama to come pick you up?" When Betsy is two years old and says, "Daddy gone," her mother replies, "Yes, Daddy is gone to work now." When Betsy is three years old and says, "See me riding," her dad says, "Look at Betsy riding fast on her red tricycle!" These expansions or elaborations of her speech help Betsy increase the complexity of her language. Such modeling is sometimes referred to as scaffolding (Berk & Winsler, 1995). Intentional support provided to learners as we engage them in literacy tasks they are not able to accomplish on their own is scaffolded instruction (Leu & Kinzer, 1999).

Story time provides another important component of Betsy's language development. Storybooks offer a rich source for vocabulary development (Karweit & Wasik, 1996), for familiarity with a variety of sentence structures, and for understanding the unique forms of written language (Snow, Tabors, Nicholson, & Kurland, 1995). Betsy often chooses her favorites again and again. Repeated readings of texts reinforce text language and familiarize children with the structure of different genres (Neuman et al., 2000). Children who haven't been read to arrive at school unable to process the dialect of book talk. They understand only context-laden language, which utilizes both the situation and nonverbal communication to add meaning to the words. When confronted with the decontextualized language found in books (Snow, 1991), these youngsters don't know how to make sense of it.

The amount and kinds of Betsy's experiences also influence her language complexity. When she plays outside, she feels the prickly softness of the grass as she rolls on it, she experiences the smooth hardness of the driveway where she rides her trike, and she squeals with delight at the flying sensation when she swings. What a great many things she has to talk about now, and what a great many words she can add to her vocabulary if someone listens and extends her speech as she tells about playing outside.

Not all children have this kind of language environment (Allington & Walmsley, 1995; Tabors, 1997; Wong Fillmore, 1991). Some youngsters have parents who don't speak much English but want their children to learn it. These parents may be hesitant to speak their native language to their children, so the children hear little language at home. Some children live in cultures in which it is appropriate to ignore them when they make sounds and even when they cry. Some come from families in which adults simply do not talk a great deal or talk in sentences that are short and lack complexity and specificity. Some youngsters do not have their questions answered at home. Some lack the coordination to create speech, some can't hear language to imitate it, and some are too fearful to speak. These children will not arrive at school with the kinds of language skills that help them succeed academically. They will need more time, more assistance, and plenty of opportunities at school to experience the kinds of language stimulation that are a part of Betsy's home life.

More to Learn

Even children who come from language environments that match school expectations have much to learn about language when they reach preschool. They may sound quite mature, but their vocabulary remains limited, as is their ability to deal with different grammatical structures. They can become confused about a new word or a word with several meanings. They may be confused by the difference between *ask* and *tell*. Have you ever told children they could ask questions after a guest speaker's presentation? They don't ask the speaker questions; they tell their personal experiences! They get confused by questions in general because questions turn around the natural order of a sentence. Passive forms also turn around familiar sentence patterns and result in miscommunication. For instance, when we say, "Betsy was given a tricycle by her dad," children look at us quizzically and wonder why Betsy's dad would want a tricycle.

Generally, children do learn a great deal of language in a short time. When they get to school, they must be allowed to continue their oral language development in the ways that have already proved successful for them. They must also be encouraged to learn written language in the same active and interactive ways through which they learned oral language. These include observing and experiencing communication as well as receiving encouragement for their own attempts at the process. Adults who accept and value the errors children make as they construct their own understandings are also essential for both oral and written language development. In addition, books and real-life experiences assist children in bringing meaning to oral and written language. Subsequent chapters will include more detailed discussions about how teachers can promote these active and interactive experiences.

It used to be commonly accepted that oral language development preceded written language development and was the basis for learning to read and write. We now realize that oral and written language are even more closely intertwined. Children actually are learning about reading and writing at the same time they are learning to talk. Learning the language of literacy assists oral language learning as much as the other way around.

HOW CHILDREN LEARN WRITTEN LANGUAGE

It's pretty obvious that teachers can teach reading better if they know how children learn to read. What is amazing is that there is so much disagreement about how children learn to read. The recent "reading wars" debate has polarized the issue, with each side citing its own research and accusing the other of flawed research. Teachers' unions, the PTA, and professional organizations for education administrators have signed onto a statement representing one side (Learning First Alliance, 1998); the professional associations composed of reading and writing experts and of experts on young children's learning defend the other side (IRA and NAEYC, 1998; Neuman et al., 2000).

The disagreement focuses mainly on how much emphasis to put on phonics as part of beginning literacy instruction. One side says that phonics is the most important part of reading and that it must come *before* any other reading instruction. The other side says that phonics is just one of many strategies used for reading and that it is best learned *during* reading instruction. This latter position is the position we accept.

There are actually many areas of agreement in the two positions. Though each side accuses the other of extremes, such as either totally ignoring meaning in reading or being antiphonics, both positions acknowledge the importance of meaning and of phonics for learning to read. The differences are mainly a matter of degree. In addition, both sides acknowledge that individual children will have different learning needs, invalidating any blanket statement prescribing one instructional practice for all.

Rather than giving you a recipe for teaching reading, this book aims to give you general information about how children learn and about the development of language and literacy. With this knowledge you will be able to observe your students in a more informed way and see for yourself how each one is processing his or her experiences with print. Only by basing your instruction on the individual child's current theories about reading and writing will your efforts be fruitful. A child-centered view of education will help you remember that you are teaching chil-

Using phonics is one of several necessary reading skills. All reading skills are learned best during actual reading and writing practice.

dren, not simply teaching reading. Teaching according to the needs of each child requires that teachers be knowledgeable about child development and about their subject matter. This combination is essential to effective teaching.

An Active Learning Process

When researchers began watching youngsters closely, they began to question traditional assumptions about how children learn. A constructivist view of learning emphasizes the personal and social as well as the intellectual nature of literacy (Gambrell & Mazzoni, 1999). As with other kinds of language learning, becoming literate is more than memorizing what an adult tells or shows a child. Children do use information and examples from adults, but they must construct their own knowledge of how print works. *Children* direct their own process of learning to read and write by actively generating and testing a series of personal hypotheses about written language. The goal for teachers is to assist children in creating meanings in response to new experiences as opposed to learning meanings others have created (Poplin, 1988).

Informal, everyday experiences with print in their lives appears to be a crucial part of children's literacy learning process (Morrow, Strickland, & Woo, 1998). These experiences include being read to, pretending to read and write, finding their favorite cereal labels at the store, and seeing how their own names are written. Youngsters do need to hear what the names and sounds of letters are, but becoming literate involves experiences with print and opportunities to think about how print works. Reading and writing are communication processes, not merely decoding and encoding sounds.

You may have noticed that we don't talk about learning to read only; learning to read and learning to write are inseparable (Routman, 1996). Reading exposes a child to models for writing, and writing involves a theory of how to create something readable. Thinking about one enhances understanding of the other, and both are learned simultaneously. Now we refer to both of these functions by the term *literacy*.

Learning Sequence

We used to think that children learned first to talk, then to read, and then to write. We now realize that there is not one point in a child's life when literacy begins; it is a continuous process of becoming (Clay, 1966; Morrow et al., 1998). The term *emergent literacy* describes the view of literacy development as a continuum. Children are working on all aspects of oral and written language at the same time. Like most children in literate households, Betsy liked to hear stories read and would play at reading even before she could talk. Certainly before she could read she was trying to write, as the other people in her family did. An emergent literacy perspective views early unconventional literacy-related behaviors as important and legitimate aspects of the developmental continuum of literacy (Whitehurst & Lonigan, 2002). We no longer talk about prereading or reading readiness experiences that separate "real" reading in educational settings and everything that precedes school attendance.

Some people believe that the forms of written language—the letters and the sounds they represent—must be taught first. Others believe that children must know the functions of written language—the ways in which it is used—before phonics and letter names are relevant. However, careful observation of children reveals that they pay no attention to adult ideas about these kinds of sequences. They do need to understand the purposes and uses of written language, but many youngsters are working hard at identifying letters while they are learning about the functions of print (Sulzby, 1986). In addition, there is significant evidence that children learn phonics from reading and writing (Goodman, 1998; Whitehurst & Lonigan, 2002) at least as much as they learn to read

Children from literate households will play at reading even before they can talk.

and write from phonics. To further confuse adults, youngsters go about this complex process in individually unique ways. Despite some commonalities, different children tune in to different aspects of written language and generate their own unique hypotheses (Dyson, 1997). The National Research Council released its report on Preventing Reading Difficulties in Young Children (Burns, Snow, & Griffin, 1998) stressing the importance of diverse forms of support for individual learners.

What this means is that schools, teachers, and workbook publishers cannot dictate how children will learn to read and write. Rather, teachers, parents, and other adults who know *and observe* a child should support that child's individual efforts to learn. As Betsy grows up, her family answers her questions about print, provides her with paper and other writing materials, lets her see the family reading and writing, and generally offers a print-rich environment filled with books and other kinds of writing. When she goes to preschool, her teacher provides much the

TABLE 1.1

Developmentally Appropriate Literacy

Appropriate Practices	Inappropriate Practices
The goals of the **language and literacy** program are for children to expand their ability to communicate through speaking, listening, reading, and writing and to develop the ability and disposition to acquire knowledge through reading. Technical skills or subskills, such as those related to phonics, word recognition, capitalization, and punctuation, are taught in ways that are meaningful to children. Teachers support the development of children's spelling ability from temporary "invented" spelling toward the goal of conventional spelling, with minimal reliance on teacher-prescribed spelling lists.	Reading is taught only as the acquisition of discrete skills and subskills. Teachers teach reading primarily as a separate subject and do not capitalize on the possibilities for furthering children's progress in reading when teaching other subjects. Language, writing, and spelling instruction relies heavily on workbooks. Children are rarely given the opportunity to revise their work, so they are unable to acquire a sense of the writing process. Children's writing efforts are rejected or downgraded if correct spelling and standard English are not used.

Source: Bredecamp and Copple, 1997, p. 172

same kind of support for Betsy's emerging literacy. Rather than predetermining what Betsy must master at a given time, both her home and her school encourage her to learn in her own way. Both environments help her see the usefulness of reading and writing; both stress the social, communicative nature of literacy, both offer experiences that further her understanding and excite her enthusiasm for learning; and both provide relevant information to help her progress. This is the developmentally appropriate approach to language and literacy (see Table 1.1).

Literacy and the Home Environment

Adults can act as models, advisors, resources, and cheerleaders to children when they learn to read just as they do when children learn to talk. Older children also can assist younger ones in becoming literate just as they help them with other language acquisition. Betsy's four older brothers and sisters don't realize that they teach the younger ones, but they do a fine job. The younger children in the family always want to do whatever the older ones are doing. When they see their older siblings reading, they want to read, too. At first, they know only that reading involves looking at the book or newspaper or cereal box. Then they discover that there is a message contained in books even beyond the fascination of the pictures. When big brother Joey was in second grade, he would invite his three younger brothers and sisters to sit on his bunk bed and entertain them by reading library books. Children in this family learned that reading was fun, and in the process, they learned how to read (Moustafa, 1997).

When Joey was at school, two-year-old Amy would ask her four-year-old brother, John, to read to her if their mom was too busy. John couldn't read actual words, but he could tell a story, turn the pages, and admire the pictures with Amy. In these sessions, both Amy and John were learning a great deal about reading. Amy was learning that books were a source of information and pleasure; John was practicing the idea of getting meaning from a book. He was aware of the print and its relationship to the content but couldn't yet decipher it. At this point in his development, John tried to put together a prize toy from a cereal box. He was having trouble, so Grandma offered to help, saying, "Let me read the directions." John replied, "I already did." Grandma persisted, saying, "Let me see if you missed anything." John handed her the direction sheet, which contained both illustrations and printed instructions, and said matter-of-factly, "I missed the words." John's statement accurately described his current level of reading; he was able to make meaning from pictures but not from print. John's approach to making sense of reading was typical for his age (Braunger & Lewis, 1997).

There's so much reading going on in this family that you might ask, "Does this family have a television?" Television is often blamed for people's not reading. The parents in this family enjoy books, but they also enjoy television and think that selected, limited viewing isn't necessarily bad. Like many parents, they know children learn new words and are exposed to a vast array of ideas and information through television. Also like many parents, they are often uncomfortable with some of this new learning. When they relent and allow their children to watch shows the parents don't approve of, an adult watches the show with the children and helps them think critically about what they are seeing. In this way, the parents use what they believe is both the good and the bad on television for helping their children grow intellectually and emotionally.

When adults make television viewing an intellectually active rather than passive experience, viewing can be a source of language and critical thinking and a vehicle for transmitting values as well as a source of information. In this way, television can provide a valuable background for literacy. However, when families use television viewing as a *substitute* for talking, thinking, and family interaction, it has negative consequences (Healy, 1990).

ORAL LANGUAGE AND WRITTEN LANGUAGE

Our conviction that oral and written language are learned in similar ways is surely becoming obvious to you by now. This parallel between learning to talk and learning to read and write guides us in deciding how best to teach reading and writing. For instance, when people wonder whether it is better to correct spelling errors in children's writing journals or to respond conversationally in writing, we have only to consider a similar situation in oral language. Which helps children learn to talk better: correcting their mispronunciations or pronouncing the words correctly in a conversation with them? If you don't know, think about how you feel about talking to someone who corrects your grammar. Most of us would avoid talking to that person. What if that person were your main source of language learning—as parents and teachers tend to be? Then you would avoid the kind of practice in talking that is essential to becoming better at it.

Children learn written language in much the same way as they learn oral language—because it is language (Cambourne, 1988; K. S. Goodman, 1996; F. Smith, 1987). This idea has become widely accepted since Carol Chomsky's early writing on the topic in 1972. Although the ways in which written language differs from oral language must be considered, understanding how youngsters learn to talk helps us understand how they master reading and writing, too. Researchers who have studied written-language acquisition (for example, Clay, 2001; Dyson, 1997; Ferreiro, 1990; Y. M. Goodman, 1986; Teale & Sulzby, 1989) have shown that young children learn written and oral language in the same manner in which, according to Piaget, they learn many other things. They learn by constructing their own rules and relationships rather than by being told about them (see Table 1.2).

Chomsky's research also demonstrated that children's drive to make sense of print is similar to their determination to utilize spoken language. Chomsky's recommendation was that children be allowed to direct their own process of learning to read, just as they direct their own process of learning to talk. Does this mean that we simply leave children alone to learn to read? No. It means that adult assistance in the process should closely resemble the type of adult assistance given children as they learn to talk (Moustafa, 1997).

When we help a baby learn to talk, do we conduct lessons on the sounds of words and then try to get the baby to blend those sounds together to make language? Did Betsy's family allow her to say only words that she could pronounce properly? Did they restrict her speech to vocabulary-controlled topics or to sentences that she could form properly? Did they group her with others who could talk only at her level? Of course not, and neither do other families. Betsy's family

TABLE 1.2
Comparison of Oral and Written Language Development

Oral Language	Written Language	Understanding
Babbling and cooing	Scribbles	Exploring the medium
Language intonations	Linear-repetitive forms	Refining the form
Native language sounds	Letterlike forms	Cultural relevance
First "words" (Mama)	Letter names as sounds	Partial accuracy
"Telegraph" sentences	Simplified phonics	Simplify for success
Creative grammar	Advanced invented spelling	Overgeneralization of "rules"
Adult speech	Standard spelling	Formal structure

encouraged her to experiment with language in any way she chose, and they rejoiced with her at each discovery. They provided Betsy with models of rich language and helped her learn through her own observation and experimentation as she tried to join in family discussions. In short, they invited her to participate in the oral interaction of the family at her current ability level.

Misconceptions About Becoming Literate

We have been discussing the processes of learning to read and learning to talk as overlapping processes. It may seem strange to think of learning to read and learning to talk as happening at the same time. It may be a new insight to realize that babies and toddlers begin the process of learning to read as soon as books and print become part of their lives. Yes, babies are learning to read, but that doesn't mean it makes sense to sit a child down for a lesson disguised as a game. Betsy's mother, Deborah, laughs at advertisements for materials for teaching babies and toddlers to read. And she was glad when the misleading radio advertisements guaranteeing results with Hooked on Phonics were changed by court order. Too many parents have wasted too much time and money on false promises.

She didn't laugh, though, when Amy came home from kindergarten feeling like a failure over her phonics workbook. Deborah was very upset when she discovered that the teacher was drilling children on isolated letters and sounds apart from any meaningful context. Deborah knows that it is harder to remember nonsense than recognizable words; like many literacy experts (such as Glazer, 1998; Moustafa, 1997; Wilde, 1997), she sees letters and sounds by themselves as nonsense. She observes her children learning phonics from songs and stories with rhymes and alliteration (sequences of words beginning with the same letter). She sees them learning the names and sounds of letters in their own names and other words that are important to them. Amy didn't have any trouble with phonics that way, but the phonics lessons at school confused her. When Deborah spoke to the teacher, Deborah learned that children in the class who hadn't been read to at home were having a much worse time than Amy with this phonics drill. Clearly, this isolated skills approach isn't useful.

Such inappropriate educational practices will persist as long as people remain ignorant of what is actually involved in becoming literate (Routman, 1996). After they have figured out how to read and write, people tend to forget how they actually did it. They usually focus on some observable details of the process and end up thinking that they learned to read and write by learning letters and sounds. Many people seem to think that reading is pronouncing the sounds of letters, forgetting that print represents meaning, not speech (K. S. Goodman, 1996). Many also believe that copying writing models is the way to learn about writing or that writing consists of transcribing sounds.

These erroneous beliefs ignore the complex intellectual activities required for becoming literate. These beliefs ignore the vast amount of understanding about the structure of written language that is essential to reading and writing.

Old approaches to teaching reading and writing ignore what children actually do to learn to read and write.

They ignore the essential role of social situations and meaningful contexts. They also ignore what children actually do when they learn to read and write: Learners use what they already know to make sense of what they don't know yet. Effective teaching helps children use what they know about language and about the world as they learn to read and write.

      Teaching practices must focus clearly on the desired goals. Most people would agree that the goal of reading and writing instruction is to create literate human beings. Literate people can read to select the more rational argument among conflicting theories and can express ideas effectively in writing. Knowing the sounds of letters and the correct spelling of words obviously is useful, but becoming literate involves much, much more.

HOW GOOD READERS READ

Most adults would say that they want children to be good readers. What is a good reader? Can we get some clues about how to create good readers by examining one?

Betsy's oldest sister, Mandy, is one such example. Her teachers in sixth grade describe her as an exceptional student and a fluent reader. Mandy likes to read and spends much time with library books. She often chooses reading over other activities. When she is reading, Mandy is oblivious to everything else around her. Her younger sisters and brothers get upset because they can't get her attention away from her books. Good readers freely choose to read and tend to concentrate as they read.

This year Mandy is reading horse stories. She got hooked on the *Black Stallion* (Farley) series, and when she finished those, she started reading every other horse story she could find. Although she doesn't have a horse and rarely has been on one, Mandy knows about horses from her reading. When she reads, Mandy can pretend that she owns a horse that carries her galloping over sand dunes or green meadows. Mandy's cousin, David, is reading another type of book—the *Goosebumps* brand of reading excitement. Both Mandy and David read mainly for pleasure. David's brother, Michael, however, has always chosen to read for information. Michael became an expert on marine mammals through his reading in elementary school, and then in junior high he switched to reading about hunting and camping. He uses the information he has gathered from reading for his weekend expeditions. Good readers find pleasure and purpose in their reading.

As we watch Mandy read, her eyes flash across and down the page. How can she possibly see every word, let alone every letter on the page? She doesn't. If she were to read slowly enough to see each letter, the process would be so laborious that she would not find pleasure in reading and would not often choose to read. If she had learned to read by thinking that she was supposed to sound out each letter and blend words together, she might have continued to look at each letter and never have become a good reader.

What about reading all the words? Mandy knows exactly what the story is about; she can tell you details and will speculate excitedly about what might happen next. But she does not labor over individual words. If she comes to a word she doesn't know, she usually can skip over it and still get the meaning from the rest of the sentence. After a few times of skipping over the same word and getting meaning from the context in that manner, she has an idea of what the word means even if it isn't part of her general vocabulary. If the printed word is part of her spoken vocabulary, she eventually figures it out using strategies that combine graphophonemic clues *and/or syntactic clues* with semantic clues related to the meaning of what she reads. Mandy makes predictions about what she reads, self-corrects, rereads, and asks questions if necessary as she adjusts her reading when comprehension breaks down.

When Mandy reads something at an easier level so that she knows all the words, she can really fly. She isn't aware of the physical process, but her eye often identifies the words merely from their general outline, or configuration. These configuration clues serve as shortcuts to identifying sight words, thus increasing reading speed and fluency. An observer might describe Mandy as a youngster who doesn't see most of the letters or many of the words she reads and even reads books with words that she doesn't know. Is Mandy typical of good readers? Research tells us yes (K. S. Goodman, 1996). Self-regulated readers use reading strategies and monitor their own comprehension as they read (Pressley, 1999).

THE CHILD'S PROCESS

Mandy shows us a model of where we're headed, but let's remember there is a complex journey from the starting point to where Mandy is. In fact, just getting to the point of understanding that letters are relevant involves a massive learning process (Edwards, 1994). Researchers around the world have carefully tracked this process among children in several countries. They have studied children's writing as evidence of their thinking and understanding. This research shows that the ways in which children construct their understanding of written language are much the same, whether youngsters are reading and writing in Hebrew, Spanish, Italian, French, or English (Ferreiro, 1990; Landsmann, 1990; Moustafa, 1997; Pontecorvo & Zucchermaglio, 1990; Siegrist & Sinclair, 1991; Teberosky, 1990).

Young children need repeated experiences with print to understand that letters are a system to represent the sounds we make when we speak. They intuitively believe otherwise, thinking that print should look like the things it describes. Children easily trust pictures to communicate on paper and only gradually come to accept the role of letters.

The study of children's evolving theories of writing demonstrates another remarkable similarity: Children's literacy development parallels the development of literacy historically (K. S. Goodman, 1996; Temple, Nathan, Temple, & Burris, 1993). Children's emergent writing demonstrates principles of representation found in the earliest writing systems: Chinese, Egyptian, and Greek. In these cultures, the symbols were created to directly symbolize the things written about. Children's early writing utilizes this theory, and common signs, such as those meaning "no smoking" or "deer crossing," support their thinking. Therefore, young children rely on drawing and symbols, such as hearts, to tell their stories before they accept the alphabetic writing system. They need repeated experiences with print to convince them that print isn't supposed to look like what it tells about. Even then, youngsters are not immediately ready to accept that print represents the sounds we make when we say words. The alphabetic system is definitely counterintuitive for young learners.

The research of Emelia Ferreiro (1978, 1986, 1990) clearly documents children's thinking as they work through various theories to make sense of a confusing system (see Table 1.3). Many other researchers have replicated her work,

TABLE 1.3
Writing Forms Chart

Form	Characteristics and Hypotheses
Scribbles	Random marks with no differentiation between drawing and writing
Drawing	Illustration tells a story
Linear-repetitive	Marks in a line, fairly uniform in size and shape (repetitive); looks like longhand
Copying standard writing	May or may not be linear but contains elements of actual words
Memorized forms	Frequently used and important words (*love, Mom, Dad,* own name, etc.)
Letterlike forms	Contains elements of actual letters, looks like letters; no more than two similar forms next to one another
Quantitative principles	The number of letters is significant: reflects hypotheses about number of letters necessary for a word; big things have big names; progresses to reflect number of oral language syllables
Qualitative principles Beginning invented spelling	Which letters are used is significant
Letter names as sounds	Reflects hypothesis that letters make the sound of their names
Simplified phonics	One letter per word or per syllable; only major sounds, few vowels
Advanced invented spelling	Attempts to regularize sound-symbol relationship; uses vowels; becomes readable
Standard spelling	Self-correction to match standard spelling models

with the same results (for example, Landsmann, 1990; Manning, Manning, Long, & Kamii, 1995; Siegrist & Sinclair, 1991; Teberosky, 1990). If teachers don't understand this information about how children think, they cannot be effective teachers. Astonishingly, many of the people responsible for creating literacy policies seem to be totally unfamiliar with Ferreiro's research that explains so much about children's literacy learning (IRA and NAEYC, 1998; Learning First Alliance, 1998; Snow, Burns, & Griffin, 1998).

BEING A RESEARCHER

WHAT IS WRITTEN IN A SENTENCE?
To find out what a child thinks is written in a written sentence, you can follow this procedure created by Emilia Ferreiro. You can be a researcher too.

You can write and say aloud a sentence, such as "Daddy kicked the ball," while a child watches and listens. Then ask about each word one at a time as follows: "Is *ball* written?" "Is *Daddy* written?" and so on. If the child says yes, a word is written, ask the child to show the word to you in the sentence. Then, whether the response is right or wrong, ask the child how he or she knew that was where the word was. You will find the same patterns other researchers noted when they did this activity with individual emergent readers. The levels identified by this study are typical of preschoolers through kindergartners. For further information, see "What Is Written in a Written Sentence?" by Emilia Ferreiro (1978).

Ferreiro (1978) demonstrated a way of finding out what young emergent readers think is written in a sentence. This fascinating study revealed that youngsters initially believe that only nouns are written. This belief relates to their idea that print represents things. Children with more literacy experience will acknowledge that verbs are also written, but only the most literate young children believe that "nonessential" words, such as *the* or *a*, can possibly be words on their own. When asked to identify which words are which, children rely on word order—context—long before they tune in to letters and sounds. This finding has significance for determining which reading strategies will be most helpful to beginning readers. *See the Being a Researcher box* ("What Is Written in a Sentence?") for further discussion.

Another of Ferreiro's research approaches involves watching and listening to children as they spontaneously explore print in writing activities (Ferreiro, 1990). Studying children's writing is easier than studying their reading. Most of what happens in reading is invisible; the action is taking place in the child's mind. However, a child's writing gives us visible evidence of what the child thinks about how print works. Reading and writing are two aspects of the written language process, just as listening and speaking are two aspects of the oral language process. And just as we measure children's oral language development through their efforts at speaking, we can determine their written language development best from their efforts at writing. One nice aspect of Ferreiro's research is that you can do the same thing she did, so you can prove for yourself what she discovered

BEING A RESEARCHER

WHAT IS THE CHILD'S THEORY OF WRITING?

To find out what a child thinks about how writing works, you need to be there when a child is writing for his or her own purposes. If the writing is done for the teacher, children tend to play it safe and not test their latest theories (Fields & Hillstead, 1995). Putting notepads in the playhouse and seeing what develops is usually productive for this kind of research. As soon as a child has finished writing, you need to get the child to tell you about the writing. If you wait very long, children forget what they wrote. Some children respond to a request to read their writing; but many will tell you they can't read. Sometimes it works to ask children what they *wanted* it to say. Use whatever approach works with an individual child to find out what that child was trying to write. Then you need to borrow the writing sample long enough to make a copy unless the child is willing to give it to you. Having the writing sample and knowing the child's intent will allow you to analyze the writing and match it to the sets of the writing forms and theories described in this chapter (see Table 1.3). Don't be surprised if you discover more than one theory being tested at a time. This research will be most productive with typically developing older preschoolers, kindergartners, and first graders.

about children's learning processes. *See the Being a Researcher box* ("What Is the Child's Theory of Writing?") for further discussion.

Once you are aware of the children's theories about print identified by Ferreiro, you can see those same theories in action in any preschool, kindergarten, or first-grade classroom. After they learn about Ferreiro's research, many teachers suddenly realize that they have been seeing this evidence of children's thinking all along but didn't recognize it because they weren't looking for it.

Of course, you won't see children's real thinking about writing if the only writing they do is copying existing print or completing other assignments with adult-imposed outcomes. The best time to observe children's theories about print is during play that includes writing materials. A large body of research provides substantial evidence for the influence of literacy–enriched play settings (e.g., Neuman, 1999; Neuman & Roskos, 1992, 1997; Rowe, 1999). Just putting paper and pencils in the play area is enough to get it started. A writing center that encourages free exploration of print will provide another opportunity for children to practice what they know and for teachers to find out what children know. Merely looking at the writing outcome won't give you much information; you

FIGURE 1.2
Is this drawing or writing?

need to observe the children as they engage in the process and talk with the youngsters about the messages in their writing. What looks like a page of scribbles or random letters may be a carefully thought-out communication. Careful and informed analysis of this writing can give teachers the key to unlock the mystery of children's thinking as they learn to read.

Is It Drawing or Writing?

As you observe, you will realize that children use all the information provided by their environment as they look for patterns that will make sense in reading and writing—or in whatever they are learning. At first, they do not distinguish between drawing and writing and may use the terms interchangeably. At this point, all their marks on paper may consist of scribbles that look much the same (see Figure 1.2). Some children will still draw when asked to write after they are capable of some

FIGURE 1.3
An example of the linear-repetitive writing form.

realism in their drawing. A child may even ask you how to write something when actually wanting help in drawing. The first big breakthrough comes when children arrive at the conclusion that writing, unlike drawing, does not reflect the shape of the objects represented.

Linear-Repetitive Forms

Once children have sorted out the differences between drawing and writing, their writing often becomes squiggly lines across the paper (see Figure 1.3). They will proudly fill up a page with this writing and may ask you to read it. These are emergent writers who have recognized the linear quality of print and are exploring that idea. This writing looks remarkably similar to the longhand, or cursive writing, commonly used by adults. Many youngsters are not concerned with the content of their writing yet but focus only on the form. When asked what they are writing, they may tell you, "A letter," or else answer, "I'm just writing." Some youngsters will obligingly make up something for the writing to say. This rereading may change, or it may stay the same each time the child repeats the reading. The latter response shows much more understanding about writing than does the former.

Letterlike Forms

Children also notice the letters in the signs, books, posters, and all the hubbub of written advertising everywhere in their environment. Approximations of letters will appear in their writing as youngsters attempt to incorporate this information into their theory of writing (see Figure 1.4). Four-year-old Patricia combines linear squiggles, actual letters, and letterlike forms in her writing (see Figure 1.5). This combination is common as youngsters work on their understanding of print.

No matter how hard schools try to have D'Nealian manuscript print or any other style of writing used consistently (Graham, 1993–1994), children will see

FIGURE 1.4
This writing uses letterlike forms.

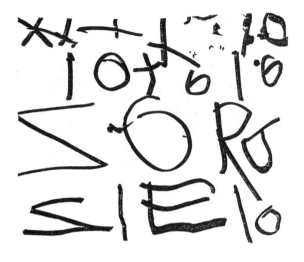

FIGURE 1.5
Like most youngsters, Patricia combines various understandings in her writing. Here she has used linear squiggles and letterlike forms as well as a few actual letters.

many different print styles as they ride down a busy street or page through a magazine. They often explore this data by copying print from signs or other writing around them. Children eventually must not only figure out which characteristics transcend writing styles but also face the chore of learning the uppercase and lowercase versions of each letter.

Letters as Representational Forms

Knowing what kinds of forms are involved in writing is still a long way from realizing that there is any connection between the letters used and the words or meanings intended. The first challenge is to realize that written marks represent the sounds of oral language—a notion very different from children's intuitive assumption that writing should look like the things written about. Traditional teaching practices, which focus on the names and shapes of letters, emphasize letters as objects rather than the more complex understanding of letters in a representational system. Television shows, such as *Sesame Street*, that show animated letters dancing around may further confuse the issue for youngsters.

In contrast, rich literacy environments that involve youngsters with actual reading and writing allow them to test and discard theories as they construct understanding of their representational system. Although children the world over demonstrate consistency in the type of theories about writing that they explore, each child's own experiences and innate characteristics affect the timing of such exploration. Typically, environmental factors include the amount of reading and writing in the child's home, whether the language of the home matches that of the school, the level of support and safety for experimentation, and the type of schooling practices encountered.

As children begin to use letters or letterlike forms for writing, they are still puzzling out the written language system. The distinctions they have made between writing and drawing create a question about how each is used. Youngsters commonly create the principle that pictures show what something looks like and writing tells the name of the thing (see Figure 1.6). Their next challenge has to do with how to make writing represent those names adequately (Ferreiro, 1990).

How Many Letters Make a Word?

Most adults assume that when youngsters focus on how to make writing represent certain words, they begin sorting out the sounds of letters. This may be what teachers are teaching, but what children are thinking about is something else. Those seemingly random strings of letters you see as part of children's writing at this point are actually far from random. They reflect a child's serious thought and creation of theories about print. Typically, youngsters construct a theory about how many letters are needed for a word to say something. They believe that a string of letters of just the right length will make a readable word. Most children will decide on a minimum number and a maximum number of letters. You will see

FIGURE 1.6

Brenton demonstrates his knowledge of writing, using both alphabetic and numeric symbols. He includes memorized forms of his name as well as three other words and has copied the date. His intent is that the writing tell about the volcano he drew.

FIGURE 1.7
This child's writing shows a quantitative principle that words contain three to six letters. It also demonstrates a qualitative principle acknowledging that different letters must be used to make words.

youngsters writing strings of three to seven letters as they explore this quantitative principle (see Figure 1.7).

At first, these strings may be repetitions of one letter. However, youngsters will soon notice that words are made up of several *different* letters, never the same letter over and over. Then their writing will contain a variety of letters, and they will demonstrate excellent observation by never putting more than two of the same letter next to one another. At this point, children are beginning to think about more than just the length of words. Some children use the same set of letters in the same order to represent any words they have in mind. As they explore and test their hypotheses, children continue to bring their writing creations to adults to read. That's a challenge!

Big Things Have Big Names

Youngsters briefly tend to be content with having the same set of letters stand for different things. But soon they begin to look for differences in sets of letters to explain what makes words different. This quest leads to more theories. As with all learning, solving one mystery opens the door to another. You might be thinking that now, finally, is the time that children learn about the sounds of letters. However, that is still not what children are thinking about, even if someone is getting them to parrot information about letter sounds. Instead, their real learning focuses on further exploring their theory that the number of letters is the key. Common assumptions are that it takes more letters to write the name of a big person than to write the name of a small person and more letters to describe a group of objects than to describe a single object (Ferreiro, 1991).

This viewpoint means that children believe that their parents' names must be long and their own short. Therefore, Christopher writes his own name very

FIGURE 1.8

Child's theory: Big things
and big people have big
names. Little things and
little people have little
names.

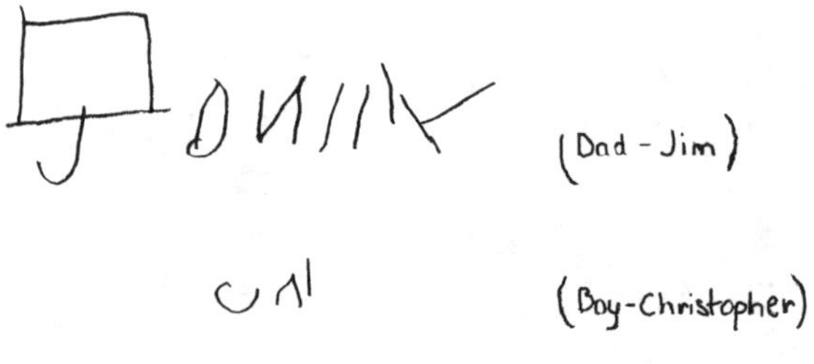

(Dad - Jim)

(Boy-Christopher)

small and his dad's name, Jim, very large (see Figure 1.8). Even after Patrick has made connections between the letters and their sounds, he writes his little sister Mary's name as *MR* and his mother's name, Katy, as *KDIO*. He obviously is adding extra letters to make his mom's name bigger than his sister's. Youngsters also assume that it takes more letters to write about a bunch of grapes than about one grape or about a flock of sheep than about one sheep. Free exploration of writing in journals or at writing centers during choice time is important for encouraging children to try out these ideas. Doing their own writing makes them more careful observers of other writing (Smith, 1989), so that when you read with children they are more apt to notice whether their theories work.

Rearranging Letters

Most children will explore their theories about different sequences of letters for different words in much more depth before they are ready to accept the alphabetic principle and learn phonics. Depending on how many letters a child knows, different patterns will emerge: Different letters might be used for different words, or only one or two different letters will be inserted for each, or the same letters will be used but in different sequences. At first, children may focus only on the letters in their own name and represent all words through various combinations of those few letters (see Figure 1.9). This approach is an approximation of the actual system but lacks important elements.

Checking and Discarding Theories

As they continue to work at reading and writing, children have opportunities to check their theories. They will soon encounter problems with those theories; for instance, Patricia's name is much longer than her dad's. They also may be perplexed by the fact that adults can't read what they have written. They know adults can read, so something must be wrong. A strong desire to become part of the literate society drives most youngsters to try again and again to make sense of the system. Well-meaning adults who give information that doesn't fit into the child's framework offer no help at all. Too often, adults are talking to a child about the sounds of letters while the child is focusing on how many marks it takes to make a word.

FIGURE 1.9
Austin uses the letters he knows—those in his name plus an *E* form and an upside down *L*—as he explores writing. Notice that his words conform to conventional standards for length and for having no more than two of the same letter next to one another.

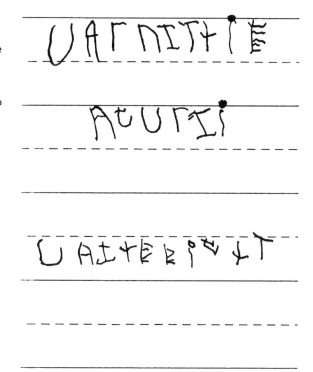

Finally, given repeated experiences with stories and environmental print, youngsters do begin to consider the sound of the word in relation to the letters used. However, they *still* may be focusing on the quantity of letters needed rather than on the phonics principles. This focus results in matching the number of symbols they write to the number of syllable sounds they hear (see Figure 1.10). This approach doesn't answer the question of why certain words are represented by certain letters, though, so youngsters must continue their work. Their own names offer an important model as children try to answer their questions. At this point, Patricia's teacher might help Patricia notice other names and words that start with a *P*. Patricia knew "her letter" before any other, and she could write her name when she was still scribble writing other words. Name writing develops earliest and provides insights about other writing.

Letter Names as Sounds

Their own first initial is often the first letter sound children figure out. As her mother reads aloud, three-year-old Sara points to an *S* in the text and says, "There's an "S." That's my letter." Sara is on her way with a new hypothesis that connects letters to sounds in words. This still doesn't mean that typical phonics

FIGURE 1.10

Syllable quantitative principle with emerging qualitative sound-symbol relationships. The child read this as, "Better watch out, better not cry, better not pout, I'm telling you why, never get mad."

I	YAH	I	YZ	POT	DA	ANT	POT	NT.
I	wish	it	was	part	day	and	part	night.

Line 1: Child's writing

Line 2: Translation

FIGURE 1.11

Can you figure out what the child knows about letter sounds?

lessons are relevant. Despite those lessons, children continue to go about their own business of making sense of things. They usually start with the theory that all letters represent a sound that is like the name of the letter. This deduction is logical because it is true for most consonants and for long vowel sounds. It is a phonics lesson that no one teaches to children but one that works more often than most that we do teach them (Clymer, 1996).

The theory that each letter makes the sound of its name leads to some interesting results when applied to *y*, which then becomes the first sound in words spelled with a *w* (see Figure 1.11). If you're confused, just say the name of the letter *y* and then say the sound of *w* to understand children's thinking. Thus, Patrick writes *yot* and reads it *what*. The letter-name-as-sound theory also makes for difficult reading for adults when youngsters decide that *h* is the logical choice for the *ch* sound. (Say *h* to yourself and see why.) Bryce combines his theories about *y* and *h* and logically writes *yh* for the word *witch*. As strange as this may seem to adults, the letter-name-as-sound theory reflects thoughtful consideration of the sound-symbol system and should be respected as such.

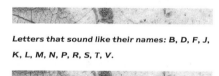

Letters that sound like their names: B, D, F, J, K, L, M, N, P, R, S, T, V.

Simply telling children the accepted spelling may not assist their learning at this point. However, if you keep on pointing out how those confusing sounds are written while you share stories and poems with children, most will eventually switch over. Continued exposure to print eventually will lead to theories more in keeping with standard convention. This transition occurs in the same manner in which hearing adult speech helps children progress from baby talk (Fields, 1998).

Simplified Phonics

English-speaking children tend to ignore the short vowel sounds in their early writing and write mostly with consonants. This practice reflects the fact that short vowels in English tend to have irregular, interchangeable, and indistinguishable sounds, shown in the dictionary as a schwa (Wilde, 1997). In contrast, Spanish-speaking children's early writing consists mostly of vowels, reflecting the dominant sounds in that language. Lessons in the sounds of vowels make much more sense in Spanish than in English because vowel sounds are consistent in Spanish.

When first exploring the sound-symbol connection in their writing, children tend to simplify the process to make it manageable. This simplification process also was demonstrated in their early speech when they spoke in one- or two-word sentences. Similarly, when youngsters begin to write by representing the sounds they hear, their early phonics-based spelling may be limited to representing one or two main sounds from a word (see Figure 1.12).

Despite the unconventional nature of emergent writing, adults finally are able to begin reading children's writing when it is based on phonics principles adults know. Unfortunately, many adults begin to value a child's efforts only at this point, rushing and discrediting everything leading up to it. Too few teachers or parents

BBKUSUSUNFME

FIGURE 1.12

This writing demonstrates the hypothesis that each letter makes the sound of its own name and that each letter represents one word. Translation: "Bumble bee, can you sing you sing your name for me?"

FIGURE 1.13

If you didn't know the child's intent, this would look like random letters. However, this is a fairy-tale format, using phonics-based spelling. The child read it from bottom to top: "Once upon a time, there lived a wolf who loved [to] eat little girls."

understand the child's previous efforts. Adults who don't understand children's emergent writing do not notice the thinking and problem solving that are going on. Even when it is right in front of us, we tend not to see what we don't know exists. Thus, children's early writing is often dismissed as scribbling or playing around.

Many adults do not value the learning process even when it reaches the phonics-based spelling level. Those who view learning as a memorization process are afraid that this temporary spelling means practicing errors (Temple et al., 1993). Consideration of how errors in baby talk disappear should dispel these fears.

Implications for Teaching

As children learn about print, they constantly formulate theories. When you understand the thinking behind children's various approaches to *reading and writing*, you will be better able to match your teaching efforts to a child's current understanding. Children's hypotheses are tested as they engage in authentic writing. When a child wants to hang a sign on a block construction to prevent others from knocking down the building, she has an authentic writing opportunity. Though children's writing is valuable evidence of their learning, the product alone won't give you much information until after a child already has things pretty well figured out (see Figure 1.13). Observing the process provides further clues. Even if you have observed the writing process, you won't be able to figure out what hypothesis a child is using unless you also find out what the child is intending to do. You can't expect children to verbalize their hypotheses, but you usually can get them to tell you what they meant to write or how they knew what a word was as they read. Then it is up to you to figure out which hypothesis a child is using. This process is a basic aspect of assessment (see Figure 1.14).

The teacher's role also is to provide support for thinking by providing opportunities for children to freely explore their current hypotheses. Making literacy tools available throughout the classroom increases the literacy opportunities available to children. Other ways of encouraging thinking include peer debate, presenting challenging questions, sharing discrepant examples, and accepting children's efforts. As we stated previously, encouraging thinking, providing

This is what Patrick wrote:

THE MOSTR Bi Patrick
a mostr lidi in otr sas he yuti to go dan to Earth
hetr trid togid ded to Earth bet he citit the gavd
wuz to sog bet then he hat e ider hwot tack a sas
sip the sassip waz no i sassip oln yot to go up
the ed

This is how Patrick read what he wrote:

"A monster lived in outer space. He wanted to go down to Earth.
He tried to get down to Earth but he couldn't. The gravity was too
strong. But then he had an idea. He would take a spaceship. The
spaceship was not a spaceship. It only wanted to go up."

FIGURE 1.14

Now that you know more about children's theories, can you read what
Patrick wrote?

meaningful experiences, and offering relevant information all are important ways
of helping children learn oral and written language. These roles of the teacher will
be discussed in subsequent chapters.

CONCLUSION

This chapter has presented information about how children learn as the basis for a
discussion of how to teach. Literacy development was described in the context of
language development, emphasizing the integrated nature of language and literacy learning. Both oral and written language were described as processes in which
children actively construct knowledge rather than passively imitate or memorize.

DISCUSSION QUESTIONS

1. Many parents of preschoolers want to help their children learn to read.
   What are appropriate ways for parents to assist the beginning literacy
   process?

2. Many early childhood programs still try to teach the letters and sounds through memorization. How can you help other teachers change to more effective teaching approaches?
3. How is reading and writing instruction changed when teachers base their teaching on research about emergent literacy?
4. What do you remember about your own experiences in learning to read and write? Were you confused when adults just sat and looked at a book and said they were reading? Did you practice writing with lines of squiggles? What did you do at home? At school?

SUGGESTED FOLLOW-UP ACTIVITIES

1. Ask a four- or five-year-old to explain something such as where rain, clouds, or waves come from. Continue your conversation past any learned explanation; try to get the child's own perception rather than repetition of adult explanations. Use the answers to analyze the child's way of thinking and learning.
2. Spend a few minutes visiting with a two-year-old, a four-year-old, and a six-year-old on separate occasions. Document the rapid changes in their ability to communicate, vocabulary, and sentence constructions. Note the children's sentence simplification processes and their own constructed principles of grammar.
3. Ask children what words are written in a sentence, as described in the Being a Researcher box "What Is Written in a Sentence?" on page 28. What theories about print do you observe?
4. Observe children of various ages as they write. Ask them about what they are writing, analyze the forms used, and try to determine their current theories about how writing works (see the Being a Researcher box; "What Is the Child's Theory of Writing?" on page 29).
5. Observe or talk to parents of young children to find out how they involve their youngsters in family reading and writing activities.
6. Compare and contrast the three policy statements regarding beginning reading that are referenced in this chapter: International Reading Association/National Association for the Education of Young Children, Learning First Alliance, and National Academy of Science.
7. Analyze your own learning. Think about how you learned to do something recently and consider how thinking, experiences, and information interacted in your learning process. Try to describe this interaction.

RECOMMENDED FURTHER READING

Duckworth, E. (1996). *The having of wonderful ideas and other essays on teaching and learning.* New York: Teachers College Press.

Ferreiro, E. (1978). What is written in a written sentence? A developmental answer. *Journal of Education, 160*(4), 25–29.

Goodman, Y. (1990). *How children construct literacy.* Newark, DE: International Reading Association.

Kamii, C., Manning, M., & Manning, G. (1991). *Early literacy: A constructivist foundation for whole language.* Washington, DC: National Education Association.

McQuillan, J. (1998). *The literacy crisis: False claims, real solutions.* Portsmouth, NH: Heinemann.

Moustafa, M. (1997). *Beyond traditional phonics.* Portsmouth, NH: Heinemann.

Neuman, S. B., Copple, C., & Bredekamp, S. (2000). *Learning to read and write: Developmentally appropriate practices for young children.* Washington, DC: National Association for the Education of Young Children.

Teale, W., & Sulzby, E. (1986). *Emergent literacy: Writing and reading.* Norwood, NJ: Ablex.

2

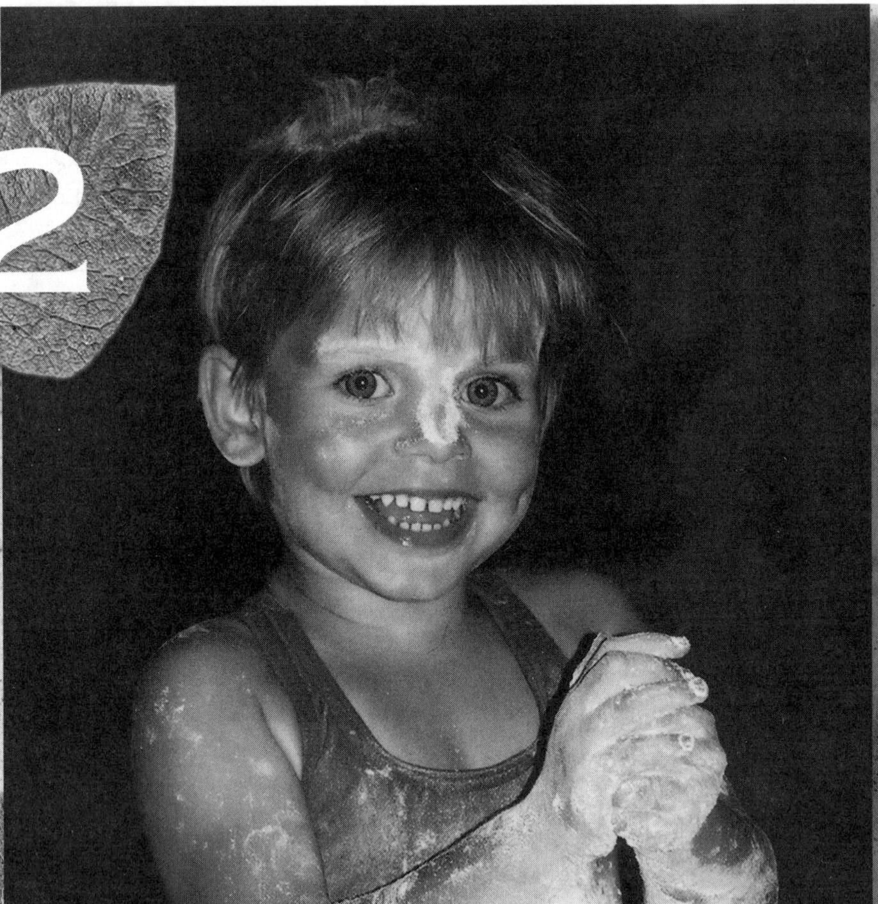

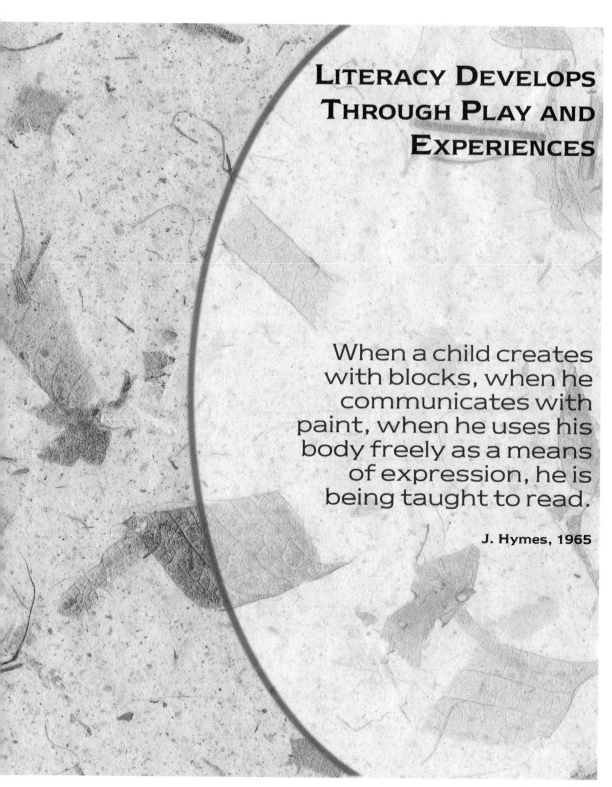

LITERACY DEVELOPS THROUGH PLAY AND EXPERIENCES

When a child creates with blocks, when he communicates with paint, when he uses his body freely as a means of expression, he is being taught to read.

J. Hymes, 1965

Developmentally appropriate practice guidelines for the early years recommend teaching in the ways that children learn; offering learning activities that are relevant, interesting, and meaningful to children; engaging children actively in learning; and allowing them meaningful choices (Neuman, Copple, & Bredekamp, 2000). These guidelines mandate early childhood programs that allow play and provide experiences with the world outside the classroom. This chapter describes authentic play and experiences and shows their link to literacy learning as well as to learning in general. You will notice that literacy materials are available for all activities (Goldhaber, Lipson, Sortino, & Daniels, 1996–1997).

The classroom environment will either support or limit children's ability to learn through play and experiences. Therefore, consideration must be given to how the physical environment is arranged. For instance, small, well-defined play spaces encourage children to focus better and to interact more in their play (Roskos & Neuman, 2002). Learning centers such as the playhouse or block area should be set off from larger areas and from the movement of the room. Storage units for play materials can create room dividers if placed so that they are perpendicular to the room walls.

What did you think when you read the quote by James Hymes at the beginning of this chapter? Are you wondering how creating with blocks, communicating with paint, and using their bodies for expression can possibly teach children to read? We hope you are wondering about that. There are more quotations from Hymes in this chapter and the next. We hope that they all make you think, and we hope that by the end of Chapter 3 you will be able to explain why these statements about being taught to read are true.

The type, number, and accessibility of play materials also affect the quality of play. We will discuss appropriate materials as we discuss various types of play and experiences. Basic considerations include having enough materials for all children, having materials to which children of different cultures can relate, and making the materials accessible to children of varying physical abilities. Some teachers are unaccustomed to planning around diverse cultures and abilities. We will be describing some teachers who are adept at including diverse cultures and abilities in their classrooms (Figure 2.1).

Ms. Reynolds welcomed Shana into the preschool environment, making sure that pathways were cleared for Shana's walker. Shana has cerebral palsy; damage to the motor portion of her brain at birth left her with limited, spastic movements in her lower limbs (Bakley, 1998). Shana receives the support of a special educator while attending the inclusive preschool and has made excellent progress in academic as well as physical development. More often than not, she leaves her walker in a corner and makes her way without its encumbrance. Watching her classmates, Shana even learned to climb the high ladder to the slide on the playground and slide down like the other children.

Ms. Montoya also tries to make her multiage-primary classroom feel homelike for all her students. She makes sure that room decorations reflect their various cultures and that posters and books similarly reflect the ethnicity of her class. She encourages parents to share items from their homes and cultures with the class.

In Chapters 2 through 5 we try to bring descriptions of classrooms to life by introducing you to some of our favorite teachers:

- Ms. Reynolds, a co-op preschool teacher (a co-op preschool is run by parents and involves parents as assistants to the teacher)
- Mrs. Hanna, a kindergarten teacher
- Mrs. Thomas, a first-grade teacher
- Ms. Montoya, a bilingual multiage-primary (ages 5–8) teacher

Of course, we know many more wonderful teachers, so sometimes their ideas and actions are credited to one of the teachers in the book. The few classrooms we describe actually represent what we've seen in dozens of classrooms. We hoped to make it more fun to read by keeping our cast of characters small and personal. Like most classrooms in the United States today, all the classrooms described are inclusive and diverse, with children of varying abilities and from a multitude of cultures.

In Chapters 6 and 7 you will meet some teachers of older children.

FIGURE 2.1
Meet the teachers.

PLAY ENCOURAGES EMERGENT LITERACY

Play is prescribed for developmentally appropriate programs in the primary grades as well as in preschool and kindergarten (Neuman et al., 2000). Teachers and parents frequently quote the statement that "play is the work of children" and pay lip service to the value of play. Yet in practice, teachers often allow play only after other schoolwork is completed, or they assign the label "play" to teacher-directed activity. Many parents complain if their children report that what they did in school was play. These problems are symptoms of widespread misunderstanding of how children learn and the role of play in that learning.

Some educators have speculated that the term *play* has a bad reputation and should be abandoned. Some classrooms use terms such as "choosing time" instead of the *P* word. Whatever we call it, children's engagement in freely chosen activities of interest is vitally important to their learning. There is no opposition between play and academics for young children: One is process, and one is content (Rust, 1997). Play is the process for learning much of the content of academics. Play is one important way in which children construct knowledge. It provides for exploration of the environment, experimentation with their ever changing theories, practice in emerging skills, and peer interaction to stimulate thought about these activities. Parents and educators who understand the value of these activities will defend play as basic to the early childhood curriculum.

Play has a unique role in literacy development (Christie, Enz, & Vukelich, 1997; Roskos & Christie, 2000). Play provides a context for practice, content for reading and writing, and a mode of learning as well. We can see play providing a context for practice when Caitlan writes a pretend phone message in the playhouse; we see play providing content for literacy when Demetrius writes about his block construction; we see play as a mode of literacy learning when Anastasia pretends to read the book from yesterday's story time. Play as a mode of learning is particularly important because it represents an attitude valuable to all intellectual development. The playful attitude encourages intellectual risk taking in formulating new hypotheses and experimenting with them. This attitude views experimentation as pleasurable and encourages further learning.

Play provides a context for literacy development practice, content for reading and writing, and a mode of learning as well.

What do we mean by play? Sometimes what looks like work to an observer feels like play to the participant; sometimes what looks like play can feel like work. What is the distinction? Generally, work is what we must do to attain something of value or avoid something unpleasant, and play is what we choose to do because it is inherently interesting or pleasurable.

We usually consider digging a ditch work, yet we see Dominic having a wonderful time digging a ditch to drain a big puddle on the playground. Because he chose to do this and is enjoying it, digging a ditch becomes play for him. On the other hand, we see a group of children in a kindergarten who appear to be playing with a set of blocks of various colors and shapes. A closer look reveals that this is not play but a lesson in following directions for finding colors and shapes. Their teacher is directing the activity and now requests that they each find a red triangle and add it to their block structures. Several of the children appear restless and have to be reprimanded to pay attention. Because this block play is not self-selected or motivating to these children, it cannot be classified as play.

Exploratory Play

Dominic's ditch digging is an example of a type of play in which children explore their environment and seek to understand it through manipulation. Sand and water play are also in this category, as are other exploratory activities that cause youngsters to fiddle around with almost anything they can get their hands on. Teachers need to provide a variety of items that are acceptable for young children's experiments so that the children can indulge their scientific curiosity without endangering themselves or damaging their surroundings. For some youngsters, explorations need to be assisted by a sand and water table that accommodates a wheelchair. If that isn't possible, then plastic tubs may make these interesting materials accessible.

As he digs, Dominic encounters the properties of dirt. It seems hard and solid where packed, but he can loosen it into powder. Where water mixes with it, the dirt becomes soft and squishy. When the dirt turns into mud, it no longer brushes off his hands and clothes but sticks to him. Dominic may find that dirt contains rocks or

Because the child chose the activity and is enjoying it, digging a ditch becomes play for him.

even something as interesting as worms. His discoveries become a foundation of knowledge that he uses to create new theories about his world. Dominic's discoveries do more than enhance his science background; they will also provide new or added meaning to oral and written language that relates to his experience. He will extend his vocabulary as he shares his experiences with others and receives their responses. He will find personal meaning in books about digging in dirt or playing in the mud, such as *Muddigush* (Knudson, 1992). He may also use his experience as a topic for writing.

Pretend Play

Pretend play refers to children's playing make-believe roles. It is sometimes called *sociodramatic play* or *dramatic play*. Most classrooms for young children have a playhouse center that encourages this type of play through props such as make-believe kitchen appliances, doll furniture, and dress-up clothes. Ms. Montoya makes sure that the play kitchen in her multiage-primary classroom includes a variety of utensils, such as a tortilla press or a wok, so that all her students' home experiences are reflected. Ms. Reynolds takes care that preschooler Shana and her walker have room to move around in the playhouse area.

Now let's watch Kelly, who has a long scarf tied around her waist to simulate a skirt. Banging pots and pans around the playhouse, she admonishes two dolls propped at the table. "Hurry up and eat," she says. "We'll all be late. I have to get to work on time." When Scott wanders in, Kelly adds, "You be the dad, and then we'll get divorced." She hands him one of the dolls and tells him to get the baby dressed. But Scott wants to cook. He drops the doll and says, "I'll fix the dinner." Kelly gets visibly upset and yells, "No! I have to go to work now. It's morning." Scott continues to try to mesh his goals with Kelly's and suggests, "Let's pretend you came home now, and I fix your dinner." Reluctantly, Kelly agrees but insists that she has to leave first and then come back.

An observer of this play scene immediately notices the amount of talking involved. It is obvious that pretend play encourages practice with oral communication. The give-and-take involved in negotiating a script and playing cooperatively requires a high degree of explicitness in speech. The negotiation process also provides children an excellent opportunity for practice in social skills, especially in becoming less egocentric. As children find out that others might not see things their way, their drive to play with other children causes them to compromise their initial positions. Realizing that theirs are not the only views of a situation represents intellectual as well as social growth.

The condensed form of time in pretend play—in which events of several days are represented in a matter of minutes—helps children think and notice connections between such events (Sinclair, 1996). Pretend play fosters general intellectual development partly because it assists with reflection—thinking things over (Piaget, 1962). Because they cannot retain ideas in their heads to mull them over as an adult might, children play them out. If Kelly wants to understand her mother's impatience of that morning, Kelly is helped by reenacting it.

Although pretend play is not the same thing as putting on a play, sometimes Ms. Montoya will notice a detailed plot emerge in pretend play, and she will encourage the children to make it into a written story. This mirrors the developmental sequence suggested by Vygotsky (1978) that begins with oral language, is demonstrated in symbolic play, and ends with the use of written language. Because this is a multiage classroom, spanning ages five through eight, youngsters who need help writing can consult with a more competent classmate. Ms. Montoya will take dictation if requested and will help children reconstruct their pretend play into a written narrative theme. This assistance allows the youngsters to explore their topic more fully and also provides them with more literacy experience. Children get to see their play and their ideas take written form, and they will practice reading as they review what was written.

Pretend play provides for literacy events in a variety of ways. Through thoughtful infusion of literacy tools in play areas, Mrs. Hanna encourages her kindergartners specifically to use reading and writing behaviors in real-life, func-

Children are reading and writing in real-life functional ways during pretend play.

tional ways during their play. She provides a moderate amount of theme-related literacy material to complement other playthings, recognizing that too many literacy props might interfere with play (Roskos & Christie, 2001). Cookbooks by the play stove and storybooks by the doll crib encourage emergent reading. The scrap-paper notepads beside the phone in the playhouse offer a constant invitation to write. Youngsters use the notepads in many of the ways they see their families using writing. They not only take pretend phone messages but also write notes to one another, notes as reminders to themselves, and grocery lists.

CHAPTER 2

It is important to note that writing in pretend play is usually pretend writing, even when the writer is capable of more sophisticated strategies. The benefit of this writing seems more related to understanding the function of print than the form. Children tend to explore their more advanced understandings of print when writing for real situations or audiences (Fields & Hillstead, 2001). Nevertheless, children's understanding of print and their visions of themselves as writers are enhanced through writing in pretend play because it offers an authentic context for literacy (Roskos & Neuman, 2002).

The play store generates lots of writing. Mrs. Hanna reminds the kindergarten children that it is important to have a list for shopping, so many grocery lists are made. Each youngster writes a list using whatever form of writing that child chooses. Some children create some readable, phonics-based spelling; others draw pictures; still others may write in squiggles; and some find the real words to copy. Most lists reflect a combination of approaches. Newspaper advertisements for sale items inspire some writing as well as some reading. Mrs. Hanna encourages literate behaviors with questions. For instance:

How can you help yourself remember what you need to buy?

How can people find out what is on sale at the store?

How do shoppers know how much things cost?

What is a receipt? Why do you need one? (Fields & Hillstead, 1995)

Setting up the grocery store involved many literacy events too. After deciding on the name of the store, a committee of children made the store sign. Then they noticed that the shelves needed labeling and that the food containers needed to have prices marked on them. A few youngsters noticed that food packages from some classmates' homes had labels written in various languages. One group of youngsters printed the money to be used in the store. The children learned much more from setting up the store themselves than if the teacher had done it for them.

Mrs. Thomas recognizes the benefits of play even though its value is not always appreciated as part of the primary-grade curriculum (Cooper & Dever, 2001). Mrs. Thomas's first graders had a great time when they set up an airport ticket counter in the classroom. Like the kindergarten play store, this pretend play center followed a relevant field trip during which the children observed passengers reading the arrival and departure schedules, ticket agents reading and writing using their computers, and baggage handlers reading destination tags. At the airport, the ticket agents gave the children a big box full of the throwaway parts of printed tickets. Everyone wanted to write tickets with these interesting scraps. In addition, some youngsters got involved painting artistic travel posters to decorate the area. Others made brochures about travel destinations. Mrs. Thomas allowed them to have a computer at the ticket counter to make things official. Several children worked together to plan and make the arrival and departure schedule chart. They brought suitcases from home to check in at the counter, and each suitcase had to be labeled with the owner's name, address, and proper destination.

Many children decided to write or dictate stories about their real or pretend trips. They expressed high interest in books about planes and stories about travel. The block area turned into a miniature airport for a while, with frequent toy plane takeoffs and landings. Playing airport turned into a theme for an integrated curriculum (Bagley & Klass, 1997). It was an exciting time.

Block Play

A block area that encourages literacy includes a supply of paper and cardboard, markers and pencils, scissors and tape, as well as books (Picket, 1998). Books showing various kinds of structures can provide inspiration for reading and for building.

Let's look at what Mrs. Thomas's first-grade students, Matthew and Dustin, are building in the block area. When we come to watch, they begin to work even more diligently. They have created an elaborate set of roadways and are attempting to add bridges and ramps. They are testing the setup with small cars and trucks. When Dustin drives a truck under the bridge, his vehicle collides with Matthew's, coming from the opposite direction. The boys decide to make traffic signs showing which way to go so they won't wreck again. They are so engrossed that they do not want to stop at lunchtime. Finally, Mrs. Thomas says they must stop for lunch, but she suggests they leave their project where it is and make a sign asking that no one touch their highway. After lunch, Matthew and Dustin return to the block area. While valuable in its own right, block building has also given these boys reasons for writing, helping them understand the value of print and encouraging practice in using it.

The fine-quality wooden unit blocks are designed to assist children in making observations about relationships in size and quantity. Building bridges or spans of any sort with blocks provides practice in perceptual skills, such as determining size and distance. Blocks also naturally lead to practice with balancing and stabilizing. The problem-solving aspect of block building offers wonderful thinking opportunities. The various shapes and sizes of blocks make them excellent classification materials—especially when they are stored according to size and shape. Blocks are important educational materials and gain in value as children progress through the primary grades. Any experiences that encourage thinking increase intellectual development, which in turn assists all learning.

Blocks can become whatever the child desires—bricks, houses, roadways, towers, or bridges. They can even be people, cars, or furniture. Some early literacy researchers believe that these experiences with symbolic representation help children understand the symbolic uses of letters to represent sounds of language. Block play generally involves a theme from which pretend play flows. Props such as miniature people, doll furniture, small animal figures, or small cars and trucks can extend block-play ideas as well as assist the pretend-play element. Block play can inspire themes for writing and art as well as for drama. Often a current theme

Blocks are important educational materials and become more valuable as children progress through the primary grades.

being explored in all areas of the curriculum will find its way into the block area. The airport is one example; a block zoo and a block farm are others. Block play can encourage reading and writing just as literacy activities can lead to block play.

Continued Value of Blocks

Were you surprised that we talk about a block area in a first-grade class? Many people expect block areas in a preschool and even in a kindergarten but anticipate big changes as children enter first grade. However, children in first grade usually are still in the preoperational stage of intellectual development and continue to benefit from having concrete materials for meaningful learning. Mrs. Thomas makes sure that her first graders have real experiences and materials to help them in their thinking and understanding. Several children in her class this year are repeating first grade. They came to her turned off to reading but excited about opportunities to play. Mrs. Thomas believes that they were stopped short in their play and must have some of their needs met through play before they can move on. Most of all, these youngsters need developmentally appropriate activities so that they can experience success and begin to feel good about themselves again (DeVries, 2001).

Mrs. Thomas believes that blocks are such important learning tools for six- and seven-year-olds that she managed to make room in her classroom for a fully equipped block area. Plenty of blocks are available so that children will not run out in the middle of a project. There are shelves for storing the blocks because Mrs. Thomas knows that dumping them into a bin makes it difficult for children to find the block they need and that dumping them together may damage the blocks. She labeled the block shelves with the outline of the size and shape of the blocks that are to be stored in each section. This labeling assists children in cleanup and calls their attention to classification categories. Mrs. Thomas enhances the block-play environment by frequently watching or admiring what is happening there. She gives her students the message that their block building is important. Her efforts are rewarded with wonderfully intricate and innovative block structures.

Mrs. Thomas considers it a shame that schools generally deprive children of this type of play just as they attain enough maturity to really create with raw materials. When she took her turn as a parent helper in her children's preschool, she saw that three- and four-year-old youngsters played with blocks more in an exploratory manner—messing around with what could be done with them. Frequently, the children simply spread the blocks around. When Mrs. Thomas taught kindergarten, she saw that with previous block-play experience and added maturity, her students were beginning to realize the potential of the blocks. Now, her first graders are becoming sophisticated in their block building.

Ms. Montoya agrees that blocks are important for her seven- and eight-year-old students as well as for her five-year-olds. She used to think of blocks primarily as math and science materials but has come to value them for language and literacy as well. She sees that block-play experience and the feelings of accomplishment that come from it provide interesting topics for discussion and writing. Of course, there is constant oral language involved in cooperative block play. As Ms. Montoya encounters more and more students who speak little or no English, she discovers that they are drawn to the block area. Apparently, blocks speak all languages. As youngsters whose first language is not English coordinate their block-building efforts with native speakers of English, the block area becomes a language-learning area.

Active Play

Mrs. Thomas's first-grade classroom is not large, but she makes provisions for large-muscle activity indoors and encourages active outdoor play at recess. Her classroom has space for a balance beam and a safe chinning bar. Students may use this equipment throughout the day. She would never consider keeping children from recess as punishment or as time to complete other work. Mrs. Thomas understands the importance of vigorous movement for proper development (Pica,

Teachers gain valuable information about children's interests, experience, and understanding by observing them at play.

1997). Frequently, she takes youngsters outside at unscheduled times for special activities involving large rubber balls or a parachute.

In the preschool where she teaches, Ms. Reynolds has set aside an area for indoor large-muscle activity. There is plenty of space for running without getting hurt, a sturdy climbing tower, trikes, large blocks, a rocking boat, and a continually challenging variety of other interesting equipment. Ms. Reynolds provides time for outdoor play too. When she taught in a child care center, Ms. Reynolds was even more careful about outdoor time because she had the children with her all day. She assumes that her half-day preschool students will have further chances to play outside in the afternoon.

When a child uses his whole body—two eyes, two hands, two arms, two legs and knees and feet—to pull himself up a scary slanted climbing board, he is being taught to read. (J. Hymes, 1965)

When she has students, like Shana, who have limited motor abilities, Ms. Reynolds makes sure that they can participate in indoor and outdoor active play too. The preschool provides scooter boards on which Shana can sit and either push herself around or be pulled by a friend (Sheldon, 1996). A wagon also allows Shana to be part of the action and move around with the others. And the school recently obtained an adaptive tricycle that Shana is very excited about.

Games

Though unstructured running, climbing, and bike riding are the mainstay of outdoor play, organized games offer occasional alternatives for those who are interested. Chasing games, such as the Chinese game Dragon's Tail, contribute to understanding of language, number, music, and social studies as well as muscle control (McCracken, 1993). Ms. Montoya and her fellow teachers value the fact that there are no winners or losers in the Dragon's Tail game. They have learned many other excellent games from the book of group games written by Kamii and DeVries (1993).

Indoor games are an important part of their curriculum too. Ms. Reynolds finds value in preschool children's making lotto games as well as playing them. Old magazines and catalogs are excellent sources of pictures for matching lotto. Mrs. Hanna helps her kindergartners cut up pictures from magazines, their drawings, or snapshots to make puzzles. Ms. Montoya buys board games and puzzles for her multiage-primary class from yard sales. Mrs. Thomas bases her first-grade arithmetic curriculum on games suggested by Kamii (1985).

Whether the games are designed to teach arithmetic or are aimed more clearly at language arts skills, children practice language and thinking. Kamii and DeVries (1993) suggest the following criteria for choosing games: Games should offer children the challenge of figuring out how to do something, children should be able to judge their own success, and all players should be able to participate actively throughout the game.

Manipulative Materials

Manipulative materials usually are located with the quiet games. The idea is to keep noisy, rambunctious work separate from that requiring closer concentration. Mrs. Hanna keeps beads, geoboards, puzzles, pegs, knitting supplies, play dough, small blocks, Legos®, Rigajigs®, and other small construction materials stored neatly on open shelves readily accessible to youngsters. These materials offer opportunities for children to problem solve and to construct knowledge about quantity, size, shape, patterns, and color. They also provide practice with visual discrimination, eye-hand coordination, and fine-muscle control, which are helpful skills but not prerequisites for reading and writing. Mrs. Hanna makes sure there are materials representing various levels of difficulty so that each child will be able to find an appropriate challenge. For a youngster with limited motor control, simply holding on to the materials is a big challenge (Sheldon, 1996). Velcro or nonskid rubberized pads can prevent materials from sliding around and make them easier to grab.

By the time children reach Mrs. Thomas's first grade, they have made progress in both large- and small-muscle coordination. However, Mrs. Thomas does not expect complete mastery, and she continues to provide opportunities to enhance coordination skills. Yes, this first grade has beads to string, play dough to squeeze, and puzzles to assemble. Mrs. Thomas knows that children in her class are now mature enough to experience greater success with these materials and to

Materials must allow for each child to find the appropriate level of challenge.

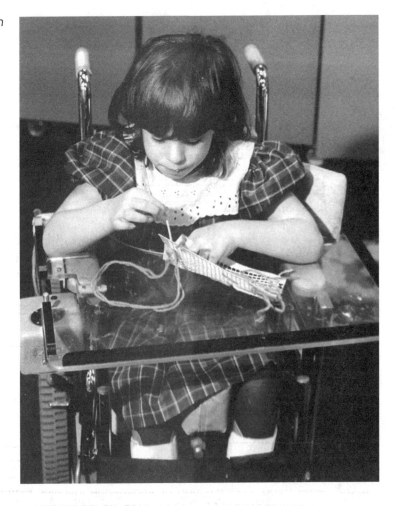

be creative rather than merely exploratory. She knows that these activities assist all students in the process of learning to read and write too. Mrs. Thomas also makes sure to figure out how Alice can participate in such activities from her wheelchair. Mrs. Thomas is helping Alice develop perceptual abilities and be part of the class despite her inability to move her body as she desires.

Most people can understand that fine-motor coordination activities are related to literacy skills. These activities have been more welcomed into the schoolrooms of young children than gross-coordination activities—until first grade, that is. After that, it is less common to find the manipulative materials that we found in Mrs. Thomas's first-grade classroom and still less common to find them used as a vital part of the program. Too often, schools relegate manipulative materials to be time fillers after workbooks or work sheets are completed. This arrangement of priorities shows a lack of understanding of how young children develop and learn.

EXPERIENCES ENCOURAGE EMERGENT LITERACY

Children and adults need to bring meaning to the printed page in order to get meaning from that page (K. S. Goodman, 1996; Leu & Kinzer, 1999; Pressley, 1998). Without some relevant experience or some personal meaning, much of the message that we read will be lost. Written words can extend our understandings, but they must build on an existing understanding. The common reaction of most adults who begin to read an article that is too technical—one that deals with unfamiliar facts and concepts—is to put the article aside. Adults and children tend to enjoy reading about the adventures of others that are similar to their own.

When a child looks ever so carefully at the scale in the store or at the life in his aquarium, he is being taught to read. When his year is a series of mind-stretching, eye-filling trips, helping him know more solidly his world, he is being taught to read. (J. Hymes, 1965)

Writing also requires experiences so that the author will have something to write about. Even authors of fiction are told to write about what they know so their writing doesn't fall flat. Likewise, children are uninspired to write unless they have something of personal interest to share.

Even more than adults, children need to build on personal experience in their encounters with written and oral language. What we know about how young children think and learn, thanks to the work of Jean Piaget, tells us that children are much less able than adults to conceptualize ideas from mere words. Primary-grade students as well as preschool children, all in the preoperational stage, require concrete-level explorations to develop understandings. When youngsters interact with real objects, they begin to think about them and develop their understandings.

Educators must make the distinction between constructing knowledge and learning facts. An adult can tell a child facts, and that child can memorize and repeat them, but such a performance does not imply understanding or necessarily involve thought. Although facts may be part of a complex understanding, they are not the same thing. Construction of knowledge involves higher-level thinking based on analysis of series of facts or events. Young children especially need first-hand experiences to encourage the hypothesis and experiment cycle of constructing knowledge (Piaget, 1973).

Sometimes adults are in a hurry for children to learn. Adults try to speed the learning process by substituting secondhand experiences for firsthand ones. They confuse passive exposure through pictures, films, or lectures with the active learning mode that Piaget's research told us is especially necessary for children under the age of eight. When these shortcut approaches result in a veneer of superficial knowledge, some adults think that the children have learned a great deal in a short time. However, like the thin layer of wood put on as a veneer over fiberboard, the superficial knowledge isn't the real thing. Similarly, knowing specific words and actually understanding what they represent are not necessarily the same thing. Just observe the results of youngsters' overexposure to television. These young children are able to talk about a number of things about which they understand little.

Firsthand experiences and observations take time. Betsy has to pour the water from one container to others over and over, on many different occasions, before she can understand that a short, wide container can hold the same amount as a tall, narrow one. Even then, the understandings she develops are only beginnings. Sometimes she will temporarily believe an incorrect idea because of her incomplete experience and immature understandings. What a temptation it is to rush in and explain to her that she is wrong and tell her the "right" answer. Knowledgeable teachers and parents resist that temptation. They know that Betsy can never discover what she has been told; she understands best what she discovers for herself. As explained in Chapter 1, these adults know that if they tell Betsy that her perceptions of reality are wrong, Betsy will only learn to distrust herself as a learner. If Betsy's immature view of the world tells her that the tall, narrow container holds more than the short, wide one, no amount of telling her otherwise will help her understand. She will believe the wise adult and believe that she is wrong, but she will be confused and cease to trust and learn through her own thinking.

When teachers and parents encourage children to explore and experiment with their environment, the children build foundations of understanding. They have experiences to think about, talk about, and write about; they expand their vo-

Cooking experiences offer science lessons, reasons to read a recipe, and something to write about.

cabulary with meaningful words related to their experiences; and they can relate personally to what others write about similar experiences. Children also gain practice in "reading"—or bringing meaning to a wide variety of experiences. They learn to read people's moods from their expressions or to read the weather from the color of the sky (Lee & Allen, 1963). Children learn to read symbols, such as the "golden arches," that relate to their experience. They also learn to read printed symbols with which they have had experience, such as the letters on the red sign that say "STOP."

The Teacher's Role

Ms. Montoya sees ample evidence in her multiage-primary class to convince her that the more experience they have with block building, the more youngsters benefit from blocks. Mrs. Thomas knows that six- and seven-year-olds need many opportunities to extend their language and thinking skills through pretend play. She also knows that play provides great reasons to practice reading and writing skills, but she does not value that any more highly than she does the other benefits of play.

Mrs. Thomas attempts to provide as many play opportunities for her first graders as possible. She knows that they are still in the "golden age" of pretend play and still have an emotional and intellectual need for that mode of dealing with ideas. Therefore, a play sink and stove are part of her room, as are dress-up clothes and other props that can be used for various themes. Her students often use desktops covered with a cloth to represent tables for playing house. Mrs. Thomas understands the continued need for water and sand play too, so she never hurries children as they wash paintbrushes or hands at the sink. Also, she never tells them not to play in the puddles or not to get dirty on the playground. She purchased a water-play table for the class, and sometimes she creates variety by filling it with rice or beans or sand. She provides further experiences with a variety of substances through frequent classroom cooking activities.

Mrs. Hanna provides a variety of props, multiethnic dress-up clothes, dolls with many shades of skin color, and a playhouse area in her kindergarten classroom. Because of limited space, she designed a structure that creates a cozy reading loft on top and a playhouse underneath. Some teachers sit at their desks during playtime, thinking there is no role for them. Mrs. Hanna believes just the opposite. She encourages pretend play through her presence as an observer and sometimes as a participant when invited. Observing pretend play not only encourages and assists play but also allows the teacher to gather important diagnostic teaching information (Neuman & Roskos, 1997).

By watching her kindergartners in the playhouse or in the block area, Mrs. Hanna gains valuable information about the children's interests, experiences, and levels of understanding about their experiences. She can pick up clues about possible emotional problems if she sees a child who replays one theme over and over again or a child who seems unable to participate in this type of play. During her observations, Mrs. Hanna finds out when children might have a narrative theme to put into writing. Occasionally, she takes notes on what they are saying and reads it back later to the children involved. These notes can become the core of a written version of their play.

As she observes play in her multiage-primary classroom, Ms. Montoya notices interesting similarities between the ways in which individual children pursue play activities and how they approach literacy activities. Some are orderly, systematic, and cautious in how they get to the top of the climbing tower or in constructing the small structures they build. These same youngsters often are the ones concerned with correctness and neatness in their writing and who proceed with orderly caution in their reading attempts. Other youngsters proceed impetuously, with seemingly little worry about the outcome, whether they are climbing to new heights on the playground equipment, writing new words, or making meaning from a new book. They make glorious messes wherever they go—the art easels, the writing center, or the block area. Some differences in behavior seem to reflect family culture and values (De Gaetano, Williams, & Volk, 1998), whereas others reflect individual personalities.

Mrs. Thomas, Mrs. Hanna, and Ms. Montoya value play as an integral part of their curriculum just as much as Ms. Reynolds does in her preschool. These fine teachers do not view play as a break from learning; rather, they see it as an essential mode of learning. None of them relegates play to a time after the "real" work of school is done. They know that this is the real work of learning; therefore, they provide extended periods of time in their daily schedules to encourage this type of learning (Christie & Wardle, 1992). Furthermore, they do not try to assign play topics, play areas, or playmates. When a task is assigned, it is no longer play; it becomes work by a child's definition (DeVries, 2001). These teachers know that free choice is the essence of true play.

Home Experiences

Children have had a lot of experiences before they reach preschool age, and once they enter school, they continue to have many experiences outside school. Some parents provide ample opportunities for their children to investigate pots and pans, plants and animals, and various textures, tastes, and smells. Other parents do little to encourage their children to explore, and some prevent their children from investigating because of safety concerns. Some families take young children on walks and excursions, whereas others don't realize the importance of such trips.

Betsy's home is ideal for exploring. Her mother understands that babies need the intellectual stimulation of moving around and touching, tasting, and smelling. Betsy's mother uses the playpen to store dangerous or delicate objects, not babies. She keeps pins, needles, and other dangerous objects off the floor and covers electrical outlets so that little people can explore in safety. Though her children do have traditional toys, Betsy's mother knows that babies are interested in exploring more than toys. They don't learn much about the real world merely from all that brightly colored plastic.

Older children in the family expand their learning experiences beyond toys by helping with chores. A two-year-old can put away canned food when groceries are unpacked, a four-year-old can sort and match socks when laundry is folded, and a six-year-old can set the table. All the children get to help in cooking at some time even though their help means more work for their mother.

Betsy and her brothers and sisters are fortunate to have a large yard for play. Their yard includes a paved area for riding tricycles, grass to run barefoot in, and dirt to dig in. Fruit trees, a vegetable garden, and pet rabbits in a cage also are in Betsy's backyard. The children in this family may choose from a variety of out-door experiences. They are allowed to pick the fruit when it is ripe and eat it when it is washed, they can eat fresh peas out of the pod or pull up tender young carrots to see if they are mature, and they can gently pat the soft, furry bunnies. On warm days, the children add the delightful sensory experience of water play when they get to fill the plastic swimming pool.

Children who live in other places have other kinds of family experiences. Lucy, who lives at the mouth of the Kuskokwim River in southwest Alaska, helps with berry picking and enjoys eating the berries mixed with sugar and shortening or blubber, the traditional ingredient, and sometimes fish. Lucy watches her mother skin seals when her father and brother go hunting and learns about the value of dried seal gut, which makes better raincoats than anything you can buy. She knows the feel of the soft fur from the animals her father traps, and she watches carefully as her mother prepares the skins to make warm winter cloth-ing. She experiences the spring ice breakup in the river and knows that it means the family will travel by boat instead of snowmobile for a while. Lucy is learning how to cut fish and looks forward to going with her family to fish camp when school is out for the summer. There are so many interesting things for Lucy to do and to learn.

Betsy's family travels by van rather than boat or snowmobile, but family outings add to her learning too. The family van has enough space, seat belts, and baby seats to take all five children safely and comfortably on errands or outings. These children go to the grocery store, the fabric store, and the hardware store. They get to ride along to pick up Aunt Marjie at the airport and to bring Mandy home from her ballet lesson. Along the way, they see bridges, trains, and con-struction work. Of course, they don't just stay in the van. They get out and explore the grocery store; they learn to identify products on the shelves and vegetables on display. They get to watch the planes land at the airport, and they get to pull the luggage off the baggage belt. These children are storing up many understandings to bring to oral and written language.

This family's everyday activities also provide the children meaningful expe-riences with written language. The younger ones watch as their mother writes the grocery list and they suggest items to include. Those who can write make notes of grocery items they notice are running low, such as their favorite juice or lunch dessert. The schedule for car pools is written and posted for daily reference. The children realize the importance of writing down the complicated plan for get-ting Joey to and from karate, Amy to and from swimming lessons, and Mandy to and from ballet. Another printed item posted prominently on the refrigerator door is the school lunch menu. The school-age children check it daily to decide whether to pack a lunch or buy one at school. Those who can't read the menu and don't yet need to nevertheless are aware of the significance of reading this notice.

School Experiences

A home environment rich in experience is the ideal model for early childhood education (Neuman et al., 2000). Schools traditionally have been organized on a factory model but current recommendations are to use the home model instead. Elementary school teachers have felt pressured to go along with the traditional approaches to education despite recognizing how poorly they fit young children. Unfortunately, too many preschools try to emulate the inappropriate public school practices. In contrast, Betsy's preschool teacher tries to create a school environment that provides many experiences similar to those Betsy has at home. Ms. Reynolds considers this effort especially important because not all children have such experiences available at home. Some of these children will be labeled "at risk for school failure" because of what they have missed. Ms. Reynolds tries to fill in the gaps.

Ms. Reynolds consciously plans experiences to help her young students find out some answers to their constant questions of *why*. She recognizes the intellectual curiosity of preschoolers and works at satisfying that curiosity in ways that will be meaningful to them. She knows that preschool students must learn through all their senses, not just through hearing. The preschool setting she has prepared is a series of invitations to experiment. It includes sand and water, paint and paste, magnets and magnifying glasses, fish and guinea pigs, and props for trying out roles seen in the real world.

Ms. Montoya also makes sure that her multiage-primary students regularly have new, stimulating experiences, both in and outside the classroom. She modifies the standard classroom offerings with new props or variations on a theme as she observes children becoming ready for new challenges. The water-play table might be set up for float-and-sink experiments for a while; at another time, it might contain funnels, hoses, and pumps for moving water in different ways; and at yet another time, it might have detergent added for blowing bubbles with straws. The sand area may contain toy trucks and road-building machinery; at other times, it may feature toy dinosaurs or zoo animals; and later, it might allow for water and sand to be combined to create a different kind of sand experience. Props in the dramatic play area change according to the children's suggestions to reflect the children's current interests based on recent field trips.

Keeping in mind the ideal home environment as a model for her classroom, Ms. Montoya involves her students in frequent cooking projects. Sometimes these are related to literature or poetry enjoyed by the class. The book *Strega Nona: An Old Tale* (De Paola, 1975) led to a pasta festival. A parent brought a pasta machine to school and supervised a cooking center where youngsters made batches of pasta dough and fed it through the machine. The next day they cooked their pasta, and on the third day different small groups made different toppings. The end result

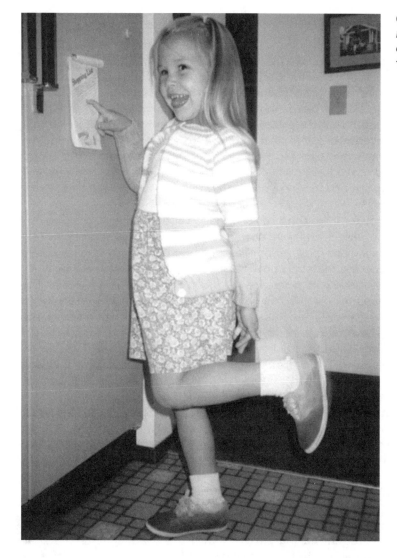

Children learn to read as a result of everyday experiences, such as reading the family's shopping list.

was a variety of pasta dishes for a pasta feast. At other times, cooking is part of a social studies or science topic. Youngsters are amazed to find that they can actually crush peanuts and make peanut butter, that they can shake cream and make butter, and that they can squeeze oranges to make orange juice. Making various ethnic foods under the supervision of a parent expert is always considered a treat too.

Cooking not only adds to children's knowledge base but also involves reading recipes and cookbooks. Some children are inspired to write their own recipes or cookbooks, using their real and imaginary cooking experiences.

CHAPTER 2

Art and Music Experiences

Visiting artists can inspire youngsters to try new art forms and techniques. Ms. Swedell's intricate weaving creates interest in learning to weave, and she willingly assists those who want to try. Stefan's dad is a potter, and he demonstrates how to make a simple pinch pot. Of course, young children cannot create beautifully finished products and often cannot even create recognizable objects. However, it is the process and not the product that is important to learning. Teachers who understand children and who care about art insist that all artwork must be the child's own work. Some teachers get sidetracked about the purpose of art activities and end up doing most of the work themselves in order to have something nice to display. Some classrooms even offer cut-and-paste work sheets in place of actual crafts or coloring sheets in place of actual art.

A good art area for young children provides a variety of paper, drawing materials, scissors, glue, easels, and paint always ready for use. This area should feature a changing variety of art-exploration challenges. Sometimes the challenge is to figure out how to use the materials provided to make something specific—What kind of bird could be made with these feathers and Styrofoam? Sometimes the challenge is to explore the potential of a new art medium—What does it feel like to finger paint with soap flakes? These opportunities for painting, sculpting, drawing, cutting, and pasting have a side benefit: They are directly related to fine-muscle and eye-hand coordination skills that children must use in reading and writing. In addition, children frequently wish to write or dictate a narrative to accompany their artwork. Though art is important in its own right, a discussion of literacy cannot overlook the link between representational art and writing.

Music events make important contributions to children's learning as well. Ms. Montoya's class really got excited when Jamaal's father demonstrated African drum playing. The children were allowed to play the drums under supervision, and they made their own drums from a variety of materials. Drum playing became a major attraction in the classroom. Drumbeats inspired dancing, and drum making inspired artistic efforts. Ms. Montoya related the study of patterns from math to the decorating and playing of drums. Some youngsters decorated their drums by trying to imitate an African decorative pattern Ms. Montoya found in a book; other children were interested in making patterns with the beats they created. Of course, some children just wanted to pound on the drums. A children's concert by famous violinist Linda Rosenthal offered another kind of live music experience.

Music is a constant part of life in Ms. Montoya's classroom, not only a special event. She uses a guitar to lead songs daily, and her class quickly has a large repertoire of songs memorized. She writes the words to the songs on chart paper so that children who wish to can follow the print while they sing. Some youngsters make up their own songs and teach them to the class. The students in this multiage-group class also have access to a variety of rhythm instruments and use them in many ways—for spontaneous parades, to lead dancing, to accompany singing, as part of pretend play, and just to explore what they can do.

Planning Outings

Ms. Montoya knows that children also learn much outside the classroom, and she wants her multiage-primary students to be exposed to other environments. She plans excursions to visit the boat harbor, the fish-processing plant, and the neighborhood grocery store. She takes advantage of unplanned opportunities, such as when the house across the street was painted and when a nearby street was dug up so pipes could be replaced. Instead of spending all her time after school running errands to buy, beg, and borrow materials for class projects, she often saves errands for schooltime. She asks an aide or parent helper to take three or four youngsters to the store for whatever is needed. The children prepare for the errand by making a list of items needed and checking to be sure they have enough money if they are buying something. These outings are valuable learning opportunities, especially for youngsters who don't get such opportunities with their parents.

For large groups, it is a good idea to plan excursions well in advance. Teachers find it worthwhile to visit the site ahead of time to decide how many children can be accommodated at one time, to acquaint themselves with possible hazards, and to analyze the potential for firsthand experiences. When she plans a field trip, Ms. Reynolds takes time to plan with hosts at the site. If a guide will lead the children on a tour, Ms. Reynolds makes certain that the guide will not spend much time talking but will show children things and let them touch whatever they safely can. She emphasizes that these young children will not learn everything about the operation they are observing but will learn a little now and more later. Experience has taught her that this caution is necessary as part of keeping well-meaning adults from trying to explain too much.

Mrs. Thomas thinks about the purpose of each field trip as she plans and tries to vary the purposes as well as the places. Some outings help children learn about processes, such as how houses are built or how bread is baked; others show behind-the-scenes activities, such as visiting a television or radio station, restaurant, or grocery store; other trips help children explore the community geographically in relation to their school and homes. Some are science excursions for studying nature (see Figure 2.2). Sometimes Mrs. Thomas and her first graders take a trip just for the enjoyment of having an adventure, smelling growing things, and feeling the breeze. All provide food for thought and ideas to draw or write about. Mrs. Thomas also tries to find books that relate to the field trips because she knows the children will be interested in them.

Ms. Reynolds is able to arrange for small groups to go on most of the outings she plans instead of taking all twenty children at one time. With a group of five children and one adult, all children can get close enough to see and hear. Their interaction tends to be relaxed, and the quality of the discussion that can occur on the spot is much better with a small group than with a large one. Sometimes all the children take turns visiting the same place on the same day; on other occasions, the teacher or parents take a different group each day for a week. Because the children have taken certain trips many times, such as going to the store to get food for snacks or

Group Story

Our walk to see the Salmon···

We saw a jellyfish on the beach. We saw a hundred salmon alive spawning. We saw a hundred dead ones. We saw some in the sea. Most were in the river. We saw an old, rusty car jack. We saw a wooden boat. We saw some pink shells. We saw a starfish in the water. Benjamin slipped on a jellyfish. Johnny's boots got stuck in the mud. There were insects on an old log.

FIGURE 2.2
Dictated stories can provide a record of a science excursion that children can enjoy reading again and again.

to the library to exchange books, usually only a few children are interested in those outings. The children know that they will get another opportunity later if they are too busy painting or pounding nails to go today. Ms. Reynolds's friends who teach in elementary school try to use this small-group model for field trips but often find that the constraints of the school system force large-group trips.

This small-group approach to field trips contrasts with another approach that Mrs. Hanna will never forget seeing during an outing to the zoo. She had her entire kindergarten class at the zoo that day, but they were spread out in groups of five, with a parent volunteer in charge of each group. Each parent leader for her class wore a construction-paper flower, and each child wore a construction-paper headband with his or her name on it. Every leader's flower was the same color as the headbands of the children assigned to that leader. The adults could easily spot their own charges in the crowd, and the children could easily spot their adult leader. While these small groups were chatting and strolling among the animals, suddenly, down the middle of the broad path between animal cages, there marched a troop of children clutching a long rope and being herded by several adults. The children were not allowed to gather in clusters around animals that particularly interested them, and certainly discussion of what they saw wasn't easy while walking single file. The adults spent their energy keeping children in line instead of talking with them. Mrs. Hanna and her students could only stare in amazement at this approach to a field trip.

Choosing Experiences

With many interesting places to visit, choosing a destination is a challenge. Ms. Montoya takes her cues from children's interests as she observes their play and listens to their conversation. Some successful trips have included the visit to the shoe-repair shop, where Ramel got his shoe fixed and the children were allowed to touch the tools and were given some pieces of leather to take back with them for playing shoe repair in school; the pizza parlor, where they helped put their own ingredients on a pizza and then ate it; the animal shelter, where they could pet the animals; and the dentist's office, where they sat in the examination chair, looked inside each other's mouths with the little mirror, and then received new toothbrushes. Each of these excursions resulted in pretend play that explored the ideas gained, and each stimulated significant drawing and writing.

Possibilities exist for brief field trips within the school building as well. A visit to the principal's office, to see what the school secretary does, to the nurse's office, or to peek inside the custodian's domain all inform and interest youngsters. Children also enjoy seeing other classrooms and meeting other teachers. Of course, children enjoy and benefit from frequent visits to the school library and the librarian.

Many preschool classes meet in church buildings. These settings offer the teachers and students the possibility of meeting the minister, seeing his or her office, and perhaps getting a tour of the chapel and sanctuary. Churches often include a kitchen, which can be useful for cooking experiences, and a recreation hall, useful for large-muscle activities. Sunday school rooms that are unused by the kindergarten or preschool during the week also interest youngsters.

Every community and every part of the country has unique features and locations that contribute to the culture of that area. These can be the basis for fascinating field trips. For instance, children living in southeast Alaska should explore the harbors and fishing boats. They should be shown around a ferry, a hydrofoil, and a tourist cruise ship; they should get to examine a floatplane and

Exploring an Alaskan fishing boat and examining an Arizona cactus are equally interesting adventures.

watch a helicopter transport machinery to a logging camp. For these children, no highways or railroads link communities, and their studies should reflect this reality. They do have knowledge of glaciers, icebergs, forests, beaches, eagles, and sea lions, however. And they have the rich cultural heritage of the Tlingit, who lived there first and still thrive there. These influences will determine which fiction and nonfiction books will be most relevant for these children. These influences will also provide topics for writing.

Children living in Phoenix, Arizona, would have a different set of relevant experiences. Instead of going to the woods to pick blueberries, they would visit the desert to examine the delicate cactus flowers in the spring and learn to avoid cactus needles. Instead of learning how to keep warm in winter, they would learn how to avoid overexposure in the summer. Instead of discovering the wonders of the beach at low tide, they would discover the difference between a riverbed when dry and after a rainstorm. The animals, birds, and trees these children see and then read and write about differ from those in Alaska but are no less fascinating. The world of Arizonan children would include black widow spiders, rattlesnakes, buzzing locusts, orange blossoms, and palm trees. The Papago, Hopi, and Navajo people native to that area weave blankets and make intricately painted pots instead of totem poles, and the relevant Native American literature and folklore is unique to this area. Both sets of experiences are equally valid for young children and contribute equally to their development of literacy.

Children do not necessarily have to go someplace for an experience; sometimes that experience can come to them. Many people are flattered when a teacher asks them to come to school to share something about themselves or the work they do. A carpenter might demonstrate how to use tools and perhaps even spend time helping interested children in the woodworking center. A plumber or an electrician would be an equally interesting visitor. Every year, Ms. Reynolds invites the mother of a new baby to bring the infant to school and let the children watch her bathe the baby in a plastic tub. This event always sparks bathing of dolls for several days as well as interest in writing and reading stories about babies. People from diverse cultures can bring artwork, clothing, or food samples to share with children. Painters, musicians, potters, and weavers can provide wonderful demonstrations for youngsters. Many such interesting people might be the parents of your students.

CONCLUSION

This chapter advocated blocks, games, manipulative materials, pretend play, exploratory play, and large-muscle play as integral parts of literacy development for children in prekindergarten through the primary grades. The value of diverse experiences in providing background and purpose for literacy also was emphasized.

DISCUSSION QUESTIONS

1. The principal walks into your class and observes block play, dramatic play, water play, and various art and manipulative materials activities all happening in a happy clamor. She interrupts your supervision of a cooking activity to ask why you aren't teaching reading according to the day's schedule. How can you help your principal understand?
2. Describe how some skills traditionally taught through direct instruction could be learned through play.
3. Why do you think Hymes says that block play, painting, field trips, and pulling himself or herself up a "scary slanted climbing board" teach a child to read?

SUGGESTED FOLLOW-UP ACTIVITIES

1. Observe children engaged in dramatic play. Note their use of props and other examples of symbolic representation. Note how the roles they play affect their vocabulary and otherwise influence their language.
2. Provide reading and writing materials and encourage their use as a part of children's pretend play. Note how children use reading and writing as part of play.
3. Encourage or help children write the story of their pretend play after it occurs. Note the benefits to literacy and to play.

4. Watch as preschool children build with blocks. Note their processes and the types of creations they make. Arrange to watch older children building with blocks. Compare their levels of manipulative dexterity, symbolic representation, goal-oriented behavior, and quality of products. Encourage literacy activities as part of block play. Note the results.

5. Plan and implement an activity with a small group to enhance the experience base of young children, following guidelines provided in this chapter. Help children use the experience to enhance their language and literacy.

RECOMMENDED FURTHER READING

De Gaetano, Y., Williams, L. R., & Volk, D. (1998). *Kaleidoscope: A multicultural approach for the primary school classroom.* Upper Saddle River, NJ: Merrill/Prentice Hall.

Goldhaber, J., Lipson, M., Sortino, S., & Daniels, P. (1996–1997). Books in the sand box? Markers in the blocks? Expanding the child's world of literacy. *Childhood Education, 73*(2), 88–91.

Neuman, S. (1995). *Linking literacy and play.* Newark, DE: International Reading Association.

Roskos, K., & Christie, J. F. (2000). *Play and literacy in early childhood: Research from multiple perspectives.* Mahwah, NJ: Lawrence Erlbaum.

Sheldon, K. (1996). "Can I play too?" Adapting common classroom activities for young children with limited motor abilities. *Early Childhood Education Journal, 24*(2), 115–120.

LITERACY DEVELOPS THROUGH ORAL LANGUAGE AND STORY

Just as speech develops
in an environment
immensely more rich
than the immediate
needs of the learner, so
the orientation to book
language develops.

D. Holdaway, 1991

CHAPTER 3

Knowledge of oral and written language conventions obviously is associated with learning to read and write. Most educators accept that exposure to language and to books is the way to help children learn about speech and print (Barnitz, 1998). Unfortunately, some adults try to impart this knowledge in ways incompatible with how children learn language. This chapter will present information and examples to help you teach most effectively in these areas.

ORAL LANGUAGE

There are two ways of learning a language: the natural way and the typical school way (McQuillan, 1998). The natural way is how children learn the language of their own families, as described in Chapter 1. This is called language acquisition, and it seems to happen effortlessly for most youngsters. The school way, in contrast, is not so effortless or so effective—as you might recall from foreign language classes. The traditional school way of teaching language is to teach *about* it rather than to use it (De Gaetano, Williams, & Volk, 1998).

Learning *about* a language is useful after you have acquired it, but it isn't a very good way to acquire it initially. We are talking about young children here, children who are still in their language acquisition stage. They may be acquiring only English, or they may be bilingual; either way, the support they need for language development is the natural kind. Language instruction that isolates pieces of knowledge about language and teaches youngsters to memorize those pieces is inappropriate. You may have seen an example of this approach in a DISTAR lesson, in which the teacher pronounces sentences in standard English and children are to repeat them until they get it right.

Some people want to take advantage of children's language acquisition period to give them lessons in a foreign language. They reason that children pick up languages early at this age and so can more easily learn to speak another language.

This idea usually ignores the difference between natural language *acquisition* and artificially *learning* a language. Indeed, young children are in the *language acquisition phase*, but that is irrelevant to how foreign languages are generally taught in school. Sure, children can pick up first and second languages quickly when young, and they do so without accent usually. But let's look at *how* they pick up these languages. They learn through using the language as part of everything they do all day long, *not* through a half-hour-long daily lesson. It takes a major commitment for schools to teach a second language to young children in a meaningful way. Where such a commitment has been made, children from monolingual homes have been able to become bilingual.

Such direct instruction in isolated skills is based on a behaviorist view that learning is memorizing and repeating what someone tells you. The constructivist view of language development is that it involves much more than imitation. Like other learning, language learning is a process of making sense of things. Learning involves creating personal meaning from experiences; it is not an accumulation of facts or skills (Piaget, 1985). Each child's meaning-making process is unique, based on a unique set of experiences. The constructivist approach to language development reflects the ways in which youngsters naturally acquire language in their homes.

What are some ways in which teachers can best assist children's continued language acquisition in school? Examples from language-rich classrooms help answer that question. First, let's observe Ms. Reynolds with her preschoolers, who come to school as competent language users. She values the language learning that her students have acquired already, so she continues and extends the processes that have proved successful in their past learning. Ms. Reynolds definitely encourages children's communication efforts in this preschool.

Adult Conversations with Children

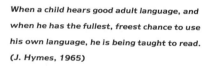

When a child hears good adult language, and when he has the fullest, freest chance to use his own language, he is being taught to read.
(J. Hymes, 1965)

Ms. Reynolds knows that the best way for children to become more proficient with language is to use it more. She also knows that interaction with adults is essential. Therefore, Ms. Reynolds and the parent helpers in her preschool classroom put a high priority on conversations with youngsters. The give-and-take of conversation gives children feedback about their communication and provides models of language.

Ms. Reynolds pays close attention to children as they talk to her, and she tries to squat or sit at their eye level for the best possible communication. She not only listens respectfully but also asks questions that encourage the children to think and use additional language. Frequently, she makes comments that extend a child's statement, elaborating on the idea and incorporating new vocabulary words. When Blair tells her that she got a puppy, Ms. Reynolds asks Blair to tell her more about the dog. After Blair's enthusiastic description, Ms. Reynolds comments, "I think you are going to have a wonderful time playing with that cuddly puppy."

Sometimes teachers have trouble understanding what children are talking about. This difficulty may arise from children's immature language skills, their use of a nonstandard dialect, subject matter unfamiliar to the teacher, or cultural differences in narrative styles. Teachers usually lack the familiarity with an individual child's personal and social world that is so critical to effective communication (Cazden, 1988). Ms. Reynolds tries to be sensitive to and accepting of all types of individual communication. Her careful listening and questioning style shows respect for children and their language. If she doesn't follow what a child is saying, she continues to ask questions until she has some sense of the child's meaning. Sometimes she has to say, "Show me what you mean," in order to understand, but she works hard at acknowledging each child's communication efforts. Another helpful aspect of her approach is that she never asks questions to which she already knows the answer, such as "What color is that dress you are wearing?" Instead, her questions are honest inquiries and a means to understand a child. These are the kinds of questions that encourage children to communicate with their teachers. Children can tell the difference between honest communication and patronizing questions.

Many of Ms. Reynolds's individual conversations with children occur incidentally as they arrive at school or while she is assisting them with boots and coats for going outdoors. Other opportunities arise as Ms. Reynolds circulates among her students while they are engrossed in their various chosen activities. She teaches the parent helpers how to encourage children's language also, yet she knows that the relationship with the one teacher who is there every day is most important to her students. Thus, Ms. Reynolds assigns the parent aides to supervise specific activities, such as baking blueberry muffins or creating collages, keeping herself free to circulate so that she is available to more children.

Adults who pay close attention to what children are saying encourage oral language development.

When Ms. Reynolds converses with children, she usually says little. Instead, she stimulates children's thinking and expression of thoughts. She is careful not to give feedback that turns off conversations. She never makes a judgmental response, such as "That wasn't a nice thing to do," when a child confides in her. She rarely gives information or a quick answer to questions either. Rather, she prolongs the conversation through questions such as "Why do you think that happened?" or simply "What do *you* think?" Her responses indicate acceptance of what is said, and she frequently verifies communication by paraphrasing what she has heard. For instance, if Marisa says, "My baby bad," Ms. Reynolds might use reflective listening and respond, "Your baby has been doing something wrong?" Then Marisa knows what message Ms. Reynolds received and can elaborate on it by saying, "Yes, he cry all night. But he just little." This information in turn could be elaborated for further conversation. The information could also result in a topic for a dictated story.

For youngsters coming to school speaking a language other than English, Ms. Reynolds's verbal interactions are designed to help them become bilingual. She helps these children continue to develop their home language while she also assists their acquisition of English. She tries to learn to express some key ideas in each child's own language, and she tries to have a parent helper available who speaks each child's home language. She doesn't teach *lessons* in English to help them learn this second language; rather, she *converses* with them in English. As she did with her own children when they were learning to talk, Ms. Reynolds speaks in short sentences to second-language learners and points out or shows what she is talking about (McQuillan, 1998).

Sometimes teachers experience difficulty in giving needed individual attention to children with so many needing their attention. Ms. Reynolds believes that two minutes of her undivided attention is worth more to a child than two hours of her attention when that child is part of a group. She strives to build trust and rapport with her students through these one-to-one encounters, knowing that trust and rapport are necessary for effective communication. She makes a point of initiating conversations with those children who make no effort to talk to her. She knows that it is natural to talk most to those youngsters who talk most to her. However, because she realizes that the more verbal children need her interaction the least, she is especially attentive to the quieter children. She has noticed, though, that some quiet children seem to feel overwhelmed by language from very verbal persons. For some children, less talk is a cultural style. Sometimes, Ms. Reynolds makes it possible for a child just to be with her, working on the child's trust before conversation. However, she is always alert to possible hearing loss when a child is quiet and unresponsive. Ear infections can damage children's hearing and delay their language development.

Mrs. Thomas also supports her first-grade children in their social construction of language. As she converses with her children, Mrs. Thomas uses open-ended questions to invite conversation instead of closed questions that can be answered with one-word responses. She recognizes the importance of providing ample wait time for children to respond in order to encourage thoughtful responses that foster discussion (Otto, 2002). Mrs. Thomas responds to what children say instead of correcting how they say it. Sometimes she repeats or rephrases children's speech, modeling correct usage and supporting further language development (Hill, 2001).

Conversations Between Children

Snack time offers an excellent chance for the kinds of conversations that assist both first- and second-language learners. The parent aides and Ms. Reynolds each sit at a table with about five children. The adults eat with the children, modeling table and mealtime conversation manners. This approach is a direct contrast with that of schools where adults stand around and converse among themselves while children eat. This latter approach ignores the learning potential of snack time. In Ms. Reynolds's class, the adults talk with the youngsters but take care not to monopolize the conversation at snack time or at any time; they encourage the children to talk among themselves even more than to the teacher. In this preschool, opportunities abound for children to talk with one another. They talk while they paint, they talk while they build with blocks, they talk while they climb the climbing tower, and they talk while they act out dramas in the playhouse area or pretend to be their favorite television heroes. The children engage in meaningful conversation and social interaction throughout the day. As they talk, children refine their ideas and inform their conclusions about their world. All the play activities and experiences described in Chapter 2 are also language-learning opportunities.

In addition to facilitating informal conversation among children and engaging in conversation with the children, teachers plan many activities to enhance language. The changing props in the playhouse—suggesting a store for a while, a doctor's office next, and a fishing boat another time—encourage new vocabulary and different types of verbal exchanges. Additionally, the many stories, songs, poems, and finger plays that children experience daily in this preschool have language development as their primary purpose. Actually, everything children do, from finger painting to playing with the pet gerbil, enhances their language development by providing motivation and content for speech. And all these activities that help children become more proficient in their first language are also helpful for youngsters learning a second language.

In her multiage class, with youngsters from five to eight years old, Ms. Montoya provides a rich foundation of play and experiences to assist children's language development. She continues the stories, dramatic play, and other language-development activities that most of her students encountered in preschool or child care programs. She plans time for oral discussion about field trips and class events. She does all this in a bilingual environment, as her class includes a large number of Spanish-speaking students. Because Ms. Montoya speaks Spanish and English, she is able to offer the best possible education program for all her students. Her school district supports this approach because of the overwhelming evidence that bilingual programs for young children mean better academic achievement as students progress through the grades (Thomas & Collier, 1997).

Opportunities to interact during play are helpful for children becoming more proficient in their first language and also helpful for children learning a second language.

Mrs. Hanna also continues the practice of encouraging children to talk among themselves as they work at learning centers in her kindergarten class. She knows that talking with others about what they are doing increases children's understanding and enhances their oral language proficiency. This type of social interaction is one of the essential ingredients for intellectual development as described by Piaget. When children compare their perceptions with those of their peers, they try to figure out which view is correct. When an adult's perception is different from a child's, the child naturally assumes that the adult is right, whether or not the adult view makes sense to the child. With peers, children assume that their own ideas are of equal value, and they will explain and defend those ideas. Instead of automatically assuming a peer is right, children go through the valuable process of analyzing the other viewpoint, comparing it to personal understandings, and modifying or solidifying their previous views (Kamii & Randazzo, 1985). Through classroom conversations with teachers and peers, children hypothesize, compare, contrast, classify, clarify, and summarize ideas (Raban, 2001).

For a few youngsters, such verbal give-and-take is not possible. For instance, Jason has aphasia and is physically unable to speak. Jason's communication challenge is increased because his small-motor control is too limited for him to be able to use any sign language. With the assistance of a communications board, Jason is learning to interact with his classmates. When he presses the right key, his communications board speaks for him and enables him to make his ideas and wishes known. This assistive technology has allowed Jason to connect with other children enough to make friends in the class. Further, helping Jason in his efforts to communicate expands the horizons of the other children; they learn a lot about trying to understand another person's viewpoint. Even for this type of extreme language challenge, the child with language difficulties is best served in the regular classroom with typically developing peers (Falk-Ross, 1997).

Listening and Diagnostic Teaching

Mrs. Hanna finds that by being a careful listener, she not only encourages more communication from her kindergarten children but also discovers a great deal about their level of language development. This information guides her in planning appropriate educational experiences for each of her students. When she discovers that some children are using more sound substitutions than normal for their age or that some are confusing words that sound somewhat alike, she realizes the need to speak slowly and clearly to those children. She also knows she needs to plan activities to enhance phonemic awareness for those children.

Mrs. Hanna doesn't become concerned when children say, "Is this aw wite?" or when someone asks to hold the "nake." She knows that production of the *l*, *r*, and *s* sounds will come with maturity. But if children continue to confuse other sounds in kindergarten, perhaps they aren't hearing them properly. Once she has determined that the children do not have hearing problems, Mrs. Hanna engages them in word games or makes a game of making the sound of the snake's hiss, the lion's roar, and other challenging sounds. Her students also enjoy playing with the sounds and rhymes in songs and poems, which are frequent attractions throughout the day. Playing with sounds assists all youngsters with phonemic awareness. Careful attention to subtle sound differences is needed as children begin to figure out which letters are used to represent which speech sounds.

Mrs. Thomas doesn't correct children's speech in her first-grade class either, even though she makes it a point to notice speech problems. She knows that the most effective way to increase language ability is through practice, and she doesn't want children to stop practicing because they fear she will correct them. Children do practice in her classroom. Hers is not a classroom in which the teacher constantly says, "Shh," to children; instead, children talk to the teacher, to each other, and to themselves.

Children can learn language from talking to their peers, but sometimes they don't know how to start a conversation with another child. Then Mrs. Thomas will help with a comment such as, "Zachary, have you told Maria about your new kitten? I think she has a black kitten too." Sometimes, Mrs. Thomas brings a small group together for a discussion. These group discussions have specific purposes: perhaps planning a cooking project or naming the new class rabbit. These situations provide excellent practice in group discussion skills, with Mrs. Thomas guid-

ing the students in taking turns and being sure everyone is heard but never domi-
nating the conversation.

Occasionally, the whole group is brought together for a discussion of a subject that affects everyone. However, most young children are not ready to function for long in a group of twenty-five. They get too squirmy and bored sharing
both the limelight and the teacher's attention with so many others. Many teachers
find it more valuable to divide the group at least in half, with a parent helper leading
one group discussion or with the rest of the class engaged in independent activities. She keeps in mind James Hymes's (1981) guideline that the right-size group
for a child has no more people than that child has had birthdays. Smaller groups
give more children a chance to participate, but even small groups of young children
can't sit still too long.

Maturation and Speech Development

By the end of first grade, you can expect that most sound substitutions and over-
generalized grammar rules will have disappeared from typically developing monolingual children's speech. This development is not the result of any specific lessons
or drills to correct the problems but is a natural process that results from children's
maturation plus their continued analysis of the language around them. Some milestones of this natural progression are listed in Table 3.1. As youngsters mature,
they become more able to duplicate the sounds of their language. Through continued exposure to the language patterns of their culture, they naturally work to discover the exceptions to grammar rules as well as the rules themselves. Mrs.
Thomas listens carefully to students to determine whether any of them are still
having difficulty and should be considered for speech help.

Until the end of first grade, or about seven years of age, some immature
speech is developmentally normal and requires no remedial intervention. Although
alert to children who require special help, Mrs. Thomas does not criticize their

TABLE 3.1

Common Milestones in Speech Development

Years	Accomplishment
3	About 300-word vocabulary
3½	*b, m, p, v,* and *h* sounds develop
4	About 900-word vocabulary
4½	*d, t, n, g, k, ng,* and *y* sounds develop
5½	*f* sound develops
6½	*v, sh, za,* and *l* sounds develop
7½	*s, w, r, th,* and *wh* sounds develop
7–8	Sentence foundation mastered (pronouns and prepositions)
8	All sounds are developed and are usually intelligible

speech. She considers the rapport established with her students to be so significant to their language development that she is unwilling to jeopardize that rapport with a critical response to a child's communication. Any needed special help can be given separately.

Vocabulary Development

Language is the primary system by which meanings are expressed (Morrow, 2001). Mrs. Montoya understands that language cannot be understood without a meaningful context. Children need ample opportunities to use language with adults and other children. Opportunities for one-on-one interactions between children and their teachers are especially important (Soundy & Stout, 2002). Active involvement in rich experiences such as those described in Chapter 2 expands children's general knowledge as well as their language. As Mrs. Montoya's children listen to stories, engage in discussions, and get involved in dramatic play and outdoor play, their vocabularies expand (Arnqvist, 2000).

Language Differences

Ms. Montoya and most other teachers have many students who come to school speaking a language or dialect other than standard English. In the years between 1985 and 1991, the number of children learning English as a second language in the United States increased by more than 50 percent. Since then, the increase has been 2½ times the rate of the general student population increase (Claire, 1995). Although Ms. Montoya knows that these children eventually will need to learn standard English to succeed in U.S. schools, she values whatever language a child speaks. She believes that accepting a child's language is part of accepting that child and that child's background.

Ms. Montoya's multiage-primary class includes children whose families recently came from eastern Europe, Southeast Asia, and Mexico. Though she speaks only Spanish and English, Ms. Montoya helps her students value all the languages in the group. She and her students try to learn something of each new language in the classroom. The children especially enjoy an activity suggested in a social studies curriculum guide (Feeney & Moravcek, 1994), learning the action rhyme "Hello Toes" (Barlin & Kalev, 1989) in various languages. Bilingual parents usually enjoy an invitation to teach the rhyme in the language of their heritage. Children benefit when teachers and parents collaborate in helping them learn the school language without losing their home language (Tabors, 1997).

As they participate in the regular class activities, limited- and non-English-speaking youngsters quickly gain proficiency with English. Interaction with English-speaking peers through play appears to be the best possible English lesson. As those learning English as a second language progress, Mrs. Hanna helps them feel proud of knowing more than one language. When Reid said, "Sergei talks funny," Mrs. Hanna pointed out Sergei's bilingual achievements and said that she certainly couldn't learn Russian as quickly as Sergei was learning English. She added, "I wish I could speak two languages like he does!" Her response seemed to make an impression on Reid as well as on Sergei.

Mrs. Hanna's first concern is that a child use language to communicate, not what language that child uses. If the child's only language is one that Mrs. Hanna doesn't understand, she works with the school district to bring in an aide who speaks that language. If that isn't possible, sometimes an older child or a parent can spend time in the classroom to assist as needed. If the child's language is merely a dialect of English, Mrs. Hanna does not feel at all hampered by the language difference. Her method of assisting literacy allows all children to learn to read and write initially in their own dialects. She enjoys the cadences and rhythm brought to English by some African American youngsters and different ones brought by a Hawaiian child in her class. When she takes dictation, she writes the sentence structures the child uses. This consistency allows the children to read back their words, matching the oral and written language. All the teachers described here accept the view that language is a personal extension of the child and that to reject a child's language is to reject the child.

Ms. Reynolds notices that youngsters learning English as a second language go through some processes similar to those that take place in learning a first language, but there are some differences as well (Tabors & Snow, 1994). Most continue to use their home language with English speakers for a time. But as they realize this isn't working, most will go through a period of not talking at all and using gestures to communicate or cries to attract attention. Then they seem to get down to the business of learning this new language. Most children will observe closely to connect the words to what is happening. This process can be greatly assisted by sensitive teachers.

Another way youngsters help themselves learn a second language is with self-imposed practice in saying the words and sounds to themselves. Then, with

Children benefit when teachers and parents collaborate in helping them learn the language of the majority culture without losing their first language.

some confidence, emerging bilingual children will begin to use some memorized expressions, such as "Wanna play?" or "What's that?" Notice that the question "Wanna play?" engages other children and offers opportunity for practice with English speakers. The question "What's that?" gets feedback for vocabulary development. Toddlers learning their first language use similar strategies. Usually these processes are the base for creative construction and communication with the new language. Like beginning monolingual speakers, bilingual youngsters will put language together in ways that reflect their current theories about how the language system works. Going between languages with different grammatical structures makes learning grammar even more of a challenge than for monolingual speakers.

Programs that offer bilingual instruction have the best long-term results for nonnative speakers of English. Children who are initially taught at school in their home language tend to have more self-confidence and more success in learning to read. Literacy skills transfer between languages, assisting with learning to read in the second language (August & Hakuta, 1997; Bialystock, 1997; Cuevas, 1997). Effective bilingual environments include not only proficient speakers of both languages but also books and other print examples in both languages. Many monolingual English-speaking parents are delighted for their children to have the opportunity to be immersed in another language and become bilingual.

Meeting the Needs of All

The age or grade level of the children who are learning a language isn't what determines appropriate language instruction. Rather, the individual development of each child determines that child's instructional needs. The only way to meet all the various needs in any class is to provide a variety of options for learning activities. Children will generally choose the option from which they will most benefit. Challenge and opportunities for success both offer motivation for learning. A combination of success and challenge leads to that delicate balance of being neither too hard nor too easy. Therefore, developmentally appropriate early-childhood programs, whether in preschool or in the primary grades, tend to provide similar types of open-ended learning activities. The children themselves may add complexity and challenge to ensure learning, or the teacher may suggest variations to an activity to enhance the learning value. Certainly the play, language, and literacy of a six-year-old are more sophisticated than those of a three-year-old, but children of both ages learn best by interacting and exploring informally in similar kinds of situations.

Mrs. Thomas knows that even first graders whose home language is standard English haven't finished their language development and still need practice. She also is aware of the significant role of verbal interaction in the intellectual development of her students. Have you guessed by now that Mrs. Thomas too encourages talking in her first-grade classroom? This approach may be quite a change from your experience with first grade. Mrs. Thomas not only makes sure that students have play opportunities that foster language but also encourages collaborative discussion while students pursue more academic kinds of learning. Youngsters in this classroom talk together as they compare the stories they have read, plan a puppet show, or discuss proper spelling while they write.

Mrs. Thomas also brings children together in groups for discussions. With first graders, she sometimes feels comfortable working with the total group, but she sees they still function best in smaller units. When she brings the whole group together, she does so for short periods and for specific purposes. As the children begin to gather, she leads the group in conversation, singing, or acting out a finger play. This activity ensures that those already sitting are involved instead of bored.

Today the topic for discussion is class rules. Mrs. Thomas creates a language-development opportunity as she guides the students in discussing essential, reasonable classroom regulations. She records everyone's ideas for rules as they are suggested. Tomorrow she will assist the children in selecting two or three ideas that will help everyone live and work together in the classroom harmoniously. After the group disbands, Mrs. Thomas confers briefly with a parent volunteer about the session. The parent tells her about a fascinating informal discussion that was taking place simultaneously with the formal one: Two girls were debating the pros and cons of a rule about interrupting someone who is reading to ask for help with a word. This information is helpful to Mrs. Thomas, who had been wondering whether she should have allowed the girls' subdiscussion to continue. This insight reinforces her belief that the most important discussions may not be those planned by the teacher.

The teachers described here believe that children's language reflects their experiences and that a child with meager experience will be a child with meager language. Therefore, the teachers make great efforts to enhance the experience base of all their students, as described in Chapter 2. Through these experiences, youngsters in their classes gain subjects to talk about, motivation to talk, and an increased vocabulary.

These teachers also accept as valid for discussion the experiences children consider important from their lives outside school. They don't limit discussion to certain sterile school topics. Additionally, all these teachers believe that children must talk in order to develop language proficiency as well as increased intellectual growth. Their classrooms are not quiet places. These teachers know that they are dealing with children in their language acquisition years.

Oral Language and Written Language

As they help children develop proficiency with oral language, early-childhood educators are helping children build understanding that assists with mastering written language. As explained in Chapter 1, it is important to remember the differences between oral and written language and how those differences influence learning. We receive many more clues to meaning when we hear oral language than when we read written language. When someone is speaking to us, we gain meaning from voice inflection as well as from facial expressions and gestures. Generally, the situation in which the communication is taking place clarifies ambiguities. This assistance is not available for making meaning from the written word. Therefore, written language must provide more complete information to make up for the lack of other clues.

Holdaway (1979) pointed out that oral and written language differ not only in form but also in function. Ideas are usually written down as a means to record

Classrooms that encourage talking assist children's oral language and literacy development.

important or memorable matters, whereas conversational oral language may serve just to pass the time. Therefore, children who are familiar only with conversational speech will use that form of language when dictating something for an adult to write. This dictation will often be incomplete sentences or refer to a picture on the page simply as "That's my house." In contrast, children who have been read to enough to notice the difference between "book talk" and "people talk" will use the language of print in their dictation. These children will dictate complete sentences that stand alone, such as "I drew a picture of my house." Being read to regularly is the best way for children to become familiar with the conventions of written language. We now turn to the subject of selecting and sharing literature for story time.

STORY TIME

It is difficult to overstate the value of reading to young children. Research repeatedly comes up with the same conclusion: Reading to children is a powerful precursor of literacy (Moustafa, 1997). Gordon Wells (1986) concluded after a fifteen-year study of children in England that their school success was highly influenced by the frequency of listening to stories read to them. Dolores Durkin's (1980) studies showed that the one common factor of children who read early was being read to frequently. Since then, many researchers have determined that children learn ways of constructing meaning for print as adults interpret stories for them (Fisher, 1998; Karweit & Wasik, 1996; Mason, 1989; Teale, 1988). Many researchers emphasize that a combination of reading to children and follow-up activities, such as creative dramatics or discussion, are particularly important for reading achievement (National Research Council, 1999). Story time is a daily staple of teachers who are attempting to provide literate environments. In many classrooms, story time is the central focus, serving as the basis for other curriculum activities. Story time offers pleasure and purpose for reading; it also helps children learn the language of print.

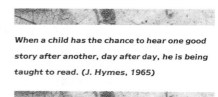

When a child has the chance to hear one good story after another, day after day, he is being taught to read. (J. Hymes, 1965)

Pleasure and Purpose

Why teach children how to read unless we teach them to *want* to read? Unless they want to read, they have no reason to go to the trouble of learning how. Unless they discover the pleasure reading can bring, children won't do enough of it to become good at it. When we read stories to young children, we introduce them to the magic of books and awaken their desire to read for themselves. When we share high-quality literature with youngsters, we give them a glimpse of the excitement, the drama, and the beauty contained in books. When we share our enthusiasm for a good story with children, we provide a model of interacting with text. When we make the print on a page come to life during a story, we demonstrate the process of reading. As children interact with adults about stories and reenact stories read to them, they gradually and without pressure construct understandings necessary to become readers.

The Language of Print

As we mentioned earlier, exposure to books helps children understand the kind of language used in writing. Readers use their knowledge of language to make sense of print, but if they don't use language in the way books do, what they know about language doesn't help them. Children who have little experience with written language are not skilled at getting meaning from words alone. They are used to getting clues to the meaning of language from their surroundings, and they become insecure and disoriented when they can't (Holdaway, 1979). When they get to school, they often have difficulty understanding their teacher's oral language as well. Because teachers tend to talk about things that are not physically present, their language has much in common with book language (Wells, 1986).

Children are not only able to understand language better as a result of being read to but are also able to express themselves better. Their increased vocabulary helps both expressive and receptive language. Additionally, children with a rich background of experiences with books are able to narrate an event and describe a scene (Wells, 1986). These skills are useful for both oral and written communication and enhance general academic success as well as literacy development.

Starting Early

Children who are read to before entering school are more likely to succeed in school (Moustafa, 1997). Reading to toddlers and preschool-age youngsters has great significance for their development in literacy. Even before babies can talk, they benefit from looking at books and being read to (Schickedanz, 1999). They are able to understand some of what is read to them, just as they are able to understand some of what is said to them, months before they say their first word. Even before babies understand the content of stories, they enjoy the process of being read to—being held closely and hearing the soothing voice of a loving adult (Fields, 1998).

The intimacy of enjoying a story with a parent or a teacher adds to the pleasurable feelings about reading that make children want to read. Attitudes toward reading can begin in infancy and can be enhanced throughout childhood. As with so much of teaching, parents should be the first and foremost influence, with teachers assisting and extending what the parents have begun. Many parents are able to teach about stories gradually by adjusting their story sharing to their child's ability to understand, just as they naturally adjust their speech to assist their young child's learning to talk. Adjusting the story time to the child's level usually means focusing on helping the child understand and enjoy the story rather than focusing on reading the exact words. This may mean talking about the pictures and relating the story to the child's own experiences at first. Later, when the child is more familiar with a given story and with stories in general, parents tend to read more of the actual print (Altwerger, Diehl-Faxon, & Dockstader-Anderson, 1985).

Look at Betsy, who at six months of age was developing an interest in books and stories. Already, she wanted to be included when someone read a story in her busy household. She had many opportunities because her oldest sister read well and was willing to entertain the younger ones, her oldest brother enjoyed sharing his new powers as a beginning reader, and her preschool brother and her toddler sister frequently requested stories. Of course, Betsy's mother and father also read to the children whenever they had a chance, and they still do.

When asked at what age youngsters should be introduced to books, Betsy's mother says that her theory about that is similar to her theory about when they should be introduced to solid food: "When they grab food off your plate and eat it, they're ready for real food." So whenever her youngsters crawl over to hear a story, they are included.

When Betsy is old enough for preschool, her teacher, Ms. Reynolds, can tell that she has been read to frequently. Not all the children in Ms. Reynolds's class exhibit Betsy's interest in books and story times. Ms. Reynolds doesn't force stories on these youngsters by insisting that everyone come to story time. Instead, she concentrates on making story time as inviting as possible, gradually luring children away from other pursuits to join the story group. As youngsters overhear the exciting plots and observe the interest of other children, they become willing to listen

Research indicates that the earlier adults start to read to children, the greater the benefits.

to stories. Until that time, Ms. Reynolds allows them to choose other quiet activities that won't interfere with story time. She also makes a special effort with those youngsters who opt out of group stories; she invites them onto her lap for one-on-one story reading during choice time or else enlists a volunteer helper for lap reading. This process emulates the home literacy model that has proved so effective.

Making Up for Lost Time

What about children who haven't had that home literacy model? Schools have too often assumed that children understand that reading is meaningful. Schools have also tended to assume that youngsters understand the language of print. Instruction based on those assumptions is meaningless to children for whom those assumptions are false. For children missing these ingredients for success, the prescription is massive doses of story time.

CHAPTER 3

Massive Doses of Story Time

Ms. Montoya wants to make sure all her multiage-primary children get to discover the power of written language "to create possible or imaginary worlds through words" (Wells, 1986, p. 156). Instead of trying to condense several years of missing language enrichment into synthetic substitutions, such as flash-card drills, Ms. Montoya attempts to provide what was missing from the previous years of life. She enlists the aid of older students in her multiage class as reading buddies and also invites parents to help provide the immersion in stories needed by some youngsters. Mrs. Hanna invites volunteers from upper grades. It is common to see a fifth grader in a pillow-softened corner reading to one or two kindergartners in her classroom. Upper-grade teachers assure Mrs. Hanna that the older children benefit at least as much as the younger ones from this activity.

First-grade teacher Mrs. Thomas also places a high priority on reading to children. Skills-based approaches to teaching reading focus on so many different tasks and skills that it is a challenge to find time for all of them, let alone for a story. But teachers who understand how to integrate teaching skills into actual reading and writing can relax the frantic pace. This approach is a more efficient way for children to make sense of written language and also to master the skills and concepts they need (McQuillan, 1998).

Teaching Children to Tune In

Mrs. Thomas arranges for volunteers to read with the first graders who lack book experience. She teaches the volunteers to interact with the children during the reading, discussing the content and the word meanings as they go. These conversations help children understand and enjoy the stories. Such interaction is an important component of sharing books with youngsters (Bergin, 2001; Whitehurst & Lonigan, 2002). These types of conversations are similar to those conducted by most parents who read to their children on a regular basis. Groups of three students seem to work well for such discussions (Karweit & Wasik, 1996).

All these teachers notice a big difference as a result of the small-group read-aloud experiences. Youngsters who previously were not interested in story time begin to show much more interest. Story time becomes relevant as children learn the idea of actively engaging their minds with stories and relating their personal experience to them. As some youngsters are simply not intrigued by fiction (Gallas, 1997), a good selection of nonfiction books is an important part of read-aloud time too. Much of children's reading for school is nonfiction, so learning how to gather relevant information from text is a valuable experience.

Sending Books Home

No matter what happens at school, home and family make the biggest impression on most children. If Mom and Dad read, reading is more important. If Mom or Dad reads a story to a child, that story is more special. But if children's books aren't in your budget and trips to the library aren't in your schedule, there are no books for reading at home. Since more than 20 percent of children in the United States live in

Children become interested in books and reading as a result of being read to and exploring texts at school and at home.

poverty (Berliner & Biddle, 1995), it is not surprising that many children do not have access to high-quality picture books at home. Many schools send books home with children in an effort to increase parent-child book reading.

Positive results have been shown in experiments in which children in Head Start programs and in kindergarten were allowed to choose a high-quality picture book to take home daily (Meier, 2000; Robinson, Larsen, & Haupt, 1995, 1996). Choosing and taking home these books more than doubled the number of picture books children read at home. Ms. Montoya is one of many teachers who have found ways to get more books into their students' homes. She wrote a grant proposal and received money to buy a large number of books to be used for this purpose. She was careful to choose books worth reading and worth looking at. Like other teachers, she was pleased with the results: Her students not only read more at home but also became more interested in books at school. And despite her worries, very few books were lost or damaged.

Selecting Appropriate Books for Children

Selecting books for home loan programs, classroom libraries, and story time can be a challenge. All books are not created equal. When Betsy's mother goes into the grocery store or the toy store, she feels assaulted by the masses of poorly written and unimaginatively illustrated books on the shelves. Just as she is careful in selecting nutritious food instead of junk food, she wants to select books that will fill her children's minds with curiosity and stimulate their thinking instead of books whose story lines and illustrations are based on Saturday morning cartoons. She knows that meaningful connections with books will occur only with meaningful stories (Egawa, 1990).

Even bookstores often have a disappointing selection of children's literature. Deborah reads the reviews of children's books in *Parents* magazine and follows the Caldecott Award winners as ways of keeping up to date on high-quality children's literature. She places special orders at the bookstore when necessary. She also makes requests at the library and encourages the librarian to order books that earned good reviews.

Her children's teachers have similar problems locating current, high-quality literature. They find reviews in professional journals helpful. *The Horn Book Magazine*, *The New Advocate*, *Young Children* (the journal of the National Association for the Education of Young Children), *The Reading Teacher* (the journal of the International Reading Association), and *Language Arts* (the journal of the National Council of Teachers of English) have reliable book review sections. A useful site on the Internet is the Children's Literature Web Guide (*http://www.ucalgary.ca/~dkbrown/index.html*), which provides an extensive set of links to children's literature resources. Mrs. Hanna likes Bobbi Fisher's list of her favorite children's literature in her book *Joyful Learning* (1998). These teachers have created their own collections of personal favorites and share them with their students year after year. When an adult personally loves a story, sharing it becomes a special experience for both child and adult.

Ms. Montoya makes a special effort to find multicultural literature that reflects the makeup of her classroom. She is delighted to see that publishers are becoming much more responsive to the need for books that reflect the diversity of our world. She likes books that include human traits that are common across cultures and ethnicity, such as *All the Colors of the Earth* (Hamanaka, 1994) and *Here Are My Hands* (Martin & Archambault, 1989). She also wants to share books with her class that encourage productive conversations about differences, such as *A Kaleidoscope of Kids* (Damon, 1995) and *Bright Eyes, Brown Skin* (Hudson, 1990).

Teachers cannot possibly find an expert opinion on every book, nor should they. You must develop your own criteria for what constitutes a good book and then form an opinion about which books are right for certain children and in specific situations. One simple guide is to decide whether you like a book yourself. Good children's literature isn't interesting just to children; it is timeless. Have you picked up a child's storybook and found that you couldn't put it down until you finished it? Are there some that you even enjoy reading over and over? Those are definitely signs of a good book.

Appealing Traits

A good book for any age is one that catches and holds the reader's interest. Suspense or tension of some sort is the classic way of hooking a reader into a story; a book without this has a poorly constructed plot. A good plot is important. For

FIGURE 3.1

Lois Lenski's simple, clear illustrations appeal to the youngest book lovers.

Source: From Lenski, L. (1946). The Little Fire Engine. New York: Henry Z. Walck. Reprinted by permission from the Lois Lenski Covey Foundation.

young children, the plot should be simple, without subplots or flashbacks to confuse them. The action should be believable without being predictable, and the problems should not be overcome too quickly. Lenski's *The Little Fire Engine* (1946) has a simple plot suitable for a young child but remains exciting from the beginning, when the fire alarm sounds, to the end, when everyone is safe and the fire is out (see Figure 3.1).

Some books can exist without suspense or plot because they offer something else. The sounds and rhythm of language can be pleasurable in themselves.

Readers enjoy such books as Wolf's *Peter's Truck* (1992) or Medearis's *Rum-a-tum-tum* (1997), and, of course, there is the fun of nursery rhymes for youngsters. Some books don't need words at all to be fascinating. Beautifully detailed wordless picture books for children are being published more frequently now. Some word-less books are designed especially for children who are in the stage of reading the pictures. Ormerod's companion books *Sunshine* (1981) and *Moonlight* (1982) offer opportunities for young children to create their own stories to accompany the pictures. Other wordless picture books are so rich in food for thought that they seem to offer something for any age. What fun it is to watch how life on the ark changes over a forty-day period as you examine Spier's *Noah's Ark* (1977). Rohman's *Time Flies* (1994) takes you on a different kind of trip, starting in a dinosaur museum. Day's series of books about the dog Carl (*Good Dog Carl,* 1988) are also delightful examples of wordless storybooks.

     Whether or not a story relies on words and plot, it should present a main character with whom children can identify. Children easily identify with Viorst's main character, Alexander, as he survives a less-than-perfect day (*Alexander and the Terrible, Horrible, No Good, Very Bad Day,* 1972). They can relate to the daily routines of the nameless little girl in Ormerod's books, and they can step into Peter's snowsuit and experience the wonder of *The Snowy Day,* created by Keats (1962). Table 3.2 lists attributes to consider when selecting a story for children.

TABLE 3.2

Criteria for Selecting an Appropriate Fiction Story

Look for the following attributes:

1. A simple, well-developed plot, centered on a sequence of events, with action predominant; a slight surprise element makes the children wonder what will happen next and can add much to a story (*Rattletrap Car,* Root, 2001)
2. A large amount of direct conversation (*In the Rain with Baby Duck,* Hest, 1995)
3. Use of repetition, rhyme, and catch phrases that children memorize quickly and easily (Dr. Seuss books, Geisel, Random House)
4. Use of carefully chosen, colorful language (*The Napping House,* Wood, 1984)
5. Situations involving familiar happenings; the new, unusual, and different may be included, but there must be enough of the familiar with which children can identify (*When Grandma Came,* Walsh, 1992)
6. A simple and satisfying climax (*Bunny Cakes,* Wells, 1997)
7. One main character with whom children can easily identify, because too many characters can be confusing (*The Story of Jumping Mouse: A Native American Legend,* Steptoe, 1984)
8. A variety of ethnic, cultural, and racial backgrounds; such stories should present realistic pictures, not stereotypes of racial or ethnic groups (*Dumpling Soup,* Rattigan, 1993)
9. Illustrations because young children "read" pictures; pictures need to accurately portray the content and mood of the story (*Fog,* Fowler, 1992)

Accuracy

We have been discussing fiction books so far, but nonfiction books should be considered too. Factual accuracy is just as important in nonfiction books for young children as it is in books for adults. Children's books don't need to be complex or detailed, but that does not mean that accuracy can be sacrificed. Mrs. Hanna uses Margaret Mallett's (1999) guidelines when she evaluates a nonfiction book for her class. She is wary of books that combine fact with fiction or fact with opinion— both combinations confuse the young reader, who can't tell the difference. She is wary of books that emphasize cuteness when they purport to inform. Mrs. Hanna recognizes the importance of nonfiction text features, such as a table of contents, index, and glossary. These retrieval devices help readers search for information, a common use for nonfiction texts. *From Sand to Sea* by Stephanie Feeney and Ann Fielding (1989) provides a model of well-researched factual information at a level appropriate to young children.

Whether the book depicts the mundane or the exotic, fact or fiction, the pictures must accurately portray the book's action, mood, and intent. Emergent readers will pay very close attention to the pictures that tell the story or provide information; therefore, the pictures need to do that. In nonfiction books, the illustrations should integrate will with the writing (Mallett, 1999). Youngsters also count on pictures to give them clues to the print; therefore, pictures need to do that too.

Illustration Quality

Donald Crews gives a wealth of pictorial information to support limited text in his factual books for young children. Beautiful color photographs are essential to Feeney and Fielding's book *From Sand to Sea*. Jim Fowler's paintings bring to life the stories written by his wife, Susi Gregg Fowler. Action-packed illustrations by Rie Munoz add humor to stories written by Jean Rogers. The detail in Steven Kellogg's and Peter Spier's illustrations delights adults as well as children. The simplicity and color in Ezra Jack Keats's and Gerald McDermott's illustrations also attract all ages. Different children's illustrators have merit for different reasons. However, not all children's book illustrations are art. Teachers and parents should be wary of overly cute art. From Disney to coloring books, illustrations without artistic merit surround children. Teachers and parents can make selections that will help counteract those influences, help youngsters develop taste, and provide worthy models for the youngsters' own art.

The values represented in the stories and illustrations are another critical issue in selecting books. Sexism, racism, and gratuitous violence are to be avoided. In the appendix to her book *The Whole Child* (1996), Hendrick offers a guide entitled "Ten Quick Ways to Analyze Children's Books for Racism and Sexism." Other guides are also available (e.g., Morrow, 1993; Temple, Martinez, Yokota, & Naylor, 1998). As Don Holdaway stated, "Literature at its best, and children's literature in particular, transcends the surface distinctions of cultural difference and embodies universal human concerns" (1979, p. 17). It is worthwhile to search for books that represent the values we wish to pass on to children.

Cultural Authenticity

Similar issues need to be considered in selecting books to authentically reflect a variety of cultures and ethnic groups (Gross & Ortiz, 1994). Simply because a book purports to be about a minority group does not mean that it will be accurate or free of stereotypes (Ramirez & Ramirez, 1994). It is difficult for those outside the group to judge those features. Mrs. Thomas has been guided in her selection of Native American literature by the eye-opening *Through Indian Eyes* (Slapin & Seale, 1992). She discovered that one of her favorite books, *Annie and the Old One* (Miska, 1971), was based on a false premise about how a Navajo child would feel about the death of her grandmother. In contrast, Goble's beautiful book *Star Boy* (1983) is true to the beliefs of the Blackfeet. Table 3.3 offers guidelines for screening books about Native Americans that Mrs. Thomas thinks could be adapted to any group.

Ms. Reynolds is concerned that most books about non-European cultures show a historical perspective rather than a contemporary one. Thus, youngsters get the erroneous ideas that their African American playmates have just escaped from slavery or that their Native American classmates cook over an open fire. However, Munsch and Kusugak do not fall into that trap with *A Promise Is a Promise* (1988). The Inuit family in this book doesn't live in an igloo but lives in an ordinary house with books and a teddy bear for the little girl. *Through Indian Eyes* also commends *The Goat in the Rug* (Blood & Link, 1976) for presenting a story that "treats Native life as though it were simply a normal part of human existence" (Slapin & Seale, 1992).

Guidelines for Sharing a Story

Picking a worthwhile book is only the first step in sharing a story with children. You need to prepare to share it effectively, you need to consider what you want children to get out of it, and you need to plan for variations in children's ability to benefit from it. You also have group management decisions to make, such as who should participate and when and where.

Effective Presentation

Ms. Reynolds rarely shares a book with preschool youngsters before she has become familiar with it herself. By reading a book to herself, she discovers whether

TABLE 3.3
Questions to Ask When Selecting Books About Native Peoples

Does this book tell the truth?
Does the author respect the People?
Is there anything in this book that would embarrass or hurt a Native child?
Is there anything in this book that would foster stereotypic thinking in a non-Indian child?

Source: Slapin and Seale (1992).

the quality is high enough and whether it is appropriate for the age and interests of her preschoolers. Ms. Montoya also wants to know the story well enough to introduce and share it effectively. She wants her lead-in remarks about the book to help her multiage-primary children make connections between their own experiences and the story. Another part of getting children involved in a story is helping them formulate questions about the outcome. Preparing adequately is important for an effective story time.

Mrs. Hanna concentrates on developing proper expression and pacing as she reads to her kindergartners so that she can convey the book's full meaning and impact. She also wants to be able to paraphrase or skip any long descriptive passages should her listeners lose interest. Whenever possible, Mrs. Hanna reads a story over several times and practices it before she shares it with children. Children are enthralled by an exciting scene that she reads with breathless haste, they are captivated by the suspenseful moment in which their teacher pauses for effect, and they gain immeasurable meaning from the expressive way she reads direct quotations to bring the characters to life. Table 3.4 summarizes guidelines for sharing stories.

TABLE 3.4
Guidelines for Sharing Stories with Children

Advance Planning
- Never share a story without being prepared.
- Plan an introduction that will link the story to children's experiences.
- Never share a story just to fill time.

Arranging the Story Environment
- Sit on a low chair or on the floor.
- Share stories in small groups more often than in large ones.
- Allow children to choose whether to listen to the story.

Effectively Sharing Stories
- Remember to point out book titles and authors.
- Help children formulate questions about the story's outcome.
- Use a conversational tone of voice and speak slowly and distinctly. Avoid a singsong or a high-pitched voice.
- Lock directly at the children. Include all members of the group, not only those directly in front of you.
- Hold the book steadily and be sure all children can see it.
- Use timing effectively; vary the tempo. As action increases and things begin to happen, accelerate the tempo. Before a moment of question, surprise, or awe, a pause can be most effective.
- Model interaction with the story. Predict or wonder about outcomes, express reactions to events, and make other comments as relevant.
- Keep the story or listening period within the limits of the children's attention span.

CHAPTER 3

Interactive Reading

Simply reading to children does not give them the full benefit of story time (Cambourne, 1988). To truly make sense of a story, children need the support of a dialogue about it (Moustafa, 1997; Whitehurst & Lonigan, 1998, 2002). Different youngsters need varying amounts of support, of course. Some need basic vocabulary assistance, perhaps because their experience hasn't included words used in the book or because they are still learning English. All young children are still developing their vocabulary, though, so it is helpful to discuss any unusual words used. Even more important is dialogue about the meaning of what is read. Sometimes youngsters need some background information before a story can make sense to them; at other times, children's related experiences may add meaning to a story.

Let's watch Ms. Montoya helping her multiage-primary children build meaning for a story. She sits in a rocking chair with a group of her students gathered around on the floor. She shows the book *Three Strong Women: A Tall Tale from Japan* (Stamm, 1990) to the children. This is the story of a fairly self-satisfied wrestler on his way to perform in front of the emperor. Ms. Montoya asks questions as she reads, such as, "Brandi, what does the word *strong* mean to you?" When she reads about "legs as thick as trees," Ms. Montoya pauses to ask the children what that means. All ideas offered by youngsters are respected and considered. When she reads that the wrestler turned white, Ms. Montoya facilitates a discussion of what that tells us about how a person is feeling. When she reads about the wrestler holding the grandmother down for half a minute, they discuss how long that is. And near the end, Ms. Montoya asks the children to predict how they think the story will end.

Effective dialogue means not just allowing but actually *encouraging* children to interrupt the story—not so much as to lose the plot but enough to help them follow it. Children have spontaneous questions and comments that make the story more meaningful to them. These comments may be too disruptive in a large group—one of many reasons for reading stories in small groups. Teachers can also interrupt the story, using planned questions to engage children's thinking about the reading and help them relate the story to their own experiences (Barrentine, 1996). The goal is twofold: to help youngsters realize that books have meaning and to demonstrate how to figure out what that meaning is. Demonstrations of figuring out meaning go beyond noticing how oral language and print correspond and even beyond learning the language of print. Teachers also need to model and involve children in reading activities, such as predicting outcomes and checking predictions.

As she reads, Ms. Reynolds maintains frequent eye contact with her preschool listeners as part of being responsive to their reactions. She demonstrates an interactive approach to reading with appropriate comments and questions, such as "Oh, what a lot to eat!" when she reads *The Very Hungry Caterpillar* (Carle, 1974) or "Do you think Daisy is afraid?" when she reads *Come Along, Daisy!* (Simmons, 1979). As she nears the end of *The Stray Dog* (Simont, 2001), she asks the children to remember "What happened the first time Willy joined the family for a picnic?" Children gather around Ms. Reynolds as she shares literature with them.

She usually sits on a low chair or on the floor to enhance interaction and cozy to-getherness. The children in Ms. Reynolds's preschool are learning a great deal about reading long before they are able to read on their own. Older children con-tinue to benefit from being involved with the kind of comments and questions de-scribed in Ms. Reynolds's preschool story time too.

Mrs. Hanna tries to individualize her interactions with youngsters even dur-ing group stories. For instance, when she reads *Muddigush* (Knudson, 1992), she asks Natalya if she likes to play in the mud—knowing that she does. Mrs. Hanna also models an active rather than a passive approach to story content, perhaps as expressions of amazement, sympathy, or outrage (Morrow, 1993).

Because reading critically as well as for comprehension is a necessity in our society, Mrs. Thomas makes sure to incorporate critical reading as part of story-time interaction. When she reads *Doctor DeSoto*, by William Steig (1982), to her first graders, she encourages discussion of whether the mouse dentist should have risked treating the fox's toothache and whether it was fair for him to glue the fox's teeth together at the end. *Oh My Baby, Little One*, by Kathi Appelt (2000), presents a topic of personal interest to children as they discuss how it feels to say goodbye to a parent. When conflicting views are solicited and respected, children learn that they can form their own opinions about what they read rather than merely accept whatever is in print. Through such interaction about stories, chil-dren can develop a variety of competencies in meaningful text construction before they can read in a conventional sense. Table 3.5 offers suggestions of questions that may help stimulate discussions.

Who Comes to Story Time?

Mrs. Hanna relies on the intrinsic pleasure of sharing a good book to bring her kindergarten students together. Like Ms. Reynolds, she doesn't require atten-dance at group story time by all children. If she wants to instill a love of reading, won't forcing stories on children accomplish just the opposite? Instead, she merely

TABLE 3.5
Questions for Possible Discussion

(Do not force discussion of questions.)

For thinking critically
- Do you agree?
- What would you have done?
- How do you feel about it?

Follow-up questions (from Egawa, 1990)
- What is this book really about?
- Does this story matter to you?
- What's on your mind after reading this book?
- What are you interested in after this reading?

CHAPTER 3

invites the children to hear a story and begins as soon as a small group has gathered. As long as they are quiet and don't interrupt the story, Mrs. Hanna does not interrupt those who remain engrossed in a previous activity or who simply prefer one of the acceptable alternatives to story time. She knows these children will be able to overhear the story as they work puzzles or draw pictures. Often one or two will leave what they are doing and join the story group as the story gets exciting. Some children find it difficult to sit still and listen without doing something else to occupy their hands, so they need to have options. Sometimes a child still isn't ready to be part of a group and prefers to listen from the side. Some children don't understand what is happening at story time and aren't interested yet. Mrs. Hanna's system provides alternatives to meet the varying personalities and maturation levels of her kindergartners. Small-group story times or one-on-one stories often provide a lead-in to group stories for youngsters not used to being read to.

Big Books help some youngsters enjoy group stories more because they can see pictures and print better. More and more children's literature is being published in oversized books for the purpose of *shared reading*, which we discuss in Chapter 4. For youngsters who are interested, Big Books provide an opportunity to follow the print as the teacher reads. The opportunity to follow the print extends some of the benefits of lap reading to group reading. As researchers discovered what children were learning by following the print during story time, teachers learned why youngsters get so upset at not being able to see the book

Being able to see the print while the teacher reads is important to a child who is trying to figure out how print works.

being read (Elster, 1994). Big Books were created to address that aspect of learning to read. It is important to remember, though, that the fact of being in a large format doesn't make a book worth reading. Teachers still need to use discretion in selections.

Reconstructing the Story

All these teachers are careful not to ruin a good story with moralizing about the message at the end, but they often plan a follow-up activity or discussion. Ms. Reynolds's students are challenged by the game of retelling the story in sequence either from the pictures in the book or with felt characters on a felt board. At this age, many youngsters also like to reconstruct the story from memory on their own, gaining valuable insights as to what reading is all about. Repeated readings of the same book, both independently and by adults, help children make sense of reading (International Reading Association and National Association for the Education of Young Children, 1998. Copple, Neuman, & Bredekamp, 2000).

Children of all ages love to take a book the teacher has just read and go off to the library corner to work at reading it by themselves. Readinglike behavior is observed in young children's early reconstruction of stories read to them. We have

Emergent readers often pretend to read a book that has been read to them over and over.

all seen emergent readers pretend to read a much-beloved story that has been read to them over and over. They not only remember the plot and sequence, they also change their language style to match book language. This childish activity, once considered merely cute, is now recognized as the way youngsters practice the language of books. Listen, and you will hear children attempting the more formal and decontextualized form of written language rather than the ambiguous oral forms that children usually use in speech. By your careful listening, you also will realize that children haven't merely memorized the stories and aren't merely imitating adults. Their story retellings focus on the personal meanings of the story and use their own immature speech patterns. This is important evidence of how children learn by constructing their own knowledge.

When children practice emergent reading in these ways, they work on the concepts that are appropriate for their level of maturity and for them as individuals seeking understanding. Some are working on the general form of written language as discussed, some are exploring the conventions of direction and position in print, and others are interpreting the written symbols themselves. When children begin the laborious work of decoding symbols, their past experience with focusing on meaning helps them avoid being "trapped into mindlessness by the slow word-by-word visual checking of early reading" (Holdaway, 1979, p. 53). The meaning of the story is both the guide and the impetus to these activities. There would be no purpose and no motivation if the story had no meaning to the child. Additionally, the reading process would become a difficult and mindless decoding task without the guidance of "What makes sense?"

Educators now recognize that emergent reading of storybooks is important enough to observe and record for assessment purposes. Elizabeth Sulzby (1985) developed a classification scheme to guide such assessment, which will be discussed further in Chapter 8. Whatever level a child is working on, teachers assist by applauding the small steps in the direction of literacy. As with oral language, it is important for adults to encourage practice rather than to focus on errors.

Children have always spontaneously worked at rereading the interesting books that adults read to them. Teaching approaches have finally taken their cue from children's own learning approaches and formalized this process. Publishers of reading materials now sell book sets with multiple copies of children's literature to facilitate such exploration of books read by the teacher. Big Book versions of stories with accompanying sets of identical little books are currently popular reading instruction materials. Story time is no longer separate from reading instruction periods.

The danger is that formalized shared book experiences (Holdaway, 1979), directed listening/thinking activities (Morrow, 1993), and other instructional activities may take over story time, destroying the pleasure found in literature and damaging the potential for learning. If this were to happen, it would not be the first time that descriptions of learning processes have been turned into prescriptions for activities. If teachers begin to force march youngsters through activities that the children previously selected for themselves, the activities will no longer be the same and will not have the same value.

Story Follow-up Activities

For group follow-up activities, Mrs. Hanna enjoys assisting children in dramatizing sections of a story as a way to internalize the meaning (Soundy, 1993). For instance, she follows up a reading of Steven Kellogg's *The Island of the Skog* (1973) with a suggestion that the children show her how the mice must have felt when they saw the monstrous creature lurching toward them on the beach. She encourages the youngsters to show emotion with their whole bodies as well as with their facial expressions. Then she asks what they might say when they feel that way. These creative dramatic experiences often reappear as children later incorporate them into their dramatic play. So the Skog might come to visit the domestic scene in the playhouse the next day, and we might find the playhouse inhabited by mice who prepare meals of chocolate waffles and coconut cherry cheese pie. Book-related dramatic play supports children's literacy learning, aiding in comprehension and recall of a story (Rowe, 2000).

Murals, individual paintings, clay sculptures, and a variety of artwork may be stimulated by a book and may, in turn, enhance appreciation for the book (Hoyt, 1992). Ms. Montoya suggested that some of her students might enjoy making a mural showing their ideas about the qallupilluits in *A Promise Is a Promise*. As part of this project, she demonstrated to youngsters how to use a watercolor wash to replicate the subtle background colors in scenes from the book. The children enjoyed learning a new way to paint as well as having an opportunity to express their ideas about the scary qallupilluits under the ice. Some youngsters enjoy using music to respond to books and other experiences. The story poem *Real Wild Rice* (Martinson, 1975) inspired some youngsters to put it to music and sing it.

Making their own version of a favorite book is a popular follow-up activity. Pattern books such as *The Important Book* (Brown, 1945) lend themselves well to a class-made adaptation. After enjoying the book, children have an opportunity to contribute their own page for a similar book. They may offer their own ideas of what's important about something they care about. Children draw their own illustrations and either dictate the written portion for an adult to write or else write it themselves in whatever forms of writing they are currently using. In another version of *The Important Book*, each page is about one child. Thus, a page might read, "The important thing about Katya is . . . ," with Katya finishing the statement via dictation or independent writing. Ms. Montoya likes to do this adaptation at the beginning of the school year and use a photograph of each child as the illustration for that child's page. Then, as children read or look at the book, they get introduced to others in the class and learn what their classmates' names look like. Class-made books are always the most sought-after books in the classroom library.

Following the Story:
Some Follow-up Activity Categories _____

- Independent reconstruction of story
- Group retelling of story in sequence

- Dramatization of the story
- Acting out the climax
- Adaptation of story into class-made book
- Responding to the book via art or music expression
- Responding to the book in writing
- Experiencing events similar to those in story

A teacher may use many activities relevant to a book as preparation for the story rather than as follow-up. Often a prior personal experience will give meaning to a story otherwise incomprehensible to young children. Playing outside in the snow and making snow angels give meaning to Ezra Jack Keats's *The Snowy Day* (1962), and picking blueberries adds to a reading of Robert McCloskey's *Blueberries for Sal* (1948) (see Figure 3.2). Children who are familiar with the salmon, eagles, and beaches of western Canada and southeast Alaska are more likely to understand Betty Waterton's *A Salmon for Simon* (1978). All these stories would likely correspond with experiences of children from Juneau, Alaska, but would not be as suitable for children from Phoenix, Arizona. Similarly, Keats's *Clemintina's Cactus* (1982) would have more meaning for youngsters from Phoenix than for youngsters from Juneau, and *Rush Hour* (Loomis, 1996) would be most relevant to youngsters from a big city.

Ms. Reynolds's preschool class enjoyed the day when class learning activities centered on the blueberries they had picked. Several children were involved in

FIGURE 3.2
After the class picked blueberries and made blueberry muffins, *Blueberries for Sal* was the story of the day.

dyeing yarn in mashed blueberries, and all who were interested took turns making batches of blueberry muffins. Everyone ate the muffins for snack. Naturally, *Blueberries for Sal* was the story of the day.

Some teachers have begun using literature as the base for their entire curriculum. They select excellent fiction and nonfiction books around a specific theme and extend that theme not only into all the language arts but also into science, social studies, art, and even math. This allows for a project approach (Katz & Chard, 1989) to education that involves children in real activities to assist them in making sense of their experiences.

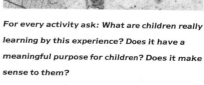

For every activity ask: What are children really learning by this experience? Does it have a meaningful purpose for children? Does it make sense to them?

The challenge of integrating curriculum around literature, themes, or any other system is to focus on authentic integration. Many teachers get sidetracked into activities that have no significance and do not extend children's understanding. Activities such as counting gummy bears during a study of bears do not help children learn about the subject of study and therefore represent a correlated rather than an integrated approach to the curriculum. To help guard against trivializing children's learning, think carefully about the activities you are considering.

Another danger to guard against is overdoing the discussion and activities related to a story. Many curriculum and resource guides suggest several days of activities related to one very short story. Though related activities help children develop meaning for what they read, let's remember that the reading itself is valuable.

CONCLUSION

This chapter presented guidelines to follow and pitfalls to avoid for both oral language activities and children's literature. Opportunities to talk were the main focus of recommended oral language activities and time with high-quality books was emphasized for literature. The important roles of adults and of other children for learning both language and literature were described. This chapter also addressed ways to incorporate language, cultural, and racial diversity into teaching both language and literature.

DISCUSSION QUESTIONS

1. A parent is visiting your classroom. Before leaving, he expresses his concern that the children aren't learning to sit still and be quiet in this setting. How would you explain why you do not value a quiet classroom?
2. Your school district gets funding to provide special assistance to young children at risk for failure in reading. Describe and defend your plan for the best ways to spend the money.

SUGGESTED FOLLOW-UP ACTIVITIES

1. Practice conversing with young children individually. Use reflective listening and open-ended questions to encourage their language.
2. Observe a master teacher guiding a group discussion. Note ways of encouraging all youngsters to participate and of teaching respectful communication.
3. Find a current list of award-winning books at your local library and examine as many of the books on the list as possible. Note the quality of illustrations that won illustrator awards and also analyze the stories for their appeal to children.
4. Using the guides in this chapter, select, prepare, and share a book or story with a group of youngsters. Ask a peer to observe and help you critique your presentation and its value for children.

RECOMMENDED FURTHER READING

Barrentine, S. J. (1996). Engaging with reading through interactive read-alouds. *The Reading Teacher, 50*(1), 36–43.

Bobys, A. R. (2000). What does emerging literacy look like? *Young Children, 55*(4), 16–22.

Dickinson, D. K., & Tabors, P. O. (2002). Fostering language and literacy in classrooms and homes. *Young Children, 57*(2), 10–18.

Fisher, B. (1998). *Joyful learning.* Portsmouth, NH: Heinemann.

Slapin, B., & Seale, D. (1992). *Through Indian eyes.* Philadelphia: New Society Publishers.

Tabors, P. O. (1997). *One child, two languages.* Baltimore: Paul H. Brookes.

4

ASSISTING EMERGENT READERS

Reading is a construction of meaning from text. It is an active, cognitive, and affective process.

J. Braunger and J. P. Lewis, 1997
(Copublished by Northwest Regional Educational Laboratory, National Council of Teachers of English, and International Reading Association.)

CHAPTER 4

This chapter looks at teaching and learning opportunities that assist emergent readers in their efforts to become independent readers. Emergent readers are still in the process of developing their understanding of how print and meaning are associated. As we describe effective teaching for children in this phase of literacy, we continue to emphasize children's active construction of knowledge in their attempts to comprehend written language. We describe the teacher's role as essential but possibly different from what you may be used to. Our view is that the teacher is the supporting actor and the children have the lead roles. We also continue to present literacy as a complex perceptual, linguistic, and psychological process rather than a set of rules to be mastered (K. S. Goodman, 1996).

Literacy, like so many other things, is greater than the sum of its parts. Reading is not phonics, word analysis, and sight words any more than a conversation is nouns, verbs, and grammar. Writing is not spelling, punctuation, and penmanship either. Reading, writing, and oral language are ways in which human beings communicate, and they are acquired through social interaction. They are also the ways in which we record and explore our ideas, feelings, and knowledge. These deeply personal and human motivations give power and significance to both written and oral language. Children want to participate fully in these aspects of their culture both for the connectedness with other human beings and for the control it gives them in their world. Teachers don't have to work hard to make kids interested in becoming literate if reading and writing maintain purposefulness in school as well as out of school. Who wouldn't work at reading when reading means knowing what is on the lunch menu today or how the story ends or who gets to bring the balls out at recess? Who wouldn't work at writing when writing gets a note back from a friend?

Children learn skills better and benefit more from practice that doesn't break reading and writing into meaningless little parts. It's very hard to remember isolated sets of information, such as sounds, letters, or numbers. That's why many business advertisements give phone numbers using a relevant word instead of merely numbers. When children work on actual reading and writing rather than on just the skills involved, the meaning and significance are retained. With this approach, fewer children get lost in their quest for learning. They aren't trying to make sense of nonsense.

Also, fewer children will get lost in the educational process when more educators respect learners' individual differences. Schools would like it if all youngsters moved from emergent reading to independent reading during first grade. Such conformity would be very tidy, but it's totally unrealistic. Some children still will be emergent readers in late elementary school, and a few will be independent readers in preschool. Thus, our recommendations for teaching have nothing to do with grade or age and everything to do with the individual child's current understanding. Recommendations for supporting young independent readers and writers are presented in Chapters 6 and 7. Regardless of what age-group you teach, you will have both emergent and independent readers among your students. Multiage classes acknowledge and capitalize on these inescapable differences.

Although this chapter focuses on reading, we are uncomfortable talking about reading and writing separately because they are so intertwined. Please keep this interrelationship constantly in mind as you read the chapters that discuss one or the other. This chapter on emergent reading precedes the next chapter on emergent writing not because reading precedes writing but because we started talking about reading in the preceding chapter and want to continue building on that discussion.

READING EXPERIENCES

A rich literacy environment offers a multitude of opportunities to read and a wide array of things to read. Experiences with these reading opportunities and materials allow children to make sense of the reading process and learn the skills needed to do so. Teachers vary the amount of support or scaffolding they provide depending on children's needs and the materials being used. During read aloud, as described in Chapter 3, teachers read to children. Teachers create opportunities to read *with* children during shared reading and guided reading. Reading is done *by* the children during independent reading and playful exploration of print (see Table 4.1). Teachers modify their support, providing less as learners assume more of the reading and providing more when the task is more difficult (Fountas & Pinnell, 1996; Tompkins, 2003). Fiction and nonfiction books will probably be the main focus of reading experiences, but reading includes signs, labels, notes, lists, menus, television guides, and other types of functional print as well. A selection of visual and auditory games for phonemic awareness and word recognition completes the package.

Shared Reading

You may be wondering what shared reading experiences are. Shared reading experiences are ways of sharing a book that encourage a group of children to observe the print and participate in the reading, each to the best of his or her ability. The teacher reads *with* the children, leading the reading as they chime in using a choral reading style. During the reading, the teacher tries to involve youngsters in thinking about the story and predicting what will happen next. Big Books, as described in Chapter 3, assist this process by making the words visible to large groups of students. Because of its size, a Big Book is easiest to use if set on an easel instead of held. The teacher's hands are then free to point to the words and help the audience follow along with the reading. Children who are trying to figure out how print works will benefit greatly from hearing the oral reading and seeing it matched to the print. Matching print to oral language requires that children look at the printed version of each word at the same time they are saying and/or hearing it aloud. This process gives them lots to think about and can help them accept the alphabetic principle, develop phonemic awareness, or increase their sight-word vocabulary. Children will benefit in different ways, depending on their current level of development.

Pattern books and other predictable books assist the process by helping emergent readers anticipate, guess, and remember what the print says. For instance, as Ms. Montoya reads *The Napping House* (Wood, 1984), she doesn't have to read many pages before most of her students are chiming in at the end of each page and saying along with her ". . . in the napping house, where everyone is sleeping."

C H A P T E R   4

TABLE 4.1

Literacy Basics

---

1. A print-rich environment
   - Adults who read for their own purposes
   - Adults who write for their own purposes
   - Frequent story-time experiences
   - Information about letter names and sounds
   - Shared reading
   - Dictation and other shared writing experiences
   - High-quality literature
   - Contextualized print
   - Functional print
   - Answers to questions about print
2. A rich oral-language environment
   - Adult language models
   - Adults who listen to children
   - Free exploration of oral language
   - Peer conversation
   - Dramatic play roles
   - Experiences for vocabulary enrichment
   - Vocabulary information as requested
3. Firsthand experiences of interest
   - Play
   - Daily living
   - Field trips
   - Nature exploration
4. Symbolic representation experiences
   - Dramatic play
   - Drawing and painting
   - Music and dance
5. Pressure-free experimentation with writing (independent writing)
   - Drawing
   - Scribbling
   - Prealphabetic writing
   - Phonics-based spelling
6. Pressure-free exploration of reading (independent reading)
   - Reading from memory
   - Reading with context clues
   - Matching print to oral language

Children and their parents have been enjoying books together this way for a long time, but now the process has been recognized as a teaching and learning activity in school. Don Holdaway (1979) is credited with creating that awareness through his research and writing about more effective beginning reading instruction. Shared reading is now formalized as part of the reading program and has become common practice (for example, see Morrow, 2001).

Favorite songs and poems written on large chart paper offer an excellent opportunity for shared reading.

Shared reading is also a good way to model the reading process, simulating parent-child story time. As children are asked to follow along while you read, they experience the directionality of print, the arrangement of print on pages, and the direction in which pages are turned. Children who are tuned in to print want and need to see the page as you read to them. These youngsters follow along carefully as they try to figure out what printed symbols go with what spoken words.

The teacher's model provides a scaffold to assist them as they struggle with the question, "What is the relationship of print to words?" The teacher's model also demonstrates the interactive nature of the reading process: the active questioning, predicting, and other meaning-making thinking aspects of reading. Multiage-primary teacher Ms. Montoya makes sure to model how to use the three kinds of clues we will describe later in this chapter: "Does it make sense?" (semantic clues), "Does it look right?" (graphophonemic clues), and "Does it sound right?" (syntax clues). Perhaps most of all, we hope that the teacher's model demonstrates the great pleasure that a book can bring. Shared reading experiences are especially important for children who have not been read to regularly at home. These students often are labeled as "at risk for failure" because they don't have the kinds of knowledge about reading that children have who have experienced story times all their lives. Holdaway (1991) developed his shared reading program with the "at-risk" New Zealand students in mind.

Of course, you can have a shared reading session using something other than a book. Favorite songs and poems written on large chart paper offer an excellent opportunity for shared reading. After several repetitions, children will have memorized the oral content; then they will begin matching the written language to the oral language. The teacher can encourage matching all along by using a pointer and pointing to the words as they say or sing them aloud. Soon youngsters will begin to exclaim over words they have identified. Children love to use the pointers themselves; reading familiar charts with decorated "magic wand" pointers is a popular free-choice activity. Many teachers have small cardboard frames available in various lengths that they encourage children to use when they identify words and letters. When Felicia announces during shared reading that she sees the word *orange* in the pumpkin poem, Ms. Montoya invites her to hold a frame around the word for all to see. Similarly, Paul is encouraged to frame the first letter in *pumpkin* after he comments that it starts like his name. Shared reading models skills in action (Bruneau, 1997).

The challenge in this type of activity is to keep the focus on the meaning of what is being read. Schools have such a long history of reductionist approaches to language arts that it is often hard for teachers to visualize more complexity (Ritchie & Wilson, 1993). And it is easy for teachers to slip back into skills drills that are separate from the content that would give them meaning. Teachers must strike a fine balance to help learners attend to both meaning and the graphophonemic clues inherent in the print. Without the meaning, though, there is no reason to decipher the print. We need to keep that perspective and that priority. Similarly, without the joy of reading, there is little motivation for emergent readers to work at their task. Ms. Montoya makes sure that she offers reading materials that are worth reading and that her reading instruction doesn't get in the way of enjoying the content.

Guided Reading

Teachers notice and build on the responses of individuals during shared reading times. Their brief interactions while circulating around the room during independent reading time (described in the next section) allow teachers a chance to teach and to make important observations of children's progress. However, by the time children are in first grade, it is common to provide more formalized reading instruction as well.

Though grouping by ability has many negative consequences, small groups can be efficient for guiding children's progress (Cunningham, Hall, & Defee, 1998). Instead of segregating children into reading groups according to ability, Ms. Montoya makes the most of the diversity in her multiage classroom. All her reading groups include readers of different abilities, and each child reads materials at his or her own level. Ms. Montoya uses interest grouping—the unifying aspect of each group is the topic the children have chosen to read about or the type of book they are reading (Opitz, 1998). For instance, Ms. Montoya has a collection of books about caterpillars that includes such variation as *Humpity-Bump!* (Murphy, 1993), an "instant reader" book from Scott, Foresman that can be read from memory using picture clues; *The Changing Caterpillar* (Shahan, 1997), a beginning book that is a little more advanced, from Richard Owen Publishers; and *The Very Hungry Caterpillar* (Carle, 1974), the beloved storybook that combines fact with fiction.

Ms. Montoya can help children think about reading skills whether they are reading the same book or not. She starts by leading a discussion of what the boys and girls already have heard about caterpillars and what they would like to find out. This sets the expectation of purposeful reading, actively checking on assumptions and seeking information. Children are then free to read the book or books each has chosen on the topic. Much of the reading is done away from the group. Ms. Montoya recognizes that valuable time would be lost if children read aloud one at a time, round-robin style. She provides some support but selects materials carefully so children can read with great accuracy on their own. When they meet again, they share information as well as strategies used in their reading. No child feels like a failure with this system.

It is difficult to address the specific strategies needed by each reader in such heterogeneous groups, however. And, like many teachers, Ms. Montoya realizes that there really is no such thing as a truly homogeneous group anyway. She knows that each child has unique academic and emotional needs and doesn't fool

Reading groups based on topics of interest, explored at different reading levels, are much more effective than ability-based groups.

herself into believing that she can meet everyone's needs in a group. So she makes a point of meeting one-on-one with her students as often as possible.

Similarly, Mrs. Thomas believes that reading conferences with individual students are the most effective guided reading time. She can target specific areas of confusion, build on strengths, and encourage personal interests for each child best one on one. She doesn't worry that she can't meet with each child formally each day. She does connect with each child informally each day, so she knows that all the children are continuing to read on their own. Her experience taking ski lessons has confirmed her view about the best use of her teaching time. She has taken both group lessons and individual lessons and has found that she's benefited more from the half hour of attention to her personal strengths and weaknesses that she gets in an individual lesson than from several hours of general group instruction.

As she reads the book *Mama, Do You Love Me?* (Joosse, 1991) (see Figure 4.1) with Ivan, Mrs. Thomas assists his understanding of reading as an active process of predicting his way through print (Cutting & Milligan, 1991). Let's listen in as Ivan works on the pages that say, "I love you . . . more than the dog loves his tail, more than the whale loves his spout." The teacher's comments and questions

I love you more
than the raven loves
his treasure,

more than the dog loves his tail,
more than the whale loves his spout.

FIGURE 4.1

The illustrations, story content, and repeated patterns in such children's literature as *Mama, Do You Love Me?* provide readers with a variety of clues for successful reading.

Source: From Joosse, B. M. (1991). Mama, do you love me? San Francisco: Chronicle Books. Reprinted by permission.

focus his attention on reconstructing meaning rather than on just recognizing words. For instance, when Ivan reads ". . . more than the dog loves his *tall*, more than the whale loves his *spot*," Mrs. Thomas asks him if that makes sense to him. She helps Ivan think about what he knows of dogs and whales and also helps him use the picture clues on the page to figure out the confusing words. She doesn't focus his attention on the differences between the words *spout* and *spot* because she can tell that Ivan is already paying attention to the letters but perhaps not enough to the meaning.

Mrs. Thomas responds quite differently when Danielle brings her the same book and reads the same pages: ". . . more than puppies, more than whales." It is clear that Danielle knows the pattern of the book and that she is using the picture clues on the page to remember the content, but it is also clear that she really is not attending to the print. This is appropriate at a certain level of emergent reading, but Mrs. Thomas thinks Danielle can move beyond that now. Mrs. Thomas varies her support depending on the needs of the learner. By pointing to the words on the page, Mrs. Thomas helps Danielle notice the discrepancy between the written word and her oral reading. Then Mrs. Thomas reads the page aloud, encouraging Danielle to read along. They find and talk about the repetition of the words *more than the* on two lines. Mrs. Thomas also has Danielle pick out the words *dog* and *whale*, asking her to note the beginning letters. Then they look briefly at the difference between the words *love* and *loves*. This is a lot for Danielle to think about, and she needs time with the book now. Danielle decides to ask her friend Anastasia to read it with her because she knows Anastasia is a good reader.

These conference times provide opportunities to record a child's current reading strategies as well as offer insights into assisting individual progress. We will postpone discussing the record keeping and diagnostic and evaluative aspects of conferences until Chapter 8, though it is difficult to discuss teaching and assessing separately.

Independent Reading

Even young children need regular opportunities for reading by themselves. An inviting library area furnished with soft cushions and an enticing display of children's books can help them enjoy books. A library area also encourages independent reading during choice times. However, as early as kindergarten, many teachers also set aside a specific time in the daily schedule when everyone is supposed to read. You might well ask, Why have a reading time for children who can't yet read? Watch a child and see. Children who have stories read to them will invariably take a beloved book and read it to themselves. The children may be the first to tell you that they are not "really" reading, just pretending—or as one child said, "I just 'bemembered' it." But, as explained in Chapter 3, researchers in the field of emergent literacy consider this readinglike behavior a significant stage in reading development.

Young children will engage in this pretend reading even before they can talk well and before they can speak in sentences (Holdaway, 1979). They will re-create the story as they perceive it, using the language at their command. Adults in the

TEACHING SKILLS DURING GUIDED READING

Ms. Montoya is listening to Kaitlin read the book *Jump, Frog, Jump!* (Kalan, 1981). She is paying close attention to which strategies Kaitlin is using well and which ones she needs more help with.

On the first page of the story there is a picture of a fly climbing from the water onto a leaf. The print beneath the illustration reads, "This is the fly that climbed out of the water." Kaitlin reads, "This is the fly that climbed *on* the water." Ms. Montoya asks Kaitlin if that makes sense: Kaitlin recognizes that it doesn't make sense, so Ms. Montoya encourages her to look at the word *out* more closely. They talk about how the word ends and look at the letters more carefully. After Kaitlin gets the word right, Ms. Montoya urges her to read the sentence from the beginning in order to make better sense of it.

Because of what the picture shows, Kaitlin's mistake tells Ms. Montoya that Kaitlin is using picture clues to help her predict what the print will say. Since *out* and *on* both begin with the same letter, this is a natural mistake, and it makes sense until the wrong word is read. While Kaitlin reads, Ms. Montoya makes notes documenting the strategies Kaitlin is currently using.

A few pages later, Kaitlin has trouble again. The sentence reads, "How did the frog catch the fly?" but Kaitlin stumbles over the word *catch*. Ms. Montoya realizes that Kaitlin doesn't remember the *ch* sound and is probably confused by the silent *t* in the word as well. This is a teachable moment—time for a phonics minilesson that will be meaningful and relevant. Ms. Montoya reminds Kaitlin about the *ch* sound and explains about the silent *t* that sometimes goes with it. Ms. Montoya makes a note of this minilesson for future reference.

Kaitlin finishes the story with only three additional deviations from the written text, two based on predictions from picture clues. Ms. Montoya notes the frequency of this pattern as she helps Kaitlin focus more on the print. The third deviation was the substitution of *a* for *the* in a sentence in which either made sense. Ms. Montoya decides to ignore that for the time being but to make a note for future consideration. Such notes as this and the one regarding reliance on picture clues help Ms. Montoya know whether Kaitlin's reading strategies are out of balance.

know will encourage any approximations of story reading, just as they encourage any approximations of oral language as the child learns to talk (Elster, 1994). Both constitute important practice in figuring things out.

Five-year-old Sasha puts on an important grown-up face and speaks with expression as she turns the pages of *The Very Hungry Caterpillar* (Carle, 1974) and reviews the story. The pictures on the page help her keep the story in sequence and are the primary source of the story for her now. When she reads *King Bidgood's in the Bathtub* (Wood, 1985), the pictures are also helpful, and she is able to re-create the main ideas of the extensive dialogue from memory. At first young children pay little attention to the print on the page but instead focus on other aspects of book reading.

Robin, a six-year-old with Down syndrome, likes to pick out several books at once and review them one after another. He tells the story to himself from memory if it is a familiar book and describes what he sees in the pictures if it is an unfamiliar one. His teacher has to work at understanding what Robin says because of his speech difficulties, but knowing the content of the books helps with this. Listening to Robin, it is clear that he understands the ideas in these books. He often tries to relate an unfamiliar book to one he already knows. For example, if there is a bear in a new book, he might call it Pooh bear.

Juanita "reads" the class books in Spanish, whether they are written in English or in Spanish. Her teacher has both Spanish and English versions of many children's literature books, but it doesn't matter to Juanita at this point. She is concentrating on the ideas in the books and doing so in the language she is most comfortable using.

An inviting library area furnished with soft cushions and an enticing display of children's books can enhance youngsters' enjoyment of reading.

There is much to learn about reading that is separate from print. First children discover that books are interesting and enjoyable. Then they quickly learn about how books work: how to turn one page at a time, where to begin, which direction to go, and that book language is different from spoken language. They pick up on the concept of plot: a beginning, a problem to resolve, and an end. They also gradually learn the more formal and complete language style used in written language. Children who do not have extensive experience with books find it difficult to adjust to the lack of external clues in written language. Unless it is a picture book, all the information must be contained in the language of books; whereas nonverbal clues and the situational context help give meaning to oral language.

As young children tune in to print, they begin to study the writing in books and to notice print everywhere. Some ask incessantly, "What does that say?" Others want to know, "What letter is that?" Individual personalities determine individual approaches to making sense of what is seen. Children impose their own drill and practice as they work at learning in their own ways. Their efforts to match the print to what it says can be complicated by early theories that only nouns appear in print and later that only nouns and verbs are written (Ferreiro, 1978; Manning, Manning, Long, & Kamii, 1995). Eventually, children realize that all the words read aloud are written, even a and the.

This realization paves the way for work on one-to-one correspondence between oral and written language. Finally, after much experience with print, it dawns on children that certain letters consistently are correlated with certain words. Then they are ready to benefit from information about how letters represent certain sounds. We used to think that letters and sounds were the starting place for learning to read. Though some people still believe that, observing children makes it clear that they have a lot of hard work before they get to that point. We also used to think that teaching letter sounds gave children the needed understanding to apply that information to reading; but now we know that children must figure that out for themselves. We can give children information about letters and sounds, but they must construct their own phonemic awareness and discover the alphabetic principle for themselves. As with all learning, youngsters construct some temporary theories about reading that no adult would teach them. These theories provide positive evidence of how knowledge is constructed.

Most typically developing children attend primarily to pictures in preschool, work on phonemic awareness in kindergarten, and begin to figure out phonemic patterns in first grade. Realistically, we know that children actually function at all levels during preschool and through the primary grades. Each child is a unique individual from a unique family, and each comes to school with a different set of prior experiences to build on. In addition, children approach the learning process in a variety of ways, depending on their individual styles of work and thought. Some children are extremely methodical and focused, whereas others are more diverse and broadly observant (Bussis, Chittenden, Amarel, & Klausner, 1985). Some have difficulty focusing at all.

Because of this wide span of backgrounds, abilities, and learning styles, broad choices of activities must be available to children. Teachers who trust their students to choose for themselves can be more certain of the right match between child and educational challenge. The difference between Ms. Reynolds's preschool class and Mrs. Thomas's first-grade class is the proportion of students working at each level rather than the kinds of learning options. Ms. Montoya's multiage classroom was designed with these kinds of differences in mind. She doesn't think of it as teaching several grades but rather as teaching children at various levels of understanding.

During independent reading time, children may be individually engrossed in a book or share the experience with one or two friends. Blair and Jessica are giggling together about a funny story they are both reading. Tyler is listening to a tape recording of a story and following along carefully in his copy of the book. A parent volunteer is reading to three children in a cozy corner.

Mrs. Thomas has been concerned about Toby, still a very early emergent reader in first grade. She watches him today during independent reading time. His frustration with reading is evident as he scans a few books with a scowl on his face. After a few minutes, he looks around the room for a group he can join. He walks around for a bit, then sidles up next to two boys reading together. These boys make room for Toby, and, as they read together, Toby's whole demeanor lightens up. He gets involved, leaning forward to be closer to the book, laughing during the funny parts, and watching as the other two boys track the print with their fingers. Mrs. Thomas is relieved to see that Toby has accepted her suggestion of partner reading; she is certain that the reading behaviors of more able readers will help Toby's progress.

Though it is not a required activity in preschool, independent reading time is very much a part of the program. One day Ms. Reynolds notices George reading to James. George, who is four and a half, is frequently read to at home; James, who is five, is seldom read to at home. This background is obvious as George shares his favorite book with James. George has had this book read to him repeatedly and has practiced reading it himself many times. He looks at the pictures to keep himself on track with the well-known story, and he knows exactly when to turn the page. As they share the book, both boys are laughing and pointing at the pictures. Two times, George stops reading to tell James that if he listens really hard, he will be able to read the book too. When he is finished, George hands the book to James and says, "Your turn." The next time Ms. Reynolds looks, James has taken over the reading and is exhibiting the readinglike behavior that George used earlier. It's amazing how much children can learn from one another.

During independent reading time, Mrs. Hanna circulates among her kindergarten students, sharing pleasure in a good book, suggesting another interesting story, and redirecting as needed. Mrs. Thomas circulates similarly but also makes time for a few individual reading conferences with her first graders each day. Whether during a conference or informally observing, these teachers are noting children's levels of understanding, their confusions, their breakthroughs, and their interests. Sometimes, these teachers are able to set an example by reading one of their own books for a few minutes.

During independent reading time, children may be individually engrossed in a book or share the experience with friends.

What Do Children Read?

Emergent readers, like all learners, are encouraged by success. Success helps them gain and keep their momentum for learning. Thus, reading materials not only need to be worth reading but also need to be readable. Fortunately, these tend to be complementary rather than contradictory attributes (Moustafa, 1997). Old ideas of readability, based on controlled vocabulary and focused on specific skills, sacrificed meaning in the process. You may remember reading boring books in first grade; some people call them "dishonest books" because they are written to teach skills rather than to share ideas. Apparently a small number of youngsters benefit from controlled vocabulary readers (Cole, 1998), but most beginning readers get important decoding assistance from the context of meaningful content (Strickland, 1998). For instance, if Sukey is stuck on a word, Ms. Montoya asks her to think about what would make sense as the starting place for figuring it out. We also know that interesting content provides the motivation to press on. If a book was put together to give practice in certain words rather than to tell a story, it may be that *nothing* makes sense. Sukey's attitude toward trying to figure out a word in such a book may be, "Who cares?"

Current practices of offering leveled books to beginning readers may be moving schools back into a focus on reading for skills rather than meaningful reading. Some teachers seem to have forgotten that the levels were created for the purpose of describing children's progress as they read literature, not prescribing it. Those teachers use the levels to limit children's choice of reading material, requiring that they read books at a specific level. Ms. Montoya values leveled books for the information they give her about what makes a book hard or easy for a child

WHAT ARE LEVELED BOOKS?

Have you wondered what leveled books are? They are books that have been analyzed according to a fairly standardized system for determining how difficult they are for children to read. Levels start at A for kindergarten or first grade and continue through level R, usually corresponding to the end of fourth grade.

The level is based on more than simply what words are in the book. For instance, level A and B books (the easiest) have a direct correspondence between the text and the pictures so that children can use picture clues extensively. A and B books also use natural sentence patterns and often are about topics familiar to children. These traits allow children to utilize what they already know about language and about the world to assist them in reading.

Moving up the levels, the vocabulary expands, the amount of print per page increases, and the pictures carry less of the meaning. By level F, typically read in mid-to-late first grade, literary language is mixed in with natural oral language structures (Fountas & Pinnell, 1996).

to read. She then uses this information as she helps children make wise choices, though she does not require that a child choose from a certain level.

Predictable Books

Familiarity with a book makes it more readable. In fact, anything that helps a child predict what comes next helps with reading. Predictability may be a result of knowing a story well, or it may come from having had an experience similar to that in a story. Pictures are another source of information that helps youngsters predict what the accompanying text will say. One type of predictable book that has recently become popular for reading instruction is the pattern book. Cumulative story patterns, such as those found in *The House That Jack Built* or *The Old Woman Who Swallowed a Fly*, have been familiar for years. Books such as *The Napping House* (Wood, 1984) or *Drummer Hoff* (Emberley, 1968) adopt that style and assist young readers through repetition of text. Probably the most easily readable pattern books are those such as Bill Martin, Jr.'s, famous *Brown Bear, Brown Bear, What Do You See*? (1983) that have a repetitive text that changes only slightly from page to page. These changes are accompanied by picture clues and rhymes that further assist in reading. Patterns, picture clues, and remembered stories offer temporary assistance to beginning readers in much the same way that training wheels help the novice bike rider—providing the support during practice that leads to more independent performance. Table 4.2 summarizes what to look for in predictable books.

TABLE 4.2
Types of Predictable Books

1. Familarity
    Essentially memorized from repeated read-aloud sessions (*The Three Bears*)
    A known situation or familiar experience portrayed (*The Snowy Day,* Keats, 1962)
2. Patterns
    Cumulative (*Why Mosquitoes Buzz in People's Ears,* Aardema, 1975)
    Repetitive forms (*The Very Busy Spider,* Carle, 1984)
3. Pictures
    Picture clues in conjunction with familiarity or patterns can make "instant readers"
    (*Brown Bear, Brown Bear, What Do You See?* Martin, 1983)

Books the teacher reads at group story time are likely to be both enticing and readable. Children of all ages love to reread a story they have enjoyed hearing. Mrs. Thomas offers her first graders small copies of the Big Books they read together during shared reading. Students eagerly snatch these up for rereading after experiencing the story with the group. What makes these books desirable to youngsters and useful for reading practice is their familiarity. Familiar books are readable books. Each child will use such books to figure out new concepts appropriate to his or her own understanding. Learners use the known to make sense of the unknown. Some are perfecting their sight-word vocabulary, some are trying to make sense of the graphophonemic clues, and some are still reading pictures.

Quantity and Self-Selection

It is a challenge to find enough books with which beginning readers can be successful (Gunning, 1998). Good teachers are always on the lookout for more good books for their classrooms; they know it is important to have many good books available (Ramos & Krashen, 1998). Though Ms. Montoya includes predictable books, she doesn't limit herself to them. She likes Bill Martin, Jr.'s, books and the *Clifford* books. Some of her students enjoy the Dr. Seuss beginning-reader books, but other children complain that the controlled vocabulary doesn't really make sense. They like Eric Carle's other books almost as well as *The Very Hungry Caterpillar,* and the children laugh with glee over Audrey Wood's *The Napping House.* Martha Alexander, Margaret Hillert, Syd Hoff, Arnold Lobel, and Bernard Wiseman are some other authors who cater to beginning readers. In other books for beginners, Shigeo Watanabe writes about a very large bear cub, James Marshall writes about hippos, H. A. Rey writes about a curious monkey, and Cindy Wheeler writes about a cat named Marmalade. Ezra Jack Keats writes about children in ways with which they can identify. James Stevenson's books range from humor and fantasy to realism. Miriam Cohen's *When Will I Read?* (1977) is a favorite that seems to reassure beginning readers. Ms. Montoya is delighted that so many of her favorites are available in Spanish too.

Many educational publishing companies are attempting to help teachers with the job of finding interesting and readable material for young readers. The Wright Group took the lead in publishing Big Books for the shared reading recommended by Don Holdaway (1979). *Mrs. Wishy-Washy* (Cowley, 1990) is probably the most popular of their books. Big Books are accompanied by several smaller copies for independent reading or use in a listening center. Most textbook companies now offer Big Books, little books, and pattern books. It is important to remember that these formats do not come with any guarantee of quality or appropriateness. We discuss criteria for selection of materials further in Chapter 9.

Just as different children learn in different ways, so they have individual preferences in books. Not only are they interested in different topics, but they also are attracted to different genres. Some like fantasy; others prefer informative nonfiction. Some struggling readers blossom when they read nonfiction on topics of interest to them (Caswell & Duke, 1998). It is important to cater to all tastes and allow children to self-select their books for independent reading (Moore, 1998). One thing all young children seem to have in common, however, is the desire to take books home to share with their parents. They are proud of their ability to read and want to demonstrate their new powers to their families. Mrs. Hanna and Ms. Montoya both have checkout systems that allow their classes to take books home freely.

Environmental Print

Remember, there is much more to read than books. There are name tags, helpers' charts, exit signs, stop signs, cereal boxes, letters from Grandma, and birthday cards. There are McDonald's arches, Baskin-Robbins flavors, and Pepsi cans. There are songs and poems and silly love notes. Reading is all around us, just as talk is all around us. Children grow up with it and gradually come to make sense of it and use it.

"Reading the room" is a favorite activity in Mrs. Hanna's class. Assorted decorated pointers, which some class members refer to as "magic wands," are available to make it more fun for children to wander around the room, alone or with a friend, pointing to and reading the messages on various signs and charts. Mrs. Hanna's kindergarten classroom is alive with print. Everywhere you look there is a poem that goes with a current classroom theme, a recipe for a recent cooking experience, a group story about a class adventure, or the day's agenda. Mrs. Hanna also entices children to want to read by communicating with them in writing. She writes notes to individual youngsters, she puts riddles on the board, and she posts notices about important events. Just because most of them can't read yet doesn't mean they can't be exposed to reading—when they couldn't talk yet they benefited from being exposed to talking. Mrs. Hanna knows that the children have been figuring out the print they see on television commercials and billboards for a long time. She values and builds on that knowledge in her classroom.

When her preschoolers go for a walk, Ms. Reynolds talks with them about street signs and advertising signs. When children play at the water table, she provides written labels for sorting items into "float" and "sink" categories. She helps her students find their own names by their coat hooks and cubbies. Even

The opportunity to choose their own books is motivating for readers.

preschoolers can read these kinds of contextualized print because there are enough external clues or past experiences linked to them. Contextualized print helps children read environmental print just as predictable books help them read stories; there is sufficient information in addition to the print to guide children's guesses about it. A stop sign is an excellent example of contextualized print. Chil-

Just as different children learn in different ways, they have individual preferences for the types of books they enjoy.

dren learn early to read those white letters on a red background, on a hexagonal sign, on a corner. Similarly, they can read many advertising logos and product brand names because of how and where they are written. Ms. Reynolds always lets her preschoolers know that they are reading when they can identify contextualized print.

By presenting a print-rich environment in which written language is used and displayed for a variety of purposes, Ms. Reynolds's preschool encourages children's natural interest in reading. As a result, the children themselves initiate much of the inquiry into print. Ms. Reynolds merely needs to be alert and responsive to their interests and questions. Sometimes children ask specific questions about written language; at other times their instructional needs show up less directly. Jevon wants to know what the sign by the block center says, so Ms. Reynolds explains that it tells parent helpers about what children learn when they play there. She also reads the sign to Jevon. When Cassie sees Caleb's name on the helpers' chart and thinks it is her turn to feed the gerbil, her teacher takes the opportunity for an impromptu lesson. Instead of just telling Cassie about the differences between her name and Caleb's, Ms. Reynolds asks Cassie to tell her how they are different. This approach enables Cassie to be self-reliant and more observant and helps Ms. Reynolds find out about Cassie's perception.

Many youngsters in Ms. Montoya's multiage-primary class can read the names of their friends on their cubbies and on helpers' charts too. They can read the recipe for making play dough—a frequent small-group activity. They also work hard at reading the weekly newsletter their teacher sends home to parents. Sometimes child-dictated articles are included in the newsletter. Many children are pretty good at reading their own dictation, and some can read what other children have dictated. They love to read the books authored by the class, in which each child illustrated one page and dictated the message on it.

Mrs. Thomas's first graders are reading the same kinds of things they read in kindergarten and for the same kinds of purposes. The difference is that more of them are able to read with fewer context clues, such as where and how the writing appears. Many first graders are developing skills with decontextualized print and can recognize familiar words whenever they occur. They also do a lot of reading as they write, reading over what they have written as they plan what to write next.

Playing Around with Written Language

"Reading the room" is one of many options available in Ms. Montoya's classroom during literacy center time, a modified free-choice time with only literacy-related activities available. Some of the other favorite literacy center choices are reading with a partner, making a tape of a story, reading along with a book on tape, and playing games with words and sounds. Literacy centers offer a variety of opportunities for children to practice reading or writing or to play around with written language. Playing around with written language allows youngsters to explore the structure of written language or to practice certain skills. Popular games for playing around with written language include fishing for words, word lotto, rime wheels, phonics riddles, and sentence-strip puzzles. These are explained in detail in the skills section of this chapter. Many of the favorite choices during literacy center time are related more to writing than to reading, so we'll leave them to the next chapter.

Although literacy center time offers many opportunities for exploring how words are put together, teacher-led games also can increase children's phonemic awareness. Mrs. Thomas has a good time with her students as they play around with the sounds in some favorite songs and poems. We'll describe these for you in the skills section too.

So far in this chapter, we've tried to give you an overview of the kinds of literacy activities that effective teachers offer their students. Whatever their ages, most of the children in these classrooms are excited about reading. By using reading for real purposes, they discover its importance in their lives. By experiencing high-quality literature, they know the richness that reading can bring to them. By playing around with words and sounds, they have enhanced their phonemic awareness and sight-word vocabulary. Because their teachers offer them open-ended literacy activities, they have felt successful in their efforts to learn. Because they are constructing their own knowledge about reading, they have a firm foundation of understanding on which to build. These emergent readers are off to a good start. Next, let's examine more closely how they have been learning specific reading skills.

VALIDATING SKILLS ACQUISITION

The skills issue has polarized the field of reading education. Holistic approaches to literacy have been widely misinterpreted and misrepresented as being antiskills, and skills-based approaches have been accused of ignoring meaning. We see this polarization as an unfortunate misunderstanding, resulting from inadequate teacher preparation and uninformed media coverage. We advocate a comprehensive approach to skills, one that ensures children's understanding of what they read as well as the ability to pronounce the words. Children learn reading skills more effectively as part of meaning-based reading than through isolated skills drill (Strickland, 1998). A comprehensive approach to teaching reading skills also teaches a broader range of skills than phonics-based programs teach. The more reading skills a reader has, the better his or her chance of success. We want children to learn all the skills, to learn everything they need to know to become fluent and avid readers.

Our criticism of the skills-based approaches isn't that they teach skills but rather that they tend to teach them in isolation from meaningful content. This approach not only makes the skills harder to learn but can also develop counterproductive reading strategies that can create serious reading problems (Moustafa, 1997). We have seen many young readers who have learned to focus on individual letters or words and who read by laboriously plodding through a recitation of sounds. This slow and painstaking process obliterates both meaning and pleasure in reading. Obviously, the reading skills are not being employed in a useful manner in these cases. We agree that reading skills are essential, and we want to be sure they are taught in ways that allow children to make effective use of them in understanding what they read.

Some people still believe that children learn to read and write as a result of mastering a set of skills. Evidence has been mounting for over thirty years that the reverse is true: Children master skills as a result of reading and writing (McQuillan, 1998). Therefore, we don't talk about skills children must have before they can learn to read. In fact, we prefer not to talk about skills separate from reading and writing at all. We are convinced that all skills at all levels are learned most efficiently as children participate in authentic reading and writing activities (Dahl & Scharer, 2000). Again, it's not that skills are not important but that there is a better way of mastering them.

When children learn to talk, to write, or to read, they are constantly working to refine their understandings of all aspects of the process. They address the entire scope of language arts at all times, with each child delving into more detail as it becomes personally relevant. Teachers need to assist children with the

Children learn reading skills more effectively as part of meaning-based reading than through isolated skills drill.

understandings each is ready for rather than with an arbitrary set of skills mandated for a grade level. Each child progresses in an individual manner, with all levels of emergent literacy evident from preschool through the primary grades.

Children work at their own levels to learn strategies that are useful in solving the problem of how to get meaning from a text. This is what most skills are. The purpose of learning phonics, for instance, isn't to be able to say the most common sounds of a letter; it is to help you figure out an unknown word and make sense of what you are reading. Some researchers, however, seem to have forgotten this purpose. They teach children phonics skills and then test them on those skills, concluding that the teaching was successful if children do well on the tests (McQuillan, 1998).

You may remember studying reading skills with different names from those currently used. Don't worry, they're the same skills; current terminology merely puts a slightly different slant on the traditional skills. For example, *phonics* is lumped together with *phonograms* (which used to be called *word families*) and with *configuration clues*. These are all placed in the more inclusive category of *graphophonemic clues*. You may have seen that word and wondered what it meant. Using your word analysis skills, you can break it into two parts: *grapho*, meaning written or drawn, and *phonemic*, referring to sound. *Graphophonemic* means the relationship between what is written and the sounds of the language it represents.

Many people who write and talk about reading strategies refer to cuing systems and graphophonemic cues or semantic cues. In this book we use the word *clue* instead of *cue*. This difference is more significant than merely adding an *l*, and it is not arbitrary. The reason for our choice of words is related to the view of learning as constructing knowledge, which we described in Chapter 1. Construction of knowledge is something that happens inside the learner's brain, not something that happens outside and is then put in. Constance Kamii (1991) helped us realize that the word *cue* refers to something external and imposed rather than internal and thoughtful. Kamii uses the analogy of an actor's following a script to describe why the term *cue* is inappropriate (1991). A cue that tells an actor it is time to speak memorized lines is not at all similar to the complex set of data that must be analyzed in the reading process.

Because *cue* is incompatible with our understanding of how learning occurs, we chose to use the term *clue* and the analogy of a detective. We decided that readers are more like detectives than actors. We like the idea that the good reader, like the good detective, must be very clever in putting the clues together. Obviously, the detective is an active thinker, not merely a memorizer.

Sight Words

With all that said, we're finally ready to talk about reading strategies. Let's start with sight words because they tend to create a good starting place for youngsters' reading. The term hasn't changed lately, though ideas about how to teach sight words certainly have. When you were young, you may have had to memorize a list of words, possibly the famous Dolch word list (Dolch, 1945). Children used to be drilled in and tested on these sight words with flash cards. We enjoyed seeing reading expert Sam Sebesta demonstrate the best use of Dolch flash cards by tearing them up and throwing them in the air. That doesn't mean we don't think it is important to learn sight words though; we just don't think that the flash-card approach is useful. Learning the most common words is best done within a context of meaningful print.

Sight words—those instantly recognizable words that no longer require effort from a child—stand out as important for beginning reading. They provide children success in their reading efforts, and they provide a starting point for learning graphophonemic strategies. Children learn most words through repeated exposure to them while reading various materials. Story time, shared reading, independent reading, and reading conferences all help learners add to their store of sight words. Repetitious pattern books are especially well suited to assisting the development of a sight-word vocabulary. Signs, labels, name tags, and other print

Children work at their own levels to learn strategies for solving the problem of how to get meaning from print.

in the environment add to a child's sight-word vocabulary as well. As children become aware of and interested in print, they are motivated to memorize some of the words around them that have personal meaning. Most young children quickly learn words such as *Mom* and *love*, for instance.

You can understand how helpful it is to recognize the most frequently used words when you realize that just ten words make up almost a quarter of all the words used in English-language printed material (see Table 4.3). The top twenty-five words constitute up to one-third of all printed material (Fry, Kress, Foun-toukidis, & Polk, 1993).

And consider this: Almost half the top fifty words are spelled in ways that make it difficult to figure them out by matching sounds to letters. For example, shouldn't the word *said* rhyme with *aid*? How about *where*? Shouldn't it rhyme

the	of
and	a
to	in
is	you
that	it

TABLE 4.3

Ten Words Most
Frequently Used in English

with *were* instead of *air*? And *what* surely must rhyme with *at*. Then there is *from*, which ought to rhyme with *Tom*, and *come*, which obviously must rhyme with *home*. We could go on and on, but don't worry, we won't. Since youngsters will be constantly frustrated if they try to apply their emerging phonemic understandings to these frequently occurring words, memorizing them is really the only answer.

The fact that these words are so common in print makes it more likely that the more children read, the more they will encounter the words and the more quickly they will learn them. This process is assisted by frequent and repeated group readings of pattern books that contain many common words, such as Bill Martin, Jr.'s, *Brown Bear, Brown Bear, What Do You See?* (1983). Follow-up activities can further assist the process for those needing or wanting extra practice. One useful activity is matching teacher-made sentence strips to the story. Another is making and frequently reading a class book that adapts the *Brown Bear* book pattern and repeats the key words. For instance, Mrs. Hanna's students love their pattern book about themselves. Each page has a picture of a child, and the first few pages read; "Amy, Amy, who do you see? I see Bryce looking at me. Bryce, Bryce, who do you see? I see Ivan looking at me." Teaching sight words with pattern books can be much more effective than using vocabulary-controlled basal readers.

Games can also help children learn to recognize common words quickly. During literacy choice time, Ms. Montoya's students frequently choose the fishing game she made for them. This game involves fishing for paper fish that have a word from a favorite book written on them. Each fish has a paper clip where its mouth should be, and the fishing poles (pointers with string tied to them) each have a magnet at the end of the line. When Tuan hooks a fish, he can't keep it unless he can read the word. If he has trouble landing his fish, his fishing buddies can give him clues. A clue can be a reminder of what story the word was in, the meaning of the word, or another word that rhymes with the word. The active and interactive nature of this game is an important part of its success.

When, to the children's dismay, many words look so much alike, games are useful. All those words that start with *wh* (*what, where, when, why*, and *who*) and those other ones that start with *th* (*then, there, they, those*, and *them*) can slow reading progress and disrupt fluency. The children have learned these words in a meaningful context, but now they need to develop quick, rote memory to distinguish among them. Because these words so often appear in context, Mrs. Thomas is willing for children to practice with them as isolated words. She has created a type of lotto game for practicing quick identification of these words. Sometimes an older reading buddy visits the first-grade classroom during language arts center

One isolated word does have meaning—the child's name is generally the first sight word a child learns.

time and plays this game with the first graders who are confusing those abstract *wh* and *th* words. Many children choose this game during literacy center time.

One isolated word does have meaning, and children learn it by itself. That word is the child's name, and it is generally the first sight word a child learns. Most children also quickly learn to read the names of other children in their classroom if name labels are used frequently for attendance, chore assignments, and identification of work and possessions. Learning names provides a store of knowledge for comparisons with new words encountered. For instance, when Bryce dictates a story about his beach trip, he can be helped to notice that *shell* begins like his friend Shawn's name. This contributes both to recognizing a new sight word and to an understanding of the nature of graphophonemic systems, better known as phonics.

Graphophonemic Clues

You have probably been hearing a lot about *phonemic awareness* as well as phonics lately. Are you confused about the difference between these two terms? The word *phonics* has been around a long time. It generally refers to the sound-letter relationships used for reading and writing. Each letter of the English alphabet stands for one or more sounds, often called *phonemes*. Phonemic awareness has to do with the ability to hear all the differences in sounds and words in speech. Both phonics and phonemic awareness are essential for successfully learning to read, though emergent reading with predictable texts doesn't require phonics (Routman & Butler, 1995).

Yes, emergent readers and writers must learn about letters and learn to hear the sounds they represent. Mrs. Thomas doesn't participate in any arguments over whether to teach phonemic awareness. She thinks it is silly to suggest that children will learn to read by learning the sounds of the letters, but she thinks it is just as silly to suggest not helping them to acquire this useful tool. Ms. Montoya has a clear idea of the role phonics plays in learning to read: It is one of several strategies that may be useful when a child confronts unfamiliar text. Mrs. Hanna agrees and explains to concerned parents that children mainly learn phonics from reading and writing, not reading and writing from phonics. This view is consistent with what Ms. Reynolds tells parents who think that their youngsters have to learn the names and sounds of letters before they can begin learning to read.

All these teachers help their students increase their phonemic awareness in deliberate and purposeful ways. They understand that phonemic awareness instruction needs to be playful and engaging so that it invites experimentation and curiosity with language. They know that phonemic awareness training alone is not meaningful. It is only one part of a literacy program and is useless unless it is in a context of real reading and writing (Yopp & Yopp, 2000). Children develop phonemic awareness as a result of experimentation with writing (Kamii & Manning, 2002). They don't learn to write and read as a result of having phonemic awareness. These teachers also provide phonics assistance at the appropriate levels for each child, and they do it by assisting children's exploration of their own theories, always within the context of meaningful words and sentences (see Table 4.4). They don't do it with "letter of the week," work sheets, or drills in isolated sounds.

For many of Ms. Reynolds's preschoolers, graphophonemic awareness remains at the stage of discovering that print, not pictures, tells the stories in the books she reads to them. Other children have discovered the print and show their interest by repeatedly questioning, "What does it say?" But remember how literacy develops, as described in Chapter 1. Children don't instantly start linking letters and sounds when they discover print. For one thing, each letter does not really have its own sound, and it isn't even possible to make the sound of most consonants by

TABLE 4.4
The Best Opportunities to Teach Phonics

Teachers *help children notice* general phonics principles during the following authentic literacy events:

- As children read and write memorized forms of words
    - Their own names
    - Their friends' names
    - Important words, such as *Mom, Dad,* and *love*
- As children match oral language to print during shared reading
    - During dictation and other shared writing
    - In memorized reading of books, charts, and functional print
    - As they read along with a tape-recorded story
- As children write with invented spelling
    - Trying out their theories about phonics
    - Constantly revising theories as a result of reading experiences

Teachers and other adults *tell* children useful phonics principles during the following authentic literacy events (limiting information to what a youngster appears ready to understand):

- As children dictate ideas and the teacher transcribes them
- As children work at writing independently
- During shared reading activities
- As children work at reading independently
- As children observe the teacher writing for adult purposes

themselves. Blending individual sounds together rarely results in a recognizable word. In addition, children must experience a lot of books and stories before figuring out that there is a system for assigning letters to the sounds in words. Before that, they have to realize that there are phonemes within words. Emergent reading of predictable books usually involves matching a story pattern with the various pictures on each page, as in the "Brown Bear, Brown Bear What Do You See?" pattern book (Martin, 1983). Although children do not need to already have phonics skills to successfully read this type of book, phonics understanding is developed through the process of this type of reading.

Although Ms. Reynolds thinks she would be wasting preschoolers' precious time by drilling on letters and sounds, she always responds to children's questions about letters. She believes that information in response to questions ensures that the child is ready for the information and also ensures that the information will have some personal meaning to that child. She is careful not to tell more than the child really wants to know.

Like Ms. Montoya, she keeps in mind that an attitude of playfulness toward language is the best way to develop phonemic awareness (Dahl & Scharer, 2000). Rather than use boring work sheets, Ms. Montoya plays games, sings songs, and chants rhymes with her primary-grade students. Children in her class

WHY ARE PHONICS "RULES" SO HARD TO LEARN?

One problem with phonics rules is that English breaks the rules so much. For instance, how often have you heard (or said), "When two vowels go walking, the first one does the talking"? This is supposed to mean we hear the long sound of the first vowel and the second vowel is silent. Are you surprised that this is true only about half the time? Just look at this paragraph so far: What do you hear in *breaks, heard, does, sound,* and *look*? The "rule" works fine for *mean, hear,* and *true,* but how does the reader know when it does and when it doesn't work?

Another often taught "rule" is that where there is an *e* at the end of a word and one vowel in the middle of the word, the vowel in the middle stands for a long vowel sound. This works fine in the words *rule* and *fine,* but this rule too works only a little over half the time (Clymer, 1996). Notice *where* and *there* and think about other common words, such as *done.* These two examples of problems with rules about vowel sounds are not unusual; we chose them because they are taught so often.

Even consonants can't be counted on to have the same sound all the time. Of course there is *c* going back and forth between standing in for a *k* and an *s,* then there is *g* going back and forth between *goat* and *giraffe.* Even *s* switches between a hiss and a *z* sound. What about *ph*? You probably think it always makes the *f* sound, as in *telephone.* But what about *shepherd*?

In short, the possibilities are mind-boggling. Just among one- and two-syllable English words there are sixty-nine letters and digraphs that are related to the thirty-eight phonemes in 211 *different* ways (Moustafa, 1997). There really is no way for readers to figure out which sound is represented by a set of letters unless there are sufficient other clues to help them.

look forward to the silly songs they make up by substituting consonant sounds in known songs. For instance, they might change the song "Old MacDonald Had a Farm" so that instead of singing "ee-igh, ee-igh, o," they sing "bee-bigh, bee-bigh, bo" or "dee-digh, dee-digh, do." Youngsters think it is funny to change the birthday song and sing variations such as "Bappy birthday bo boo" (Yopp, 1992). On Ramel's birthday, they sing "Rappy rirthday ro roo," and when they sing to Felicia, the song is "Fappy firthday." On field-trip bus rides, children love to sing silly songs such as "Willoughby Wallaby Watya, An elephant sat on Katya. Willoughby Wallaby Waul, An elephant sat on Paul." They are gaining phonemic awareness as they are having fun.

Rhyming words help students hear likenesses and differences in words. Rhymes with the same spelling (called *rimes* or *phonograms* or *word families*) can

[handwritten margin note: Songs has phonemic awareness also certain games.]

RHYMES OR RIMES?

Teachers are told that teaching rhymes helps children learn to read. Some accept the idea but apparently do not understand the role rhymes play in learning to read. They treat rhymes that have the same spelling pattern (rimes) the same way they treat rhymes that are spelled differently from one another.

Words that rhyme and that have the same spelling pattern have common rimes (also called phonograms). Therefore, knowing how one looks in print helps with reading the other. This is true of the following sets of rhymes from the book *Bowl Patrol!* (Janovitz, 1996): *cat* and *scat*, *slurp* and *burp*, *stop* and *drop*. These rimes can be emphasized for reading and writing.

However, rhymes with *different* spelling patterns are not useful tools for word recognition. Consider these sets of rhymes from *Bowl Patrol!*: *bowl* and *patrol*; *hi* and *bye*; *leap* and *deep*. This type of rhyme is valuable for auditory language activities, though. Hearing all kinds of rhymes is part of phonemic awareness, and these can be emphasized in speech.

also provide a very useful boost to word recognition. Knowing a few common phonograms can help with reading many words. For instance, knowing how to read *hot* can help in reading *pot, dot, cot, tot, lot, not, got,* and *rot* as well as *shot, blot, trot,* and so on. In fact, the thirty-eight most common phonograms can make 654 different one-syllable words when combined with different beginning consonants (Fry, 1998). This kind of phonics information is easier for young readers to learn and to use than is single-letter blending (Vacca, Vacca, & Gove, 1995).

Mrs. Thomas offers books, poems, songs, and games that focus on auditory rhymes and written rimes to her first graders too. Many of the predictable books utilize rhymes, and Mrs. Thomas often features them during shared reading times. She also helps children who are interested to make riming word wheels (see Figure 4.2).

While writing Halloween stories, Heidi has been inspired to see how many different words she can make that rhyme with *bat* and *cat*. Heidi enjoys sharing her riming wheel with others in the class during literacy choice time. They spin the outer wheel to play a game of guessing which word it will land on. She and Anastasia decide to work together to find other word patterns that can be made into rime wheels. They discover that not all rhymes work for their game. When they worked on rhymes for the word *boo*, they found that *too* worked fine, but *shoe, new,* and *blue* each needed separate rime wheels. Oops, why doesn't *sew* work with *new* and *few*? There is a lot to learn about the confusing English language letter-sound system.

Did you ever think about pig latin's being phonemic awareness practice? It is just another way of playing around with the "onsets and rimes" by putting the

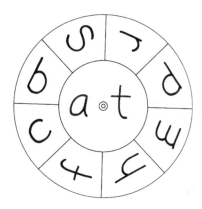

FIGURE 4.2
Riming wheel illustration.
The outer circle turns and
creates different words.

consonant at the end (Moustafa, 1997). *Ids-kay eel-fay ery-vay art-smay alking-tay is-thay ay-way*, but they can't do it unless they can hear and separate the sounds in the words.

Books of riddles (Thaler, 1990) offer another way of playing with phonograms. Can you guess the answers to these? 1. What large monkey hides in a cape? 2. What is the biggest part of being crude? 3. How do you make mice cold? (Answers: 1. An ape; 2. Being rude; 3. Take away the *M* and make ice.) Youngsters who are working on these kinds of ideas think these riddles are hilarious.

Riddles are a fun way to teach phonograms or rimes.

Mrs. Thomas encourages further word analysis by beginning another chart. This chart displays compound words that children have recently dictated, written, or discovered in their reading. She encourages children to add to the chart as they discover more words that are made by putting together two shorter words. In a card pocket below the chart are tagboard strips on which students can write the separate words that make up their compound word. Taking these word strips out and putting them together like a puzzle is an attractive activity to many of the first graders. Trevor is amazed at what happens when he recombines just a few common words and discovers the words *nothing, something, somewhere,* and *nowhere.*

Good readers rely on a variety of clues as they read. Most teachers call children's attention to phonics, word families, and other word analysis clues but sometimes overlook word *configuration* clues. Mrs. Thomas knows that the general shape of a word, possibly coupled with the initial letter, is often sufficient information to the reader engrossed in the meaning of the material. Although this shortcut to sight-word identification is generally intuitive, Mrs. Thomas helps children notice the general shape of words as they write and read together. She comments on the two tall, giraffe-neck letters in the word *giraffe;* she points out that the double os in *look* remind her of eyes looking at her; she mentions when a word is very long or very short. Once children begin noticing the shape of words, they continue to store up this useful information on their own, and it contributes to their fluency. The relevant question to teach children to ask themselves regarding graphophonemic clues is, "Does it look right?"

CHAPTER 4

Semantic Clues

None of the graphophonemic clues is really useful unless employed in combination with the answer to the question, "What would make sense?" The reading strategy based on this question is commonly known as using context clues—*the most used reading strategy*. Because this semantic reading skill relates directly to the meaning of what is read and therefore reflects the true purpose of reading, Mrs. Hanna, Ms. Montoya, Ms. Reynolds, and Mrs. Thomas are all enthusiastic about helping children learn to use it effectively.

Remember the description of a good reader in Chapter 1—Mandy reading her book without knowing all the words? Because Mandy knows most of the words, the ones she recognizes give her sufficient clues to make a reasonable guess at those she doesn't know. If her guess is wrong enough to affect the sense of what she is reading, she goes back and tries again. Then she might apply her graphophonemic knowledge. She could always go to the dictionary, but how much fun would reading be if she had to spend much time with that kind of interruption? After Mandy encounters a word several times, she will have a good idea of its meaning, whether or not she knows the correct pronunciation. As with most of us, Mandy's reading vocabulary exceeds her speaking vocabulary. Just as our oral vocabulary increases through hearing words used in context, we increase our reading vocabulary through seeing words used in context. Looking up words in dictionaries gives us definitions but does little for our ability to use words appropriately. Think about reading words you can't define yourself in order to verify the value of meaning clues. (We assume you are using them while reading this text when you come to such words as *scaffolding, semantic,* and *graphophonemic.*)

Even before children are reading, they can become familiar with the idea of filling in a missing word in a sentence. Oral-context clue games make useful transition-time fillers as well as reading-skill builders. Mrs. Hanna often plays guessing games with her kindergartners while they wait in line for the bus. She incorporates semantic clues into the games, asking children to fill in the missing words in her sentences. "We are going _____ now," she says. "We will ride on the _____ bus." When there are several possible correct answers, she accepts all of them at first. Later, as children develop phonemic awareness and begin to make relationships between letters and sounds, she encourages combining that information with guesses at what makes sense. She gives clues, such as, "It starts with *h*," or "It rhymes with *fellow.*" Can you use these clues to fill in the preceding blanks?

Guessing games about what a sign says are also challenging and fun for youngsters who are trying to make sense of the print in their environment. Here the semantic clues they use have to do with what makes sense in the context of where and how the print is used. This is another way of getting in touch with the meaning of print. When they go for walks, children are full of ideas about the signs they see. They know what the STOP sign says and a few others; they have ideas about many store signs from visits there. Ms. Reynolds encourages their logical thought rather than ending it by simply telling them the answers. Ms. Reynolds also encourages discussions about signs and labels in the classroom, such as the safety rules in the

IN CHILDREN'S SHOES

Play a game to test the theory that you use context clues when you read. Retype any short reading selection, leaving a space for every fifth word. (You could use correction fluid, but that would give a clue about the length of the word.) Have a friend do the same, with a different selection. Then exchange reading materials and see whether you can read the missing words.

Next, with a different selection, use a series of symbols (such as &*#@, in any order), one per letter, instead of a space, to represent the missing words. You will probably be able to "read" those symbols in context (Moustafa, 1997).

Finally, list those symbol sets separately. Can you read them? Does it help to go back to the reading selection for clues? You have just put yourself in the shoes of a child who is learning to read.

woodworking center and the labels for where tools belong. She helps children notice the usefulness of signs in the school too, such as EXIT, OFFICE, BOYS, and GIRLS.

words that give ideas to complete a sentence

Ms. Reynolds often demonstrates the use of semantic clues during story time. As she reads, she sometimes stops to allow the children to fill in a word. Her preschoolers especially enjoy chiming in on rhyming words in stories or poems. When Ms. Reynolds reads *Mama, Do You Love Me?* (Joosse, 1991), she might read the little girl's question, "What if I stayed away and sang with the wolves and slept in a cave?" Then she would read the Mama's response, "Then, Dear One, I would be very _____ ." The children like guessing the best word for how Mama would feel if her little girl did things such as running away or turning into a walrus. Of course, they all chime in on the repetitive phrase, "But still, I would love you." Many children will review a book after the teacher has read it, working to match their memory of the story to the print on the page.

Mrs. Thomas demonstrates the value she places on semantic clues when her first graders read aloud to her. When a child stops on a word, Mrs. Thomas first asks, "What word would make sense?" rather than, "What are the sounds of the letters?" If the child's guess is close in meaning but incorrect, for example, suggesting *mail* when the word is *letter*, Mrs. Thomas often ignores the error to keep the flow and meaning of the story. However, she may decide that a child will benefit from going back to the missed word after the story is finished. She would validate the child's reading by a comment such as, "You made a good guess about this word. What you read makes sense and sounds right." Then she might ask, "What letter would you expect the word to start with if it was *mail*?"

Mrs. Thomas is guided by the individual child's needs in giving feedback. A child who is confident and excited about reading can profit from more correction than a child who is insecure about reading. For an insecure reader, Mrs. Thomas

Children learn to use semantic clues when teachers encourage them to think about. "What would make sense here?"

usually just supplies the missing word to assist fluency and to help the child focus on meaning. She works to help children focus on the print and the meaning at the same time. Mrs. Thomas usually saves her minilessons on skills for the end of the reading so as not to interrupt the flow. Then she uses her observations of the child's error patterns to offer some relevant tips.

Ms. Montoya keeps in her mind a list of questions she uses to help readers focus on the various clues when they run into a reading roadblock (Fisher, 1998). When she wants to help a child focus on meaning, she asks the following kinds of questions:

What would make sense?

What other words could make sense?

What does the picture tell you?

[handwritten margin note: Very important for making sure that the child understand what he/she reads.]

Syntax Clues

Another aspect of meaning in print is reflected in the question teachers ask a child about a reading confusion, "Does it sound right?" In this case, sounding right has to do with the order in which words are written. This order relates to the grammatical structure of a language and creates expectations of what kind of word should come next in a sentence. In English, the sequence generally is noun, verb, object. So, if you read, "She _____ him," you expect the unknown word in the middle to be a verb of some sort. If the word starts with the letter *k*, you might use phonics to narrow it down to *kicked, kissed,* or *killed.* The previous sentence or the next one surely would help you figure out which word was correct. But your starting place is the expectation of a verb and a verb with an object. You know it won't be "She kitty him" or "She kind him," for instance, because neither sounds right.

If context clues from the previous sentence suggest that the next step will be kissing, persons proficient in the English language will know that the word could not be *kissing* because that would require the word *is* to be inserted first. Similarly, it couldn't be just *kiss* without a word such as *will* in front of it. That leaves *kissed* as the word that your brain, using your knowledge of English syntax, instantly will sort out from the several options. Of course, if standard English is not your first language, this process may be far from instant or easy.

You may have filled in many a work sheet or diagrammed many a sentence practicing this sort of thing in school; but really, familiarity with language is gained from using it, not from work sheets. Remember the language-development activities described in Chapter 3? They are critical to children's familiarity with language syntax, whether the children are learning a first language or a second language. The main idea behind language-development activities is to encourage children to *talk*; the silent classroom is counterproductive to learning of many kinds. Story time, also described in Chapter 3, is the other main contribution to a child's knowledge of English syntax.

Hearing the language of literature is especially important for youngsters who do not speak standard English in their home environments. Stories provide a model of language that matches the language of books written in English and helps develop accurate syntactic expectations for English-language print. However, for children whose first language is not English, research clearly supports allowing them to learn to read in their home language initially (for example, Snow, Burns, & Griffin, 1998; Thomas & Collier, 1997).

FROM THE NAEYC POSITION STATEMENT "RESPONDING TO LINGUISTIC AND CULTURAL DIVERSITY"

Language development is essential for learning, and the development of the children's home language does not interfere with their ability to learn English. Because knowing more than one language is a cognitive asset (Hakuta & Garcia, 1989), early education programs should encourage the development of children's home language while fostering the acquisition of English.

For the optimal development and learning of all children, educators must accept the legitimacy of children's home language, respect and value the home culture, and promote and encourage the active involvement and support of all families, including extended and nontraditional family units. (National Association for the Education of Young Children, 1996a)

Personal Schema

Tyler's experiences caring for salamanders create an understanding of salamanders that helps him when he reads about them. When he reads, his understanding helps him realize when he misreads something—what he reads won't fit into his personal schema. For instance, if Tyler read, "The salamander flew . . . ," he would stop himself and self-correct. His next try might be, "The salamander froze until the danger was past." We frequently refer to readers self-correcting as a result of realizing that what they read did not make sense. How do you know when something doesn't make sense? That information is not on the page; it is in your head. Your personal experience base, including knowledge gained from prior reading, is an essential component of the reading process (F. Smith, 1994). In this case, Tyler knew that salamanders can't fly.

Teachers can assist children's development and conscious use of their personal schema for reading. All the meaningful and engaging experiences provided in your classroom add to the knowledge and understanding a child brings to reading. These were discussed in depth in Chapter 2 and include not only field trips and guests but the entire active, process approach to education as well. All curriculum topics should add to children's personal knowledge base and be appropriately integrated into the language arts. After all, readers need something to read about. A teacher's comments and questions about what children read can help the children become more aware of how their own experiences relate to what they read. Mrs. Hanna frequently asks children to think about what they already know regarding a topic in a book they have chosen. Ms. Montoya finds that having her students for three years instead of one helps her know more of their experiences that might relate to their reading. She can remark about Jazzmin's daddy being a dentist when they read *Dr. DeSoto* (Steig, 1982). She can also ask Amber about the dentist who helped her stuck baby tooth come out and whether that dentist used a method different from Dr. DeSoto's method. When Patricia chooses a nonfiction book about horses, Mrs. Hanna can talk with her about how it compares with Patricia's own experience with horses.

Integrating Strategies

All the reading strategies we have discussed are valuable, and good readers use all of them (McQuillan, 1998). Effective teaching helps children learn how to integrate all strategies at once (see Figure 4.3). For instance, when children have some graphophonemic skill, they combine that information with their idea of what word would make sense and come up with the right one. In determining what would make sense, they use syntax and semantic clues to select an appropriate word of similar meaning. Most teachers find these three questions useful when a child stumbles on a word:

Does it make sense? (context clues and personal schema)

Does it sound right? (syntax clues)

Does it look right? (graphophonemic clues)

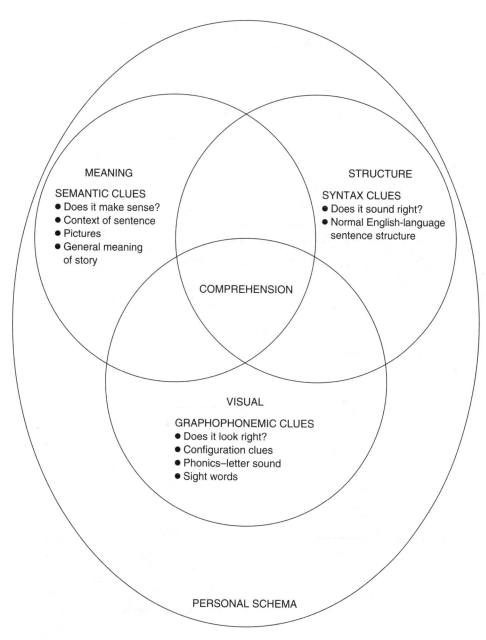

MEANING

SEMANTIC CLUES
● Does it make sense?
● Context of sentence
● Pictures
● General meaning
  of story

STRUCTURE

SYNTAX CLUES
● Does it sound right?
● Normal English-language
  sentence structure

COMPREHENSION

VISUAL

GRAPHOPHONEMIC CLUES
● Does it look right?
● Configuration clues
● Phonics–letter sound
● Sight words

PERSONAL SCHEMA

FIGURE 4.3
Integrating literacy clues.

If the answer to all three questions is yes, reading continues. Through a combination of strategies, fluency increases, and children gain satisfaction from the process. Children quickly learn to ask themselves these questions as they read independently too. Mrs. Thomas helps children become more aware of what strategies they are using as a way to help them become more proficient with the various clues. When she notices a child self-correct when reading aloud, she often asks about it at the end of the story. She might ask, "Why did you change what you read?" The child generally answers something like, "I knew it was wrong." This is the lead-in for Mrs. Thomas to ask, "How did you know it was wrong?"

When good readers, such as Mandy, misread a word, changing its meaning, they quickly realize something is wrong because the word doesn't fit with the rest of the story or the sentence. They then check to find the error and make sense of what they are reading. How do good readers know when a word doesn't fit in with the rest of the story? They rely on their own experiences that formed their own personal schema. They focus on all necessary clues and use a balanced set of reading strategies. As you work with children, you will notice that they all have different strengths and weaknesses in using these strategies. Children whose home language is not standard English will have less success with the syntax clues, for instance; they will need to use other clues more. Children with hearing or perceptual disabilities will need to focus on the clues that are accessible to *them*, which means a strong reliance on context clues when confronting an unknown word.

Comprehension

Comprehension is a result of successfully integrating all the reading strategies (Pressley, 2000). None of the reading skills has any value unless a person can understand the message in what is read. The bottom line is that communication is what comprehension skills are all about. Traditionally, teachers have been directed to test children's comprehension through questions about what they read. Most of these questions tend to be at the literal level—what happened, when, where, who, how many, and so on. Actually, you can skip these mundane questions and go on to those that require children to think about, rather than merely remember, what they read. It is clear that children must use the literal information as a base for their further thinking about a story; therefore, both levels can be covered simultaneously.

Ms. Montoya often asks her students what they think will happen next as they read with her (Fisher, 1998). This question encourages active, predictive strategies for reading and at the same time gives her feedback about the children's understanding. At the end of a book, whether it is one she read to the group or one a child read independently, Ms. Montoya asks general overview questions such as the following:

What is this book about?

What are some of the important things that happened?

What are some things you learned? (Remember, not all books are fiction.)

Does this book remind you of any other books?

Do you know of other books written by this author?

Questions that require critical thinking also require basic understanding of what was read. If a child can participate in discussions about what was right or wrong in a story, you know that child comprehended the story. These "grand conversations" (Peterson & Eeds, 1990) about text help children develop more varied responses to texts. The more traditional "gentle inquisitions" wherein teachers ask for recall of specific factual information limit student responses (Leu & Kinzer, 2003). Chapter 3 described some critical thinking questions in relation to story time. Similar kinds of questions are appropriate in conjunction with shared, guided, or independent reading. When Tyler and Mrs. Thomas talk about *The Salamander Room* (Mazer, 1991), their discussion focuses on whether Brian, the boy in the story, should be allowed to keep the salamander he found. They also consider the practicality of Brian's ideas for making his bedroom into a salamander room. This approach to checking comprehension does much more than that: Mrs. Thomas is demonstrating how to use active and critical thinking in conjunction with reading. This demonstration contributes to comprehension as well as checks on it, and it helps children become discerning about what they read. Advertising campaigns increasingly require this kind of thinking in conjunction with reading.

The question "What do you think will happen next?" encourages children's active predictive strategies for reading.

It's never too early to start. The old view was that practice in comprehension skills begins when a child begins to read independently. With current understanding of emergent literacy, teachers realize that comprehension skills are developing long before a child can read by conventional standards. The infant's ability to make sense of oral language is the actual beginning of this skill. It is developed and expanded to written language whenever an adult reads to the child.

Story time offers an excellent opportunity for teaching and assessing comprehension skills. Teachers can tell much about children's understanding and involvement through their nonverbal behavior. Tanya's rapt attention while Ms. Reynolds reads aloud contrasts sharply with Kelly's squirming and fiddling with things. Children's comments and questions during and after a story are also revealing. Scott volunteers an excited guess about what will happen next in the story. Betsy makes a text-to-self connection (Harvey & Goudvis, 2000) when she tells of an experience she had that was similar to the one in the story. But Abbey just wants to know what's for snack. Ms. Reynolds was impressed when Tanya made a text-to-text connection between a fictional story about a train and information from a nonfictional concept book about trains.

The follow-up activities described in conjunction with story time in Chapter 3 relate to comprehension skills. Opportunities for retelling stories while looking at the pictures in the book let children practice thinking about the meaning in what they read. Children also enjoy retelling stories with flannel-board figures, with puppets, by dramatizing them, and through various art media. Some youngsters are interested in making up new endings or otherwise writing their own versions of popular stories. Timmy had fun dictating "Timmy and the Terrible, Horrible, No Good, Very Bad Day." Ms. Reynolds learns a lot about her students' levels of comprehension through observations and discussions with children during these activities.

Peer-group discussions help readers look at the meaning of what they read in more depth and from different perspectives (Tompkins, 2003). Whether a group is reading the same book or different books on related topics, sharing reading responses enhances comprehension (Morrow & Gambrell, 2000). Some teachers formalize group discussions by having each person assume a specific role (for example, Daniels & Bizar, 1998). One child is discussion director, planning questions to discuss. Another child selects favorite parts of a book to read aloud to the group. Another child is in charge of pointing out connections between the reading and real experiences or noting similarities with other books. Finding new, interesting, funny, important, or hard words in the reading is a job for yet another child. Each group also includes an artist who illustrates a favorite part of the book. Whether these are separate jobs or shared by all in a group, they are beneficial approaches to peer discussions.

Many teachers organize their curriculum around themes or projects of interest to children. The classroom library offers a selection of fact and fiction books related to the current topic. As children read in depth about a topic, from a variety of sources, their understanding of what they read increases. For instance, The Salamander Room, which Tyler was reading, is just one of many books about lizards and similar creatures currently in Mrs. Thomas's class library. Tyler and several of his classmates became interested in studying lizards as a result of their questions about dinosaurs and whether anything like them still lived. They are extending their understanding by caring for some salamanders in a classroom terrarium. This experience generates much thought and discussion, which Mrs. Thomas encourages the children to put into writing. The more they experience and think and write, the more understanding they bring to their reading. And the more understanding they *bring* to a book, the more they *get* from it.

CHILDREN WHO PROGRESS MORE SLOWLY

What about children who *don't* seem to get it despite your best efforts? Do you start drilling them with work sheets and flash cards to get them to catch up? This is precisely the approach undertaken in the past, with dire results. Children who have difficulty with literacy usually are most in need of comprehensive approaches that emphasize meaning (Sacks & Mergendoller, 1997). For instance, the New Zealand schools adopted more holistic approaches in an effort to better meet the needs of the native Maori population, for whom skills-based approaches were failing totally (Holdaway, 1991). We hear many teachers in the United States say that the children who surely would have failed using old approaches now have a chance to make sense of reading.

Nonacademic Roadblocks to Success

Children may have difficulty becoming literate for many different reasons, including cultural and language differences that make the expectations, explanations, and words of school incomprehensible (Carger, 1993; Pellegrini, 1991; Walker-Dalhouse, 1993). Some cultural differences are related not to ethnicity but rather to social class and economic status. According to the National Research Council report on preventing reading difficulties, reading problems are disproportionately high among minority children, non-English-speaking children, and children who grow up poor (Snow et al., 1998).

According to the National Research Council report on preventing reading difficulties, reading problems are disproportionately high among minority children, non-English-speaking children, and children who grow up poor. (Snow et al., 1998)

Sometimes, children experience difficulty in school because of unmet emotional needs (Greenberg, 1998) or physical problems. Other "non-academic roadblocks to success include: poor attention, poor home support, frequent absences, and disorganization" (Gaskins, 1998, p. 542). However, some youngsters who have been read to daily, who speak the language of the school, share the culture of the school, and have no known physical disability nevertheless have difficulty learning to read. You probably can't do much about the nonacademic causes of reading difficulties, but you can accept each child's efforts and help each child progress in whatever ways are possible for that child (Bredekamp & Rosegrant, 1995; Truax & Kretschmer, 1993).

Each child is unique and has unique reasons for success or failure in school.

Lumping all these children into the "low" group and depriving them of interesting reading activities is not the answer. Roller (1996) characterized such groups as giving poor readers so much skill work that they actually do very little reading. Each child is unique and has unique reasons for success or failure in school. Grouping all low achievers together is based on the erroneous assumption that there is one common problem. Though creating separate groups for slow readers is common, it is the worst possible thing to do (Cunningham et al., 1998). The resulting damage to self-esteem and motivation to learn is often irreversible. These are the two things you need to nurture for success: children's self-respect and their desire to learn. Without these, educational efforts are wasted (May, 1994).

Effective Teaching Approaches

It may sound radical, but the best teaching for children who are experiencing difficulty is the same as the best teaching for children who are progressing nicely (for example, Moustafa, 1997; Snow et al., 1998). For instance, children who have some form of dyslexia especially need a balanced approach to reading strategies in order to utilize their strengths. Drills on letters focus on their weaknesses, whereas learning to use syntax and semantic clues allows these youngsters to draw on what they know to figure out what is difficult for them. Instructional methods considered sound for students reading in their native language are recommended for students reading in a new language (Fitzgerald, 2000). Good teaching is good teaching.

All young children benefit from exposure to high-quality literature, models of standard oral and written language, opportunities to explore their theories of literacy, and adults who encourage their efforts (Winter, 1997). We have said several times that the children who benefit most from these in school are those who have not experienced them prior to school. For instance, some youngsters know little about reading because they haven't been read to. The obvious solution is massive doses of being read to, accompanied by the kinds of booktalk that literate and doting parents have with their youngsters over bedtime stories. Children who have not been read to deserve the same opportunities to construct their understandings of print that others have had (Moustafa, 1997).

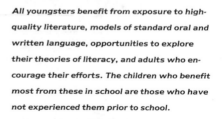

All youngsters benefit from exposure to high-quality literature, models of standard oral and written language, opportunities to explore their theories of literacy, and adults who encourage their efforts. The children who benefit most from these in school are those who have not experienced them prior to school.

The widely used *Reading Recovery* program (Clay, 1993b) approaches prevention of reading failure from a holistic perspective with a special concern for the child's self-esteem. It targets first graders who seem to have the least understanding of literacy and gives them special attention to try to get them caught up before they feel left behind. Basically, teachers trained in this program do the same things that good teachers do in their classrooms, only they do it with one child at a time for a full thirty minutes every day. The teacher first works to develop a good rapport with the child, then engages the child in meaningful literacy experiences. Teacher and child read books together to build fluency and confidence. They focus on meaning rather than just on words or letters, yet those components are not ignored. Children write as well as read in this program, which we will discuss further in the next chapter.

Some teachers say that there wouldn't be a need for special Reading Recovery programs if all teachers had such good training in reading methods and if class sizes allowed that kind of individual attention (Allington, 1993). Certainly, issues of teacher preparation and class size have an impact. Many teachers are attempting to implement Reading Recovery approaches in their classrooms. Ms. Montoya received special training to be a Reading Recovery teacher. Though her district no longer funds the one-on-one sessions, she is well prepared to apply the principles in her classroom. Mrs. Thomas is using a program called *Early Intervention in Reading,* which is based on Reading Recovery ideas but used with a small group instead of one on one. However, there are no quick fixes for most reading problems. Youngsters identified as "at risk" in first grade will continue to need high-quality educational experiences in subsequent grades (Gaskins, 1998).

Home-School Mismatches

It is unacceptable that children from ethnic or racial minorities and non-English-speaking children are overrepresented among children with reading problems. This suggests that schools are not adapting to the children who come to them but instead are inflexibly expecting all children to conform to one mode. Although we believe that the best teaching for children experiencing difficulty is the same as the best teaching for children who are progressing nicely, that doesn't mean treating all children the same. We have emphasized that each child is unique and deserves to be respected for the individual he or she is. All children "deserve literacy programs that build on and expand their language and culture, with a view toward helping them understand and value their heritage and respect the heritage of others" (Strickland, 1994, p. 333).

Teachers who value diversity are able to use the diversity within their classrooms to enrich the learning environment (Abbott & Grose, 1998). Yet they face a challenge to find the commonalities among children while honoring differences. For instance, when Ming lost a tooth, all his classmates could relate to the experience. Such a common experience can be the source of exploring differences, such as the word for "tooth" in different languages or different customs for celebrating the loss of baby teeth. As Ming and his classmates shared their similar yet different experiences of losing a tooth, their sense of community and their acceptance of differences both were strengthened.

The sense of community is essential for assisting youngsters to learn English as a second language (ESL). Social interaction between English-speaking and ESL students is the most productive way for ESL students to learn English (Tabors, 1997). However, like many teachers, Mrs. Thomas tries to have the language learning go both ways. She makes a point of asking her students who speak a language other then English to help her learn to say and write some words in their language. Mrs. Thomas points out that these children are becoming *bilingual:* an important word for an important accomplishment. She wants to be sure that her English-speaking students honor instead of ridicule the attempts of those working at learning a second language. Mrs. Thomas also wants to make it clear that children don't need to give up their home language in order to learn the school language (Goldenburg, 2002). Children will benefit from having both languages (Fillmore, 2000).

Ms. Montoya has the advantage of being bilingual. She speaks Spanish and has many Spanish-speaking students. Thus, she is able to help those children learn to read and write in Spanish initially, building on what children already know. This is a hallmark of successful programs that work with English-language learners (Genishi, 2002). It is a much easier task to transfer literacy to a new language than it is to learn a new language and learn to read simultaneously (Krashen, 1992). Ms. Montoya has a friend teaching in California who was among those confronted with the 1998 state law requiring that all teaching be done in English. Teachers were even threatened with penalties for speaking to children in any other language. Talk about an ethical dilemma (Feeney & Kipnis, 1990)! This situation brings to mind the old Bureau of Indian Affairs schools where Native American children were punished for speaking their native language. Native American groups are now working against serious odds to reverse that loss in order to keep their languages and cultures from disappearing (Goebel, 1996; Wilson, 1996).

Differences of culture may be more difficult to transcend than language differences. The tools, products, and social practices that bring order and purpose to our lives define our sense of culture (Gallas & Smagorinsky, 2002). Different ways

Teachers who value diversity are able to use the diversity within their classrooms to enrich the learning environment.

of thinking may not be recognized but may simply create barriers to communication that hinder children's learning. Some teachers may think Native American children who don't answer questions don't know the answers. However, these youngsters are more likely not answering because of cultural considerations. For instance, in some Native American cultures it is considered rude to give a quick answer to a question. To do so would be a sign of disrespect to the person asking the question because quick answers indicate that the question and the questioner are not taken seriously (Stokes, 1997). Some Native Americans wouldn't answer because it might make their friends who don't know the answer feel bad. The value is concern for others rather than the mainstream American value of winning.

Classrooms in most communities of the United States represent a mix of cultures and languages from around the world. Though Hispanics and African Americans are in the largest minority groups nationally, many classrooms also include Native American children, children whose families are recently from Southeast Asia and eastern Europe, and those from elsewhere in the world. (Of course, all but Native American children are from families who came from elsewhere not too long ago.) Several cultures and languages may be represented in one classroom, creating rich opportunities for learning.

Children with Learning Disabilities?

More than 2.4 million children in the United States are labeled "learning disabled" (Pikulski, 1996). More than 80 percent of these children are described as having serious problems with reading. The International Reading Association has questioned the definition of "learning disability" and the process of labeling children as having neurological problems. Lack of medical verification of such damage is cited as a serious concern. Another concern is related to the assumption that reading problems are due to an intrinsic central nervous system dysfunction. Such a diagnosis, even if it could be proved correct, is discouraging to the child and the family. It creates a lack of hope, which destroys motivation and makes it less likely that the child will succeed. The label itself can have negative consequences for the child's education, such as lowered teacher expectations and segregation into instructional programs that include little actual reading (Pikulski, 1997).

Ms. Montoya agrees that labels can be harmful and prefers to try to figure out why a child might be off track in learning to read. She looks for something more specific and helpful than a "learning disability" as a cause (Spear-Swerling & Sternberg, 1996). She checks for visual and auditory processing problems and tunes in to the individual child's thinking. She tries to help youngsters with learning problems get back on track as quickly as possible, without any labels or segregated instruction.

Differently Abled Learners

The focus on keeping children of differing abilities from being segregated for instruction also applies to those who are intrinsically differently abled. It is widely accepted that when children with disabilities are educated alongside their same-age peers, they are more likely to learn typical behaviors, mannerisms, and work habits (Soriano-Nagurski, 1998). Instead of being taught separately in special-education classrooms, children with disabilities are now part of regular classrooms throughout the United States. Like other kinds of diversity, these differences can enhance the learning opportunity for all students if teachers are given sufficient support. Support comes in the form of special-educator involvement, classroom aides, reduced class size, and specialized training.

When Mrs. Thomas found that Lori, one of her new students, had a severe hearing loss, Mrs. Thomas was given a microphone that amplified her voice so that Lori's hearing aids could pick it up better. Mrs. Thomas took lessons to learn *cued speech* so she could communicate with Lori better; eventually, with the help of the classroom aide who accompanied Lori, the other children in the class learned to use cued speech a little also. Lori's classmates were given enough information to understand why Lori needed some special assistance. Cued speech is one approach to communication for the hearing impaired; it is different from sign language in that it enhances lip reading. Lori's parents chose this approach because it assists in learning spoken language, on which written language is based. They believe that this will help Lori learn to read and write more easily. Cued speech can assist with learning to read because it corresponds exactly to the words read (Blasi & Priestley, 1998).

Robin's mother, Karen, is his strong advocate. She insists that he is a child more like other children than different, though he was born with Down syndrome. Robin enjoys going to school with other youngsters his own age and is learning steadily—at his own pace. Robin wants to be with his classmates and objected to having to ride a separate bus for "special" kids. When his mother sought permission for Robin to ride the regular bus, she was told that safety precautions made that impossible. Karen didn't give up; she pushed until she was told that Robin would have to pass a safety drill before he would be allowed to ride the "real" bus. Karen and Robin practiced and practiced for the drill. Robin's teacher and his classmates all practiced for the drill. What a great day it was when Robin passed with flying colors! This small victory was important for Robin's academic success because it increased his self-esteem and helped him and his classmates see him as part of the group (Soriano-Nagurski, 1998).

During literacy center time, Robin and his friends enjoy re-creating favorite scenes from books read at school. As Robin uses small toy animals from the farm set and puts them through the actions in the book *Mrs. Wishy-Washy* (Cowley, 1990), it is clear that he understands the story. It is also clear that Robin's presence in the classroom is an asset to the whole group.

Nick's mom is also deeply involved with her son's education. Nick has autism, a developmental disability that significantly affects verbal and nonverbal communication as well as social interaction (Colasent & Griffith, 1998). Like Robin, Nick can understand and retell stories he hears, but he tends to refer to the characters as objects. Nick can make sense of stories better when they are connected as part of a theme of study, such as a series of stories about the dinosaurs that interest him. Nick's mom hasn't read the research demonstrating that children with autism benefit from holistic language and literacy processes (Colasent & Griffith, 1998), but she has observed it for herself. She is delighted with Nick's progress in his first-grade classroom and credits the way language and literacy are taught there. She values the opportunities for meaningful conversations in the class environment, the connection emphasized between the reading and writing processes, and the abundance of print.

When children with disabilities are educated alongside their same-age peers, they are more likely to learn typical behaviors, mannerisms, and work habits.

The stories of Lori, Robin, and Nick demonstrate important principles for successful inclusionary classrooms. Teachers need adequate support and preparation to appropriately meet the special needs of differently abled youngsters. The joint statement by the International Reading Association and the National Association for the Education of Young Children (1998) emphasized the importance for teachers of young children to be knowledgeable about literacy issues. This is crucial for teachers working with differently abled students, as even modest professional development can influence teacher's knowledge, which in turn influences students' achievement (McGill-Franzen, 2002). Children with special needs must be helped to become an integral part of the classroom community. Teaching practices that help most learners make sense of literacy also assist most differently abled children to learn.

Accelerated Learners

Another type of child with special needs is the accelerated, or gifted, learner. We are careful not to shortchange these children in the type of program described in this text. When we encourage children to read and write all they can in response to topics in which they are truly interested, there is no limit to the level of literacy that can be attained. Advanced students quickly lose interest in an artificially sequenced program or one that tries to move groups through material simultaneously. Flexibility and open-ended expectations on the part of the teacher are as important to the self-esteem of an above-average learner as they are to that of a below-average learner. Being *different* can make children feel bad, even if those differences stem from giftedness. Differences are highlighted when teachers expect all learners to perform the same tasks in the same way.

Meeting the Needs of All

Round-robin reading comes to mind here. Do you remember those incredibly boring episodes when everyone in the room had to take turns reading a section from some book? You were supposed to be following along with the reader and know the place when the teacher called on you. We don't actually know anyone who ever did know the place.

Children who were good readers had finished the whole piece by the time the second person had read the second paragraph. Those youngsters were reading something else that looked interesting in another part of the book or else daydreaming. Children who were not good readers were having trouble following along, mostly because they were paralyzed with fear over having to take their turn. Their minds were busy trying to figure out an escape route. This is an example of an approach disrespectful of individual differences. Any time schools expect the same thing from all children, they are failing to meet the needs of most of them.

CONCLUSION

In the classrooms described, the teachers do not define reading as saying words no matter how accurately or with how much expression. These teachers are so committed to the concept of reading as an active rather than a passive process that they are not satisfied with readers who merely repeat facts from what they read and demonstrate good literal comprehension. These teachers encourage the critical thinking and reading between the lines that result from interaction with print. They want children to question and to criticize, to exclaim and to cry; they want children to be *involved* with reading.

An enriched conception of early literacy expands our ideas of the skills involved. We know that children must do far more than use the graphophonemic clues on the page and know which way to turn the pages; they must also bring to the printed page their understandings of language, of what they are reading, and of their world. By integrating all these pieces simultaneously, children can experience reading as communication between the author and themselves.

New information about learning has given value to the emergent-reading processes of pretend reading and reconstructing a text from memory. New views also recognize that children are practicing actual reading strategies in these processes.

DISCUSSION QUESTIONS

1. A parent says he has heard that you are not using phonics workbooks and is worried that his child won't learn phonics. How would you answer his concern?
2. A child takes home a pattern book she has memorized and proudly reads it to her parents. She comes back to school crushed, saying that her family said she wasn't really reading. What explanation should have been given to parents before the child took the book home?

SUGGESTED FOLLOW-UP ACTIVITIES

1. Prepare a story from a Big Book and conduct a shared reading lesson with children. Involve the children in following the print and matching oral to written language by using a pointer to focus on each word as it is read. Observe children's level of participation to determine their awareness of print.
2. Observe and listen to emergent readers reading familiar predictable books with their friends. Note the clues they attend to and try to determine their current understandings.

3. Familiarize yourself with different types of predictable books. Try to find out by observing various children what makes a book readable for them.

4. Ask a young reader to read aloud to you. As you help the child with unfamiliar words, practice focusing attention on meaning clues first, with graphophonemic clues giving secondary assistance. Note the kinds of errors the child makes and try to determine the strategies he or she is using.

5. Note the current and possible uses of functional print in classrooms you visit.

RECOMMENDED FURTHER READING

Allington, R. L., & Walmsley, S. A. (Eds.). (1995). *No quick fix: Rethinking literacy programs in America's elementary schools.* New York: Teachers College Press; Newark, DE: International Reading Association.

Cunningham, P., Hall, D., & Defee, M. (1998). Nonability-grouped, multilevel instruction: Eight years later. *The Reading Teacher, 51*(8), 652–664.

International Reading Association and National Association for the Education of Young Children. (1998). Learning to read and write: Developmentally appropriate practices for young children. A joint position statement of the International Reading Association and the National Association for the Education of Young Children. *Young Children, 53*(4), 30–46.

Moustafa, M. (1997). *Beyond traditional phonics.* Portsmouth, NH: Heinemann.

National Association for the Education of Young Children. (1996). NAEYC position statement: Responding to linguistic and cultural diversity — Recommendations for effective early childhood education. *Young Children, 51*(1), 4.

Strickland, D. (1998). *Teaching phonics today: A primer for educators.* Newark, DE: International Reading Association.

Yopp, H. K., & Yopp, R. H. (2000). Supporting phonemic awareness development in the classroom. *The Reading Teacher, 54*(2), 130–143.

Assisting Emergent Writers

If confined to using words they can spell correctly, they cannot write—certainly not anything worthy of the thoughts they think.

Cathy M. Roller, 1996

CHAPTER 5

In the previous chapter, we described how children learn to read by reading. In this chapter, we will discuss how children learn to write by writing. In the preceding chapters, we looked at read aloud, (storytime) shared reading, guided reading, and independent reading: reading to, with, and by students. In the emergent writing chapter, we will look at writing for, with, and by children as we examine shared writing, interactive writing, guided writing, and independent writing. The parallels in these lists point out the similarities in the learning processes for learning to read and learning to write. Shared reading and writing provide modeling and scaffolding to assist the child's thinking, guided reading and writing offer relevant feedback and guidance for children's independent efforts, and independent reading and writing allow children needed practice and opportunities for trying out their current theories. As children are actively engaged in writing and/or reading, the teacher determines the appropriate level of support based on skilled observation of the learners and a clear understanding of the scaffolding required of each method. You will notice that learning to write, like learning to read, requires three different types of learning processes: opportunities for children to think as they try out theories, experiences with writing, and information about writing.

This chapter focuses on emergent writing and the kinds of writing activities that help youngsters become comfortable with themselves as writers. In the next chapter we will describe methods of helping children learn to write in more conventional ways.

Remember as you go that writing and reading are intertwined. The more people read, the more they know about writing; and the more people write, the more they know about reading. In fact, writing involves reading, as you review what you just wrote before writing your next sentence. Of course, we are talking about *real* writing, not copying something off the board for spelling and handwriting practice. In the past, some teachers confused copying with writing, and many thought they were teaching writing when they taught penmanship. Now, however, more teachers are coming to value writing as an important communication tool and to realize that even young children are capable of authorship. These teachers aim toward helping each child believe in him- or herself as a writer.

What kind of teaching helps youngsters believe in themselves as writers? It is teaching that helps them construct personal understanding of the process. Constructing knowledge about writing means creating and testing theories while working at writing. We can't emphasize enough the fact that children learn to write better by writing more. The classroom that helps children find reasons to write and gives them freedom do so is the classroom that fosters children's understanding and produces proud and capable young writers.

SHARED WRITING

Observing adult writers is one useful way to get information about how writing works. Children learn a lot about literacy from literate adult examples. They especially need examples to help them learn the many arbitrary conventions of written language, such as the spaces between words, left-to-right sequence, capital letters, and punctuation. One way to provide examples is to write children's ideas for them while they watch and help (Morrow, Strickland, & Woo, 1998). This *shared writing* is not done in a way that suggests that youngsters cannot write for themselves, but it occurs in addition to their doing their own independent writing. Taking dictation from children (writing *for* them) who are able to write for themselves can be compared with continuing to read stories to children who are learning to read by themselves. This activity provides more useful information and some assistance to children's learning. Providing support enables children to focus on the creative, composing aspect of writing as opposed to getting overwhelmed by the mechanical, physical aspects of getting the words down on paper. Another way to look at the process is that taking dictation and providing other demonstrations of writing helps children learn to write in the same way that talking to them helps children learn to talk. They need models for both kinds of language.

Mrs. Hanna makes sure that children can see as she writes their dictated ideas.

When we write as children dictate their ideas, we are assisting their growth in all areas of the language arts: speaking, writing, and reading (Groth & Darling, 2001). They are using their oral language skills to dictate, they are observing how writing is done as they draft and the teacher writes the text, and they are able to read the completed product. Shared writing builds on the language-experience approach, which has been common in classrooms for young children for nearly forty years (Lee & Allen, 1963). Ample classroom talk is fundamental to language experiences and promotes thinking and concept formation (Heller, 1999).

As we describe shared writing activities in several classrooms, you will notice a continuum for how much writing the teacher does compared with how much children do. You will also notice that shared writing can occur with a large group, a small group, or individual children. Each has its own benefits.

Preschool Authors

Ms. Reynolds also values helping children get their ideas into writing. She views this process as an important part of the print-rich environment in her preschool program. As we walk into her classroom, we see her engrossed in conversation with Tanya in the art area. Apparently, Tanya spent a great deal of energy creating a collage this morning and wants Ms. Reynolds to make a sign describing it. Ms. Reynolds writes on a piece of tagboard as Tanya tells her about the different items glued onto the collage. As Ms. Reynolds writes, Tanya watches, stopping her narrative occasionally to allow the writing to catch up. Although the result is a giant run-on sentence with minor grammatical errors, Tanya grins proudly when she hears her words read back from the paper.

After Ms. Reynolds moves on to assist other children, Tanya reads the sign from memory several times to herself. Then she gets her friend Justin so she can read the sign to him. Still intrigued with the written form of her own speech, Tanya gets several crayons of different colors and traces over the letter forms that Ms. Reynolds wrote. Colorful wavy lines cover the original writing. The words are now difficult to read, but Tanya thinks the result is beautiful.

While Tanya is making her sign colorful, Ms. Reynolds responds to a request to get the bunny out of his cage. She stays with the youngsters who are petting him and responds to questions and comments about the rabbit. As the discussion focuses on proper ways to treat the classroom pet, she suggests that the children make a sign by the cage about how to treat bunnies. The four youngsters seem enthusiastic, so Ms. Reynolds quickly brings over a portable easel with chart paper already on it. She writes with a marking pen so that the writing will be visible to the group.

Each child contributes a rule of personal importance. Kelly says, "Don't touch his nose." Betsy says, "Don't squeeze him." Timmy adds, "Just feed him lettuce." Caleb warns, "He might poop on you." All these contributions are written down just as stated by the children. Then they all read them together as Ms. Reynolds moves her hand under each line of print. The children and Ms. Reynolds carefully hang the new sign on the wall beside the rabbit cage, and all the authors importantly point it out to other children in the class.

When Ms. Reynolds composes her monthly newsletter for parents, she quotes these and several other compositions in describing class activities. She credits the authors, who then experience a wider audience and a different printed form of their thoughts. Although neither the individual collage description nor the small-group rabbit rules were preplanned as language-experience lessons, they show that Ms. Reynolds is receptive to opportunities for children to translate their experiences into oral and then written language. A classroom environment that encourages this type of activity results in frequent spontaneous requests by children for adults to help them write. The writing is always authentic and meaningful to the children.

As a group, the four-year-olds are more interested in art-project captions and story dictation than are the three-year-olds. Three-year-old Seth, however, became excited about spiders after hearing several fact and fiction books about spiders read at story time. He spent some time poring over the pictures in the books and then went to the paint easel to work. When he had finished painting lines all over his paper, he asked an adult to label his picture "Seth's spider with spider web. Eats baby spider webs." Some preschool children dictate lengthy descriptions or stories, which Ms. Reynolds helps them make into small books with construction-paper covers. These books are placed in the reading corner. Ms. Reynolds also places books of children's drawings and emergent writing in the class library.

After children have authored their own books, they enjoy inviting friends over to the library area and reading their books to them. Generally, the reading consists of a remembered version of the dictation or writing, but some children

Seth learned about spiders from looking at books in his preschool library. He decided to communicate his ideas through painting and then he dictated what he wanted written on his picture.

recognize a few specific words in their stories. Whether reading from memory or from letter clues, they are learning that their ideas can be put into writing and can be read. As children see books dictated by other children, they often discover that some of the same words are in their own and their friends' books. Sometimes they can then read parts of someone else's book. As we have said, it is hard to separate writing skills from reading skills.

INTERACTIVE WRITING

Interactive writing is farther along the continuum of writing "with" children than shared writing. Shared and interactive writing both make vital links between reading, writing, listening, and speaking by highlighting that what we say can be written down. Like shared writing, the teacher and child(ren) decide together what will be written and use the child(ren)'s own words to highlight the learners' experiences and oral language (Sipe, 2001). However, interactive writing involves the children in the actual writing of the text. As children and teacher compose together they "share the pen." Children contribute what they know about spelling, letter formation and mechanics, and the teacher scaffolds them by supplying what they lack. The success of interactive writing is dependent on a teacher's knowledge of the learners' understandings (McCarrier, Pinnell, & Fountas, 2000).

Kindergarten Activities

Frequently, interactive writing occurs spontaneously to meet the needs of an individual child or a group involved in a project, but sometimes Mrs. Hanna initiates interactive writing. A shared experience, such as a field trip to the grocery store, may provide the occasion for large-group dictation. Mrs. Hanna first engages children in a lively discussion about the trip and then leads them into thinking through the experience sequentially. She asks questions such as "What happened when we first got there?" and "What happened next?" She writes down what the children tell her, using their grammar and vocabulary. She frequently stops at familiar words, such as *the*, and invites children's participation, asking, "Is there anyone who wants to write that word for us?" When they come to the word *store*, Mrs. Hanna invites Steven to write the beginning letters. Writing on large chart paper allows the writing to be large enough for all to see, and posting the charts encourages children to read them over and over. Youngsters will return to these charts when they "read the room" with their pointer wands, and they will refer to them for spelling words when they write independently.

Making a class book about Halloween costumes demonstrates the continuum from dictation to independent writing. Some children want Mrs. Hanna to write for them, while others write in their own way for themselves. Others want varying amounts of teacher assistance. Ashley wrote about her princess costume, "Mi Mom mad me a perses drs." Sam prefers to have his teacher write while he dictates an account of his spaceman outfit. Mrs. Hanna writes his exact words as he watches with interest and speaks slowly to allow her time to write. Just as she is ready to write *spaceman*, Sam proudly volunteers that it starts with an *s*, like his name. Mrs. Hanna suggests that Sam write that letter and makes a mental note of Sam's progress. However, she tries not to interrupt Sam's flow of ideas; her main goal is to get Sam's ideas written down. She focuses on the meaning of children's words rather than on the specifics of how to write them for now. Yet she carefully forms each letter in a consistent manner when she writes because she knows that her students are still sorting out which variations in letter forms are significant. For instance, an *n* looks a lot like an *h*, and the differences between a *u* and a *v* can get confused.

As she does with all the children, Mrs. Hanna encourages Sam to watch as she writes what he says. She leaves the paper in front of him and reaches over to write in front of him. Because she is right-handed, she reaches in from his right so her hand won't block his view. She wants Sam to be able to see how she holds the pencil, how she forms the letters, and where on the page she begins writing. As she writes, Mrs. Hanna reads aloud what she is writing. Table 5.1 summarizes these important steps in taking dictation from young children.

The Halloween costume book sparks several scary Halloween stories by individual children. Most of the youngsters create several books on their own about various topics. The classroom aide laminates the finished products and binds them into nice-looking books with plastic bindings. Each child-authored book goes into the classroom library along with the collection of fiction and nonfiction books as well as many other student-created books. Some of these other books were written and dictated by children as individual projects, and others are group books containing individual thoughts on a common theme. All are frequently read.

Sometimes it is difficult for Mrs. Hanna to find enough time to help all the children herself, so she gets help from parent volunteers and older children whom she has trained to do interactive writing. As much as she values long and

TABLE 5.1
Dictation Procedure with Individual Children

1. Encourage discussion to formulate ideas first.
2. Write exactly what the child says.
   - Accept run-on sentences.
   - Accept ungrammatical sentences.
   - Use standard spelling in spite of mispronunciations.
3. Make sure the child can see you write.
   - Be sure your hand is not in the child's way.
   - Be sure the paper is in front of the child.
4. Write legibly and form letters consistently.
5. Read dictation back to the child when finished.
   - Run your hand under words as you read.
6. Encourage children to take the completed transcript to another adult to read.

involved stories, Mrs. Hanna cannot give each child unlimited attention. Volunteer assistants are especially helpful for finishing long writing projects when the teacher's attention is needed elsewhere. If the topic allows, Mrs. Hanna sometimes asks a child to limit the writing to one or two main points. This approach gives children practice in organizing ideas and in sharing the teacher's attention with others.

Proficient Writers

Even proficient writers benefit from interactive writing. Mrs. Thomas writes the daily news each morning through interactive writing with her first graders as they gather for a class meeting. After a brief discussion of events in people's lives, the class decides on one or two to write up. After they decide what to write, Mrs. Thomas involves the group in figuring out how to spell the necessary words, always asking them how they figured out which letters to use. Answers provide her with information about children's understanding and also provide valuable modeling for youngsters who haven't figured out the system yet. Volunteers come up to the chart and do some of the writing as others offer advice and feedback. If something is written incorrectly, correction tape over the error allows it to be fixed easily. Mrs. Thomas emphasizes the need for capitals and punctuation marks during this writing process. She notices how quickly most of the children pick up on these ideas and begin to use them in their independent writing.

Proficient writers also benefit from shared writing. David signs up for an individual conference with Mrs. Thomas because he wants help with a long story he has been writing. Having written two pages independently, using invented spelling, he is growing weary of the effort involved in sounding out each word, figuring out which letters might correspond to those sounds, and then laboriously forming all those letters. Still eager to finish putting his ideas down on paper, David asks to dictate the rest to Mrs. Thomas. Although they aren't sharing the pen, David is sharing in the writing process. He is drafting the story! David's level of sound-symbol understanding guides Mrs. Thomas as she requests his involvement in spelling the words. However, as always, Mrs. Thomas's main purpose in taking dictation is to get the communication onto paper. As this is David's intent too, he feels delighted with the finished product. Mrs. Thomas helps David make a cover for his book, with the title and author's name printed boldly on the wallpaper sample he has selected for the cover. After David has practiced reading his story aloud, Mrs. Thomas arranges for him to go to the kindergarten and read it to children there. David feels proud of his work.

Older Emergent Writers

Older emergent writers especially benefit from shared writing procedures. Mr. Larson uses it successfully with his late bloomers in second grade. They have exciting stories in their heads and get frustrated by the mismatch between what they want to write and what they can write. An adult "secretary" can keep enthusiasm for authorship alive while demonstrating the important skills these youngsters need to learn. Additionally, reading their own stories provides valuable emergent reading practice with material of interest to the children. These young-sters don't like most of the books they are capable of reading since the easy-to-read books are usually geared toward younger children. Stories and reports they and their friends produce during shared writing meets a need for appropriate read-ing material. The more they read or write, the better they will get at both, so it is important to keep all children involved in literacy activities.

Dictating their ideas as an adult writes can be especially helpful for speak-ers of nonstandard English. Older youngsters may still be in the emergent literacy phase because they speak a dialect of English. The mismatch between their oral language and the language of print makes it hard for them to read. Because their dictated material utilizes their natural language pattern, it is easier for them to read what they have dictated. This gives them reading material in their own lan-guage, which matches research recommendations for beginning reading instruc-tion. When youngsters are attempting to figure out how print works, they need to match the spoken words to written ones. Consider how hard this is if the way you put together a sentence is different from the way a book puts together a sen-tence. Their own writing offers these children the perfect solution for initially mak-ing sense of print as readers, and shared writing offers the opportunity for them to produce their own writing.

INDEPENDENT WRITING

Writing on their own allows children to explore the information they have accumu-lated from adult models and other experiences with print. When children write, they are able to use a trial-and-error approach to making sense of written lan-guage. This "kid writing" (Y. Goodman, 1985) requires serious thought. They try out their current theories about written language while they practice writing, much as they try out their understanding of oral language as they practice talking. When adults allow children to use this trial-and-error approach, the children build firm understandings of significant concepts and then are able to transfer these un-derstandings to a variety of related situations.

Testing Theories

When well-meaning adults try to keep children from "wasting time" by making mis-takes, they deprive children of significant learning experiences. Telling children principles far removed from their current understanding truly wastes the chil-dren's and the teacher's time. Understanding may be replaced by rote memory of a few facts. Because children cannot easily transfer specific facts to other situa-tions, they will have to learn more facts by rote. This approach brings the addi-tional danger of discouraging thought by suggesting to children that they cannot figure out things on their own but must rely on an authority. Good teaching, in-stead, fosters children's own thinking and assists their deeper understanding.

When you think of beginning writing as an initial experimentation with the written word, your expectations for young students change. Instead of expecting beginners to form letters correctly and spell words according to custom, you can

Writing on their own allows children to explore the information they have accumulated from experiences with print.

appreciate each small step toward standard written expression in both form and function. You can rejoice with a young child over approximations of intent in writing, a shopping list of what appear to be scribbles, just as you do with a toddler who makes an imprecise attempt to say a new word.

Initial Explorations

Ms. Reynolds encourages independent writing by both three- and four-year-olds. They have access to blank paper, marking pens, crayons, and pencils. Ms. Reynolds understands the importance of children's freely exploring written language to unlock its mysteries. She enjoys watching children play around with print in the same way in which they explore with clay or blocks. These preschoolers are

FIGURE 5.1
Two examples of young children's signatures.

free to squeeze and smash clay, to stack and scatter blocks, and to scribble and scratch with writing utensils. The parent helpers are used to the idea of process being important, whether or not there is any product. Parents are therefore comfortable with the lack of "correct" writing in the writing center.

The teachers and parent helpers in the preschool have learned to read children's attempts to write their own names (Green, 1998). They decided that a grown-up's writing a child's name on a painting after the child has already done so is disrespectful of the child's writing. So, as part of empowering children's use of print, they learned the distinctive signature of each child in the school. In the process, they decided that the children's signatures are as readable as the signatures of many adults (see Figure 5.1).

The wide range of writing forms that Ms. Reynolds observes in children's paper-and-pencil work fascinates her. The writing includes random scribbles and drawing, linear markings, letterlike forms, and conventional letters. Most youngsters actually use a combination of forms in their writing. Many children already write their own names with some accuracy, but most tend to turn the letters around randomly. Some children are ambivalent about the difference between drawing and writing. Tabatha says, "I drawing my name," and Abbey announces, "I writing a picture" (see Figure 5.2). Some children confidently experiment with letters and letterlike forms, whereas others limit themselves to tracing or copying correct forms. Some fill pages with rows of squiggles, and still others apparently have no interest at all in writing yet.

Some differences are attributable to levels of understanding, but the role of individual personality and style of learning accounts for other differences. Some children don't think at all about what their writing might say; others will decide after they are through that their scribbles look like something specific. Some will ask an adult what their writing says, and some know exactly what they want it to say.

FIGURE 5.2
(Top) Tabatha said that she drew her name. (Bottom) Abbey said that she wrote this picture.

Different youngsters attend to different aspects of writing and have different purposes as they write. Some children focus on form, detail, and accuracy, whereas others are carried away with the stories they have to tell.

Dominic has created a combination of scribbles, drawings, and letter forms that he explains orally in elaborate detail (see Figure 5.3). By listening carefully, Ms. Reynolds discovers that Dominic has a well-developed story in mind but simply lacks the technical skills to put it into standard readable form. Ms. Reynolds is delighted with Dominic's writing progress. Dominic knows what writing is for, he understands that symbols are used to communicate ideas, and he has the ability to express himself.

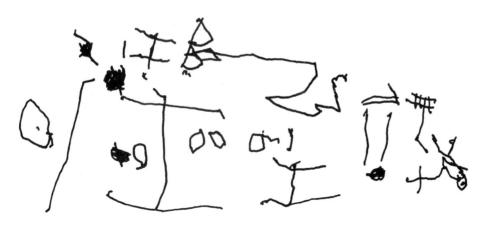

FIGURE 5.3
A letterlike form of emergent writing.

Tanya's writing has no plot; it is limited to marks that she has designated as symbols for people and for things important to her. Tanya's theories about print lead her to consider print as representing things rather than language. Ms. Reynolds isn't worried because she knows this phase is natural. She is worried about Justin, though. His paper has only perfectly spelled words on it because he will only copy words from around the room. He lacks the confidence to try writing on his own and always anxiously asks, "Is this right?" Ms. Reynolds wonders whether his parents' efforts to teach him the alphabet and sounds at home are causing Justin's concern about correctness. All she knows for sure is that Justin's concern is getting in the way of his ability to explore and learn about written language.

Conventional Forms Appear

Betsy's sister Amy, who's just started kindergarten, has discovered that spaces appear between segments of writing and that specific kinds of marks make certain letters. Amy has noticed that some writing is made from combinations of straight lines, some from curved lines, and some from both. She has been exploring these observations during the past year, moving from making long rows of circles to creating more letterlike forms.

Amy frequently chooses to work in the writing center. There she alternates between copying words she knows from around the room and creating new ways of putting her own ideas into print. She particularly likes to write her own name and the names of her friends. She has become skilled at making the letters in her own name and has noticed that these same letters are also in some other names. For a while, she was merely reordering the letters in her own name when she wrote. (For an example of this writing form, see Daniel's writing in Figure 5.4.) She used these same letters in some sequence to spell any word she didn't know. She still sometimes uses

FIGURE 5.4
Daniel explores
writing, using
"his" letter, *D*.

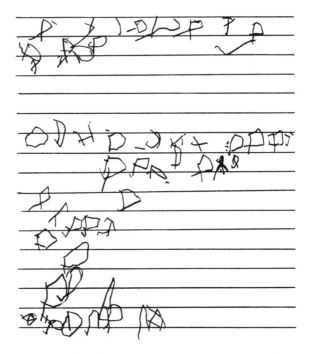

random assortments of letters that bear no apparent relationship to the sounds of words in the message she may "read" from her paper. Her work and that of her class-mates is not just playing around prior to really learning to write; these exploratory stages are essential elements of learning to write. Children's approximations of print are refined through practice and personally constructed ideas as they develop into conventional print (Leu & Kinzer, 2003).

Maria has played with print long enough to discover that a relationship exists between sounds and letters. She writes stories in which most of the major sounds are represented by a letter that has a name similar to that sound. The letter-name-as-sound theory is not taught by adults, but children construct it through their own logic. Regardless of what is taught by adults, youngsters go through their own processes of making sense of print, of language, and of the world. Adults who un-derstand children's process of becoming literate can appreciate the intellectual feats represented by these "incorrect" theories.

Dien has mastered the distinguishing characteristics of letters but has only a vague awareness of a symbol-sound relationship. He has figured out that writing uses a few characters over and over again. His writing conforms to standard writing in that it is a series of letters with not more than two alike adjacent to one an-other. He also has apparently created the theory that words need between four

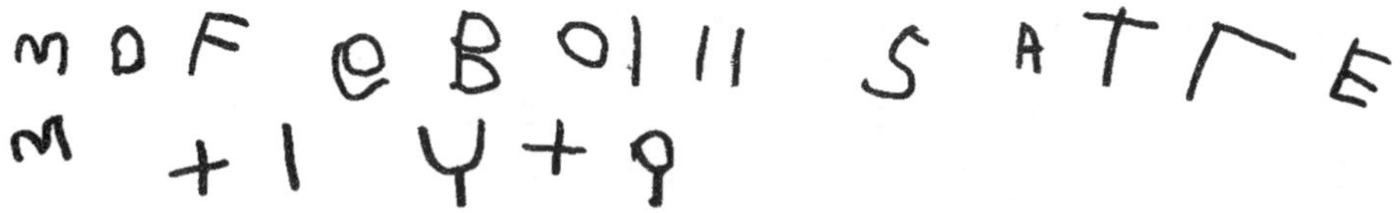

MDF @BOII SATLE
M +I Y+P

FIGURE 5.5
This child's writing conforms to conventions well enough that we might think we could read it.

and eight letters. This common emergent writing theory is more clear evidence that children construct their own understanding regardless of what adults think they are teaching (Kamii, Long, Manning, & Manning, 1990). Dien's work looks so much like adult writing that we may be tempted to think we can read it (see Figure 5.5). However, the groups of letters do not spell words, and we have to rely on Dien to read his work to us.

Bryce's concept of the relationship between letters and sounds hasn't reached the point at which he knows that each sound is to be represented by a letter. Sometimes he represents a word with one letter; sometimes he represents syllables with one letter. Sometimes he takes the easy way out and does pretend writing with rows of squiggles. He must continue working before he can select appropriate letters for the sounds he hears and then work some more before he can master standard spelling conventions *and* the many exceptions to the rules.

Carlos is exploring print in Spanish, his home language. During the course of the school year, Ms. Montoya notices a few differences between his emergent writing and that of children writing in English (Kamii et al., 1990). Carlos also explored the idea that words require a certain number of letters, but when he moved on to representing sounds with letters, he wrote mostly with vowels. Carlos also was able to clearly represent each syllable in his words with a letter. English-speaking children's emergent writing, in contrast, uses mostly consonants, with few vowels. Their attempts to represent the chunks of sounds they hear in words do not correlate well with syllables. These differences are related to the differences between the two languages; in Spanish, vowel sounds and syllables are much clearer than they are in English. Most vowels in English are the mushy schwa sound and are difficult even for adults to identify. This English-language pattern results in many unstressed syllables that blend together when spoken.

Becoming Writers

During first grade, most of Mrs. Thomas's students will become writers. Although their ability to write according to standard conventions will vary greatly, all children in Mrs. Thomas's class come to consider themselves authors (see Figure 5.6).

The aly cat   There wus a cat hoo livd in the aly it wus sckrufy and sagye and wet it dug in grabij cans it just found bons and uther shuch things it slepd on emty grabij cans won day a grl found it she fed it melck and gave it a aoft bed to slepe in it graoo farey plump and fat it becam to big for its bed it drace vary litll melck pepl stil kaerd for it it was not so fat . Ashley

Ashle
by
Sthy
Ashley

FIGURE 5.6

Can you read this invented spelling? Put in your own punctuation to discover the plot. Note the confusion caused by the keyboard: The *i* is used for the *l*—it looks like an *l* on the keyboard. The *a* in *soft (aoft)* is a typo, probably made because the *a* is next to the *s* on the keyboard.

They all write, and they all are encouraged to read what they have written to their classmates. Their desire to have others read their writing becomes a major impetus to learning more about spelling and punctuation.

Adam is a first grader who understands many conventions of print. He has helped write several class books patterned after familiar stories. In December he wrote his own version of the song "Santa Claus Is Coming to Town." Adam incorporates many standard spellings with his phonics-based spelling; he also uses spaces between words and some punctuation. When he reads a first draft, he recognizes when he has left out a word, and it is common for him to edit by changing or adding a word. Adam is so excited by his new ability that he tells his teacher, "I

wass	a pon	a tm	ther
woss	som	polpl	

FIGURE 5.7

This child's writing shows familiarity with the "once upon a time" story format.

just don't have time to draw pictures anymore, I have too many things to write words about!"

The content of what children write in this classroom is amazing. Even children who rely on pictures and use few words have wonderful stories to tell. Mrs. Thomas sees a direct relationship between the literature she shares with her students and the type of writing they do (see Figure 5.7). From their knowledge of fairy tales, these children have a useful model of story structure, and many of their stories start with some version of *wuzupnatm*. From stories such as *Curious George* (Rey, 1941), they gain favorite characters to write about. From other stories, they learn how to use direct dialogue or a narrative form. Nonfiction books encourage children to write about real experiences or to research and write about topics of importance to them. Television also serves as an inspiration for children's writing. Mrs. Thomas allows children to write about whatever interests them, even if it is a Saturday morning cartoon character or plot.

Most of Mrs. Thomas's students are trying to match the sounds of their language with letters to write it. Some children are just beginning to explore this concept. Many are working at the letter-naming level, like Maria in the kindergarten class. Some have made the discovery that the names of letters and the sounds aren't always the same. Whatever the child's level, Mrs. Thomas values and encourages each child's attempts at writing without criticism of the product. She knows that criticism during the shaky early attempts can discourage further efforts to make sense of writing. She also knows that their temporary phonics-based spelling (also called invented spelling) helps children think about how words are spelled and assists their growth in literacy (International Reading Association and National Association for the Education of Young Children, 1998).

Instead of criticizing early efforts, Mrs. Thomas continues to encourage youngsters to create and test their own theories as they practice writing. She also provides models of conventional writing through her own demonstrations, via minilessons, and through constantly exposing the children to books and other print. She knows that their own desire to make their writing readable will keep children striving toward those models. Mrs. Thomas keeps in mind that the more children work at writing, the more they will analyze

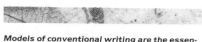

Models of conventional writing are the essential partner to exploration with writing. This partnership provides the framework for all writing instruction.

the writing they see in books and all around them (F. Smith, 1983). Duckworth reminds us of the importance of a child's theory building for his or her development of understanding. Thus, models of conventional writing are the essential partner to exploration with writing. This partnership provides the framework for all writing instruction.

CHAPTER 5

Fear of Failure

Previous feedback about her writing has made Felicia so concerned about spelling and letter formation that she won't explore with print. During journal writing, Felicia begs her teacher to tell her how to spell the words she wants to write. Ms. Montoya's sympathy for Felicia's fear of failure makes her want to give in, but her desire for Felicia to become truly literate and not to be merely a copier of words makes her hesitate. Ms. Montoya tries to show that she accepts mistakes during various school activities. She calls attention to her own errors, such as misplacing a book or miscounting materials. She publicly admires children's writing with phonics-based spelling and pretend writing. Ms. Montoya tells all the children to write in whatever way seems right to them and not to worry about adult spelling for now. She explains to youngsters that they don't have to spell perfectly when they are just beginning. Gradually, Felicia relaxes and tries to write on her own, and Ms. Montoya is relieved.

Some youngsters do come to view themselves as failures when they progress more slowly than others. These children naturally don't want to write because they perceive writing as demonstrating their lack of ability (Roller, 1996). Writing is a humiliating experience for these children. Ms. Montoya realizes these late bloomers need lots of additional support. As mentioned previously, shared writing is helpful, as is collaborating with a more proficient friend.

Collaborating with a more proficient friend can help a late-blooming writer develop confidence and skills.

Nate may not be good at putting things down on paper, but he has an amazing imagination for creating exciting stories. As he works with Tim to get those ideas onto paper, he watches closely to make sure Tim is getting it right. Of course, Nate is doing a lot of reading and carefully observing a lot of writing during this process. Ms. Montoya knows that the most important part of getting reluctant writers moving is helping them find something they personally want to write about (Roller, 1996). Choice in literacy tasks promotes motivation (Morrow, 2001), and choice in writing topics may be even more important than choice in reading materials.

Authentic Writing

At the beginning of the chapter, we recommended helping all children find reasons to write. You may have suspected that we didn't have in mind writing to please the teacher as a reason to write. Writers of all ages are motivated by having personally meaningful topics to write about and an audience to write for. It might be personally meaningful to Omar to write a letter to his grandmother, to Jazzmin to make a phone directory of her friends, to Tyler to write a book about salamanders, and to Betsy to produce a "Keep Out" sign for her bedroom door. The purpose doesn't matter as long as it is one the child cares about.

Not all purposes come from the youngsters, however. Teachers are constantly thinking about ways to encourage children to write. Ms. Montoya thinks about writing activities as well as reading and math activities that would be relevant for each topic of study in her classroom. She is also constantly alert to reasons for writing that might come from children's personal interests and play activities. This chapter describes various types of authentic literacy events that help children find purposes for writing. Notice that we said *authentic* literacy events. Authentic means the kinds of writing done for real-world purposes rather than for contrived school purposes. We believe that kids can tell the difference.

Freedom to Write

We also recommended giving children freedom to write. What do we mean by this? You might think we mean giving them enough time to write. Time is essential to good writing, and schools rarely allow enough of it. However, the freedom we are most concerned about is the freedom from *fear*. Are you surprised at that statement? If you watch youngsters in a traditional classroom, you will see that many are unable to write because they are afraid of failure. These children can't express themselves on paper because they feel constrained to use only words they know how to spell correctly; additionally, they can't concentrate on the content of their writing because they are focusing all their energy on producing good handwriting. These problems are a result of writing instruction that emphasizes perfection of mechanics—spelling, handwriting, and punctuation. To make matters worse, they get only one chance—no second and third drafts. (We hope you appreciate that we used more than one draft in writing this book.)

Being a risk taker is a conspicuous trait of prolific writers, and risk takers are not fearful. They charge ahead with whatever skills are at their command, and they get their ideas down on paper, worrying about details like spelling later. Teachers who honor emergent writing assist children in risk taking and thus assist them as writers. Thus, Ms. Reynolds offers a well-stocked writing center for preschoolers, even though most of them are unable to write anything an adult could begin to read. Recognizing the importance of their processes, Ms. Reynolds respectfully discusses their writing and drawing with youngsters in her class. Similarly, children in Ms. Montoya's multiage group feel comfortable writing at whatever level makes sense to them. Their teacher talks with them about the content of what they write rather than simply evaluating it for errors. If you have forgotten the many forms of kid writing, you may want to go back and review that section of Chapter 1.

Journal Writing

Writing in a journal is an excellent way for youngsters to develop that courage and confidence as writers that we have been talking about. Journals by nature are personal expressions written for personal purposes. This private aspect of journals is critical to their success in building confidence since such writing is for yourself and is not subject to outside evaluation. Mrs. Hanna has given each kindergarten child a journal—a small, blank booklet with a sturdy contact-paper cover bearing the child's name. Mrs. Hanna encourages all youngsters to write in these journals, even those children for whom writing is drawing or scribbling. What or how they write doesn't matter. What does matter is that they spend energy exploring their theories about writing. She has found that writing in her own journal during daily journal-writing time not only provides a model of adults as writers but also keeps children from asking her how to spell words. She can more easily encourage students to think for themselves about spelling if they know she is too busy writing to spell for them.

Though most anything is acceptable as a journal entry, there are some rules for journal time. Each child must draw or write something, names are to be written on each day's entry, and the date is to be stamped on each. In Ms. Montoya's multiage-primary class, children individually bring their journals to their teacher to share their work when they are finished writing. She takes notes while they read their writing to her; these notes are valuable documentation of each child's writing development.

Sometimes she thinks a youngster needs a nudge to move from drawing to writing. When Caitlan again shares the same sort of pictures she has been drawing for a couple of months, Ms. Montoya asks her to write down some of what she has said about the picture. This writing may be no more than the names of the people pictured, but it's a start. The teacher's expectations of children are determined by her knowledge of each child's background and progress (Girling-Butcher, Phillips, & Clay, 1991). Ms. Montoya has a system for helping her more proficient writers move into conventional spelling in their journals. As a reference, in the front of their journals, she helps them list some words they use frequently. She sees children using this crutch and then discarding it as they memorize the spelling.

Sometimes a child needs a nudge to move from drawing to writing.

Mrs. Thomas responds in writing to her first-grade students' journals. These responses are not evaluative comments, such as "Good job" or "Great handwriting." Mrs. Thomas responds to what the children have written as she would in a conversation. She focuses on the meaning of the writing instead of the mechanics, recognizing that children understand the communicative nature of writing long before they can conventionally produce it. When Demetrius writes, "I PLD Ol 6 TeTh aWT WaThe Mi haNDS," Mrs. Thomas writes back, "You lost six teeth! Was it hard to pull them out with your hands?" Notice that her comments honor the child's communication and also model the correct form of the words he was writing. This is an effective way of assisting a child's writing development, just as a similar oral response to an oral communication assists language development. As they hear adult speech models, children modify their baby talk to be more adult; similarly, they modify their spelling to be more like adult spelling when they have relevant examples.

When asked how she finds time to respond to each child's journal, Mrs. Thomas says that she has time because she doesn't have to correct work sheets. She not only believes that journals are much more educational than work sheets but also enjoys reading them much more than work sheets.

Making Books

Making books is also a lot more enjoyable than doing work sheets and gives children a purpose for writing. There are so many different kinds of books to make. Some books are whole-class books; some are written entirely by one child. Some are takeoffs on other books; some are accounts of personal experiences. Some are big and some are small, some are rectangles, and some are fancy shapes. Some are stapled or bound, and some are folded in magical ways. All are fun for children and encourage them to want to write.

We talked about making a class version of *The Important Book* (Brown, 1945) in Chapter 3 and mentioned Timmy's own version of *Alexander and the Terrible, Horrible, No Good, Very Bad Day* (Viorst, 1972) in Chapter 4. The children in Ms. Montoya's class decided to make their own *Snowy Day* book after becoming familiar with Keats's original (1962). All those who were interested contributed a picture and a caption of their favorite thing to do on a snowy day. Some liked to make angels and snowballs, like the little boy in the book, and others contributed other ideas, such as cross-country skiing or helping Mom shovel the driveway. In writing their captions, children were free to write on their own, to ask a friend, to look in the pictionary, or to find the words in other books. The criterion for acceptability was the child's own satisfaction. The finished book was laminated, bound, and placed in the class library to be enjoyed by all. Of course, Ms. Montoya read it at group time before it went into the library.

Mrs. Hanna's class has just gone on a field trip to the museum. As a follow-up to the experience, she engages the children in conversation about the things they saw there. Then she invites each to draw and write about his or her favorite thing for a class book. Many youngsters choose to dictate part of their narrative and have an adult help them write, but others are happy with their own kid writing. For those who ask an adult to do the writing, the composing experience is still practice with writing. Those who do their own writing generally are interacting with their friends while they are writing. They give and get advice about what to write and how to write it. This peer interaction is an important part of learning to write because it stimulates thought about how best to get ideas onto paper effectively.

Sometimes if a child has trouble thinking of something to write, a wordless picture book can offer inspiration. Ms. Montoya got this idea from one of her professional books (Roller, 1996) and has tried it with success. Writing words for *Good Dog Carl* books (Day, 1988) has been a lot of fun and led to a lot of laughs. Spier's beautifully detailed wordless books offer a different kind of writing inspiration. Writing such books in a multiage-primary classroom encourages children at various levels to collaborate. Younger children who benefit from the oral language practice can work with older children who benefit from figuring out how to put the story into writing.

Mrs. Thomas's first-grade class has been studying fish recently. She makes blank books with colored construction-paper covers in the shape of fish. At choice time she holds one up and mentions that these are available at the writing center for any children who want to write their own fish books. Needless to say, many youngsters are attracted by the interesting shape and bright colors; they want to make a fish book, and so they write about fish. Dustin's book contains facts he has learned about fish, and Heidi writes about going fishing on her family's boat. Both youngsters sign up to read their books to the class in the author's chair that day.

Sharing writing with an audience and getting constructive feedback is an important part of learning to write. Though their audience is appreciative, both Dustin and Heidi find out that they need to explain parts of their writing better in order for

Making books can be motivation to write.

their classmates to understand their ideas. Dustin decides to write his revised version on the computer; he thinks it will be easier than writing it by hand again.

Research Writing

The fish books just described are a form of research writing. They helped the children record and report information (Richgels, 2002). Writing done in response to information-gathering procedures is what we are calling research writing. This writing can take the form of individual or group books similar to those already mentioned. Tyler's book about salamanders is the result of his experience observing and caring for them, augmented by some fact and fiction reading. His book shows that he knows a lot about both salamanders and writing.

Mrs. Thomas's students enjoy using their research information to make riddle books to share with their classmates. These usually take the form of a "Who am I?" sort of riddle. Children write two or three clues on the outside of the book and put the answer and an illustration on the inside. During a study of sea life, Bryce and Ivan worked together looking up information and writing these clues: "1. I hug rocks. 2. I have eyes on the end of my arms." Opening the book, you see a picture of a starfish (see Figure 5.8). At sharing time, these boys and others who have written riddles enjoy sharing them with their classmates, who have fun guessing.

FIGURE 5.8
A pop-up riddle
book.

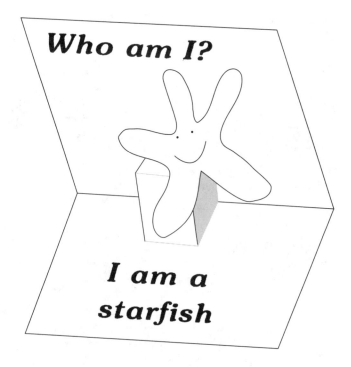

Doing research using the Internet can be a productive way for youngsters to gather information, although much of the information available is geared toward older children and adults. Sites where young children write for other young children are a good source of appropriate Internet material (e.g., Little Planet Times at *http://www.littleplanet.com* is an interactive on-line newspaper for kids, by kids). Mrs. Thomas's students made their own home page about the glacier near their school, and youngsters all over the world can learn from it. They have found similar projects by children in other places (e.g., Kids' Space at *http://www.kids-space.org*). They also use e-mail to request information and to make friends with children from around the world. The Internet encourages both reading and writing as well as the exchange of viewpoints that stimulates thought for learning (El-Hindi, 1998). Mrs. Thomas uses a "recommender system" to investigate the quality of information on the Web. This involves recommendations from trusted sources. An example of an educational recommender system can be found at *http://it-edtech.ed.usa.edu/alteredvista* (Owens, Hester, & Teale, 2002). She also refers to Karen Bromley's (1999) Web sites for writers.

(No throwing ["frowing"] rocks)

FIGURE 5.9
A functional writing sample.

In Mrs. Hanna's class, children not yet able to read conventionally do research using their own firsthand observations during science experiences. Even though they have limited reading and writing ability, they too can make riddle books. When they study trees and seeds, Mrs. Hanna takes her students on walks to collect samples of leaves and seeds from a variety of local trees. The children help create a display in which each set of samples is carefully labeled. Then they work in teams to examine the samples and write up their observations as clues for guessing which tree they are describing. One important clue frequently mentioned in various forms is "It hs poky nedls."

Keeping records of experiments and experiences is another form of writing. Ms. Montoya's students have planted beans and are measuring their growth. Each child has a partner, and together they record observations of their plant's growth in a logbook. Part of the log takes the form of narrative accounts about how green the plant is or how it is growing toward the light source; a graph tracking the plant's growth is another aspect of the log. Similarly, recording the change from caterpillar to butterfly is an exciting use for a science logbook. The amazing experience of seeing a butterfly emerge from a cocoon and then setting it free generates significant drawing and writing in the classroom.

Functional Writing

We talked about reading functional print in Chapter 4. Now let's talk about writing it. Signs are one category of functional print. Children are used to seeing signs everywhere, and therefore they naturally make signs of their own. There are signs in the pretend zoo, such as "elofetss" and "seols" or "BeRRFVe ANAMollS." (Can you read them? They say "elephants," "seals," and "Beware of Animals.") There are signs in the block area, such as "DO NoT Rek," and signs about rules for the playground (see Figure 5.9).

Lists are another type of functional print. Lists showing who has had a turn and who wants one are useful in most classrooms. Even preschoolers can write their own names so that they can recognize them and contribute to a wait list. For

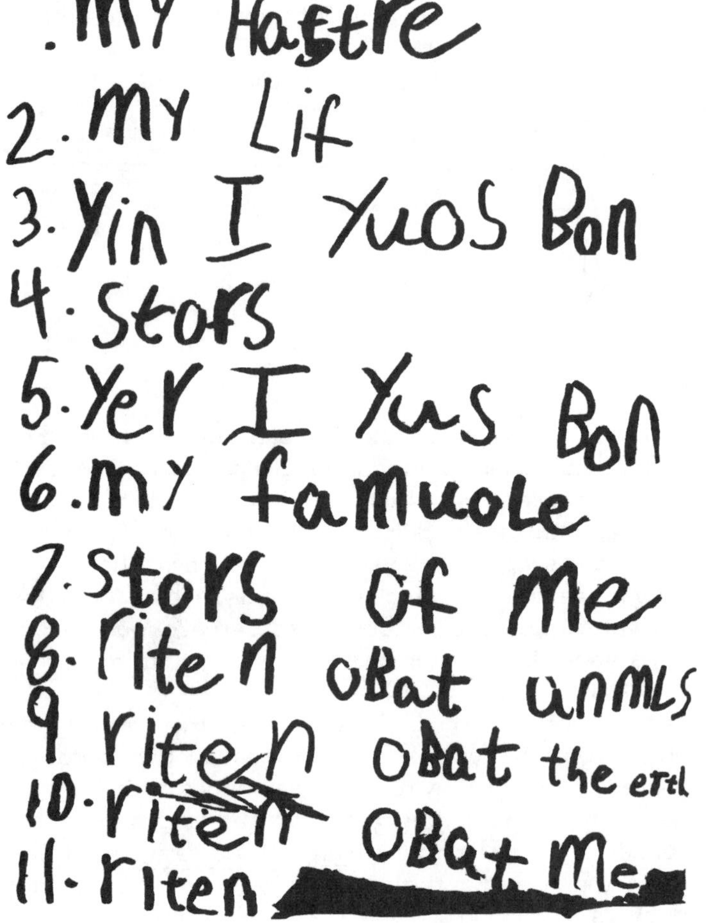

.my Hastre
2. my Lif
3. Yin I Yuos Bon
4. Stors
5. Yer I Yus Bon
6. my famuoLe
7. Stors of me
8. riten oBat unmls
9 riten oBat the ertl
10. riten oBat me
11. riten

FIGURE 5.10
You can even write lists of things you want to write about.

instance, Dien and Jevon want turns on the minitrampoline, and Jordan is using it now. Ms. Reynolds gets a piece of butcher paper and tapes it to the wall near the trampoline. She encourages Dien and Jevon to sign up for turns, promising that they will be notified as soon as it is their turn. This keeps peace in the classroom as well as helps youngsters learn about the usefulness of print. They find out that their names on a list can represent their claims just as well as their standing in line does. They also learn that once their names are written on the list, they stay in the order written. These are important discoveries. There are other kinds of lists too: things to take on the field trip, things to bring for putting on a play, and birthday guest lists. You can even write lists of things you want to write about (see Figure 5.10).

Jazzmin's decision to make a phone directory to help her call her friends was her idea but no less valuable than a teacher's plan. A phone directory is a good example of functional print in our society. Much of youngsters' writing during play is pretend uses of functional print. For instance, they write menus when they play restaurant, make tickets when they put on a play, and write checks when they play store. These examples are valuable writing events, helping children learn just as much as if they were directed by the teacher. Teachers who understand the value of writing in play make sure to offer writing materials along with other dramatic play props. Writing in the playhouse is an important part of independent writing even if it is pretend writing.

Personal Communication

Here comes the end to another sacred truth about school. First, we told you children are supposed to talk to each other in school instead of being quiet. Now we're going to tell you to encourage children to write notes to each other. Yes, note writing generates lots of interest in writing. Mrs. Thomas accidentally discovered this when a couple of girls in her class started a "love note" fad. It quickly caught on, and soon notes were everywhere. From this event, Mrs. Thomas got the idea of encouraging children to write notes by creating a class mailbox for mailing notes. Youngsters take turns with the job of delivering mail to the correct storage cubbies. Mrs. Thomas models this kind of writing when she writes notes to parents and asks children to deliver them.

Letters are important too. Omar's letter to his grandmother is just one example. Many children have loved ones who live far away and who may even write letters back. Getting a letter in response to a letter is motivation to write more. Thank-you letters are an important letter form also and are used to thank hosts for field trips or guests who bring special events into the classroom. Sometimes Ms. Montoya takes dictation for a group letter as a way to demonstrate letter writing, and sometimes she encourages each child to write a personal thank-you letter. Mrs. Hanna encourages her students to write to authors of books they especially like, telling what they most like about the book. (Frequently, youngsters will get a response to these letters as well. See, for example, Scholastic Network at *http://www.scholastic.com* or Ask the Author at *http://ipl.org.youth/AskAuthor*.)

E-mail messages seem to get quicker and surer responses from authors and others; therefore, this is a favorite way to communicate in writing. Lupita likes to send e-mail notes to her mom at work; doing so makes her feel closer to her mother and adds to her sense of security in the school environment. Annie frequently writes to her sister, who is away at college. Sometimes children write to others in their own room or to friends in another classroom.

Ms. Reynolds models letter writing for any preschoolers who are interested when she sits at the writing center and creates the weekly class newsletter for parents. She doesn't write it at home in the evening because she knows it is valuable for youngsters to see the process and hear her talk about what she is doing.

There are many reasons for you and your students to write letters; be alert to possibilities related to any curriculum area or school event.

Painting and Drawing Relate to Writing

Drawing is a way of representing ideas visibly and often provides a bridge into representing ideas through print. When children are encouraged to talk about their pictures, their drawing can become richer and is more likely to hold a story (Oken-Wright, 1998). Encouraging children to talk about their drawing involves respectful attention to what the child's intent is. Questions such as "What is it?" or comments such as "What a beautiful picture!" can have negative results. It is important to watch and listen to figure out why a child is drawing and how that purpose might be extended to literacy. A useful response to a child's drawing is, "What's happening here?" This question sets up the expectation that something is happening, something that can be told about in story form.

Ms. Reynolds provides many opportunities for personal expression in her preschool through drama, music, and art as well as writing. Betsy loves to paint and works at the easel almost every time she comes to school. She is still experimenting with the way the paint drips down the page and what happens when she paints one color over another. But Ms. Reynolds sees that Betsy is beginning to move from exploring this medium to using it for a purpose. One day, Betsy says that her painting is a picture of her mom. Making a symbol for a person with paint is a step toward writing, and so is knowing that the letters her teacher wrote say "Mom" (see Figure 5.11).

Although controlling paint is a challenge for Betsy, she is quite confident with a marker. Using the markers at the writing table, she tells complex stories with detailed drawings and symbols. Ms. Reynolds often sits at the table with the children as they work and listens to them talk about their work. Generally, it just looks like a lot of scribbles and mess until the child tells what's happening. Certainly no one else could ever decipher Betsy's self-expression efforts, but she has clear ideas about her intent. Ms. Reynolds values Betsy's work and listens respectfully to her explanations. Ms. Reynolds values Betsy's symbolic representations both as drawings and as a step toward writing.

The link between drawing and writing doesn't end with preschool. Ms. Montoya sees how her students of various ages intertwine the two forms of expression. Drawings seem to stimulate writing, and writing seems to stimulate drawing. Often, drawing seems to serve as a prewriting process as a child thinks through an idea by illustrating it first. For youngsters with limited writing ability, drawing can provide the detail and elaboration that they are unable to communicate through writing.

Writing Centers

Many classrooms have writing centers. Writing centers are places where writing may occur, but mostly they are the place where the writing materials are kept handy. These materials may be used for a variety of purposes and in most any part of the room. If Danielle needs paper to write phone messages in the playhouse, she

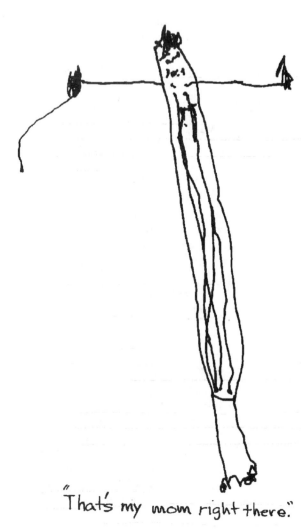

FIGURE 5.11
Making a symbol for a person with paint is a step toward writing, and so is knowing that the letters the teacher wrote say "Mom."

"That's my mom right there."

gets a notepad from the writing center. If Dominic needs to make a sign to protect his block structure, he can find a piece of tagboard and a marker in the writing center. Special-interest items, such as Mrs. Thomas's fish-shaped books, can be placed in the writing center to encourage writing, but they needn't be used only there.

Let's look at Mrs. Hanna's writing center setup as an example. Unlined paper seems best for most of her students. They are so busy trying to make letter forms that the additional challenge of staying within lines discourages them. Mrs. Hanna's students can select from a variety of sizes, shapes, colors, and textures of paper.

She recycles paper that has been used on only one side in order to provide quantities of paper while maintaining a clear conscience with regard to the environment. Many different kinds of writing utensils are also available. Most of the children prefer to use the water-based marking pens that make distinct lines and come in bright colors. Mrs. Hanna also provides pencils and crayons. The crayons are regular size rather than the fat kind often recommended for small hands, which Mrs. Hanna finds are actually harder for youngsters to manage than the smaller ones. Glue, staplers, tape, and paper clips complete the basic writing center setup.

In addition to the basics, there are many other popular writing center materials. As with most kinds of materials, it is best to rotate some of them regularly rather than have everything out all the time. Some possibilities for writing center additions are stamps and stamp pads, business envelopes and order forms from junk mail, cut-and-paste patterns for making envelopes, "stamps" such as those from Greenpeace or Easter Seals, catalogs and order forms, cardboard and wallpaper for making book covers, small notepads, business cards, and almost anything else you might find in your desk or in your junk mail.

A computer is also a writing center. Unfortunately, many classrooms have only one computer, and it too often is used for workbooklike games. Word processing is a much better use for a computer. If you think a computer helps you to write, think how much help it can be to a child who has difficulty figuring out which direction a letter faces and who has trouble controlling a pencil. Writing by hand is incredibly labor intensive for beginners, and some children can write much more prolifically with a computer. The printed-out results look so grown-up that youngsters feel even more pride in their work. When a child wants to polish a piece of writing by doing another draft, the computer is especially useful. If the piece was originally written on the computer, the child can easily make revisions. If not, Mrs. Thomas tries to find time to be the child's typist while helping with editing.

Mrs. Hanna makes a computer available to her kindergarten students also. She has been fascinated by the different ways in which youngsters approach literacy via the computer. She agrees with Labbo's (1996) categorization of children's approaches to the computer screen: as a landscape to be explored, as a canvas to be painted, as a playground, and as a stage to narrate plays.

Children feel grown-up working at a keyboard, even if it is the keyboard of an old typewriter. Usually, typewriters that end up in classrooms these days are electric, but occasionally youngsters can be found struggling to punch down a key of an old manual typewriter. Ms. Montoya laughed the day she saw Katya searching all over the manual typewriter for a place to turn it on. Katya was impressed when she found out it was a machine that ran without electricity.

GUIDED WRITING

We consider it guided writing whenever a teacher assists a child with a composition and enhances that child's ability to write more effectively. This assistance can be a quick word of encouragement or the answer to a question as the teacher

A classroom post office, complete with pretend stamps for sale, encourages youngsters' letter writing.

moves around the room during independent writing. Or it can be a formal conference with a child who wishes to discuss a writing project.

Children will learn writing skills much more effectively through feedback on writing to express their ideas than through drills on isolated sounds. They will learn spelling, handwriting, and even punctuation as they strive to make their writing understandable to others.

Mrs. Thomas focuses her teaching on the communicative intent; correctness of form is just one aspect of effective communication. Mrs. Thomas knows that richer writing and meaning occur in longer, "connected discourse" than in isolated words or short phrases (Armington, 1997). Therefore, she encourages writing in-depth stories and reports. She also encourages children to read their compositions to others as part of the writing process. For children who seem ready for it, she teaches them to edit their work and to keep in mind the question, "Is this what I want to say?" When Kristen reads, "I like to hug her with my bear," Kristen says to herself, "You know this doesn't make sense. I guess I could cross out the *her*."

Punctuation also plays a role in effective communication. When Ms. Montoya noticed that Lupita had begun putting periods at the end of her compositions, it seemed like the time to discuss the placement of periods. She asked Lupita where periods went, and the Lupita promptly answered that they went at the end of sentences. The problem was that Lupita didn't know how to find the end of sentences. A brief lesson on listening for pauses when she read her writing aloud helped a little, though Lupita ended up with periods after some clauses too. Ms. Montoya knows that these things take time, and she is satisfied with the progress for the time being. She makes a note to help Lupita notice where periods appear in stories she reads until Lupita is able to make sense of the idea. The best time to teach is when students have an opportunity to apply what they are learning to an authentic literacy activity (Tompkins, 2003). Lupita will write more stories and continue to work on periods. Minilessons such as this, focused on individual children's own writing concerns, are more effective than general group lessons.

When youngsters are tuned in to an audience for their writing, they are motivated to learn standard conventions of print. They have a reason for spelling in ways that others can read and a reason to use punctuation thoughtfully. They also have a reason for making the print legible. Teachers teach skills effectively and efficiently when they assist youngsters in their efforts to edit their work for an audience.

The editing process is most appropriate for youngsters who are past their emergent writing stage and have attained more confidence in themselves as writers. Therefore, we will save further description of editing conferences for Chapter 6, in which we talk about more proficient writers. The writing process involves several drafts and a polished product. For emergent writers, the first draft is usually as far as the child can go.

WRITING SKILLS

Now that you have an idea of the kinds of writing activities that best assist emergent-writing development, let's examine those activities more closely from the skills angle.

As with reading, skills aren't the focus when children write, but that doesn't mean that youngsters don't learn writing skills (Calkins, 2000). In fact, they actually learn to *use* skills to improve their own writing, not merely to fill in the blanks on work sheets or to pass a spelling test. Too often, old approaches to skills instruction resulted in just that, but there was little transfer to actual writing (Moustafa, 1997). Skills development does require practice, but practice is more useful as part of actual writing than as filling in work sheets (Leu & Kinzer, 2003). Another significant part of skills development involves the demonstrations and models of competent writers. Demonstrations of writing are much more effective ways of teaching writing than are lectures about it.

Effective teaching of writing skills helps youngsters use those skills in their writing rather than to fill in work sheets or pass spelling tests.

In this section we give examples of how writing skills are most effectively learned. This discussion will focus on both how children learn as they work at writing for themselves and how they learn from adult example. Did you notice all the various skills being demonstrated and encouraged during the shared and independent writing activities described? In case you missed some, we'll be specific and point out when phonics, spelling, punctuation, handwriting, and composing skills are learned and taught. As we look again at some writing activities, you will find children constructing their own understandings of some issues, and you will find teachers providing direct instruction as relevant. Both are valuable aspects of learning.

When writing with four-year-olds, Ms. Reynolds often mentions details such as the shape of a letter, the fact that a word starts like a child's name, or where on the page she begins writing. Although she points out the spaces left between words, most four-year-olds find that idea difficult to grasp. After all, you don't hear those spaces when you talk. Ms. Reynolds doesn't expect children to master any of these concepts yet; she merely helps them begin to take notice. She knows that she cannot speed conceptual learning; it has to come from experiences that assist children in the development of hypotheses that they will challenge, discard, and replace through further experience. Writing with adult assistance helps children who cannot yet write something readable to see themselves as writers, causes them to notice more, and therefore helps them learn more about how writing is done (F. Smith, 1994).

Concepts About Print

With the occasional child who shows readiness through interest, Ms. Reynolds will follow the dictation process with a game of finding words in the dictated piece that start with other letters that the youngster knows. However, many preschoolers are not able to distinguish between the letters and have only a general idea of acceptable letter forms. Only a few have any understanding that letters represent the sounds of language. Ms. Reynolds knows that with continued exposure to reading and writing situations, these children will refine those understandings and become literate. She doesn't try to rush them past their discovery of foundational concepts and into specifics of letter names and sounds. She certainly doesn't use phonics work sheets or flash cards. She wants them to build on firm foundations for a lifetime of rewarding reading.

Ms. Reynolds understands that children need help to develop the concept of separate words as part of learning to decipher phonics principles. Since no spaces exist between spoken words, children tend to lump together phrases such as "once upon a time" and consider them a single word. When they find out their understanding isn't correct, they often overcorrect and think that each distinct sound in a word makes up a separate word. Because of this confusion, children experience difficulty in matching oral and written versions of language (Clay, 1975), and until this confusion clears up, children cannot progress in discovering sound-symbol relationships. Ms. Reynolds carefully says each word as she writes it during dictation, and she leaves distinct spaces between words. Later, when she and the child read back what was written, she runs her hand along under each word as they read it. Through these kinds of experiences, repeated over and over, children gradually formulate the basic concepts on which to base understandings of phonics and other word-recognition tools.

Mrs. Hanna doesn't expect most of her kindergartners to benefit from instruction focusing on details about print either. Many are still building their personal foundations of understanding about written language. Most have learned the names of the letters and can recognize them in both capital and lowercase form because they have watched television shows that have that emphasis. Many are still working on the concept of words as separate pieces of language. Demonstrating the idea of separate words through shared writing is a meaningful way of helping children sort this out.

FIGURE 5.12

Bret drew and wrote about "A-T walkers" (from *Star Wars*). Notice he has the *A* and the *T* but tries both the *Y* (letter-name-as-sound theory) and the *W* (conventional form) for *walkers*.

Phonics

Children learn phonics best by writing with their own invented phonics-based spelling (Richgels, 2002). It is apparent in their independent writing that most of Mrs. Hanna's students have learned letter names, but few have progressed beyond letter names as sounds (see Figure 5.12). Because many letter sounds are the same or similar to the letter name, this is a good start. During shared writing, Mrs. Hanna often asks children to contribute the starting letter of words that begin with one of these easier sounds. Because children's comments during shared writing are not restricted to answering the teacher's questions, Mrs. Hanna learns about children's perceptions of letters and sounds from their comments. She learns even more from analyzing their phonics-based spelling strategies. She sees children applying and refining their knowledge of phonics as they write with this kid spelling. As she observes their ways of representing words, Mrs. Hanna gains information that guides her in planning follow-up activities appropriate for each youngster.

Amy demonstrates that she is moving beyond letter names as sounds by saying, "I know what that word starts with! It starts with *y!*" as Mrs. Hanna helps Amy write about what she did "yesterday." Now her teacher knows to involve Amy in discussions about letters that do not make their name sounds but are nevertheless regular enough in the sounds they represent to be fairly easily learned. Amy progressed to this point through continued exposure to correct spelling in books, on signs, during shared writing, and in word play rather than through drill in these letter sounds. When she figures out for herself that the conventions of her language indicate a certain symbol for a certain sound, she truly knows the rule. Mrs. Hanna knows that the best way of teaching phonics is through repeated experience with written forms of language meaningful to the child. She knows that isolating the sounds from words and meaning in workbooks or flash-card drills is counterproductive for most children (Strickland, 1998).

Apparently, some children thrive on work-sheet phonics drills. Doesn't this refute the theory that such teaching procedures are inappropriate? Actually, the fact that some children are able to make sense of those isolated pieces of information about the sound-symbol system testifies to the effectiveness of children's own approaches, not of the workbook approach. Those who succeed with the phonics drill are those who have experiences reading and writing as part of their daily environment; they have learned the basic premises of written English through their own thoughtful exploration of print. The workbook exercise merely allows them to demonstrate what they already have learned. For those children, the specific information about letters and sounds has attained a meaningful context.

Some teachers who wouldn't consider using work sheets nevertheless plan their curriculum around the "letter of the week." Apparently, they don't realize that this is just another form of meaningless encounter with letters. Finding words and stories that match a letter is backwards from the sequence in which children learn about print; it also contradicts our understanding of how children learn in general (Wagstaff, 1998). Instead of having youngsters think about all the things that start with a certain letter, teachers should put their energies into helping youngsters figure out how letters are part of actual written communication. Letter-of-the-week activities take time away from opportunities for authentic and meaningful activities related to children's interests (Fisher, 1998). Besides, children don't encounter letters one at a time in the outside world, nor do letters do anything interesting by themselves—except dance around in misguided efforts at educational television.

As Mrs. Hanna encourages her class to notice letters and sounds during shared reading and writing activities, most of her kindergartners progress to the point of recognizing the regular consonant sounds at least at the beginnings and ends of words; some students recognize the more prominent sounds in the middles of words too. The long vowel sounds are easy because they follow that helpful rule of having the same name and sound. Short vowel sounds are another matter, however. Mrs. Hanna thinks confusing kindergartners with this mass of irregularity and indistinct sounds is cruel. Because vowels in unaccented syllables all have basically the same schwa sound, knowing which vowel appears in which word is really a matter of memory through familiarity rather than of learning rules (Wilde, 1997). Mrs. Hanna allows children to take their time with this frustrating aspect of phonics and considers it inappropriate for the kindergarten curriculum.

Even most of Mrs. Thomas's first graders aren't ready for short vowel sounds. Because children use many other word-recognition skills in addition to phonics, Mrs. Thomas doesn't find it necessary for her students to know every sound in a word in order to be successful readers. Nonetheless, she assists her students in extending their understandings of phonics principles and of other word-formation principles. She too works on helping children construct these understandings through repeated reading and writing experiences. Informal comments during dictation, games, and discussions during follow-up activities all provide information children can use to figure out how to express themselves in writing.

Spelling

The application of phonics in writing is spelling; therefore, all the phonics games and activities described in Chapter 4 assist with spelling. But remember, neither phonics nor spelling rules (or broken rules) make any sense until a child has finally come to the realization that the written code represents the sounds of the spoken code (Griffith & Leavell, 1995–1996). This *alphabetic principle* is constructed individually through many repeated experiences with print. Instead of making sure youngsters have this firm foundation, too many teachers forge on with meaningless instruction that leaves children in the dust.

Emergent writers who are aware of the alphabetic principle are working on the immense complexity of the sound-symbol relationships in the English language. Because of this complexity, spelling has been called a type of knowledge rather than a skill (Wilde, 1992). In learning to spell, we have to grapple with the use of silent letters as markers, as in *light* and *bite*; the use of different letters and combinations for the same sounds, as in *just* and *giant*; the use of the same letter for different sounds, as in *cat* and *city*; and a wide variety of confusion over the irregularity in English spellings (see Figure 5.13).

It takes a course in history and geography to understand why English words are spelled as they are. For instance, we spell *phone* with a *ph* instead of an *f* because of its Greek origins and because the Greek letter phi was transliterated into *ph* in Latin (Wilde, 1992). Another tidbit: *Daughter* is spelled as if it rhymes with *laughter* because once upon a time it did. We especially like the bit of historical trivia that says it was once considered a sign of brilliance to be able to think of many different ways to spell a word. Other information to ponder: English was spoken long before it was written, and then it was put together with the Latin alphabet, which doesn't fit English. English is a mishmash of derivations from many languages, which keep their original spellings to show their origin. After centuries of creative spelling, standardized spelling is a recent convention. The young child's way of spelling words as they sound was once the accepted norm among educated adults.

Although much spelling defies categorization and simply has to be memorized, there are certain patterns in the English sound-symbol system that children can figure out as they read and write (Glazer, 1998). One of the best ways to learn to spell is to read a lot and be immersed in correct spelling until the way common words look becomes as familiar as your friends' faces. The other best way to learn to spell is to write a lot. Writing gives practice in thinking about spelling, which also makes readers more aware of spelling when they read (F. Smith, 1983).

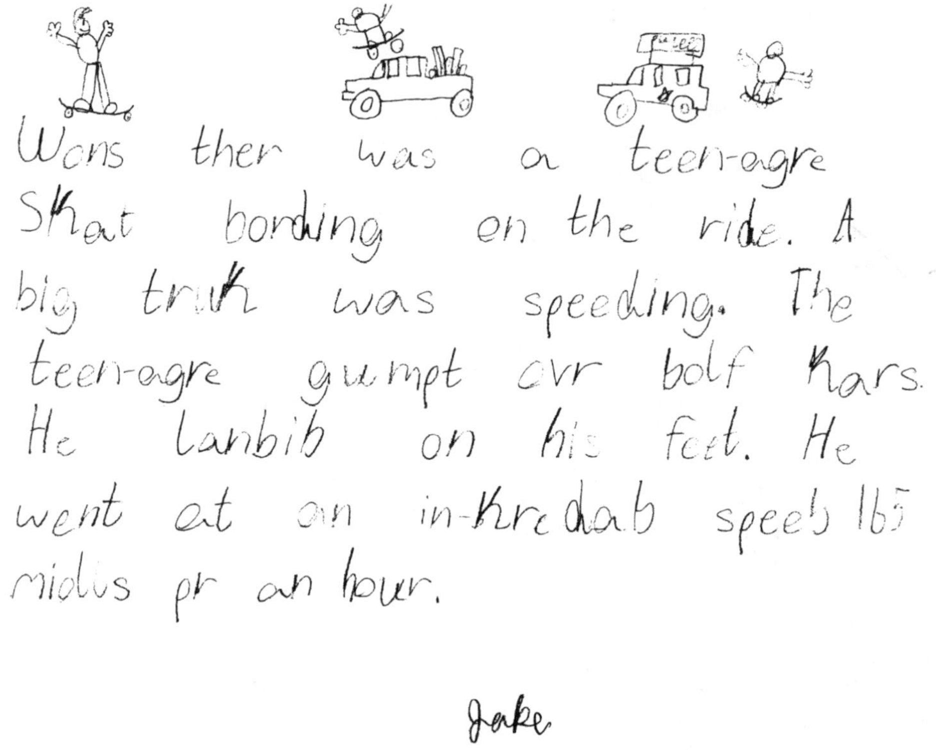

Wons ther was a teen-agre Skat borbing on the ride. A big truk was speeding. The teen-agre gumpt ovr bolf kars. He lanbib on his feet. He went at an in-kre dab speeb 165 miblus pr an hour.

Jake

FIGURE 5.13

Jake encounters spelling irregularities and complexities; for example, he shows confusion with the beginning letters in *jumped* and *cars*, using *g* and *k* instead of *j* and *c*. Note alternative form of the word *road*.

Tyler is grappling with the inconsistencies of spelling in a systematic way as he writes. He carefully says each word several times as he listens for the sounds to write down. When Tyler writes that he wants to *jriv* a car, Mrs. Thomas compliments him on hearing the sounds in the word *drive*. If he asks, Mrs. Thomas may acknowledge that the word isn't really spelled that way, but she will admire Tyler's spelling as a "good" way to spell. Mrs. Thomas frees children to write and to explore writing by not insisting that they spell words correctly at this point. She doesn't work on perfecting spelling until young writers demonstrate readiness for it. Until then, Mrs. Thomas makes a distinction between the "right" way to spell and a "good" way to spell. When Tyler uses his best knowledge of sounds and the letters that represent them to spell a word, his efforts constitute a "good" way to spell. His teacher congratulates him for his efforts and focuses her attention on the message of the writing rather than on the spelling. This is exactly the way adults encourage children to learn oral language—adults respond to the content of what children say rather than to the errors they make in saying it. If children's baby talk and incomplete and

TABLE 5.2

Some Ways to Teach Spelling

- **Dictation and shared writing**
  Commenting on some of the spelling as you work
- **Responding to children's journals**
  Modeling standard forms of words children wrote as part of response to their message
- **Reading with big books**
  Calling attention to how some words are like other words
- **Encouraging children to read independently**
  Allowing opportunity for standard forms to become part of children's visual memory
- **Encouraging children to write independently**
  Allowing opportunity to explore and refine their understanding through phonics-based spelling
- **Helping children polish their written compositions**
  Giving direct feedback about standard spelling of words that individual children use frequently in their own writing

---

ungrammatical sentences were corrected every time they spoke, children probably wouldn't talk very often and therefore wouldn't make much progress in speech.

Mrs. Thomas knows that spelling words the way they sound is not merely a mistake to be tolerated or ignored for fear of discouraging a child's efforts. Phonics-based spelling plays an important role in the process of deciphering the sound-symbol system of written language (Dahl, Scharer, Lawson, & Grogan, 1999). Mrs. Thomas explains to parents and administrators that this active exploration of the system will enable children to construct a personally meaningful and useful set of encoding and decoding rules. Research shows that this kind of spelling is the best way for youngsters to learn phonics and other word-recognition skills (for example, Glazer, 1998; Strickland, 1998; Wilde, 1997).

Mrs. Thomas's students do make progress in standard spelling through their observation of print, through discussions with peers about how to spell, and with Mrs. Thomas's assistance (see Table 5.2). Children who write tend naturally to compare their spellings of words with spellings in books and elsewhere, gradually revising their own spelling until it conforms to what they see (see Figure 5.14). For example, Trevor looks critically at what he has written: *scol*. He comments, "I know that's not right because it's not long enough." He then refers to a book in which he knows the word is written. Previously, he hadn't noticed any discrepancy between his spelling of this word and conventional spelling. As long as he was satisfied with his own version, Mrs. Thomas knew he wasn't ready for more information.

Children seem to inspire one another in their writing. We can observe this as Heidi and Anastasia discuss their writing, sharing ideas and viewpoints. Mrs. Thomas is confident their writing will be better for the interaction. In this class-room, students make faster progress because their teacher encourages them to collaborate on spelling while they write. Several children who are writing at the

the frot seps and noct   on

the   dor oped bot

i ded   see ene bote

i nwdest   tat i wos nocen

on the hol wa dor i openo the

dor and i so a ghost

plaen the peano i   slole wokt

en i wos rele scard i notest

tat on tes brocen beth tar

wos a scol i trnd dac and

the dor wos lokt i thect

jest nabe i kod vows the

scol to owpen the dor i

owpend the dor i ran and

ran i got awt and ievd

hapole evr aftr

FIGURE 5.14

This child has begun to incorporate some standard spellings into his writing. He also knows a lot about phonics and uses it to compose long, involved stories with spellings such as *nwdest* or *notest* (for *noticed*) and *spooce* (*spooky*) and *scol* (*skull*).

same table will discuss and compare ideas about how to spell any word in question. The process of explaining their own rationale for spelling a certain way, coupled with the process of considering and accepting or refuting a classmate's differing ideas, greatly enhances children's understandings about spelling.

A "word wall" is a valuable resource for children who want to work on their spelling. Children consult the word wall as a quick way to find the correct spelling of a word while they are writing. Ms. Montoya and Mrs. Thomas both have versions of word walls. Ms. Montoya helps children group words by common *phonograms*. Remember those? We described them in Chapter 4 and explained that phonograms are more useful and natural to use than trying to blend separate letters into whole words. You might have known them as *word families* or might remember them better by the term *rimes*. One of the most common rimes is *ay*. Depending on what consonants or consonant blends you put in front of the letters *ay*, you can make twenty-six different words, such as *day, play, say*, and so on. When Ms. Montoya and her students notice rimes in stories they read together, they post them together on the riming word wall (Moustafa, 1997). These can be a big help in thinking about spelling. Of course, you have to have separate sections for *low*, *know*, and *slow* and for *how*, *now*, and *cow*. What about the rhymes *though* and *toe*? What about *bough* and *bow*? Now, is that *bow* as in "take a bow" or as in "he wore a bow tie"? No wonder spelling is so confusing!

The English-language riming word wall isn't useful for her Spanish-speaking students, so Ms. Montoya helps them make a word wall with favorite words from stories read in Spanish. These are grouped by syllables instead of rimes because syllables are the salient feature in Spanish words (Moustafa, 1997). Youngsters learning to read and write in their home language of Spanish are supported in their spelling efforts by this word wall. Whether grouped by rimes or syllables, as just described, or by initial letter or topic, as described next, the words can be confusing without some contextual clue. One way to help children keep the words straight is to have them make picture clues representing the story they associate with the word.

Mrs. Thomas focuses on words that children frequently use in their writing, working with youngsters to post the correct spellings of those words in alphabetical order. When Trevor posts the word *school*, it is in the *S* section; and the word *drive* is in the *d* section. One wall is for any frequently used words, and another reflects words related to current topics of study. While they study birds, words such as *nest*, *eagle*, and *soar* are posted on the current topics wall. When the topic switches to sea life, different words appear, such as *ocean*, *mussels*, and *anemone*.

Additionally, Mrs. Thomas assists individual students in focusing on the correct spellings of words they use frequently in their own writing or dictation. She helps each child create a "word bank." The children make file boxes out of milk cartons for their word cards and use alphabetical dividers to help them organize their words by beginning letters.

Remember Ms. Montoya's system of helping individual children record often-used words in the front of their journals? That's yet another way to help youngsters who are ready for conventional spelling to move in that direction. In all these situations, the emphasis is on real writing, but the value of conventional spelling for effective communication is acknowledged as a goal.

Writing Mechanics

In addition to learning uppercase and lowercase versions of the twenty-six letters and the forty-four sounds represented by those letters, children must learn the mechanics of writing. Ms. Montoya often notes with amazement how perfectly some of her students can write in mirror images. Mirror-image writing would be difficult for her to do, but if a first grader accidentally starts on the right side of the paper, that child may naturally and easily write everything exactly backward (Wilde, 1997). So Ms. Montoya carefully points out where on the page writing and print begin, and she points out the return to the left side after coming to the end on the right. Most of her older students have internalized this guideline, but many of the younger ones write until they come to the edge of the page and then write down the side.

Some children have more trouble with these mechanics than others. Heidi is tidy and methodical not only in her writing but also in her play with items such as

CHAPTER 5

blocks and other manipulatives. Her writing stays in neat lines as it is supposed to. Anastasia, on the other hand, is exuberant and messy in everything she does. Her writing goes in every direction, rather like her thoughts.

Most older youngsters in Ms. Montoya's class are able to deal with the concept of space between words, but some focus on other aspects of writing and forget that one. These youngsters can benefit from activities similar to the cut-apart sentence exercise that Mrs. Hanna did with Amy, Maria, and Bryce: After a child reads a whole sentence, it is cut apart so that each word is separate. This makes a puzzle for children to put back together word by word. Some children initially use periods as markers between words. Ms. Montoya must help her students deal with punctuation too, but although some youngsters incorporate it in their writing (see Figure 5.15), most of them aren't ready to do more than simply notice it.

Conveying Meaning

We gave you many examples of how teachers model writing forms during shared writing, but it is important to model function and process as well as form. Because the composition process involves much more than spelling and proper placement of words on a page, children also benefit from demonstrations of deciding what to write. This is why youngsters need models of adults composing their own writing. Children need to do more than simply see the writing; they need to hear the writer share the composing process aloud. Just as children learn by observing their parents writing notes and lists at home, they benefit from the same kinds of models in school. Children who *don't* experience such adult modeling at home especially need it at school.

Fax on Faxgivinge

by Patrick McCormick.
Fax fur the hrviest.
Fax fur the fod.
Evy ey bady les sll bat.
On the 28, av November.
Fax for all the hrviest.
Fax for all the fod

FIGURE 5.15
Patrick worked on punctuation when he wrote this poem, "Thanks on Thanksgiving": Thanks for the harvest. Thanks for the food. Everybody let's celebrate. On the 28, of November. Thanks for all the harvest. Thanks for all the food.

When composing parent newsletters, with her students' help, Mrs. Thomas thinks aloud to help her students understand the thought processes behind writing. She often involves youngsters in thinking through questions important to the composition process. She gets them to think about the events of the week that might interest parents and about what announcements need to be made. As she composes, she asks herself aloud whether what she has written will make sense to parents. She also talks through some of her spelling and punctuation decisions. She might say, "That sentence is too hard to read unless you know to pause there; I guess I need a comma." Her comments on spelling distinguish between words that look as they sound and those that are impossible to sound out.

Ms. Montoya writes the daily schedule on the board as part of the opening session each morning. She comments about the content as she writes, wondering aloud if visitors to the classroom will understand the day's plan. She involves the youngsters in deciding whether the wording is clear enough. She also asks children to help her remember when she needs a period or quotation marks. Mrs. Hanna often adds a riddle to her daily schedule and, as she writes it, muses aloud about what those reading it might think. "Does this clue tell too much?" she asks. "Will anyone be able to make a guess from this clue?"

Even in preschool, Ms. Reynolds makes sure that children see her writing and using that form of communication as she continues the process of socializing youngsters into a literate world. When Justin proudly announces that he succeeded in putting together a certain difficult puzzle, Ms. Reynolds congratulates him and writes a note to his parents about his achievement. Justin watches as she writes and listens as she reads the note back to him. When he hears his mother read it later, he has a greater sense of what writing is about.

What children gain from adult demonstrations depends on the current understanding of each youngster. As youngsters become more sophisticated, they are ready to notice the teacher's procedures for adapting writing to a specific audience as well as how to punctuate for meaning. At first, they notice only that writing goes from one side to the other and then starts over again. Different children will get different kinds of information from the same literacy event. Children absorb only the information they can currently utilize and observe only what they are ready to see. The same writing model will be seen by one child as squiggles and by another as an important composition guide. All learners must fit new data into existing theory systems. Through this process, the learner's brain modifies information so that each person gets something different from the same lesson.

CHALLENGES TO EMERGING LITERACY

The smooth road to success in U.S. schools is to have an environment at home that closely matches that of the schools. Those who have the easiest time are generally children who talk like the teacher, who have been involved with books and writing at home, and whose parents have values similar to the teacher's. However, more and more, this description does not fit a large number of children in our schools (see Figure 5.16).

When youngsters write for an audience, they are motivated to learn standard conventions of print.

Some children whose home culture and language match those of their schools have difficulties nevertheless. For some children, the cause is clear—a hearing loss or Down syndrome, for instance. For others, the cause is a mystery to solve and address. Some youngsters have combinations of challenges, such as cultural differences coupled with fetal alcohol syndrome or poverty plus prenatal exposure to cocaine. All these children come to school, and all of them can be in your classroom. All of them can learn; meeting their unique needs and believing in their potential are the necessary components (Allington, 1998).

My store ubawt my lif

I levt wef my mom

se ded u los uv bad degs

so my gramu kod poles and day tuk hr a way

sow I wus en koort end I levd wef my ant

but my dad got kuste

dan we got to ulasku

dan I want to skow

dan I had frans

YES!

de and

The translation is:

The story about my life

I lived with my mom

she did a lot of bad things

so my grandma called the police and they took her a way

so I was in court and I lived with my aunt

but my dad got custody

then we got to Alaska

then I went to school

then I had friends

YES!

the end

FIGURE 5.16
This child's writing tells the story of a child whose life has not been easy. It also shows some evidence of English pronunciation influenced by having Spanish as her first language.

Poverty

One-fourth of all preschool children in the United States live in poverty. On any given night, between fifty thousand and two hundred thousand children have no home (Kameenui, 1998). More and more, single parents are struggling to provide for the needs of their families. Clearly, not all youngsters are going to have nightly bedtime stories or homes filled with reading and writing materials. Not all youngsters will come to school adequately fed, clothed, and rested. Not all will have their emotional needs met; many are neglected or even abused. School policies must address these issues as part of any educational plan. A child hungry for food or attention cannot attend to academics.

Some children do not come to school ready to learn. Mrs. Thomas has to defend these children's need for time to construct their own knowledge. She also has to defend the need for authentic literacy experiences more vigorously when she is teaching children whose homes haven't provided the literary knowledge provided in homes such as Betsy and Amy's. Children who have not developed understandings about print as part of their background experiences often receive inappropriate catch-up teaching efforts that merely provide intensive doses of information to be learned by rote (Roller, 1996).

Some educators, in their eagerness to help those youngsters catch up, seem to hope that knowledge can somehow be injected, as a timesaving tactic. Yet when teachers use this shortcut approach, they doubly deprive youngsters who have previously missed out on important literacy-socialization experiences. These youngsters missed out on literacy at home, and then they miss out again at school when they are not allowed the time and experiences to internalize understandings about written language. Ironically, those children who least need free time to explore print, those who already understand it, are more likely to be allowed the freedom to continue their explorations. Those who most need that opportunity are too often kept busy with remedial drills and segregated from their more able classmates (Kameenui, 1998). Mrs. Thomas continues to work at counteracting this practice. She strives to allow each child to have the necessary experiences for building firm foundations of understanding (Au, 1997).

Vanessa is flourishing with this approach to literacy. When she reads her long, dictated story to the class, she remembers every word. This child had the lowest level of literacy knowledge in the class at the start of the school year; she didn't even know when print was upside down. Yet through the open-ended activities of this classroom, she feels successful, is making good progress, and feels good about herself. Vanessa is involved in shared writing and independent writing just like her more advanced classmates, but she participates at her own level. She also receives directed instruction aimed at her own understandings and confusions as part of guided writing. Vanessa, like others who have further to go to become literate, benefits from a classroom in which she participates in the same kinds of activities as the other children (Yaden, Rowe, & MacGillivray, 2000). The only difference is that she and her classmates are treated as individuals, with individual learning needs and styles.

Diversity

A typical classroom in the United States today will include several youngsters whose home language is not English and one or more differently abled children. These children must be helped to write in whatever way is possible for each individual.

Diverse Languages

In previous discussions of shared writing, we have referred to the benefits of children's seeing how their *own* talk is written down. Some children come to school speaking a dialect of English, such as those spoken by some African American, Hawaiian, or Alaskan village children. Others come speaking Spanish, Tagalog, Russian, Chinese, or one of many other languages. Monolingual English-speaking teachers will be able to figure out how to write the dialects of English but will need help for other languages. We believe it is worth the effort to enlist the aid of a parent, older sibling, or other volunteers to help beginning writers see their own words made into print (Barnitz, 1997). This process also then creates reading material in their own language. After youngsters have figured out how print works, they can be helped to transfer that understanding to standard English.

Diverse Cultures

In writing, as in reading, cultural differences may create more problems than do the more obvious language differences. Some African American youngsters come from a culture in which storytelling differs quite a bit from most teachers' expectations. Researcher Anne Dyson (1990) documented a mismatch between a teacher's and a kindergarten girl's ideas of story. The teacher had difficulty following the child's dictated narratives, which were not linear but instead had an episodic quality and utilized rhythm and rhyme. This young African American girl had an excellent sense of a good story in her own culture, but it didn't match her teacher's understanding of a good story. If we are to help all children succeed in school, we must learn to respect the knowledge that all children bring with them to school.

Native American youngsters may be more used to learning from watching others than from having something explained (Casbon, Schirmer, & Twiss, 1997). For these children, the shared writing process would be valuable. But teachers who value risk taking in trying out writing theories may be disappointed. It is more common for Native American children to reflect on what they observe and practice it in private. Many of these youngsters prefer to perform the task publicly only after they feel confident about their ability (Stokes, 1997). Accepting all children into our classrooms means accepting diverse ways of learning. Accepting diverse ways of learning means honoring and providing for them.

You don't have to be from a minority culture to have a way of learning and thinking that doesn't match school expectations. Many highly creative individuals experience failure in U.S. schools. Children who have a unique way of doing things or of viewing situations may have their thinking rejected in classrooms in which one right answer is the goal. Good teachers cannot be egocentric in their thinking; they must strive to understand and honor how each child is thinking (Armington, 1997). Teachers who cannot do this doom many youngsters to failure because of the teachers' own inflexibility.

Diverse Abilities

Inclusion means making every child a part of your classroom community. This is a big challenge, and the schools must make a significant commitment to ensure that teachers and classrooms are ready for all children. It can be exciting to see the progress made by youngsters despite a physical challenge.

Flexibility is necessary when working with students who are differently abled as well as with those who have different learning styles. Adaptations of curriculum, environment, and teaching approaches may be necessary to meet children's special

Inclusion means making every child a part of your classroom community.

needs. Assistive technology, such as can be offered by computers, may be needed to enhance some children's ability to participate in class activities (Winter, 1997). Because there is so much teachers need to learn about how best to assist a child with special needs, parental involvement is especially important for these youngsters.

CONCLUSION

The most important academic idea for all children to learn is that writing and reading can be useful communication tools and satisfying activities. Even more important than immediate academic progress is that each child learn to believe in his or her ability to be ultimately successful with these processes.

We have presented an approach to teaching writing that encourages children to formulate and explore their own hypotheses about the process. Models of writing, both from reading materials and from adult demonstrations, play an essential role as children learn to write. Children's reading gives them models of correct writing forms, and adult demonstrations emphasize the thinking involved in the process of writing. Spelling, punctuation, and penmanship skills are taught as part of effective communication rather than as the main focus of writing instruction. Though children's own explorations are the primary source of their learning, the teacher's role is to encourage those explorations and to help youngsters improve their own writing through comparison with conventional forms.

DISCUSSION QUESTIONS

1. A fellow teacher questions your kindergarten journal-writing program, saying, "They don't even know their letters and sounds yet. How can they write?" Explain the value of journal writing for emergent writers in a way this teacher can understand.
2. A parent complains because her child is bringing home writing papers with phonics-based spelling. She says you are teaching her child bad spelling habits. How do you explain the approach to writing that you are using?

SUGGESTED FOLLOW-UP ACTIVITIES

1. Provide blank paper and writing materials to preschool, kindergarten, and first-grade children and encourage them to write. Observe and ask questions to discover the various theories they use in their writing. Can you determine through this process what they think writing is, how they think it is done, and what they think it is used for?
2. Ask to borrow (or copy) samples of children's writing and compare these papers with children's writing samples collected by others. As a group activity, classify the samples of children's writing according to forms described in this chapter and in Chapter 1.
3. Encourage a child or a small group of children to tell about an experience or make up a story. Help them write it down. Follow the dictation or shared writing procedures described in this chapter. What did you learn about the child or children in this activity? What did you learn about the dictation process? What were the children learning?

RECOMMENDED FURTHER READING

Au, K. H. (1997). Literacy for all students: Ten steps toward making a difference. *The Reading Teacher, 51*(3), 186–194.

Bradley, D. H., & Pottle, P. R. (2000). Supporting emergent writers through on-the-spot conferencing and publishing. *Young Children, 53*(1), 20–27.

Dahl, K. L., & Scharer, P. L. (2000). Phonics teaching and learning in whole language classrooms: New evidence from research. *The Reading Teacher, 53*(7), 584–594.

Oken-Wright, P. (1998). Transition to writing: Drawing as a scaffold for emergent writers. *Young Children, 53*(2), 76–81.

Owens, R. F., Hester, J. L., & Teale, W. H. (2002). Where do you want to go today? Inquiry-based learning and technology integration. *The Reading Teacher, 55*(7), 616–625.

6

SUPPORTING INDEPENDENT WRITERS

Children turn to writing with . . . pleasure when they are in control of the process—when they are able to write and draw on topics of their choosing, and bring the elements of their imagining and play worlds on the page.

Ruth Shagoury Hubbard, 1996

Having watched children get started as readers and writers, let's follow this approach to literacy through the primary grades. If you are a teacher who believes that children learn what is relevant to their own experiences and interests, you will continue emphasizing those experiences and interests in classroom activities at any grade level. If you believe that children learn in an active rather than a passive mode, you will continue the exploration-and-discovery approach to learning beyond first grade. If you believe that children learn best when they have confidence in themselves as learners and experience joy in the learning process, you will nurture successes rather than point out failures for second- and third-grade writers as well as for younger students.

Chapters 2 and 3 showed how children's literacy is nurtured though play, large-motor activity, and real experience. Chapters 4 and 5 described how children become literate through their experiences with language and print. These experiences should not stop just because a child has become literate. Being talked to, listened to, and read to continue to be important for a budding reader and writer. Having opportunities to climb and jump, build block towers, and dam up mud puddles also continues to provide insights, understanding, and enthusiasm for writing, talking, and reading.

The next two chapters will describe how children learn to read better through additional writing experiences and learn to write better through additional reading experiences.

Remember Betsy's brothers and sisters? Remember Joey? Let's visit his class and observe how his second-grade teacher, Mr. Larson, nurtures reading and writing. Later, we'll also visit Mrs. Williams's room across the hall. If Joey gets his wish, this will be his third-grade class next year.

AN ENVIRONMENT FOR WRITING

Joey's teacher, Mr. Larson, has several goals for creating a classroom that encourages, nurtures, and teaches writing. His first goal is to develop positive attitudes and an appreciation of beginning writing—in himself, in his students, and in the parents of his students. Second, he wishes to provide a rich spectrum of experiences from which his students can draw when they write. Finally, he must provide the classroom structure for writing—time, materials, and routines. When these goals are in place, the children will have plenty of opportunities to write, and Mr. Larson will have an optimum environment for teaching.

Attitudes That Encourage Writing

Beginning writers are generally enthusiastic, creative, and eager to improve, but they are far from proficient (Fraser & Skolnick, 1994). If Mr. Larson made his *second-grade* students wait until they could spell correctly, write legibly, and use proper punctuation, years would pass before they could possibly become writers. By waiting until they became proficient, children would waste valuable time when they could be gaining the benefits of actually writing: understanding the purposes and procedures of communication through print. They would also miss out on opportunities to explore spelling, punctuation, and word choice and to practice handwriting. Probably the biggest waste would be their lost enthusiasm and confidence.

Acceptance

An environment conducive to writing means an accepting environment (Mallett, 1999; Tompkins, 2003). In an accepting environment, Mr. Larson understands that first drafts by nature are messy and contain what most adults consider errors in spelling and mechanics. He understands that some writing is for personal purposes and needn't be shared. His class schedule includes time for thinking and inspiration and never requires lockstep participation in a prescribed topic or format. Class members learn to share their writing with their peers and to be constructive listeners and responders. The *process* of writing is valued as much as the products and accomplishments of the young writers.

Encouragement

Mr. Larson knows how to encourage kids to write. He is willing to fight through hundred-word run-on sentences with no punctuation and little recognizable spelling to find out what a child is trying to say. He then responds to the writer's message rather than to the writer's mistakes (Frank, 2001). Mr. Larson may comment that he can tell from Joey's story about fishing with his dad that Joey felt scared when they almost capsized in some rapids on the river. What about the twenty-five misspelled words and the twenty missing periods Mr. Larson seems to ignore? Is he contributing to a generation of writers whose writing no one can read? No one wants that, of course, but neither do we want people who can pass spelling and punctuation tests but are afraid to write.

How do we get the best of both worlds? We rely on Joey's own desire to communicate through his writing. When he is enthusiastic about his ability to express his feelings and share his experiences through writing, he will want to make sure others can read what he has written. After Mr. Larson has responded to the meaning and purpose of the writing, when appropriate, he will help Joey revise and proofread his story in preparation for sharing it with others. At this point, Joey will be open to Mr. Larson's instruction in composition, spelling, punctuation, and other writer's tools.

Modeling

Mr. Larson makes his classroom writing workshop time even more safe for young writers by modeling being a writer himself (Au, 1997). He lets his students see him write, make mistakes, get frustrated, and have to revise and, perhaps, throw away writing attempts. Mr. Larson will often read something he has written to the class or to one or two students to get feedback. He finds student input especially helpful when he tries to describe class activities for the parent newsletter. Mr. Larson's writing isn't limited to newsletters, however. He composes funny rhymes and stories about students and class activities, and he occasionally writes down stories he has made up to entertain his own three little boys. Mr. Larson is a good model of a competent, amateur adult writer who can share both the hard work and the occasional glory of being a writer.

Respect

Because he is a writer himself, Mr. Larson has the greatest respect for any child who is writing, and he expects children to respect each other as well. Early in the year, the class discussed writing etiquette and, as a group, created guidelines for being a member of a community of writers. It takes time to form a community of writers (Gillet & Beverly, 2001). Mr. Larson knows it is time well invested. Over the years, many rules have been generated by Mr. Larson's classes. Whichever rules are chosen for the year, Mr. Larson models the attitudes for his students and teaches the children how to be respectful of and helpful to one another. *See the "Ideas for Respecting Each Other as Writers" box.*

Purpose

Helping students establish their purposes for writing is essential. When children have a message and an audience in mind, they want to write (Calkins, 1994; Fletcher & Portalupi, 2001; Graves, 1994). Neither Mr. Larson nor Mrs. Williams assigns writing topics or even insists that all children write at a given time. These teachers know that the desire to write must come from the child's own interest. They have found that allowing children not to write when they don't feel like it does much more for attitudes about writing than insisting that every child write every day. Of course, their goal remains to have children writing daily.

To help children establish purposes for writing, these teachers provide a stimulating environment in which much happens to write about. Animals in the class, field trips, visitors to the class, science experiments, and new books contin-

---

IDEAS FOR RESPECTING EACH OTHER AS WRITERS

Listen when others are reading.
Give positive suggestions.
Ask real questions for clarification.
Be a good editor.
Get help from each other.
Help others when they ask you for help.
Don't bother someone who is reading or writing.
Share materials.

If they put me in the zoo
what could I do?
I could be a Elafint
or a Sercas trainer
or maby a little scinyor.
I would fly and jump.
Or maby ride on a hump.
And sing with the Birds
and eat erbs
And crackl! crackl! snackl! snackl!
If they put me in the zoo
wat could I do?

FIGURE 6.1
Poem by Summer Koester.

uously provide exciting subjects. Books and poetry shared with students have the dual effect of providing ideas for content and ideas for form. Youngsters may try to write in the style of a much-enjoyed author, such as Judith Viorst, or start writing poems similar to the humorous ones by Shel Silverstein (Figure 6.1).

Independence

A hallmark of process writing programs is that children are expected to develop and exhibit a great deal of autonomy (Graves, 1994). Mr. Larson and Mrs. Williams expect children to select their own topics for writing. They teach their students to read, evaluate, and revise their own writing and to give and take response from their peers. They must learn to work in small groups without the teacher and to accept help from visitors to the classroom. Mr. Larson and Mrs. Williams teach strategies and processes and expect children to learn to make their own decisions in selecting them. Young writers learn to find their own writing materials and to keep track of their writing folders themselves. Finally, these teachers require their children to take part in formal evaluation procedures and in reporting their own progress to their parents. Obviously, trust and high expectations exist when teachers give up so much of their "power" to their students.

A Developmental Philosophy

Normal children develop on different time lines (McDevitt & Ormrod, 2002). Mr. Larson allows his second graders to keep the kind of control over their learning that their kindergarten and first-grade teachers allowed. This means that most of his teaching is responding to what each child is trying to do. For example, Carlos's reading skills have developed so that he is now able to learn plenty of information from books. So Mr. Larson has steered him toward *What's Inside My Body?* (Royston, 1991), which Carlos reads himself. During their next conference, Mr. Larson will work with Carlos to brainstorm a good way to present, in writing, what Carlos wants to share with the class. Thien, on the other hand, is trying to write sentences about the pictures he draws. Mr. Larson ignores the fact that many of Thien's classmates went through this stage in kindergarten and encourages his sentences. Thien's picture of the eggs hatching, captioned "TDY THE JKKENS PEKT OT," hangs proudly from the ceiling above the chicken cage. Thien has good reason to be proud of his work—he has learned to speak and write in English in only two years of school!

Beginning writers are not proficient writers, but they can quickly become proficient by doing more writing.

Mr. Larson recognizes that children develop at different rates, and he supports all his students as they develop. He knows that normal children begin to read and write anywhere from age four to age eight, and he does not place any stigma on the late bloomer. In Thien's case, Mr. Larson celebrates the fact that Thien has progressed enough in the English language to begin reading and writing. Mr. Larson has seen second graders who were already labeled failures by age seven because they were not reading or writing fluently. He laments such labeling and never allows the late bloomers in his classroom to be viewed as remedial or special-education students just because their developmental clocks are different from those of other children.

Sharing the Attitudes with Parents

Mr. Larson also recognizes that many of the parents and community members he encounters are unfamiliar with, confused by, or even hostile about his approach to literacy. A major goal, then, is to provide experience and education for adults in the classroom. Mr. Larson invites all parents to participate in his class during writing workshop and provides them with ways to be helpful. Those who are available during the day listen to writers read their work, provide guidance in small groups, and circulate among the children as they write. Others may be called on to type up children's stories or to copy them and bind them into classroom books. Still others might arrange an occasional poetry reading or writers' breakfast. Mr. Larson finds that the more he exposes parents to the children's work, the more they understand the developmental approach, in which writing is not necessarily perfect. In addition, Mr. Larson shares his program at open house and other parent functions and discusses aspects of writing in letters to the children's parents. Of course, positive assessment techniques, as we'll discuss in Chapter 8, show parents the benefits of his balanced approach to teaching writing.

Content That Encourages Writing

The first thing you see when you walk into Mr. Larson's class is a chicken-wire enclosure in the center of the room. Five tiny chicks hop around under a pair of heat lamps. On the way to his seat, Joey stops to pick up a chick, kisses its beak, and gently puts it back. Joey knows a lot about these chicks; he and the class have been watching a dozen eggs for the past month. In his science folder, Joey has charts he made of the weekly development of the embryos, along with a written journal describing each stage of their development. He learned how chicks grow and hatch from spending time observing them, from listening to Mr. Larson, from reading library books, from research on the Internet, and from daily talking with his friends as they waited for the chicks to hatch. Today Joey is wondering how long it will take for the chicks to be full grown, and he plans to bring this question up during this morning's class meeting. Joey is lucky that his teacher considers chickens an important topic for writing. Mr. Larson provides a variety of possibilities for writing topics—children's interests, social studies, science and literature, and children's personal lives and experiences.

CHAPTER 6

Children's Interests

What may appear at first to be a classroom steeped in science activities is actually one with reading and writing as its focus. Mr. Larson bases his language arts program on his children's and his own interests. Instead of focusing on what a reading or writing program says should be studied each week and month, Mr. Larson tunes in to what the children are interested in (Koeller & Mitchell, 1996, 1997). He arranges for exciting things to go on in the classroom and then bases reading and writing on these happenings. For example, last October, after Mr. Larson read *Whale Brother* (Steiner, 1988) to the class, the children voted to study whales. In November, Carolina's family visited relatives in Mexico, so while she was gone the class followed her trip with an in-depth study of Mexico. Since several children in the class had new brothers and sisters, January had two "baby weeks," highlighted by visits from the babies, a text set full of books about baby siblings, and a class book of poetry about infants. May is "outdoor education month," and the class will take hikes in different ecosystems each Friday. Their observations are often recorded in their daily journals.

Content Integration

Mr. Larson finds that organizing writing and reading around good books or around science or social studies topics gives the class time to meet more content curriculum demands, is never boring, and provides the class with a continuing common ground for discussion and learning. He knows that second graders are not interested in reading and writing just to be reading and writing; in fact, neither is he. Instead, they are all interested in what they can learn and enjoy *using* reading and writing. Mr. Larson is interested in local plants and animals, art, and hiking. He doesn't have to wait until summer vacation to enjoy the things he loves; instead, he does them all year with the second grade. Although his classroom is small, there is still room for a parakeet and a minigreenhouse. An art gallery hangs above the coat hooks. Mr. Larson's enthusiasm for the projects is contagious—he says he gets excited about learning, and that excitement seems to spread through the class. Mr. Larson uses content as the vehicle to teach reading and writing processes by providing interesting activities for children to do, to talk and think about, and then to read and write about (Harvey, 2002; Routman, 2000). Mr. Larson and Mrs. Williams have found that their process-oriented math programs require writing, and they agree that problem solving via writing is a powerful learning opportunity (Whitin & Whitin, 1997).

Mr. Larson and Mrs. Williams recognize that nonfiction enhances understanding. Learning is about understanding things, not just knowing things (Gardner, 1991). Investigating the read world encourages children to inquire further, which will lead to deeper understanding. Stephanie Harvey (2002) advocates sharing wonder and passion about the world. This morning, as Joey and his friends come into the room, they cluster around their teacher with information they have to share. Yesterday the children generated questions about chickens; last night they researched them. Today they are eager to tell about the rules for keeping chickens in the neighborhood, about how to tell if a chick is male or female, and if handling them too much could make them sick. Mr. Larson is almost overwhelmed with all the answers and asks each child to sit with a friend, tell what he or she has found out, and then write discoveries in a personal journal. Wonder and passion about the world are contagious in Mr. Larson's room.

Literature

Mr. Larson also knows that writers are readers and that readers are writers. He does not separate out these two processes but instead constantly stresses their interconnections. Often after reading a book to the children, he'll casually point out tricks the writer used to make the story, poem, or article work. This week, when he read *Whale Brother*, he asked the children to think of other stories in which a boy has to go out alone in the world to prove himself. The children thought of *Jack and the Beanstalk*, which some of them had read in a small group. After they discussed the similarities and differences in the stories, some of the boys began to write their own stories using a "quest" story structure. Children who read widely and listen to a variety of stories read aloud are exposed to rich vocabulary, beautiful phrasing, and a plethora of types of writing. When a seven-year-old looks at an old-fashioned Christmas card and says, "It's a picture of a parlor," we know the child probably heard that word in literature, not in everyday talk.

Personal Journals and Correspondence

Mr. Larson schedules time for writing in personal journals every day. During journal time, children are free to write as they please (Rasinski & Padak, 2000). Mr. Larson reads these journals only at the invitation of their owners and never corrects the journal entries. Most second graders love to share their journals with their teachers, and Mr. Larson's children are no exception. At the end of the school day, they may leave their journals in a special basket by Mr. Larson's desk. Most evenings, Mr. Larson makes time to read and respond to all the journals.

Reading and responding to journals has become one of Mr. Larson's favorite parts of teaching. He enjoys having a few private moments in each child's world and feels he comes to know each individual better this way. He has disciplined himself to respond honestly to what the children are trying to say, not how they say it. Often this means echoing their messages, as in Figure 6.2. Sometimes children are struggling to understand their lives, and Mr. Larson believes his nonjudgmental replies in their journals can help them understand their feelings.

But most of the time, these dialogues in the journals are just plain good fun. The children look forward to reading Mr. Larson's replies when they come into class in the morning and are disappointed if he hasn't had time to read the journals.

Mr. Larson hopes that in time the second graders will expand their dialogue-journal topics, especially to tell him about the books they are reading. He encourages children to pass their journals to each other for response too, sort of like the note passing that was so deliciously fun and strictly forbidden in his elementary school days.

*Writers are readers, and
readers are writers.*

This year, Mr. Larson has also started a home-school journal. Each Friday during workshop, the children are asked to write briefly about the most significant thing that happened at school that week. The journal is sent home, and parents are invited to respond and return the journal on Monday. This real communication allows parents a personal view of what is going on in school. The home-school journal also provides parents with a good weekly look at writing development over the school year.

Warm-Ups

Despite this rich classroom environment, there are still several children in the class who bluntly state that they don't like to write and don't know what to write about. Others are still afraid to fast-write and ignore spelling difficulties. With

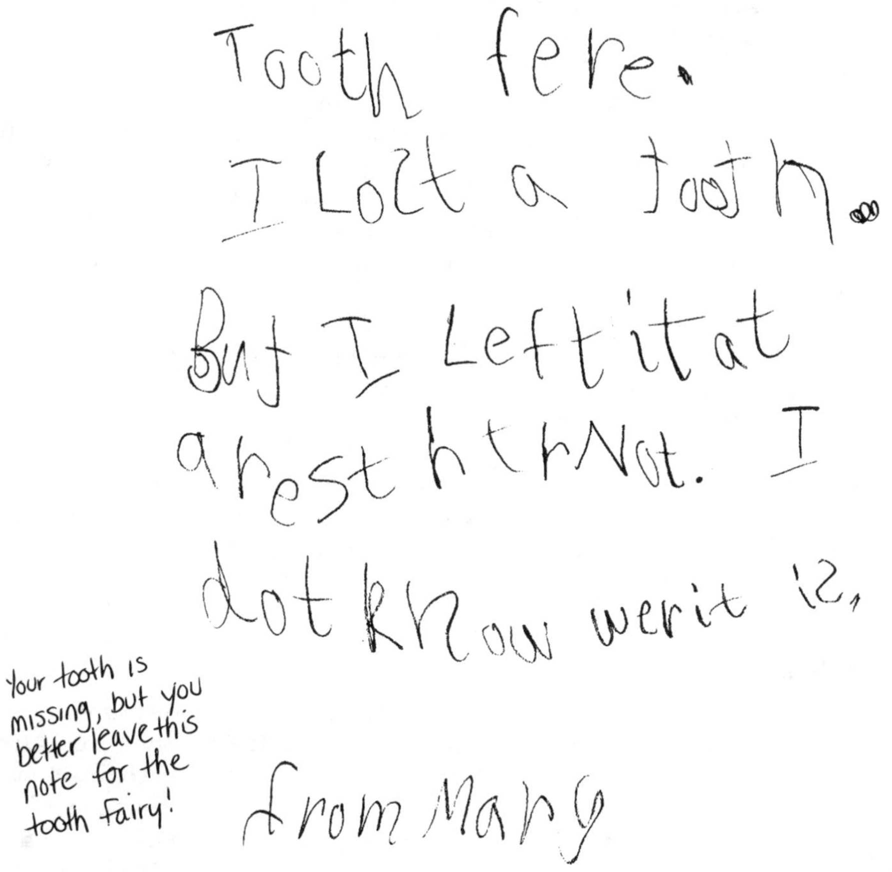

Tooth fere.
I Loct a tooth.
But I Left it at
a rest h t rNot. I
dot kNow werit iz,

Your tooth is
missing, but you
better leave this
note for the
tooth fairy!

from Mary

FIGURE 6.2

The teacher responds to a student's letter to the "Tooth fere."

these children in mind, Mrs. Williams takes time each day to lead her third-grade class in playing around with words and language. She tries to find as many interesting modes of writing as possible and gives a little writing warm-up each day. Yesterday Mrs. Williams was in conference with Shawn, a boy who has little interest in writing but a great deal of interest in other things. Mrs. Williams wrote down a riddle that Shawn asked her, and they both laughed over the absurdity of it. Mrs. Williams suggested that the other kids would love these riddles and encouraged Shawn to make a list of all his favorites and then write some of them down for a riddle book. Because each item was a short and manageable writing segment, Shawn felt more comfortable with this task. The next day, Shawn shared the riddles he had written down with the class and said he needed more riddles for his book. Mrs. Williams suggested to the class that each child submit a favorite to Shawn and appointed him editor of the riddle book. It will be Shawn's job to review the riddles for inclusion in his book and later to be in charge of the book's publication.

Short writing such as this often serves as the best starting place. Mr. Larson's second-grade class is having fun with bumper-sticker messages. The students look for them when they go driving with their families and when they ride on the school bus. They try to remember their favorites to write on the supply of "bumper-sticker paper" Mr. Larson keeps on hand. Making up messages of their own, they have revealed some of the unique aspects of second-grade humor. Mr. Larson and Mrs. Williams know that what the children are writing is silly, but the important fact is that they are writing.

Mrs. Williams encourages her third-grade students to analyze magazine and television commercials and to write their own. She knows that television commercials grab children's interest with their catchy jingles and fast pace. Commercials offer children a high-interest topic for writing. She helps youngsters think about persuasive techniques used in advertising and asks questions such as "Will you really have as good a time as they show people having if you drink that brand of pop?" Mrs. Williams's students respond by making up their own advertising skits and rhymes with outrageous claims for fictitious products.

Webbing

Mr. Larson has found that visual webbing activities often help children find a clearer picture of what they wish to write about (D'Angelo-Bromley, 1996). After reading *Coyote in Love* (Dwyer, 1997), Sasha wanted to write about the main character, Coyote, but she was having trouble getting started. Mr. Larson suggested a web about Coyote. Together, they quickly produced a schematic drawing that summarized Coyote's character, his problem, and the resolution of the story, and Sasha was ready to write (see Figure 6.3).

Mr. Larson uses webs for many purposes: to introduce a story or something interesting in social studies or science, as a read-along tool during shared reading to emphasize the plot or character development, and as a way to assess what children know. He finds that this nonlinear, visual presentation of information is useful for many young children. In fact, he has used similar processes himself to organize and learn information in his graduate classes.

Materials

Besides emotional safety and a content- and literature-rich environment, children need materials for writing. We described writing centers in Chapter 5. Mr. Larson and Mrs. Williams have their own versions of writing centers in their classrooms too. In a designated bookshelf, they provide a variety of papers, bookbinding materials, glue, tape, scissors, and an abundance of writing tools—pencils, felt-tipped markers, colored pencils, and pens. No child can ever use the excuse "I don't have a pencil" for not writing! Each classroom has computers that are used almost exclusively for writing, revising, and publishing.

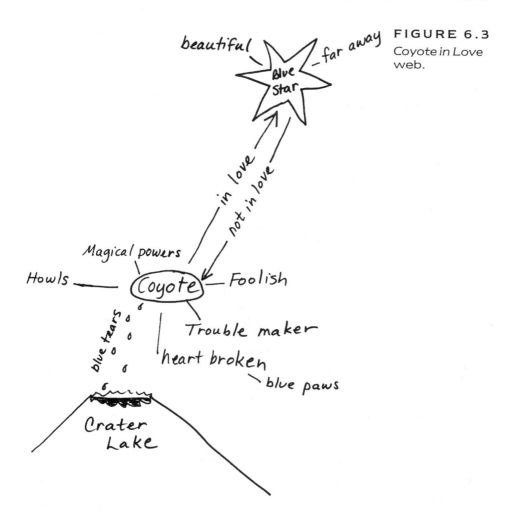

FIGURE 6.3
Coyote in Love web.

Their second- and third-grade classrooms are stimulating, safe, and literate places for Joey and his friends. Let's take a look at how Mr. Larson and Mrs. Williams actually set up their writing workshops.

ORGANIZING THE CLASSROOM FOR INDEPENDENT WRITERS

You have seen how Ms. Reynolds, Mrs. Thomas, and Ms. Montoya structure dictation, shared writing, and guided writing into their school days. As children develop from emergent to beginning writers, they crave and need time for more independent writing. Mrs. Williams provides this through writing workshop. Within the workshop format, children learn a process for writing, and guidance is provided via minilessons and writing conferences.

The Writing Workshop

Although reading and writing go on all day in this class, Mrs. Williams has designated a special time after morning recess for writing every day. Generally, this period lasts from thirty to forty-five minutes. She often starts with sharing something she's written or encouraging one or two children to read their polished projects to the entire group. Sometimes, Mrs. Williams uses this time to give a minilesson to all the children, for instance, reviewing the use of an apostrophe in contractions or sharing some exciting leads or opening lines.

After a short time of listening or sharing, the children are on their own for writing workshop. The writing activities vary, but Mrs. Williams asks the children to try to spend some time each day writing in their journals and some time working on a project. To facilitate the process, a huge "DON'T DISTURB: WRITERS AT WORK" sign hangs over one corner table. Here children can expect to work without interruption from other children or the teacher. On the table are large jars of pencils; nearby are shelves with paper and other supplies. The computer is reserved for writing, and many of the children have learned to use *Kidspiration*, a word processing program. Talking and sharing with friends, groups, or teachers is of course encouraged but not near this quiet writing center.

Some days, Mrs. Williams uses writing workshop time to write herself. But most days, she works with children one on one. She may circulate around the room, kneeling down beside her young writers for brief questions or instructions, or she may have more formal writing conferences at her desk. The bulk of her time is spent focusing on individual children. Luckily, Mrs. Williams has been able to enlist several parents and one classroom aide to be in the room during writing workshop. These adults work one on one with children too as well as keep an eye out for disruptions that might make children lose focus on their writing.

In Mr. Larson's room, the children have their own writing folders, which are supposed to remain in their cubbies at night. In these folders are drafts of current projects, a list of possible topics, and a log in which Mr. Larson asks the children to fill in what they have done each day. Journals can be kept in here too. Beside Mr. Larson's desk is an open file box in which he has a large hanging file for each child. This is where he keeps special finished projects, clipped with their drafts, dated, and ready to share with parents during conference time.

These files of students' papers help Mr. Larson communicate the same positive message to parents that he communicates to his students. As he explains the goals of the writing process and invites parents to observe the children in class, he provides examples of the types of writing children do and the progress they have made. He is able to explain the peer-editing process and show parents the "student edited" stamp. The teachers want to help parents become involved in what their children are learning, and they try to enlist the parents' help. Certainly, parents continue to influence their children's attitudes and motivation.

Children can expect to work in the writing center without interruption.

Even in such a stimulating, accepting environment, second and third graders may need more help in developing the desire and self-discipline to write every day. Pencils disappear, drafts get lost, and a talkative friend can easily distract a child from the task at hand. Mr. Larson and Mrs. Williams believe that an organized room and a few systems can help children learn to develop their own ability to organize. When you visit Mrs. Williams's room, you'll probably be overwhelmed with all that's going on there. Mrs. Williams says that neither she nor the children could tolerate all this action if it weren't for the important organizing that is done behind the scene. Children need to be taught where to go for help. They must know where materials are kept and how to use their writing folders. They must learn to use a writing process (which we'll discuss next). Finally, they must clearly understand the boundaries of acceptable behavior within the writing workshop (Graves, 1994).

Writing workshop is often a noisy, busy time. It took Mrs. Williams a while to get used to writing as a noisy rather than a quiet time. But the results are well worth the initial stress: folders bursting with drafts and finished products and children who are confident in their powers as writers. She remembers well her experiences as a child: the groans that accompanied the teacher's announcement that it was "time for creative writing. Now write a story!" Instead, Mrs. Williams now hears groans when she reminds the children that they have five minutes to wrap up what they're doing. Many children list writing workshop as their second favorite time of the day, with recess coming in first!

CHAPTER 6

A PROCESS FOR WRITING

Mrs. Williams finds that the open-ended process writing approach supports her view of how young children learn (Spandel, 1996). Let's observe youngsters working in many of the stages of the writing process (Table 6.1). Some third graders are mature enough to proceed through all the stages; others are content to simply write a first draft.

Prewriting Experience

Many students are working on the first phase, the *prewrite experience*. Aaron and Ruben are discussing soccer prior to writing about their involvement on a soccer team. (Their actual experience of playing soccer also served as an important part of the prewriting experience for this topic.) They review events of the last game, remember interesting plays, and brainstorm together, recalling events to include in a story. They make a list of special words needed for this story: *referee*, *goalie*, *forward*, *halfback*, and *score*. Prewriting experiences can take many forms—some, like a field trip, are organized by the teacher. Many other experiences can come from the world outside school.

Fastwrite

Michelle works on the next phase, *fastwriting*, which will result in her first draft. Some teachers call this a "sloppy copy" because the important thing is simply to get something down on paper. If Michelle were writing in her personal journal or doing some other writing that she didn't plan to share with anyone and had no desire to polish, this could be her only draft. Sometimes the writing experience is

TABLE 6.1
The Writing Process

Prewrite	Participate in an experience Talk about the experience Brainstorm Think about audience, form, and purpose Webbing	
Fastwrite	Put notes and ideas on paper Prepare "sloppy copy," or first draft	
Share, respond, and revise	Read and share first draft with others Receive feedback Change and rewrite draft using feedback	This stage may be repeated more than once
Edit	Proofread and polish details of final draft	
Publish	Prepare final copy Share with others	
Evaluate	Assess effectiveness of process and product	

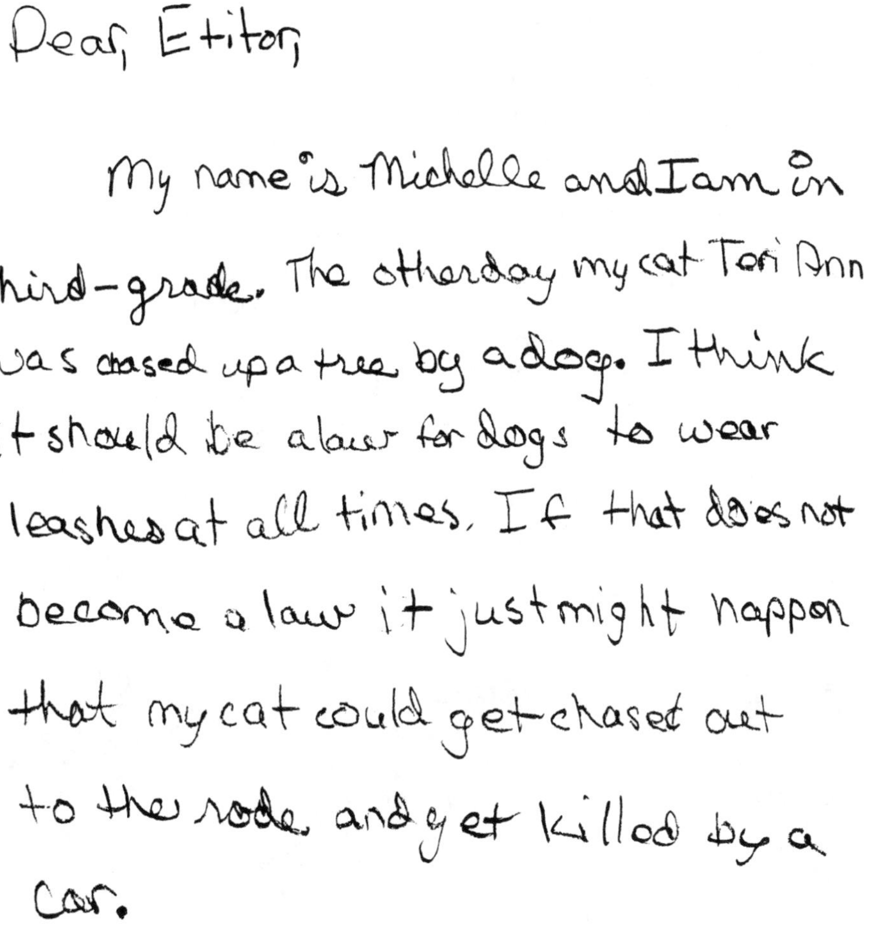

Dear Etitor,

My name is Michelle and I am in third-grade. The otherday my cat Tori Ann was chased up a tree by a dog. I think it should be a law for dogs to wear leashes at all times. If that does not become a law it just might happen that my cat could get chased out to the rode and get killod by a car.

FIGURE 6.4
Michelle's letter to the "Etitor."

valuable for just getting ideas or feelings on paper, so spelling, punctuation, and style are unimportant at this stage. Today Michelle drafts a letter to the editor for the local newspaper. Her letter requests better enforcement of the leash law for dogs; she is upset about this because a dog chased her cat up a tree yesterday (Figure 6.4).

Respond and Revise

In this case, Michelle wants to write as correctly as possible, clearly stating her case. So she moves into the *response* phase. After rereading what she has written, she reads the letter to her friend Kenesha to find out if she has clearly stated her message. Kenesha tells Michelle which parts she understands and points out a sentence that doesn't make sense to her. Together the girls plan some changes that they think strengthen the letter. Michelle then *revises* the letter and plans to read it to a group for further feedback.

The next day, Michelle meets with a small group to read her letter draft; the others in the group are also in the respond and revise phase of their writing. Each child takes turns sharing a draft and requesting peer responses. They have practiced the procedure with Mrs. Williams and now can meet without her. Their comments emphasize the positive, and we hear statements such as "I liked the part about how glad your cat was to get down from the tree" or "You really made me feel how scared your kitty was." Other comments help focus on clarifications needed, such as "I don't understand how the law will protect your cat." Michelle makes further changes in her letter as she moves through the *revision* process. She does not hesitate to add or delete sentences or to replace a word with a better one. At last Michelle feels satisfied that her letter makes her point. By the end of this year, she will be comfortable with totally reorganizing a paper.

There is little question that revision is the most difficult part of the writing process—we can testify to that in our experience in rewriting new editions of this book! For young writers, there are three main types of revision: adding, deleting, and changing. Adding is simple, changing is manageable, but deleting is an ex-

In a writing response group each child takes a turn sharing a draft and requesting a response.

I liked the part about_____ because . . .

Could you tell me more about . . . ?

Would you explain . . . ?

FIGURE 6.5

Ideas for responding to writing.

tremely painful process for young writers who usually see more as better. Mrs. Williams finds that only repeated demonstrations of the revision process, using her own or students' writing, help children understand the value of deletion. As writers mature, other, more sophisticated processes of revision can be developed.

One of the more difficult parts of the writing process for these third graders to learn was working in response groups. Mrs. Williams knew that just telling them to work in these groups would never work, so she first invited a group of fifth graders in to model how their response groups function. After this demonstration, Mrs. Williams and the children brainstormed and then made a poster of a list of questions and comments that were positive and appropriate as responses (Figure 6.5).

Another day, Mrs. Williams asked a small group of children to try to be her response group for a story she had written about their field trip. As the rest of the class watched and commented, Mrs. Williams coached the children in asking her appropriate questions and giving her encouraging yet honest feedback. Soon some of the children were asking to form their own response groups. Many third graders still have a very difficult time responding in groups without their teacher, but by now all the children at least have the idea of how response groups work.

Edit

Michelle doesn't plan to ask for any further feedback on content, although when she wrote a fairly long play recently, she went through the response-and-revision process several times before she felt satisfied with her final product. Now she is ready for the fourth phase, *editing*. This is the time for polishing her paper by proofreading details such as spelling, grammar, punctuation, paragraphing, and handwriting. Mrs. Williams helps with the proofreading, involving Michelle in the process through comments such as "Do any of the words look funny to you?" Mrs. Williams wants her students to learn spelling both as a visual image of how a word looks and as an intuitive, kinesthetic knowledge of which letter to write next. She never uses oral spelling drills or even written practices of writing words over and over to "practice" spelling. She knows that neither of these approaches will carry over to the actual use of spelling in writing. Later in this chapter, we will look at more details of how these teachers embed spelling instruction in the editing phase.

The amount of proofreading for punctuation varies with different students. Michelle is fairly sophisticated in her understanding of punctuation, but other students may be ready for only some basics. Mrs. Williams encourages all students to read their work aloud to determine where punctuation marks might be needed to direct the reader. Long pauses may require periods; small pauses may require commas. The inflection and tone of voice will indicate question marks and exclamation marks. When children learn punctuation and paragraphing as part of making their writing more clear to others, they truly understand concepts of punctuation and are able to use them in future writing. At times, Mrs. Williams sees a punctuation or word-choice problem that a number of children are making in their writing and chooses to do a minilesson with these children. Later in this chapter, we will see a minilesson in action.

Publish

Neatness and handwriting count on the final draft. If Michelle wants the editors of her town's newspaper to take her letter seriously, she knows her work must be legible and clear. Michelle carefully rewrites her letter to make it ready for the next-to-last phase, *publishing*. Other types of publishing include making copies of a story or poem for the class or school library, displaying a captioned art project outside the classroom, sending a factual report of information requested by younger students to their classroom, putting on a play or puppet show, or simply sending a letter to an intended audience.

Mrs. Williams is always concerned that children view writing as real communication and therefore works to find real modes of publication. In her class you can see a class newspaper, pen-pal activities, and large-scale production of the student's original books, and she is always looking for other legitimate ways of sharing work in the classroom.

Mrs. Williams's students love the Author's Chair, which is scheduled once a week (Graves, 1994). Children voluntarily sign up for this special time to share their completed work with the rest of the class. This week LaMarr sits in the special chair, sings a song he has written about his favorite basketball team, and passes out copies of the lyrics he wrote. He then receives special attention and feedback and a round of applause. He leaves school feeling good about his writing and about himself. No child is required to have a turn in the Author's Chair, but by the end of the year most of the second and third graders are eager to be recognized in front of others for their writing accomplishments.

Mrs. Williams encourages students to use the classroom computer for word processing if their written work is lengthy. Using word processing makes the revision and polishing processes much easier since the entire paper doesn't need to be rewritten each time a child makes a change. Of course, having been done on the computer, the final product looks professional, offering a perfectly typed copy.

Evaluate

Several weeks later, Michelle's letter and several others for and against a leash law appeared in the newspaper. Mrs. Williams cut out the page from the paper and put it in Michelle's writing folder. Later on, when she and Michelle were going through the folder, Mrs. Williams asked Michelle if she thought the letter had done any good. When Michelle replied that the dog that had chased her cat was now fenced

Using word processing makes the revision and editing processes much easier.

in the neighbor's backyard, Mrs. Williams said she thought that the letter had changed the owner's mind. Mrs. Williams is gently guiding Michelle in the reflective process of self-evaluation.

Mrs. Williams also pulled out a copy of a letter Michelle had written to her grandparents at the beginning of the year. In comparing the two, Michelle notes that she now knows how to start a paragraph. Mrs. Williams points out that Michelle is now able to write to a public audience and that's why the letter was published. Michelle leaves the conference feeling proud of herself, and Mrs. Williams records Michelle's accomplishments in her notebook. She makes a note to herself to share the two letters with Michelle's mother next week at parent conferences.

You have seen how Mr. Larson and Mrs. Williams constantly integrate content into their writing programs. Writing is a powerful way to learn subject matter (Vacca & Vacca, 1999). After all, without interesting things to write about, why bother? By second or third grade, teachers must also purposefully help children pay attention to spelling, punctuation, grammar, and the mechanics of writing as well as to elements of the craft of writing. Mr. Larson and Mrs. Williams know that

GUIDELINES FOR TEACHING WRITING

Children strive to write so that others understand their meaning. Always respond to the meaning of a child's message first. Then arrange opportunities for feedback to help children revise their writing so that others understand it.

Children use their natural language when they begin to write their thoughts. Accept all of children's writings until they are confident that they can write. Then gradually introduce polishing for more effective communication and standard language usage.

Children continue to discover how language works when they write frequently and for various purposes. Provide opportunities for children to use their writing to explore alternative ways of expressing thoughts.

Children write more often, and more effectively, if they are aware of progress and success in writing. Focus on specific areas of progress in responding to a child's writing; encourage this same focus in feed back from peers.

teaching such concepts in isolation is inefficient and developmentally inappropriate. Still, they must help children approximate their writing to conventional standards. Second and third graders have enough experience with print to recognize and demand that their work be "right." Therefore, their teachers must teach conventions in the context of children's writing. Textbooks, work sheets, and curricula don't work—they provide no relevant context, and children do not make the transfer to their own writing. What does work is embedding appropriate instruction, on a group or individual basis, into the writing process. Let's look at how Mrs. Williams teaches letter-writing conventions in her class.

The Minilesson

Mrs. Williams's class has been invited to be pen pals with a third grade in Florida. The children have agreed that everyone in the class will write a letter, and Mrs. Williams sees this as a perfect opportunity to do a minilesson on letters. Mrs. Williams is aware that some people have switched from the term *minilesson* to *focus lesson* (e.g., Routman, 1996; Bromley, 1999). She prefers *minilesson*, as it emphasizes the brief nature of the instruction. Mrs. Williams has written a letter to the teacher in Florida that she is showing on the overhead projector to her class. In five short minutes, she shows important parts of a friendly letter—the date, greeting, and closing. She shows how she used a comma in the greeting and another one after "Sincerely yours" in the closing. The children then begin work on their letters, referring to the sample letter chart Mrs. Williams has posted. When she conferences with children, she looks specifically for their use of these conventions and points them out to the children.

On another day, Mrs. Williams approaches a much more difficult topic—revision. She knows that revision is the hardest part of writing for many writers, so she plans a minilesson to demonstrate how she revised a newsletter that she had prepared to send home with the children. Using an overhead projector, she shows the children her original notes and then her first draft on the word processor. She shares with the children that after reading it out loud, it seemed to her that many sentences seemed to repeat themselves. She asks the children to help her identify these sentences. After finding three pairs of sentences that say the same thing, Mrs. Williams models how she crossed out the redundant sentences and rearranged those that remained. She then shows the children her revised copy of the newsletter. In future conferences, she will remind children of her revision process as she helps them revise their own writing.

In these minilessons, Mrs. Williams uses direct instruction with her third graders. Many people who study the constructivist approach to literacy get the impression that direct instruction is inappropriate. However, we know that there are many things about writing that cannot be figured out logically by children. Punctuation is an example of this type of conventional knowledge. The children all have the common purpose of writing a good letter. The teacher has limited group instruction to less than five minutes, which is a lot less time than it would take to show each child individually. Her model is a real letter she has written, and the children are aware of its purpose. Motivation is high because the children want their letters to be read and understood by a real audience. The children apply their skill right away; there are references in the classroom to help them. In the end, they know they will have a set of letters that their pen pals will be able to read and that they will receive real feedback.

Mrs. Williams is conservative about using direct instruction with small and large groups, and when she does, she follows a few simple guidelines (Table 6.2). The main guideline is that the instruction needs to be related to the kind of knowledge involved. Coming to an understanding of how to read and write, as discussed in Chapter 1, cannot be learned through instruction but must be constructed by the individual child. In contrast, social knowledge, such as spelling conventions and punctuation, can be taught within a real context.

TABLE 6.2
Guided Writing Using Direct Instruction with a Group

Use only for knowledge that must be taught through direct instruction in order to be learned.

Provide direct instruction when the entire group has a common need.

Keep minilessons under five minutes.

Provide context with real examples and real purpose.

Apply the skill immediately and check the children's understanding.

Provide written examples for future reference.

A minilesson uses direct instruction to show children things about writing that they cannot figure out logically.

The Writing Conference

We hope it is clear to you that group minilessons are only a small part of the guided writing that Mr. Larson and Mrs. Williams do each day. You have probably noticed that most of the guided writing we have described in these last three chapters has occurred in one-on-one situations. Here is the heart of instruction in the classroom: the student-teacher conference. Conferences are simply times for a child to meet individually with the teacher. Many conferences are informal: The teacher roams around the room, stopping to briefly answer questions or point something out before moving on to another child. Other conferences are more formal: The child may meet the teacher at a specified place in the room and may have signed up days in advance for this time alone with the teacher. Conferences are a critical component of writing instruction (Frank, 2001). As we discuss writing conferences, keep in mind that all our teachers integrate writing and reading so much that it's hard for us to separate writing conferences from reading conferences—often both processes are addressed together.

Mr. Larson has a special conference table that is set out of the line of traffic in order to be secluded but still provides him a view of everything going on in the classroom. He posts a sign-up sheet there so children can easily schedule themselves for an appointment as they feel the need or desire for one. If a child goes for a week without signing up for a conference, Mr. Larson seeks out that child and spends time casually discussing his or her reading and writing. Mr. Larson tries to make the discussion nonthreatening and supportive to encourage the child to request a conference. Some children seem to sign up all the time. Do they want additional attention, or are they too dependent on teacher direction or praise? With these youngsters, Mr. Larson tries to figure out the cause of constant requests and then deals with that cause. Generally, he urges his students to try to work a day without teacher direction between conferences.

Conferences may last for only a minute or two or for as long as fifteen minutes. They usually last from five to ten minutes, and Mr. Larson is able to meet with about ten children daily. Are you shocked that he doesn't try to work with each child each day? Mr. Larson has found that giving his undivided attention a few times a week to each child is far more valuable than meeting daily with that child in a group. This way of working with the children means that none of their time for reading and writing is wasted. Of course, he circulates among the whole class between conferences and interacts with students incidentally during those times too.

Mr. Larson keeps his files and records for conferences in the conference area so that he can pull out an old sample of a child's writing for comparison with today's work. Children can see their progress when they have these comparisons. Mrs. Williams keeps her records of conferences in a notebook with a section for each child, just as Mrs. Thomas does. She records children's feelings about writing and reading as well as their skill. She likes students to see what she is writing down about their progress, so she takes notes during the conference sessions. On occasion, she adds notes after a spontaneous interaction outside the conference session when she didn't have her notebook handy.

Sometimes a child has writing to discuss, sometimes reading, and sometimes both at once. Whichever literary endeavor the teacher and student discuss, the teacher tries always to provide specific, positive feedback. Mrs. Williams cautions that positive feedback must be specific rather than general. With general praise, we run the risk of making children dependent on outside approval rather than helping them learn to rely on their own judgment. So while meeting with Jennifer, Mrs. Williams says that the turkey dinner Jennifer described made her mouth water. She tries to refrain from making such meaningless statements as "What a good story!" or, worse, "You're a good writer."

Mr. Larson has a reputation for boosting the self-esteem of kids who especially need it, and he is a master at positive feedback. He firmly believes that his purpose during conferences is to be supportive, constructive, and specific as he helps students take their next steps toward their goals (Calkins, 2000). He always

Teachers find that giving their undivided attention a few times a week to each child is far more valuable than meeting daily with that child in a group.

notes the progress a child has made rather than the errors. He never tries to improve writing with a red pencil or to improve reading with lists of words missed. Instead of talking about errors, he discusses what needs to be learned by saying, "Now I think you are ready for . . . "

Children usually sign up for a conference with a specific purpose—requesting help in finding more information on a topic, wanting feedback on writing, or sharing a story that was particularly enjoyable. The teacher values the child's purpose and uses it as a starting place to extend the youngster's knowledge and understanding. For instance, when Ruben was trying to find information about comets, Mrs. Williams helped him become more proficient in using the table of contents and the index in books. She also felt that was an appropriate moment to send him to the school librarian, who helped Ruben learn how to find things at the library. When information or skills are important to children, they will learn them.

As children become more proficient and confident in using written language, their purposes change. Now that Melinda can write most of the words she uses without laboriously matching the sounds of language to the letters, she is

FIGURE 6.6
Sweet Puppy.

more free to concentrate on the meaning and form of what she writes. She no longer has to think about each word as she writes it, so she thinks about how to communicate more effectively. Mrs. Williams's responses to Melinda during conferences help her think through the content and the way her thoughts are structured. Developing syntax, style, and the choice of words to express her thoughts comes next. Refining word usage to paint pictures that show rather then tell the reader what she is trying to say is an exciting continuation of developing Melinda's skill as a writer. Mrs. Williams doesn't spend time with details such as spelling until after Melinda has finished the important process of getting her ideas on paper.

Writing Conferences in Action

Let's go back into Mr. Larson's room and eavesdrop on one of his conferences today. Sam has volunteered for a conference for the first time, and Mr. Larson looks forward to what he brings—a picture and caption he made after hearing *The Velveteen Rabbit* (Figure 6.6). After Mr. Larson read this story about a beloved stuffed animal, the children were invited to bring in their favorite toys and write about them. Mr. Larson was surprised at how many children like Sam brought in stuffed animals.

Mr. Larson:	All right, Sam, looks like you have a favorite dog. Would you read your story to me?
Sam:	Okay. (*Reads*) My favorite toy is my Sweet Puppy. I like my Sweet Puppy.
Mr. Larson:	Gosh, Sam, my favorite toy was a stuffed dog, too!
Sam:	I got Sweet Puppy for Christmas.
Mr. Larson:	I can see from your picture he's kind of an alert looking dog.
Sam:	Yeah, he's like a watchdog, but he's kind of worn out.
Mr. Larson:	How'd he get so beat up?
Sam:	Well, he's old.
Mr. Larson:	Is there anything else you'd like to write about him?

Sam:	Yeah, he fell in the bathtub once, and when we got him out he was all wet. So my grandma put him in the dryer, and then he fell apart and . . .
Mr. Larson:	Whoa, Sam. Could you write that down?
Sam:	Okay.
Mr. Larson:	Look here, Sam, before you go, let's add you to the list of everyone's favorite toys. (*Writes in his notebook as Sam watches, "Favorite Toys, Sam—Sweet Puppy."*)

Notice that Mr. Larson was not at all dismayed at Sam's writing. He knew that Sam, a transfer student, had not had a language-rich environment either at home or at school. Sam's writing is at a level well below that of his classmates. But Sam had something to say, and Mr. Larson was ready to listen. Notice how he probed Sam for more information—and Sam had plenty more to say. Finally, Mr. Larson accepted Sam's invented spelling but also modeled the standard spellings of *favorite* and *sweet* when he added Sam to the favorite-toy list. Sam later added several sentences to his paper and proudly read it to the class during sharing time. Mr. Larson filed this paper away and will use it as a benchmark to compare with later papers. Notice that Mr. Larson never corrected or suggested changes. As Sam begins to be a writer, Mr. Larson is interested only in encouraging him to write as much as possible.

Across the hall in the third grade, Zachary has been working on a story about his cat all week. He has written several drafts of the story and has even asked his mom to help with correct spellings. Not satisfied yet, Zach has requested a conference so that Mrs. Williams can help him type his story on the word processor. Before he sits down at the computer, Mrs. Williams asks Zach to read his story to her. When he is finished, Mrs. Williams tries to find out why he wants help.

Each child's writing has something to say, and the teacher's job is to listen.

Mrs. Williams:	What do you like about your story?
Zach:	Well, I like it about my cat, and I like the part about Lisa's mother in our garage. But Kelly thinks it's too long, and I do too.
Mrs. Williams:	So you want to make it shorter?
Zach:	Yeah.
Mrs. Williams:	Well, there are a couple of things you could do: You could just cut some of it out, or you could rewrite some of the sentences. What do you think?
Zach:	Could we do it without writing it over?
Mrs. Williams:	Let's use the computer here and see what we come up with. (*They sit down at the computer, boot up Zach's disk, and begin.*) On the first page here, is there anything that really isn't important to the story?
Zach:	Well, it probably doesn't matter about Texas (*crosses it out*). So the title is "The Way I Got Lisa."

Fortunately, Mrs. Williams and Zach had time to work through Zach's story together. At Zach's request, Mrs. Williams typed it in and showed Zach how to revise words and paragraphs with the word processor. Zach became so involved that when Mrs. Williams had to take the class out for recess, Zach continued. In Figure 6.7 you can see the result of Zach's revision.

Zach loves to write. He is also a perfectionist. His writing is exceptional for a third grader. Mrs. Williams is glad that his exuberance for writing has not diminished during his four years in school and that she can challenge him to write even better. Zach has profited immensely from the writing-process stages that Mrs. Williams has taught this year and is the first child in the class to really be able to edit his own work. Mrs. Williams is also glad that word processing is available for all the children in her class so that the tedious tasks of rewriting can be avoided as much as possible.

In the final copy, Zach corrected a grammatical error on the first page. As he read his story out loud, he noticed "had fell" didn't sound right and made an appropriate correction. Zach's final paper has a real sense of story, and extraneous details have been omitted. This is a paper that both Zach and Mrs. Williams are proud of.

In these conferences, Mr. Larson and Mrs. Williams have focused on strategies that Sam and Zach are currently working on and ignored areas that might need attention with other children. Each boy received about five minutes of personalized attention to his own needs and spent the rest of his writing time writing.

Mr. Larson and Mrs. Williams find that conference time is the most productive teaching time of the day. They both work hard to do as much as possible within a five- to ten-minute time frame so they have time to work with each child each week (Table 6.3). Each individual writing conference is as unique as each student and each piece of writing. Mr. Larson and Mrs. Williams love the personal contact that conferences allow. In Chapter 7 we will continue our look at conferences when we

The Way I Got Lisa

by Zachary

There was a little cat in our garage. It had fallen out of her mother's nest. So we brought her inside. My mom called the vet, and when we got there we went inside and it got its shots. And they told us she was a girl. I named her Lisa.

Then we went next door to Randall's. We got the special kind of milk for Lisa because she was only about four weeks old.

Then a few days later when we were outside we heard something, it was like a pit pat. Then we found out it was Lisa's mom. A few days later a cat came down in our garage. Everyday we fed her. After about four weeks my grandma called the animal control. They came and took Lisa's mom and her kittens. We didn't see them again.

The End.

FIGURE 6.7
How I got Lisa.

focus on reading, and in Chapter 8 we'll discuss how conferences are used for assessment as well as for instruction.

EMBEDDING INSTRUCTION

What makes good writing? Spandel (1996) lists six "primary traits" that are commonly agreed on to describe effective writing: ideas, organization, voice, word choice, fluency, and conventions. Our responsibility as teachers goes beyond providing a conducive environment, time, materials, and a workshop format. Our responsibility is to teach children, as appropriate, how to improve their writing. To do

TABLE 6.3
Guidelines for Writing Conferences

- Let the child take the lead
- Respond to the child's message
- Ask questions that teach
- Work at appropriate stages of the writing process
- Let the child make the changes

this, we must embed instruction within the context of their own writing when we conference with individual children or provide a minilesson.

The Writer's Craft

When we look at children's writing, we might notice a strong, fresh voice, a vivid description or a great opening sentence. Beginning writers, like any writers, can be guided in various aspects of craft (Fletcher & Portalupi, 1998). Fletcher (1999) emphasizes the importance of highlighting the reading-writing connection as learners explore the writer's craft. It takes time—time to read, time to talk, and time to write. Let's consider a few aspects of craft that are crucial to beginning writers.

Audience

Not all writing is for others to read. Mr. Larson encourages children to keep notes on topics they would like to write about for other audiences—from letters to friends to reports or poems for the class newspaper. Using these ideas, Mr. Larson helps the children understand the concept of a writing audience. Students learn not only that they as individuals are an audience for their own private writing and that the teacher and classmates are an audience for public writing but also that a *specific* or *known audience* differs from a *general* or *unknown audience*. Mrs. Williams spends time asking children to think about who will read their writing and what those people will know and not know about the subject. She tries to get students to consider viewpoints other than their own, but she knows that not all third graders are mature enough to be able to do that. When children can identify broad ideas of possible audiences for their writing (such as their classmates, parents, a mail-order repair department, and so on), they may see a variety of writing possibilities (Fletcher & Portalupi, 2001).

Voice

Mrs. Williams and Mr. Larson both prize *voice*, a child's unique style of writing. The youngsters may not be sophisticated enough to discuss the concepts of voice and style, but they can recognize that their voice might vary with the audience. Most important, children respond to their teachers' appreciation and acceptance of their personal ways of expressing themselves. Both teachers know that they could easily squelch children's individuality if they attend too much to how children write rather than to what children have to say. They understand the importance of avoiding the transfer to "teacher's voice" in the story (Frank, 2001).

By reading and discussing works by various authors with different styles, students begin to appreciate differences in writing. When children get a chance to meet the author of a book they have enjoyed, their ideas of a personality behind writing grow. Hilary Hyland came to Mrs. Williams's class and told about writing her book *The Wreck of the Ethie* (1999). She made a big impression when she explained how she decided what to write and about throwing away her first efforts. Knowing that writing isn't easy even for published authors, but that it is rewarding to them and worth the effort, are important concepts for children to learn.

Encouraging Growth in Spelling

Spelling is a loaded subject area (Wilde, 1997). Of all the areas of instruction in today's schools, spelling is a top concern for parents and critics of education. "Look at this—ten misspelled words in one short paper!" "Don't they teach spelling anymore?" "When I was a boy, we had tests on twenty words every week and spelling bees every year—what happened to those?" "Where are the spelling books and the spelling homework?" "Kids just use spell checkers—they don't teach them how to spell in school anymore!"

Do these comments sound familiar? Mr. Larson and Mrs. Williams face a public that demands higher standards in "basic skills" and at the same time is woefully uneducated in the current research and pedagogy of teaching spelling. Parents, standards, and curricula expect an end to invented spelling and a switch to standard spelling beginning in the second grade. Let's face it: Unconventional spelling sticks out and is a target of critics of education. Although teachers may celebrate a child's invented and transitional spelling, the public sees only *wrong* spelling. Mr. Larson and Mrs. Williams face two major tasks in teaching spelling. The first is to help their students learn conventional spelling. The second, and perhaps the more difficult, is to inform and educate parents and the public. Success in the former task, of course, lends support to the latter.

Looking at Children's Spelling

Mr. Larson has piles of stories that his avid second-grade writers produce every day. At the beginning of the year, he looks carefully at examples of each child's spelling to assess what the children know about spelling. Some people might be dismayed at Mary's report on *Charlotte's Web*, but Mr. Larson, as we shall see, observes much to celebrate (Figure 6.8). (We use the convention of capital letters to represent children's spelling. In addition, we'll use the // to indicate a phoneme. Since international phonetic spelling is not common knowledge, we'll use the most common English phonetic letter or letters to represent individual phonemes.)

Let's analyze this spelling with Mr. Larson (who, by the way, is delighted with Mary's summary of her main character and her emotional response to the plot).

SARLIT WIS A HEROW.	Charlotte was a hero.
SHE SAV A PIG.	She saved a pig.
AT'S TEREBL THAT SHE DID.	It's terrible that she died.
BUT 3 FUV H(e?)R BABES RTAD.	But 3 of her babies returned.

FIGURE 6.8
Charlotte's Web, by Mary.

SARLIT tells us that Mary knows

1. That each phoneme is represented by a letter
2. The letters that represent the sounds of /r/, /l/ and /t/
3. That the phoneme for the /sh/ sound starts with s
4. That each syllable contains a vowel
5. That the /r/ sound contains a vowel
6. That the /schwa/ sound (the unaccented "uh" vowel sound in English) is represented by a vowel

WIS additionally tells us that Mary knows

7. The representations for the sounds of /w/ and /z/
8. That the sound /z/ is represented by the letter s at the end of a plural word

A HEROW adds to Mary's list:

9. The representations for the sound of /h/
10. Long vowel sounds are represented by the vowel's alphabetic name
11. Many words ending in the /o/ sound end in -ow, as in *know, blow,* and *row*

The next three lines demonstrate that Mary also knows

12. The representations for the sounds of /s/, /v/, /p/, /g/, /d/, and /b/
13. Conventional spellings for several high-frequency words
14. The word family for the rime -ig, as in *dig, jig,* and *pig*
15. That the apostrophe is used to create contractions

Mr. Larson has compiled quite a list! A trained linguist would probably add more to this list, but for purposes of primary spelling assessment, Mr. Larson has recognized many important aspects of Mary's spelling development: many phonemes that Mary can hear, many letters that she can use to represent sounds, several spelling conventions of the English language, and several high-frequency words that Mary has learned to spell.

Now Mr. Larson changes focus to some areas in which Mary has not yet solidified her knowledge. Note that she shows some but not complete knowledge of these generalizations:

1. The /sh/ sound can be represented by either *sh* or *ch*
2. The ending /d/ sound in the past tense is represented by *-ed*
3. Conventional spelling of the word *of*
4. Short vowel sounds

Finally, Mr. Larson notes that occasionally Mary does not seem to attend to all phonemes in some words, as in SAV (*saved*) and RTAD (*returned*).

What is Mr. Larson to do with this information? First, it is obvious that Mary has many phonics "rules" and many generalizations of written English in her repertoire. Her developmental spelling shows that she hears and represents most of the phonemes accurately and that she is paying attention to conventional spelling. Her spelling, although difficult to decipher at first, is really quite remarkable.

Mr. Larson would never tamper with Mary's completed report on *Charlotte's Web*. However, he makes note of some spelling conventions he might check on in the future:

*   Sight-word spellings of *it, was*, and *of*. (These will most likely fall into place as Mary continues to read and write a lot.)
*   Forming the past tense. (Again, Mary will continue to refine her knowledge in this area. She will most likely begin to "hear" the final /d/ sounds as she internalizes the spelling convention for past tense.)
*   Making plurals with words that end in *y*. (This would be a good minilesson.)
*   Alternative spellings for the /sh/ sound. (This will come up later in more complex words, such as words that have /sh/ spelled with *ti* in the middle. For the time being, Mr. Larson might point out to Mary that the standard spelling for *Charlotte* is on the cover of the book.)

Mr. Larson's greatest concern with Mary is that she learn to hear all the phonemes in the words she writes. He will continue to informally monitor her progress.

You probably noticed that Mr. Larson knows quite a bit about phonics himself. He would be the first to confess that phonics was not a favorite subject of his in school. In fact, he wasn't allowed to have a reading book at school until he memorized the sounds of the consonants and long and short vowels! He recognizes that this sort of task for a child is counterproductive to reading development. On the other hand, an adult understanding of phonics is essential if a teacher is going to be able to accurately analyze children's phonetic spelling (Wilde, 1997).

How Can We Teach Spelling?

Teachers know that spelling programs with prescribed word lists, daily exercises, and end-of-week tests don't work (Heald-Taylor, 1998; Hillal Gill & Scharer, 1996). Research shows that words "mastered" on spelling tests are frequently misspelled in daily writing. If spelling books and published programs don't work, then what does? We are aware of many schools and districts in which improving spelling has been made a priority. In lieu of following spelling books, what *can* teachers do? Or, more specifically, how would you teach spelling to Mary and her classmates, our developing second- and third-grade spellers?

Reading and Writing

Mr. Larson and Mrs. Williams agree with Mrs. Thomas that the best activities for learning to spell are reading and writing, and the more the better. Through independent reading, not only will children encounter a broad view of the range of spelling possibilities, but they will also encounter those difficult high-frequency words—that's right—very frequently. High-frequency words, or function words, are words that have no referential meaning but put the content words (nouns, verbs, adjectives, and adverbs) together. They are not exciting words, but they become very easy to learn and read when children read for meaning. (Imagine trying to help a child sound out or learn to spell *the*, *of*, or *one* using by-the-book phonics. Just as Mary did, they'd produce DA, UV, and WUN.)

Individual Direct Instruction

Anyone who works with children on their writing knows that a most frequently asked question is, "How do you spell _____ ?" Primary teachers have trained themselves to encourage children to "guess and go" rather than just spell out the words. However, sometimes teachers would rather just give the spelling so that the child will be able to go on with the thought. The teacher might write the word in the child's dictionary or word list or point to it on a word wall. In other instances, teachers might use this opportunity to show and teach a child how to spell a word. Glazer (1998) suggests that a direct approach is sometimes an expedient manner in which to tell and teach at the same time. Based on work by Grace Fernald and Sylvia Ashton-Warner, the method is multisensory and immediate. When a child asks for a word needed in writing, the teacher guides the child in tracing in the air and saying the word at the same time. So, when Sam asks for *birthday*, Mr. Larson holds Sam's writing hand and directs him to point with his first finger. Mr. Larson holds Sam's hand as together they write *birthday* in the air while they say the word together. They do this several times, and then Mr. Larson asks Sam to trace *birthday* in the air himself. Satisfied that Sam has traced the word exactly, Mr. Larson gives him a card and watches as Sam correctly writes his new word. Mr. Larson repeats the process if necessary, and then Sam goes on with his writing, with his important word spelled correctly not only on his paper but also on a card he can use later if he needs to. Glazer cautions that this method should be used exactly as described.

Word Study

Both Mr. Larson and Mrs. Williams give brief informational spelling lessons in group settings. Minilessons are arranged when the teacher notices that a number of children are struggling with a spelling convention. For example, Mr. Larson has noted that several children have been experimenting with the /e/ sound at the ends of such words as *baby, city,* and *funny.* Mr. Larson asks the class if they can think of some names in the class that end with the /e/ sound. Mary, Billy, and Zachary volunteer their names, which Mr. Larson writes on the board. "How do we spell the e sound in these names?" he asks, and the children respond with "*y!*" Mr. Larson then asks for more words that end with the same sound. As the list on the chart grows longer, Mr. Larson challenges the children to think of a word with this ending sound that doesn't end with a *y.* Mr. Larson asks the children to tell a neighbor what the "rule" is and listens in as they share. The children construct their own generalizations after sorting words that fit the pattern and words that don't. They are more apt to remember these "rules" as opposed to memorizing an arbitrary set (Ganske, 2000). Mr. Larson takes extra care to note if the children are applying this convention in their writing later that day. A child who does not do so might receive a brief individual review, such as we described earlier. The "Y Ending" chart is placed at a level so that children can add other words to it, and a special little chart is hung nearby for exceptions to that rule.

Since Mrs. Williams's day is so full of reading and learning in science and social studies, she realizes that it is important for children to understand and know how to read and spell content words. The class study of Alaskan animals offered many interesting examples of words for consideration. For example, *mouse, lynx, moose, goose, mosquito,* and *caribou* make for good discussion of the many ways to form and spell plurals in the English language. Mrs. Williams presents this information embedded in study of the animals and helps the children create a temporary word wall in which all the Alaskan animals (and their plurals if irregular) are listed and categorized. Spelling anomalies, such as *ptarmigan,* are also highlighted.

Both Mr. Larson and Mrs. Williams find that many children still benefit from study of rime or word families. Mary has contributed to the *-ig* and *-ow* lists. Mr. Larson has put focus on words from other languages, and Carlos has proudly submitted *Juan* and *La Jolla* to the "Borrowed from Spanish" list. These lists familiarize children with common spelling patterns and serve as spelling references for words that don't follow English generalizations.

Much attention is currently focused on word study (Fountas & Pinnell, 1998; Invernizzi, Abouzeid, & Bloodgood, 1997). We are concerned that teachers not go overboard trying to "cover" a planned word-study curriculum. We believe the children will tell us, through their writing, what they need to know.

Strategies

The sure thing that Mr. Larson and Mrs. Williams agree will aid children in becoming better spellers is the use of spelling strategies. Children who have progressed beyond emergent writing and reading are all too often aware that their phonetic spelling is not the same as conventional spelling. They sometimes become hesitant to spell a word "wrong" and may choose less exciting words they can spell or become overly dependent on asking adults for spellings. Because independence and creativity are important goals in their programs, Mr. Larson and Mrs. Williams encourage children to rely on strategies commonly used by competent adult spellers (Marinelli, 1996; Wilde, 1992, 1997).

1. *Placeholder/invented spelling.*   Continued use of "spell and go" or phonetic spelling allows children to maintain the flow of their writing and use a wide range of vocabulary. Because important papers can and will be revised, initial spelling is not nearly as important as getting ideas down on paper.

2. *Using knowledge of spelling patterns or conventions or of word meanings.* The minilessons and informal, individual spelling instruction given to children help them recognize words that belong to families or that use special conventions such as contractions. Knowledge of words having common roots, such as *cycle*, helps spellers distinguish spelling of *bicycle*, *tricycle*, and *life cycle* from *icicle*.

3. *Using human resources.*   Teachers should refrain from telling children how to spell on a regular basis and thus making children dependent on them. Instead, children should be encouraged to spell as they think a word should be spelled or to ask another child. It is legitimate, though, to tell a child how to spell a word when teaching the spelling, as in the Fernald-Ashton Warner method described earlier, or in the final stages of proofreading.

4. *Using textual resources.*   Any print-rich classroom is a valuable resource of references for words. Children easily learn to find spellings of words in contextual settings—in books, on signs, and in captions. We have talked about word walls and charts used in the classroom as references for spelling and for word family and spelling conventions. Many teachers encourage children to keep individual resources of spelling words. These may be homemade dictionaries, note cards clipped together in a ring, or cards in a file box. Word banks such as these allow children an individual reference and give practice in alphabetizing.

Dictionaries, of course, provide children with correct spellings, but a dictionary user must be able to make a reasonable guess about the spelling of a word in order to successfully find it in a dictionary. Children who have access to computers can easily be taught to use the spell-checker function. Spell checkers do not teach spelling, nor do they make children dependent. Spell checkers require that the writer make decisions about the correctness of a spelling.

5. *Generation, monitoring, and revision.*   Probably the most sophisticated of the strategies, this involves the most thinking about a spelling. Children can be encouraged to write down several guesses about the spelling of a word and then to choose the best one. Later, during the editing process, conventional spelling can be confirmed.

6. *Memorizing.*   We all know that some words simply must be memorized. The vast majority of words in our spelling vocabulary are correctly memorized simply through use. For example, the word we just used, *through*, is considered a spelling demon. Most people learn to spell it over years of practice.

Although some experts (Fountas & Pinnell, 1998; Glazer, 1998) advocate weekly spelling lists, we agree with Sandra Wilde (1997) that young children naturally learn to spell about five new words a week through writing and that spelling-word memorization and quizzing is a less effective use of classroom time. However, if weekly spelling lists are required by the school district, they should be short (five words or less) and individualized for each child. Spelling words should, of course, be in the child's oral and reading vocabulary (Figure 6.9), and, when found in the child's writing, all the phonemes should appear in the child's phonetic spelling (Fresch & Wheaton, 1997; O'Flahavan & Blassberg, 1992). Additional ideas for teaching spelling are found in Figure 6.10.

Refining Grammar and Mechanics

When we were children, we were supposed to learn correct grammar by copying sentences and picking the correct verb. Mrs Williams remembers punctuation exercises that involved copying a paragraph and supplying the correct punctuation marks. We're sure you can see how ludicrous this seems now and how this kind of exercise must have stifled our ability to write.

Today's children who have been encouraged to write are courageous and creative, but they still make mistakes in grammar, and they still need to learn how to punctuate a sentence so it makes sense to the reader. Have you thought about how we can help youngsters learn these conventions without resorting to the same type of grammar lessons and work sheets that were useless to us as children?

Mr. Larson uses the same approach to grammar and mechanics as he does to spelling. He simply works at individual problems as he conferences with his students. When he sees a grammatical error, he might first ask the child to say the sen-

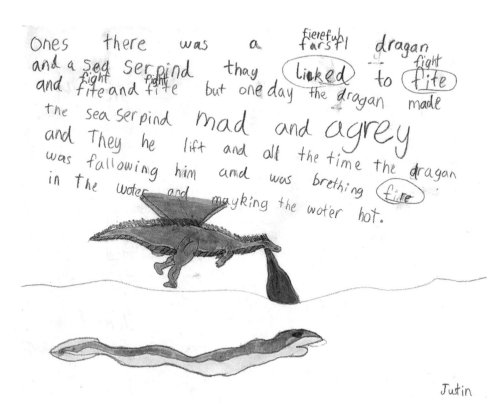

FIGURE 6.9
Justin's dragon paper.

tence out loud. Does it sound right? Often the error is corrected this way. But other times the grammatical error is part of children's oral language—you've heard "me and my brother" or "my dog, she." If you work with students whose first language is not English, you've probably heard a number of unusual constructions. The first thing to remember about these grammatical constructions is that they are part of a child's best attempt to communicate. If we correct too many of them, children will get the message that we are listening to *how* they speak rather than to *what* they have to say. Mr. Larson feels he often has to make a judgment call in whether to correct. His first response is to attend to the meaning of the message, repeating it if possible in standard English. If he decides to suggest a change, he'll preface his suggestion with a remark like "In books, it's written this way." Emphasis is always on the purpose, which is communication. Mr. Larson tries to use standard grammar in normal conversation with children and to point it out in books. He knows that second and third graders are still refining their understanding of grammar at this age and that, with lots of exposure, the standard grammar will eventually be learned.

- **Modeling correct spelling**
  While writing children's dictated ideas
  When responding to children's journal entries
  Anytime you write anything
- **Continuing to accept invented spelling**
  Thus freeing children to become writers, which makes them more aware of standard spelling
- **Helping children edit their writing**
  Demonstrate proofreading for errors in your own writing
  Help children compare their own spelling to standard forms
- **Helping children select spelling words from their own writing**
  Create personal spelling lists of frequently used words
  Make personal spelling files or books
- **Giving individual minilessons relevant to children's own writing**
  Point out common spelling patterns and word families
  Explain spelling rules and conventions applicable
- **Showing how to use spelling resources**
  Demonstrate use of pictionaries or dictionaries
  Allow children to help each other with spelling
  Help youngsters think of places where they could find a certain word spelled correctly
- **Providing spelling resources**
  Make charts of words from content units and field trips
  Display wall charts of common words that do not follow spelling "rules" (*what, where, the, their,* and so on)
- **Making sure that children love to read**
  The more they read, the more they see standard spelling

FIGURE 6.10
More ways to teach spelling.

In addition, as they get older, children will learn when it is appropriate to use their home dialects in a situation and when it is advantageous to use standard grammar.

Mrs. Williams finds mechanics a much easier topic to deal with than grammar. All children are excited about learning how to make their written work understandable to others. Since kindergarten, children have learned about periods and capital letters as their teachers have taken dictation or gone over written work with them. As children become more adept writers, we see them attempting to use more punctuation marks, experimenting with capital letters, and imitating special written forms, such as business letters. Their teachers routinely show children in minilessons and guided writing conferences how punctuation, capital letters, and paragraphs are used (Wilde, 1992).

CONCLUSION

Becoming a better writer is more than improving spelling, grammar, and punctuation. What is important is that children write consistently and write a lot and that we respect and respond to what each child says. As children master the skills of writing, teachers and children become freer to concentrate on improving writing—finding new forms, new topics, and new depth. We can encourage children to find their own unique voices and to find better ways to say what they have to say, from developing catchy beginnings and endings to using all their senses to describe, from developing strong plots to finding unusual metaphors. This chapter has described how a classroom writing workshop works for young writers. In the next chapter, we'll look at reading in the primary grades and show how a literature program supports the writing process.

DISCUSSION QUESTIONS

1. A third-grade student turns in a poorly written paper done hurriedly. The paper shows no thought or care for spelling, handwriting, punctuation, or even content. What should you do?
2. You are attempting to encourage creative writing in a second-grade classroom. One of the children fears to write any word without knowing the correct spelling. She refuses to make a guess at spelling. Consequently, she writes very little and frequently interrupts the teacher to request correct spelling. How can this child be freed to learn through her own exploration of print?
3. Can you think of situations in which direct instruction can be used appropriately in primary grades? Explain.
4. Your second and third graders write widely and often. How can you determine which of their many pieces would be appropriate for revision, editing, and publishing?

SUGGESTED FOLLOW-UP ACTIVITIES

1. Help a child or small group of children find a purpose for writing that involves an intended audience. Assist the writer(s) in analyzing the resulting work in terms of effective communication for that audience. If possible, arrange for the writer(s) to share the work with the intended audience.
2. Assist a child who wishes to polish something he or she has written. Follow procedures described in this chapter.
3. Write something of your own and share it with children. Ask for their feedback and model the revision process using an overhead projector.

4. Learn how to bind books using cloth or contact-paper-covered cardboard covers. Use taped or sewn bindings. Help a child create a book from some special writing.

5. Engage children of differing writing abilities in private discussions about their writing. Ask what topics they usually write about and how they decide what to write. Ask if they write outside school and for what reasons. Find out if they use any procedures for polishing when they share their writing with others. Ask what they like about their writing and what more they want to learn in order to write better.

6. Choose a paper written by a beginning writer. Analyze it and list everything you have observed that the child knows about spelling and conventions.

7. Prepare a letter to parents explaining your spelling program. Discuss the importance of phonetic spelling and your alternatives to a traditional spelling program.

RECOMMENDED FURTHER READING

Calkins, L. M. (1994). *The art of teaching writing.* Portsmouth, NH: Heinemann.

Culham, R. (1998). *Picture books: An annotated bibliography with activities for teaching writing.* Portland, OR: Northwest Regional Educational Laboratory.

Fletcher, R., & Portalupi, J. (2001). *Writing workshop: The essential guide.* Portsmouth, NH: Heinemann.

Fraser, J., & Skolnick, D. (1994). *On their way: Celebrating second graders as they read and write.* Portsmouth, NH: Heinemann.

Routman, R. (2000). *Conversations: Strategies for teaching, learning, and evaluating.* Portsmouth, NH: Heinemann.

Spandel, V. (1996). *Seeing with new eyes.* Portland, OR: Northwest Regional Educational Laboratory.

Wilde, S. (1997). *What's a schwa sound anyway? A holistic guide to phonetics, phonics, and spelling.* Portsmouth, NH: Heinemann.

7

CREATING A CLASSROOM FOR READERS

"I waited all my life," said Jim. "Now I can read."

**From *When Will I Read?*
by Miriam Cohen, 1977**

CHAPTER 7

In the favorite children's book *When Will I Read?*, Miriam Cohen (1977) shows us a primary classroom where the teacher encourages emergent literacy through play, environmental print, and other developmentally appropriate classroom activities. However, the bottom line is that children are eager to "really read." When at last this happens, be it in kindergarten or third grade, a new and exciting world opens for children. They can read independently!

In this chapter, we'll look at how our teachers structure an independent reading program for children who are "really reading." As we've discussed earlier, independent reading develops within each child's individual time line, sometimes as early as kindergarten and sometimes as late as the upper elementary grades. For purposes of our study of the reading development of young children, we will focus again on the classrooms in which Mr. Larson and Mrs. Williams teach. Some children in these classrooms are not yet independent readers; however, these children still need independent reading. So, our goal in this chapter is to describe not how children learn to read but instead how reading becomes a tool to experience literature and to learn from information books. You will also notice that once children can "really read," our teachers do not group their students for reading instruction. Instead, their focus is on individualized reading instruction during independent reading. Grouping is used for study of literature and content, when teacher input, discussion, and group interaction enhance learning information and understanding ideas.

In Chapter 6, we looked at how Mr. Larson and Mrs. Williams encouraged children's writing. We hope it's clear to you that a major factor in their success is that their second and third graders see a clear purpose in their writing. With motive in place, refinement in form, style, and conventions is much easier to encourage. With reading too, purpose is paramount to success. Today's children are lucky to have a wealth of children's literature that is richer than ever before. Teachers are lucky too because the almost limitless choices in reading materials provide purpose for every child.

At the heart of a developmentally appropriate reading program is individuality. This means that children must be free to choose what they read and how they will respond to it. In turn, the teacher must focus individual attention on each child. As with writing, individual attention is given through the reading conference, the heart of an individualized reading program. The reading conference provides the core time of interaction between teacher and child—the opportunity for teaching appropriate information and strategies that will refine a child's ability to read for pleasure and purpose. In the preceding chapter, we eavesdropped on writing conferences in Mr. Larson's and Mrs. Williams's classes. Let's take a look at a couple of their reading conferences as well.

READING CONFERENCES

It's almost lunchtime, and there's an air of restlessness among our twenty-five second graders. Mr. Larson has been circulating around the room, checking children's record sheets, answering questions, and helping children find just the right book in the classroom library. Mr. Larson aims to check in on every child informally every day. Luckily, he often has parents and sixth graders in during reading time to help out. All is calm now, so Mr. Larson decides to squeeze in one more formal conference and sees that Casey's name is next. As Casey gathers his stuff together, Mr. Larson leafs through his file, reminding himself that Casey has only recently begun to read independently. He is glad he has time to meet with Casey today.

Unlike many of his classmates, Casey was a late starter in reading. Because Mrs. Hanna and Mrs. Thomas recognized and accepted his less mature development, Casey arrived in second grade with his self-esteem intact and has made great strides this year. For the past month, he has been into Dr. Seuss books. He reads them to his mom, to his sixth-grade buddy who comes to the room once a week, to the special-education teacher, and to anyone else who will listen to him. He sits right down at Mr. Larson's desk and proceeds to read out loud from *The Cat in the Hat* (Seuss, 1957). Mr. Larson expected this and has positioned himself so he can read over Casey's shoulder, marking on his notepad the few miscues Casey is making. After Casey has been reading for a couple of minutes, Mr. Larson notices that Casey has read *sold* for the word *should* and is hesitating, looking at Mr. Larson in some confusion.

Mr. Larson:	Whoa, Casey, what's the fish telling the cat, here?
Casey:	I don't know, it doesn't make sense, "He sold not be here."
Mr. Larson:	How could you make the sentence make sense?
Casey:	"He sold it here?"
Mr. Larson:	The *s* and *h* make a sound like *shhhh,* here.
Casey:	Oh, "He *shol,* no, he *should* not be here." Oh, "He should not be about. He should not be here. When your mother is out."

And Casey reads on.

Mr. Larson noted here that Casey was not keying into the beginning sound of the word *should* and had made a nonsensical guess at pronouncing the unknown word. Casey knows that what he reads should make sense, so he pauses, waiting in a sense for Mr. Larson's help. Mr. Larson tried to get Casey to make a reasonable guess at the troublesome word based on the context of the story. Casey's pretty good at this, but Mr. Larson noticed that Casey didn't seem to know the *sh* sound. He quickly demonstrated it to Casey, who picks up where he left off and reads on without further help from Mr. Larson.

Imagine if Mr. Larson had stopped to teach a traditional basal phonics lesson here! He could have spent a half hour on a lesson on the *sh* sound, with lists of words and practice sheets. But instead, Casey got his fifteen seconds of strategic instruction and went on reading, practicing the new sound.

Mr. Larson is always amazed at how children such as Casey are so adept at picking out just the books they need. Right now, Dr. Seuss books seem to be perfect for Casey's need to solidify his intrinsic knowledge of phonics because of the

TABLE 7.1
Format for a Reading Conference

Creating a Classroom for Readers

---

1. Discuss the book with the child, ensuring comprehension and helping the child extend meaning
2. Have the child read out loud and give help or instruction as needed
3. Discuss additional activities or suggest related readings

---

stress on rhyming, repetitive words, which Mr. Larson calls "word families." Casey is transitioning from an emergent to an independent reader, but he does know that what he reads should make sense—even silliness like *The Cat in the Hat.* He knew when to ask for help, took the assistance, and continued with his task—reading.

After Casey has finished reading the section he has prepared, Mr. Larson suggests he record in his personal dictionary the words from *The Cat in the Hat* that have an *sh.* He might want them so he'll know how to read them and later spell them for something he's writing, or he might want to show them to his mom. Now Casey is eager to get back to his desk to draw a big picture of the mess the cat has made and to take a look at a new book Mr. Larson has found for him, *A Hatful of Seuss* (Seuss, 1996), which contains stories with more involved content.

Notice how Mr. Larson let Casey take the lead. Casey indicated to Mr. Larson what he needed to learn, not the other way around. The substance of a guided reading lesson should come from the learner. Reading conferences provide an excellent forum for a guided reading lesson. Children who are allowed to be in charge of their own learning seem to have a sense of when they need help. Casey leaves his conference confident and intent on his next project. Table 7.1 lists steps to take when you are having a reading conference with a child.

It's time for lunch now, and Mr. Larson reminds the class to put their dialogue journals in his basket and to leave their writing folders on their desks. Mr. Larson has had formal conferences with ten children today and has had time to check in with everyone. He's tired too from such intense teaching and is ready to relax and eat his lunch.

Across the hall, Mrs. Williams is holding her final conferences for the morning also. She has encouraged her third graders to make their own appointments with her, once a week for reading and once for writing. On the calendar now is Jennifer.

> **Mrs. Williams:** So, what did you bring to show me today?
>
> **Jennifer:** I finished *Sarah, Plain and Tall* [MacLachan, 1985]. I loved Sarah.
>
> **Mrs. Williams:** Well, tell me about her.
>
> **Jennifer:** Well, there's this family, and they have two kids, and the mother died and their father is looking for a new mother,

During a reading conference, the teacher can position herself so she can read over the child's shoulder and record miscues.

and this lady named Sarah comes on the train to live with them. She's tall, and she say's she's plain.

Mrs. Williams: What does *plain* mean in this story?

Jennifer: Well, it usually means like plain, you know, not pretty. But I liked Sarah. She liked flowers and planted a bunch of them.

Mrs. Williams: What was the problem in the story?

Jennifer: Well, I think the problem is if the kids will like her when she comes to be their mother. They do like her, and she stays.

Mrs. Williams: Is Sarah like your mother?

Jennifer: Well, no. Sarah was really young, I think. Also, my mother goes to work. But I like my mom, and they liked Sarah. Also, I think this story happened a long time ago. Maybe like *Little House on the Prairie.*

Mrs. Williams: So—it sounds like you liked it?

Jennifer: Yeah! I loved it!

Mrs. Williams:	Maybe you'd like *Ida Early Comes Over the Mountain* [Burch, 1980]. It's about a girl who is like a nanny to a bunch of little kids. I think Mrs. Sanders has it in the library.
Jennifer:	Okay, can I go to the library now to get it?
Mrs. Williams:	On your way, Jennie! Oh, and have a look at this book I found just this summer, *Searching for Laura Ingalls* [Lasky & Knight, 1993]. Do you think I should read it to the class?

And Jennifer leaves for the library. Jennifer is a sophisticated reader, and Mrs. Williams enjoys conferencing with her—they talk about children's books as friends talk about their favorite best-sellers or as families talk about movies at home. Anyone who loves books and stories is hungry for conversation about them. But this conference was not just idle book talk (Hornsby & Sukarna, 1988). Mrs. Williams was checking that Jennifer was comprehending not only at the literal level but at higher levels of thinking as well. She tuned in to Jennifer's inferences when she asked her about the problem in the story and later asked her to evaluate the book in terms of her own life and other books she's read. Jennifer has no problem finding books, but this time Mrs. Williams has responded to her interest in pioneer stories and has suggested another, more difficult book that Jennifer might enjoy. In this way, Mrs. Williams is nudging her toward more mature books.

Notice too the reading strategies that have been touched on in this conference: Mrs. Williams checked on vocabulary and on finding the main idea. Mrs. Williams had reviewed Jennifer's section in her conference notebook when she was preparing for the conference. She had noted that they'd been working for over a month on identifying the main idea, problem, or plot of stories. Today, Jennifer was able to tell the problem without a long narrative about all the subplots in the story.

Kagan is next. He declared, early in his literate life, that he "only reads nonfiction." Lucky for him, much of today's nonfiction is a lively combination of fact and delightful fantasy, appealing to both the pragmatic and those hungry for humor or story. His choice today, *The Magic Schoolbus and the Electric Field Trip* (Cole, 1997), is an example of such literature. Kagan explains that he wants to make an engine with his dad for the science fair and that he's chosen his book from the "Electricity" section in the library. Mrs. Williams listens as Kagan reads his favorite part of the book. She then asks Kagan to explain how an electromagnet works (she really doesn't know this herself—it's a genuine question). Using drawings in the book, Kagan explains his understanding of an electromagnet. When Mrs. Williams asks if all motors must have electromagnets, Kagan can't answer. So together they look through the book for this information. Mrs. Williams is modeling how to scan a book quickly. When they've found a tentative answer, Mrs. Williams asks Kagan to go over to Ms. Joy in the custodian's office to verify his conclusion.

Does this sound like a reading conference to you? Or is it a science lesson? To us, these should be indistinguishable. Kagan is practicing reading and using reading to learn about electricity and motors (Moss, Leone, & Dipillo, 1997). He's received some individual help in a study skill and is encouraged to use real resources to guide his research. He is excited about what he's learned and motivated to learn more.

Mrs. Williams finds that reading and writing conferences are the most intense and productive teaching times of the day. She must sit with one eye on the class but also focus her attention on individual children and their immediate needs. She has learned that keeping a notebook helps her remember what's happened in previous conferences and also gives her an overview of the progress each child has made over several months. Mrs. Williams finds the conference approach so much more efficient than the reading groups she used to use. She remembers feeling frustrated and guilty when she taught the children skill lessons that only some of them needed or when children had to sit and wait for others to finish reading so that the group could discuss a section of the book.

Like Mr. Larson, Mrs. Williams still has to work hard to keep all conferences within five to ten minutes so she can work with every child each week. Sometimes when she has a moment, she sneaks a look at the novel she keeps on her desk. This isn't just modeling. Mrs. Williams loves to read, both children's and adult books. She knows that occasionally showing her enthusiasm for her own reading adds to the creation of a literate environment (Au, 1997). She's made a conscious decision, though, to spend most of language arts time interacting with her children.

Years ago, when Mrs. Williams stopped using a basal reader (sometimes called literature) series to organize her reading program, she worried that her children might not learn reading skills. She also wondered whether time spent in response activities and reading out loud each day was beneficial. After several years of using an independent program, she has found that the children read just as well as before and that their attitudes toward reading and the amount of reading they do have all improved. Mrs. Williams thinks this is because they spend reading time doing real reading and responding, not wasting their time listening to other children in reading groups, answering artificial questions, or doing boring workbook pages. In fact, she marvels at how successful children were at learning to read despite these inappropriate practices (Bredekamp & Copple, 1997). Mrs. Williams knows that children enjoy reading more now and that this powerful motivation provides a momentum that comes from everyone in the class, not just from the teacher. And she no longer worries about children missing important skills because she knows that by using reading conferences, she can teach skill lessons.

Conference Processes

Conference sessions generally are a mix of discussing the content of children's reading, instructing them on knowledge or strategies they have demonstrated they could benefit from, and listening to them read aloud. Mr. Larson often checks reading comprehension by requesting students to tell him about the most interesting (or funny or exciting) part. He also asks questions to encourage critical thinking and reading between the lines in literature or to ascertain whether children are understanding the topics presented in information books. He is especially

TABLE 7.2

Types of Questions Useful for Reading Conferences

1. How do you feel about what you are reading?
2. What interesting things did you find out from reading this?
3. What was exciting (or funny) about this story (or article)?
4. What are the main points in the story (or article)?
5. What kind of people are the characters?
6. Do they seem like real people that you might meet or have for friends?
7. How do you think the author felt about the people and the situation?

concerned that a transaction has occurred between the reader and the text, that is, that the child has a powerful response (Block, 1999). Mr. Larson's questions are often similar to questions you might find in a teacher's manual, but they are aimed at an individual child's own reading selection. Mr. Larson's ultimate goal is for children to determine themselves what they will share with their teacher in the reading conference (see Table 7.2).

Mr. Larson tries first to get the student to initiate the discussion or volunteer information. He uses the questions only to probe for something not brought up. Also, he stays alert for insights about how a child is managing the reading process. He knows that many children cannot tell him what bothers them when they read.

Word-Recognition Strategies

Mr. Larson encourages youngsters to read a passage aloud to him. He never asks children to read aloud to a group unless they have a chance to prepare first since oral reading requires more skill than silent reading. However, private oral reading gives Mr. Larson clues about word-identification strategies the children are using. Mr. Larson takes notes about miscues as the child reads, jotting down the type of mistakes made rather than how many. He wants to know whether words substituted make sense in context or whether they are simply similar in appearance. He got worried when Ron read *tree* for *three* since the substituted word made no sense. But when Sue read *pond* for *lake,* Mr. Larson didn't worry at all. If the sentence and story make sense with the substitution, the reader is reading for meaning, and that is what the reading process is all about. But if Ron says a word that makes no sense and doesn't correct himself, Mr. Larson knows Ron is only reading letters. We will discuss this process, which is called miscue analysis, further in Chapter 8.

When Aaron read the word *reptile* in a book about alligators, Mrs. Williams asked him how he figured out that word and made a note of his response. When children need help figuring out a word, both Mr. Larson and Mrs. Williams encourage them to use the strategy of either skipping the word and saying, "Blank," and later returning to the word or making a guess based on what would make sense and then using phonics clues to check their guess. This approach keeps the meaning of the reading rather than the sounds of letters in the forefront. These teachers never encourage vocalizing individual letters in an effort to put sounds together. They know the worthlessness of that approach. These teachers also encourage children to ask each other for help. They always wish to foster independence and autonomy. They never suggest that children look for pronunciations in the dictionary, as the symbols used there are inappropriate for children (Wilde, 1997).

Intonation, Fluency, and Pronunciation

Mr. Larson finds that listening to his students read aloud gives him other useful information about their reading progress. While a child reads, Mr. Larson listens for intonation; he notes whether the reading sounds similar to natural talking and whether the intonation reflects the meaning of what is read. He listens for fluency, that is, the natural flow, or cadence, of language. If a child is reading slowly and hesitantly, the level of the material may be too difficult, or the child may be relying too much on phonics. Mr. Larson can monitor these processes during reading conferences and offer help. For example, Carlos can practice his fluency by preparing a selection by rereading it many times until he is ready to read aloud to a kindergarten buddy (Samuels, 1997). Mr. Larson can offer quick phonics information when necessary or explain how to tell when quotation marks show that someone is talking. Mr. Larson also notices pronunciation so that after the child has finished reading, he can help with any mispronounced words. Obviously, the teacher doesn't interrupt a reader to correct mispronunciations. Mr. Larson is delighted when he finds words that children don't use in their oral speech but they have discovered in literature. For example, it was obvious that Joey understood the meaning of *chaos* but was pronouncing it as it is spelled. A little friendly correction helped Joey add a brilliant new word to his speaking vocabulary.

If pronunciation problems stem from dialect or language differences, Mr. Larson ignores them unless the child requests help. Only after a child expresses a desire to develop standard dialect in oral or written language does Mr. Larson consider correction appropriate (Townshend & Fu, 1998). When the child requests help, teacher assistance is much more effective during preparation of oral reading than as criticism afterward. Mr. Larson shares Mrs. Hanna's convictions that children perceive criticism of their language as a personal rejection. He also agrees with her that to keep the child talking and writing is in the child's best interest, whether the speech or writing is standard English or not.

So we see Mr. Larson and Mrs. Williams using conferencing to provide individual instruction in skills, to deepen understanding of text, to plan temporary skills or interest grouping, to encourage continued progress, to provide feedback to children, and to enjoy children's reading and writing with them (Taberski, 2000). Conferencing is also a primary mode of assessing student progress, which we'll discuss further in Chapter 8.

C H A P T E R   7

AN ENVIRONMENT FOR READING

In the second grade, reading time is much quieter than writing time, when many children are working in groups. Now during reading, most of the children are intent on their individual books. We see Maria Elena and two other children working on a poster outside the room and Mr. Larson quietly talking with LaMarr, but otherwise the students are reading on their own.

Melissa is reading *Ramona and Her Father* (Cleary, 1977), a library book about a girl her own age. Since she loves a good story, her purpose is just to enjoy reading and to find out what happens. Lying on the rug in the classroom library corner, she is engrossed in her story. Felipe's purpose in reading today is to find information about comets. He has gone to the school library and checked out several reference books that listed comets in the index. The librarian helped him find an edition of *Odyssey* magazine that had an article on comets. Now Felipe has spread these materials on a table and is looking at the pictures. These two children are experiencing different but equally valid purposes for their reading. In each case, the purpose is the child's own purpose: something that child wants to do.

Mr. Larson and Mrs. Williams both use a workshop approach (Harwayne, 2000) as the format for their reading programs. This means that most of the time allotted for reading each day is devoted simply to authentic reading: the reading of real books. Mr. Larson mentions that his philosophy grew from a terse statement by Charlotte Huck (1996), "Children learn to read by reading." He realizes that all proponents of a holistic approach to reading support this theory. Therefore, he feels justified in not using basal readers, workbooks, phonics charts, or flash cards as the basis of a reading program. Instead, he uses a simpler yet vastly richer system: reading books!

Independence

An environment conducive to reading provides freedom. Students have the freedom to choose what to read, to decide when and where to read, and even not to keep reading what they've started. Why are these student freedoms important? Let's face it, we never *want* to do what we *have* to do. Adults have to free kids from *having* to read so they can *want* to read, so they *will* read. Children can never become proficient readers unless they read more than what is required in school. The child who sneaks a book and a flashlight into bed at night will be truly literate.

The second- and third-grade classrooms we are observing provide choices for what to read and offer options within the room of where to read. What's more, children even have some choice of when to read. Mrs. Williams does not use reading a book as a filler after other work is done. She allows for at least forty-five minutes of independent reading time a day and does her best not to let assemblies and other interruptions deprive the class of their precious reading time. Mrs. Williams always has a paperback book on her desk so that when time permits, she can sneak in a few moments of reading herself. By never canceling reading and writing times and by modeling reading and writing herself, Mrs. Williams is communicating to her students the importance of literacy (Au, 1997).

Quality Literature

Mr. Larson has filled his room with books. He doesn't confine books to the class library area because he wants his students to think of books all the time. He makes sure that books about chickens, at all levels, are by the chicken cage; he displays books about rockets and planets beside the solar system chart Felipe brought to share; and he puts all kinds of books along the chalkboards. Mr. Larson has noticed that children respond more to books that are displayed showing the front picture rather than shelved so that only the spines show.

Mrs. Williams's classroom has reminders about books and their contents on posters and charts hung around the room. She encourages her students to make posters, book jackets, costumes, and displays in lieu of book reports to let other children know about especially good books. She also copies poetry she thinks they might enjoy onto wall charts for their casual reading.

Both classrooms have specially designated library areas where most of the class books are kept. Both Mr. Larson and Mrs. Williams have made their class libraries inviting and pleasant places. Old rugs, cushions, and beanbag chairs provide

Students should have the freedom to choose what, when, and where to read.

cozy places for reading and browsing through books. The teachers feature books by displaying them on top of the bookshelves, where children can easily find them. The teachers frequently exchange the books that children have tired of or that they didn't care for in the first place. Also, the teachers select books on topics that interest individual children. Decorated book boxes containing a variety of books and interesting materials on a specific topic create special attractions in Mrs. Williams's room (Opitz, 1997).

Today, as Mr. Larson and the children are discussing what to do when the chicks grow up, he pulls out some books on raising poultry and mentions that he found them at the school library. Mr. Larson constantly models using libraries and helps his children be comfortable in the school library. He talks with the librarian, Mrs. Sanders, to ensure that she is aware of what is going on in his class (Giorgis & Peterson, 1996). Once a week, when they go to the library, they receive instruction on how to use the library, they hear a story related to their themes, and they check out books. The librarian has posted a schedule of times when children may go into the library alone or in small groups. Mr. Larson also likes to take at least two field trips a year to the local public library. In the fall, he makes sure that all children have a library card and that they all know how to find the children's section in this big library. A second visit is usually scheduled near the end of the school year so the librarian can give the second graders information about summer reading programs and story times and let them know that someone is always there to help them find a good book.

Choosing Books

In both the school and the public library, the librarians have taken special care to teach young children how to select books. They have pointed out sections of the library containing "everybody" books and "easy-to-read" books. The easy fiction, marked on the spine with yellow tape, is on low shelves in one corner. These books are often just the thing for first and second graders who are practicing their developing reading abilities. Right now, Joey is browsing through the "Easy Fic" section and has chosen a favorite of his, *Little Bear* (Minarik, 1957). Joey loves this book because it looks more grown up to him than the picture books his teachers read to him. The short chapters and big print are as inviting to him as the sensitive drawings by Maurice Sendak. Molly picks out *The Stupids Step Out* (Allard, 1974), a hilarious book Mr. Larson has read to the class.

Some of Joey's classmates choose books from the regular fiction section. Mrs. Sanders taught them the rule of thumb: pick a book that looks good, open to a middle page, and begin to read. For every word you don't know or can't figure out, put down one finger. If you get to your fifth finger (thumb) before you've finished the page, put the book back; it's probably too hard for you. This little rule, devised by Jeanette Veatch (1968), is easy to learn and helps children feel in charge of their own book selection in the school library.

Mrs. Sanders is also aware that children are attracted to books by their topics and authors. She has shown the children the nonfiction section and how the different topics are organized within this section. These children are probably too young to use the Dewey decimal system efficiently, but they do know where the animal books, the biographies, and the poetry books are. An avid reader herself, Mrs. Sanders loves to talk to the children and her friends about her favorite children's authors. She encourages children also to select their library books by looking for favorite authors. Her goal is that all children in the school will be independent, informed, and comfortable using this library.

AN INDEPENDENT READING PROGRAM

The children in Mr. Larson's class have put away their writing materials and settled in comfortable places around the room with their books. LaMarr sits on the sofa reading *Curious George* (Rey, 1941) for the fifth time. Amy is slouched on pillows in the reading corner, mouthing words as she reads *Maggie's Moon* (Alexander, 1982). Amy only recently began to feel confident enough to read on her own. Before that, she spent much of her reading time at the listening center. Mason is there right now; he is wearing headphones, listening to a tape of *Why Mosquitoes Buzz in People's Ears* (Aardema, 1975) and following along in a paperback copy of the book. Matthew, on the other hand, never did like those headphones—he reads alone at his desk, absorbed in *The Hardy Boys: The Great Airport Mystery* (Dixon, 1985).

Carlos is reading *Los músicos de Brema* (Gross, 1979) to Ms. Gonzales, the bilingual tutor. He speaks Spanish as his first language, and although he's been learning English from Joey and his friends, Carlos has been lucky to have an adult who reads and writes with him in his native language. Children who do not speak English as a first language should begin their reading experiences in their native language if at all possible. When they become independent readers in their first language, and when they can speak English fairly fluently, the transition to reading in English becomes natural.

Molly isn't even in the room; she's down the hall reading *Morris Has a Cold* (Wiseman, 1978) to an enthralled kindergartner. Molly has practiced this story and can read it without hesitation. It's hard to tell which child is enjoying the story more. Multiage reading activities such as this, often called peer tutoring, are academically advantageous for the younger child but most likely even better for the older child, who has seen a clear purpose for preparing an oral reading (Tompkins, 2003).

The children in this class have all kinds of reading styles, interests, backgrounds, and abilities. Mr. Larson finds that an individual reading program helps every child read what he or she is interested in, at an appropriate ability level. Matthew and Shennelle are good readers; in fact, they hardly ever stop reading. Sometimes Matthew will read three or four books a week. Mr. Larson is delighted to see this enthusiasm and encourages these children to read widely. Amy and Mason, less mature readers, are choosing books with predictable patterns, such as *A Dark, Dark Tale* (Brown, 1981) and *The Napping House* (Wood, 1984), which they've heard the teacher read. They still enjoy a chance to read to any adult who'll listen and display enthusiasm equal to Matthew's. LaMarr has checked out *Curious George* books every week of this school year, and he tells us that he has read

Ultimately, a teacher's goal is for children to determine themselves what they wish to read.

Curious George Rides a Bike (Rey, 1952) seven times. Mr. Larson doesn't interfere with LaMarr's choices. He knows that as LaMarr rereads the same book, he's practicing reading, gaining fluency, and developing his concept of a story. Carlos hasn't tried to read in English yet, but he listens intensely when Mr. Larson reads out loud and he has read all the Spanish picture books in the public library. What all these children have in common is a strong motivation to read, so that's what Mr. Larson encourages them to do.

What if these children were put into reading groups, as we were, with oral reading as the focus? Matthew and Shennelle would probably be bored with the stories in their readers. They would become adept at keeping place as reading progressed around the circle while they thought about more interesting things. Maybe Matthew would have a paperback hidden inside his book to keep him occu-

When a young child reads to an older child, they both benefit.

pied while he waited for his turn to read. Maybe Shennelle would become vigilant about other children's errors, pointing them out when they read aloud. These children would probably rush through their work sheets and other assignments so that they could get back to their reading. They might cause a teacher to ask why such good readers weren't doing well in reading.

What about Amy? She would probably be placed, like Carlos, in a "low" reading group made up of a small group of children with completely different needs. They would plod through oral reading sessions and waste endless time listening to each other stumble through lifeless stories. Amy and Carlos would soon figure out that no matter how much they learned and progressed, they'd still be in the bottom reading group. By second grade, they might already have decided that they were "dumb." Amy might withdraw; Carlos might bother other children.

Such a scenario gets very depressing, doesn't it? Mr. Larson, Mrs. Williams, Ms. Montoya, Mrs. Hanna, and Mrs. Thomas are all glad that none of the other primary teachers in their school use basal programs any more. The use of ability grouping is no longer recommended to promote effective literacy instruction

(Reutzel, 1999). The children in Mr. Larson's room read for about forty-five minutes every day, usually before lunch. It is important to build children's reading stamina. This is done through sustained reading (Calkins, 2001; Santman, 2002). Mr. Larson and the children try to arrange each day so that nothing interrupts reading time. Mr. Larson knows of a school that has everyone in the entire school read independently for the first half hour of the school day—that includes teachers, principal, children, secretaries, nurse, custodian, and even visitors. He remembers visiting this school and being asked to sit on a bench in the hall until reading time was over—luckily he had a paperback in his knapsack! A whole-school reading time isn't possible in his school, but Mr. Larson still tries to maintain reading as an inviolate time of the day. It is never replaced with other activities. In fact, on this year's field trip to the beach, the children brought their books for forty-five minutes of rest and reading before lunch.

Flexible Grouping

You might think that these classes have no reading groups. When Mrs. Williams gave up the basal reader, she eliminated fixed reading groups, but many of the class activities still happen in groups. Today, Thu, Aaron, and Melinda are working on a play that Melinda found in one of the old textbooks. They are reading it through in parts and will later make plans for inviting other children to take up the minor characters. They will present the play as a radio drama to the other third graders.

Mrs. Williams will meet this afternoon with a literature group of five children who have been reading *Rosie and Michael* (Viorst, 1974), a story about a boy and a girl who are special friends. This group has also read all the *George and Martha* books (Marshall, 1977) and has made their own *George and Martha* book for the class library. Today they want to learn about setting up a poster on how to be a friend. Next, Mrs. Williams will share a list she was given by the librarian of some more books about friends. After discussing what makes a good friend, these children will later choose to write stories about their own friends that focus on the qualities of friendship.

Mrs. Williams and Mr. Larson each have dozens of sets of six copies of the same book. These are used by literature circle groups. Mrs. Williams invites each child to participate in a literature group once a month. Mrs. Williams gives a book talk on a number of titles and lets the children select the text they are interested in reading (Reutzel, 1999). The groups all read the same book during their independent reading time or at home and then meet in class to discuss the book. Sometimes Mrs. Williams comes to the groups armed with questions, but she prefers it when the students come up with questions for each other (Wiencek & O'Flahavan, 1994). One way to facilitate children's interaction is to have each child take a turn making an opening statement about his or her thoughts on the book.

Mrs. Williams belongs to a book group herself and notices that the third graders do basically the same thing the adult group does—they compare notes on a book, discussing what they like and dislike and how the book relates to their lives. From these discussions often come suggestions for other books the group would

Reading and writing workshops allow individualization of academic needs and nurturance of self-esteem for bilingual, gifted, and at-risk children.

enjoy. Mrs. Williams finds that she enjoys her private reading much more now that she gets help from her friends, and she observes that this seems to be happening for her third graders too. She is especially excited when children recommend books to each other. Whatever the format of the discussion, however, both Mr. Larson and Mrs. Williams encourage children to come up with their own questions and avenues for discussion (Wade & Moje, 2000).

Mr. Larson uses flexible grouping. Groups form and disband for various purposes. Groups are used for writing response, for writing minilessons, for art or drama projects, for research on similar topics, and occasionally for practice in reading strategies. No child is ever stuck in a "low" group. Mr. Larson encourages groups

ALTERNATIVES TO ROUND-ROBIN READING

There is little evidence that the traditional oral-reading circle is of any educational value. However, many teachers still consider the ability to read orally an important skill. What are some ways to retain oral reading in the program?

ORAL READING FOR DIAGNOSTIC PURPOSES
Children can read orally to the teacher in a one-on-one situation.
Children can read orally to a tape recorder, parent volunteer, or older child.

ORAL READING FOR INFORMATION SHARING
Children can read the lunch menu, daily bulletin, and newspaper items.
Children can confirm an answer by reading it from a book.
One child (a good reader) can read out loud while others listen with their textbooks closed.
Children can read passages from reference books or trade books.

ORAL READING FOR ENTERTAINMENT
Two children can share one book, reading to each other.
Children can participate in choral reading.
Children can read poems or essays for an audience.
Children can participate in reading a radio drama, in play reading, or in readers' theater.

ORAL READING AS PART OF THE WRITING PROCESS
Children read their own writing in progress to partners or response groups.
Children share original creative writing or reports in the Author's Chair.

TIPS ABOUT ORAL READING
Have children prepare in advance anything to be read for an audience.
Remember that oral reading decreases comprehension.
Teach children how to read punctuation and inflection.
Give children the opportunity to listen to good readers (tapes and CDs).

of mixed abilities. Usually the children choose their own groups, but Mr. Larson requires everyone to work in a writing response group once a week and in a literature circle group once a month. When studying social studies or science topics, Mr. Larson encourages mixed ability groupings by providing boxes of a variety of books on a subject (Opitz, 1997). No child is ever left out or left behind because of language differences or less developed reading ability (Schifini, 1996).

Mr. Larson will never have the time to read with his students as often as he'd like, whether in small groups or as individuals. So he actively recruits individuals who will read with and to his children and who will listen to his children read. He schedules classroom volunteers during reading and writing time. These parents, foster grandparents, and college students don't need much special preparation for helping with reading—what they do need is time, patience, and guidance to let the children figure out things for themselves. Mr. Larson also insists that his students go to each other for help, even when adults are in the classroom, to foster independence. In addition, he always schedules time for "reading buddies"—children from both higher and lower grades who spend half an hour a week reading together with his children. Both younger and older children benefit from such cross-age tutoring (Taylor, Hanson, Justice Sewanson, & Watts, 1997).

Comprehension Strategies

Mr. Larson believes that the goal of reading is comprehension and that the goal of comprehension is to construct meaning. He knows that proficient readers extend their understanding beyond the literal level of the text. He emphasizes the strategies identified by Stephanie Harvey and Anne Goudvis (2000) with his students. These include making connections between prior knowledge and the text, asking questions, visualizing, drawing inferences, determining important ideas, synthesizing information, and repairing understanding when a reader is confused. Mr. Larson models these strategies during read-alouds and shared readings by occasionally thinking aloud as he reads. He provides guided practice during reading conferences.

When several children are practicing a similar reading strategy, Mr. Larson might form a temporary study group. When the teacher has prepared or collected special materials for practicing a strategy, it can be efficient to share those materials with several children at once, and the children have the benefit of working with peers. Group sessions that allow youngsters to construct their own knowledge often depend on peer collaboration far more than teacher instruction to achieve a given goal.

Last week, Mr. Larson worked with Mason, Isaac, and Sam to help them use context clues. He noticed that these children were hesitant about guessing at unknown words and tried too hard to sound them out. To help them use picture and sentence context, Mr. Larson gave them comic strips with words missing and encouraged them to guess what went in the blanks. Later, during conferences, he reminded the children to use that guessing strategy if they got stuck on words when they were reading out loud to him.

Response to Literature

Do you remember Maria Elena and her friends who were working on a poster outside the room during reading time? Were these girls reading? They were working on an important part of an independent literature program, *response to literature* (Huck, 1996). When we turn a reading program over to our students, when they choose books they want to read for pleasure or for information, we expect that the children will respond in some way. Often a response to literature is just a thought—a child may wonder what happened to Wilbur after his friend Charlotte died or imagine wild things in his or her own closet. Other children respond by asking questions: Do you remember Ramona asking Miss Binney how Mike Mulligan went to the bathroom in *Ramona the Pest* (Cleary, 1968)? In a literature discussion group, children have a chance to listen to their classmates' responses and to share their own feelings about their readings. Teachers like Mr. Larson are delighted when children argue over books and recommend good books to each other. Sometimes during class meeting, a child will share a book with the whole class. This morning, Amy shared *Crow Boy* (Yashima, 1955). Sometimes she daydreams and watches the crows hopping around outside the room, and it impressed her that Taro, the hero of the book, did the same thing. Amy shared her impressions of crow calls, and before she was finished with her report, Joey and LaMarr both wanted to see the book.

Mr. Larson never assigns written book reports, but he does encourage the children to write about special books they've read. Sometimes comments on books show up in the dialogue or home-school journals. When this happens, Mr. Larson writes back, reflecting on what the child has said and asking for more. One month, after the class had been reading folktales, Mr. Larson noticed that many of the children's stories began to include folkloric elements, such as "once upon a time," princes and princesses, and three wishes. Reading literature has a powerful influence on the content of children's writing (Lancia, 1997). Discussing literature helps build knowledge of the writer's craft (Portalupi, 1999).

Flexible groups allow teacher and children to work together for a variety of purposes.

Sometimes Mr. Larson encourages children to make a poster or some type of advertisement for a book they think others will like. That's what Maria Elena and her friends are doing. They've written what reads like a movie advertisement from the newspaper for *No Jumping on the Bed!* (Arnold, 1987). These girls have never lived in a New York apartment building like the one in the book, but they were giggling over the book as they passed it among themselves, and they decided that Mr. Larson should order lots of copies for the class library. Mr. Larson challenged them to prove to him how funny the book was, and this poster is the result. Now they are decorating their six-foot-tall poster to show various floors of the apartment building Walter fell through and laughing as they paint. These girls are responding in writing as well as with art.

Response to literature takes many forms besides thinking, talking, and writing. Mr. Larson, like all the other primary teachers at his school, encourages children to express their impressions of stories through art. Murals, maps, animal cutouts, and all kinds of posters cover the walls and the hallway outside the room. Mr. Larson invites the children to do all the bulletin boards and room decoration. Inspirations from reading seem to show up everywhere. When Mr. Larson put clay out yesterday, many of the children made chicks and eggs, but Amy made a crow. Children also enjoy making dioramas, shadow boxes, displays, and costumes about their books. Last Halloween, all the children in Mrs. Williams's class dressed up as book characters.

Thu's mother spent a week last October with Thu's class helping the children make puppets from old light bulbs, pieces of cloth, and papier-mâché. Most of the children made scary Halloween monsters that they used to act out Jack Prelutsky's *Nightmares* (1976). One year, Mrs. Williams's class made puppets to act out different folktales. Puppets seem to open the door for creative dramatics. Even the quietest child will act out a part behind a puppet.

Mrs. Williams encourages other dramatic activities, such as readers' theater, pantomime, and play reading. Many children in second and third grades are not interested in presenting plays for other children, but they love to read out loud. Plays are a natural way to satisfy this desire and to give children practice in reading with expression. When a group does ask to do a play for others, a teacher or a parent helps them stage it so that no child is put on the spot to memorize lines or be embarrassed in front of others.

Groups usually meet in the afternoon during activity time to work on various projects. Some of these projects involve the whole class; others are initiated by small groups. This can be a noisy part of the day, but Mrs. Williams finds that she enjoys the sounds of children busy at their work. Besides, she knows that an active response will help these children remember, understand, and appreciate the books they've been reading.

Response to literature must involve an open-ended reaction to the work of literature. The teacher may suggest or provide the medium of response (a radio play, use of pastels on black paper, and so on), but the direction of that response must belong to the child to be authentic. Open-ended activities encourage children to express their own reactions and emotions, not those of the teacher.

Response to literature takes many forms. Primary teachers encourage children to express their impressions of stories through art.

Vocabulary Development

Mr. Larson and Mrs. Williams believe that the best way to increase an independent reader's reading vocabulary is to let them read widely and often (their colleagues who work with emergent readers agree; see Chapter 4). They know that traditional vocabulary instruction consists of defining words in sentences. Typically, the words have little connection to what students already know; finding definitions and using words in a sentence doesn't ensure understanding, and it is definitely not fun (Rasinski & Padak, 2000). Mr. Larson and Mrs. Williams recognize that concrete experiences provide ample opportunities to learn new words and concepts. After a field trip, Mr. Larson uses shared writing in the form of a language experience story to develop vocabulary as well as concepts. Mrs. Williams knows that her students do much of their vocabulary development at home. Whenever they read, students are building their vocabulary (Johnson, 2001). By providing students time to read, write, and talk about their experiences, teachers provide vocabulary instruction (Heller, 1999).

Enrichment Activities

When you begin to read children's books, you'll see that some books simply must be accompanied by activities that the teacher can organize for the class to do. For example, *Stone Soup* (Brown, 1947) and *Blueberries for Sal* (McCloskey, 1948)

GUIDELINES FOR HELPING CHILDREN LEARN TO READ

Children work hard at reading whatever is important to them.

Children learn to read by reading. **At first they may understand the thought and express it in somewhat different words. As they continue reading, gradually they become more accurate. As they experience the process and talk about it, it becomes clearer to them.**

Children learn to read intuitively. **Since learning to read is largely intuitive, as most learning is at this age, explanations, directions, and direct teaching may do more to confuse than to help. After children have established successful reading processes, they can discuss ways to gain greater depth and evaluative ability.**

Reading involves understanding written thoughts. **To find out how well children read, ask them to tell you about what they have read. Ask follow-up questions in terms of the purpose for which they were reading.**

Children need to develop self-confidence as readers. **When children select their own reading materials and can talk about what they have read, they experience success. When helping children who have difficulty, emphasize how much they were able to understand on their own.**

Each child's development and experience with reading are unique. **Since no two children learn at the same rate, listening and responding to them individually and in small groups are more useful than group instruction.**

When children read effectively, they understand the meaning but may or may not report it in the exact words of the print. **As long as children do not seriously distort meaning, don't make an issue of it. If there is distortion, allow time for children to self-correct. If children do not question the meaning of the distorted sentence themselves, then is the time to raise the question of meaning.**

Children learn to read most effectively when what they read is important to them. **When children choose their own reading material, it is automatically more important to them than what might be assigned, and they want to find out what it says. They concentrate on getting the meaning.**

wouldn't seem complete in a primary classroom if the teacher and children didn't make a big pot of stone soup or a batch of blueberry muffins. After reading *The Quilt* (Jonas, 1984), it is fun to have children pick out or decorate fabric squares that can be sewn into a huge classroom quilt. *Peter Rabbit* (Potter, 1902) and *Rabbit Hill* (Lawson, 1944) seem to call for planting a garden or at least some carrot seeds. As you read children's books, always be aware of the art, cooking, sewing, or building ideas that can enrich the meaning of the book for children. Many children's books, such as Peter Spier's *The Fox Went Out on a Chilly Night* (1961), are based on songs and music. Wouldn't it be a shame to miss a chance for a good song, game, or dance that a book like this suggests?

When considering teacher-directed enrichment activities, remember that every activity should have as its purpose a deeper understanding of literature. Activities that precede a reading can help build a context and provide focus. Activities presented during a reading aid understanding and enthusiasm. Follow-up activities help summarize the meaning of a book and help children make connections. Remember, though, that teacher-initiated activities do not necessarily allow for individual children's response and do not replace open-ended response to literature activities.

Reading to Learn

Many primary teachers say that their focus must be developing foundations in literacy and mathematics and therefore that they just don't have time to teach science, social studies, and critical thinking. Mr. Larson thinks differently. He always makes sure that any area of content study is supported by reading and writing. One way he can do this is to stock his room with books on the topics of study and invite children to read widely in these books. If the books are of different levels of difficulty and if their range is varied, every child will be enticed to read and learn about the topic. In addition, since content information comes from a variety of sources, the children can function as a learning community, sharing and comparing information.

The classroom science books may lead to collections of shells, insects, or leaves; observation charts of the weather; and experiments about sunlight. When the class decides to study whales, Mr. Larson collects all the whale books he can find. He takes the opportunity to show children how nonfiction books are organized and how to use the table of contents, the index, and chapter headings. He assists children in making charts of information they've gleaned from their reading. When the children discovered that some of the whale books discussed orca whales as friendly, intelligent, and sociable whereas others labeled them dangerous enemies of people, Mr. Larson helped them compare these different points of view in the different texts and separate facts from opinions.

Social studies trade books lead to maps, charts, and time lines; to comparisons with children in other countries; and to field trips in the community. Reading about and responding to the lives of famous individuals can provide insight into others' lives and times as well as their own (Koeller & Mitchell, 1996–1997). Health books lead to children's keeping track of the food they eat and when they brush their teeth. Picture books about math illustrate much more than counting: *Fraction Action* (Leedy, 1994) illustrates concepts, and *Math Curse* (Scieszka, 1995) helps children identify with math anxiety. Do you see how closely related reading and writing are to the other subjects you must cover in the primary grades? There's no need to make content areas separate in a literature program; in fact, they're hard

If science and social studies materials reflect different levels of difficulty and if their range is varied, every child will be encouraged to read and learn about the topic.

to keep separate. Remember Mr. Larson's chickens? The children learned science and math concepts and processes through observing those chickens in addition to practicing reading and writing about chickens. Many teachers who use an integrated curriculum say that they have more time to do all things they want to because their curriculum isn't chopped up into little sections.

THE TEACHER'S ROLE

We have already discussed the heart of an independent reading program: the conference. We have also described the important role of the teacher in setting the physical and emotional environment conducive to reading. Work on the physical environment involves time before and after school for selecting, sorting, and displaying reading materials. At the beginning of the school year, teachers arrange a library area so that children perceive it as semisecluded and comfortable. Maintaining this positive emotional environment and fostering the freedom for children to choose what, when, and where to read become a teacher's ongoing job.

If you aren't tied down to meeting with three reading groups, you are free for individual reading conferences and for spontaneous interaction with individuals. You can circulate while children work, asking a question here, making a suggestion there. You can spend time guiding children in working independently. For instance, you can help them select books of interest and of appropriate difficulty. You can help children learn to keep their own record sheets of the books they have read. You can help them learn to work in groups and provide guidance so they can learn the limits about where they can work, how noisy they can be, and what materials they can use. You can model the importance of reading by sharing your own favorite books and by reading yourself when you have a spare moment. If you provide guidelines and organization, an individual, activity-oriented program such as this has a much greater chance of success.

Read-Aloud Time

One of teachers' big responsibilities and greatest joys is to read out loud to their children. Even though most second and third graders can read independently, they still love to listen to their teacher read to them. You probably know how satisfying it is to share a good book with a group of rapt listeners. Second and third graders still like picture storybooks but are also fascinated with chapter books. Beverly Cleary's *Ramona the Pest* (1968) is a great way to start young children with chapter books. They will feel smug in their knowledge about the misadventures of Ramona as she starts kindergarten. Read to your children every day, several times a day. You will be giving your youngsters models of good stories, exciting vocabulary, and beautifully constructed sentences that will not only entertain but also contribute to the richness of their oral language and their writing. And you will provide a common literary experience for everyone in the class (Rasinski & Padak, 2000).

Mrs. Williams always starts the day by reading out loud to the whole class. She chooses books that she thinks will stretch her listeners, not ones they'll read on their own or that their parents might read to them at home. Right now she's reading *Koko's Kitten* (Patterson, 1985), a book recommended by the public librarian. As the class hears the story of Koko the gorilla, who communicates in sign language, many themes emerge to explore and discuss: Can animals really "talk"? Can they "love" another animal? Children in the primary grades generally enjoy books for their surface stories, but the adept teacher can enrich a story by exploring deeper themes in discussion.

Read-aloud time is one of the favorite times of day for everyone. Ruben likes to imagine pictures in his head; Molly draws elaborate pictures of the stories she hears. Jennifer just likes to relax and listen. For Mrs. Williams, this is one of the most satisfying parts of the school day—she loves the calm feeling of having everyone concentrating on the same thing. With so much going on in class, this is one of the few times when the children have common ground, and Mrs. Williams often chooses a book that represents what the class is studying in science, social stud-

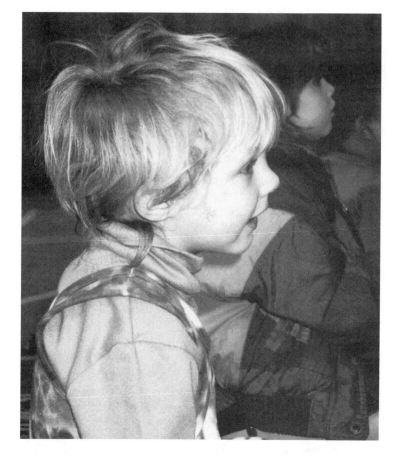

Read-aloud time is one of the best times of day for everyone.

ies, or literature. She chose *Koko* because the class has been talking about how animals communicate.

Many teachers also enjoy telling stories. When you are not holding a book between yourself and your listeners, you'll have an almost magical connection with them. We all know what it feels like to catch a child's eye while we read out loud. In storytelling, you maintain constant eye contact, and, like an actor or a comedian, you respond to your audience—to their giggles and their fears—in a most intimate way. Mr. Larson recently took a storytelling class and learned two folktales. His children beg him to tell his stories over and over again, so he is busy learning another story.

A Literature Curriculum

Teachers often organize a literature curriculum for their class and sometimes even for their school. Some, like Mr. Larson, want to be sure that children are reading in a variety of genres so that they are aware of the full range of literary experiences. During this school year, Mr. Larson has highlighted a different genre each month: folktales, animal stories, mysteries, information books, poetry, fantasy, historical fiction, modern fiction, and biographies. He introduces the genre by reading a good example to the class and then asks Mrs. Sanders, the librarian, to pull out lots more books of that genre. Remember Matthew and his Hardy Boys mysteries? He may never have discovered mysteries if it hadn't been for a literature curriculum.

Mrs. Williams prefers to focus on an author of the month. When she read Tomie dePaola's *Watch Out for the Chicken Feet in Your Soup* (1985), many of her third graders were so impressed that they picked up other dePaola books (there are over a hundred to choose from!). Mrs. Williams creates an author display each month and encourages her students to write letters to the featured author. Once in a while, Mrs. Williams is able to coordinate her author of the month with a school visit from that writer. This year, Ann Dixon, a local Alaskan writer, shared her newest book, *Trick or Treat* (1998), with the children before it was even published! The author approach gives the children a strategy. They will tell you that one of the best ways to find a good book in the library is to look for a favorite author. This year, they'll learn about at least nine authors in great detail.

When you choose challenging literature to read out loud, whether you choose by genre, author, or topic or even when you follow a list of specific books, you have the opportunity to stretch your listeners by offering them literature they might never have chosen themselves. Many of the books teachers read out loud are too difficult for the children to read on their own or have topics that are new. Mrs. Williams tries not to read books her students are already reading but instead chooses those that will give them an enjoyable challenge.

By second and third grade, children have constructed a great deal of knowledge about literature that they probably couldn't verbalize. They know about characters and that their changes create a story. They know that certain words create images or feelings and that book language is different from oral language. They know they can find themselves and their own joys and fears in stories. They know that myths explain the unexplainable. They know that books can become models for their own writing and that sometimes their own writing sounds like books they've read (Figure 7.1). Some literature programs and teachers' guides belabor such knowledge, encouraging the teacher to "teach" these intangibles. We hope you will help your children read widely and deeply and encourage them to take what they learn and apply it to their lives, their writing, and their knowledge of the world. We hope you will not spend time "teaching" such concepts as rhyme in poetry or setting in prose but instead will simply encourage and support children in using these literary devices in their own writing.

Individualized Guided Reading

If the teacher doesn't have reading groups, doesn't assign required stories, and doesn't teach basal skill lessons, what does the teacher do to help children learn specific reading information and strategies? Certainly not assign workbook or ditto pages! Neither Mr. Larson nor Mrs. Williams believes in workbooks. They see

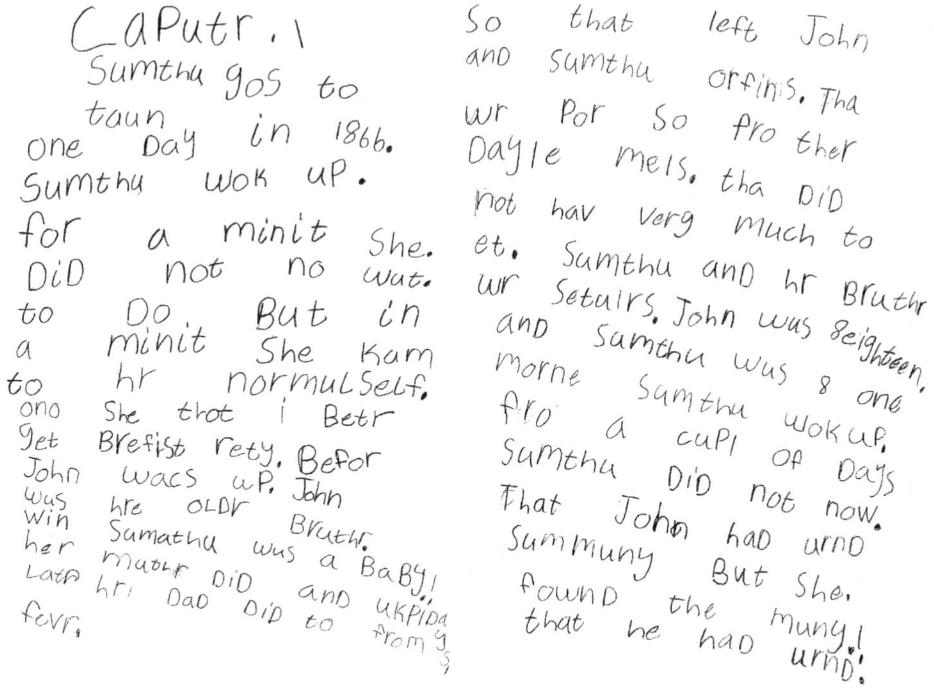

CaPutr . 1
Sumthu gos to
taun in 1866.
one Day
Sumthu wok uP.
for a minit She.
DiD not no wut.
to Do. But in
a minit She kam
to hr normulSelf.
ono She thot i Betr
get Brefist rety. Befor
John wacs uP. John
was hre OLDr Bruthr.
win Sumathu wus a BaBy!
her muthr DiD and ukPiDa
Latr hri Dad DiD to
fevr.   from g

So that left John
and Sumthu orfins. Tha
wr Por So Pro ther
Dayle mels, tha DiD
not hav verg much to
et. Sumthu and hr Bruthr
wr Setuirs. John was 8eighteen,
and Sumthu wus 8 one
morne Sumthu wok uP,
fro a cuPl oF Days
Sumthu DiD not now.
That John had urnd
SumMuny But She,
FounD the muny,!
that he had urnd!

FIGURE 7.1

Literary models from children's reading are often translated into their own personal writing.

little carryover to actual reading or writing from the isolated drills provided in workbooks, except perhaps a negative attitude toward reading and writing. Mrs. Williams says, "If you must use workbooks, just don't call it reading or writing." She has had children in her classes whose past experiences have led them to equate reading with workbooks.

Instead of using skill lessons and work sheets, Mr. Larson and Mrs. Williams, like the primary-grade teachers in the previous chapters, do the vast majority of their teaching individually, either during informal checking in with children as they work or during more formal reading and writing conferences. You've probably already figured out that through careful individual attention to spelling errors in writing and to graphophonemic miscues in reading, you can quickly and purposefully see what a child's immediate needs are. Then you can help the child with the phonics instruction and strategies he or she needs. When you show a child during a conference how to indent a paragraph, to look at a long compound word as two parts, or to see the difference between first-person and third-person writing, you're teaching information about language. When you model making a chart of comparisons between two characters, show how to skim a page, or demonstrate how to use an index to find references to a specific topic, you're teaching strategies. Teachers must be vigilant to constantly identify and address each child's needs but also must never waste a child's time on skill lessons or work sheets that the child doesn't need. What a shame when the child could be reading or writing instead!

Supporting Children with Special Needs

Sometimes a child just doesn't seem to progress. When this happens with one of his children, Mr. Larson works hard to determine whether the cause is a school-based or a home-based one. Discussions with parents often lead to mutual efforts on behalf of the child. If a situation outside school is causing learning problems, families can be helped to find counseling and other resources.

If the problem lies within the school, Mr. Larson considers it his job to try to correct it. He has seen some youngsters who had trouble reading because they had a mistaken idea of what reading was. Their previous experience led them to believe it was naming words rather than a thinking process. In these cases, Mr. Larson pro-vided experiences to counteract this previous learning. He has found that going back to taking dictation from a child sometimes helps a youngster make that missing connection between print and meaning.

Sometimes a child has not learned procedures for self-help. The youngster may become discouraged and stop whenever an unknown word is encountered, not knowing what to do next. If this seems to be the problem, Mr. Larson focuses on helping the student learn to ask questions such as "What word would make sense here?" and "What word that starts with that letter would make sense?" Mr. Larson also says not to worry about a word if the story makes sense without knowing what it is. Finally, he reminds the child that there are twenty-four other youngsters in the class who can help, if the child asks.

Some children may have motivational problems. A child may be trying to read material that is of no personal interest or may not believe that any reading is worth doing. A child may be totally turned off by any kind of schoolwork. If a teacher only needs to help a child find something more interesting to read, the problem is simple. But if the problem stems from a negative attitude toward read-ing or school in general, then the problem is serious. Mr. Larson has spent a good deal of time and energy trying to determine why one of his students has negative feelings about learning. He needs to know if these feelings reflect past failures with learning, home attitudes, or emotional problems with authority. Until he has this information, Mr. Larson may have a hard time helping that child.

Mr. Larson tries to keep kids turned on to learning. He tries to involve them in activities that they have selected, and he attempts to maintain teacher-student relationships that keep kids open to his suggestions. He knows that when chil-dren like their teacher and think their teacher likes them, they are influenced by the teacher's enthusiasm and suggestions. He also thinks that encouraging self-direction and personal responsibility for learning keeps kids involved and inter-ested in school.

Mr. Larson doesn't put kids with reading problems in a group that isn't expected to do much. He believes this kind of grouping will just make sure that they will never do anything. Mr. Larson also hesitates to endorse traditional remedial procedures, especially those that pull children out of the classroom to drill them on isolated letters, sounds, or words. He fears that this type of instruction will make learning meaningless and more difficult. However, Mr. Larson is comfortable with one pullout approach, the Reading Recovery program (Clay, 2001). This short-term program focuses on meaning in reading rather than on isolated skills. Mr. Larson has learned much about the roots of reading problems and ways to deal with them from talking with the Reading Recovery teacher. Though the program serves first graders, Mr. Larson thinks it is important that he provide some of the same kind of assistance to his second graders.

Mr. Larson has also known some excellent remedial reading teachers who used other approaches and who worked with reading problems within the regular classroom. Mr. Larson welcomes help in his classroom from Mrs. Whitmore, the Title 1 teacher. Sometimes he and the specialist together can discover a gap in understanding and remedy it with such special attention. Any extra help can ease the burden of trying to provide for each child's interests, level of knowledge, and style of learning.

In addition, Mr. Larson must help parents understand and deal with their children's learning problems. Periodically, parents ask if their child is dyslexic. Then Mr. Larson explains that the term *dyslexia* has no meaning other than "does not read." When Tom's parents were convinced that Tom was dyslexic because he sometimes wrote letters backward, Mr. Larson explained that children just becoming familiar with print often fail to notice which way a letter faces. He assured them that most reversal problems disappear by themselves after more experience with print. Naturally, Mr. Larson knows that some children do have physical and perceptual impairments to learning. These youngsters must be accepted as they are and helped to make adaptations in order to achieve whatever their potential may be.

There are children who are clearly at risk for school failure for a variety of reasons. Usually, these children themselves are fine, but their values, experiences, and expectations about learning don't match those of the schools. Flexible, developmentally appropriate approaches to education can help bridge these differences and remove some of these children from the "at-risk" category. Labels do not serve these children well; opportunities to engage in real reading and writing, coupled with appropriate instruction, do (Allington & Baker, 1999). Standardized tests have had the most negative impact on these children because of the cultural bias inherent in those tests. Holistic teaching and assessment methods are more able to meet the needs of a diverse population of learners.

Oddly enough, the formula for meeting the needs of bilingual and gifted children is the same as that for at-risk students. Bilingual children need materials and role models in their home language, but their processes for learning to read and write are the same as those of monolingual children. Flexible, developmentally appropriate approaches allow gifted children to advance at their own rate, choose challenging and enriching materials, and then analyze them with the depth and

Bilingual children learn reading and writing through the same processes that monolingual children use.

breadth they desire. Reading and writing workshops allow the same individualization of academic needs and nurturance of self-esteem for many different kinds of learning needs.

Encouraging Parental Involvement

Mr. Larson and Mrs. Williams know that they cannot be the only supporters of reading and writing—parents and family members are powerful models and teachers as well. Parents can be involved on several levels: by simply knowing what is going on in the class, by becoming cognizant of how and why teachers do what they do, and, finally, by actively participating in instruction (Hannon, 1998; Rasinski & Padak, 2000).

Mr. Larson sends home a weekly newsletter. In it, he announces classroom activities, themes, and materials needed. He makes liberal use of short articles written by his students and provides information on community activities, television shows, and books that might be of interest. Parents are appreciative of this consistent direct communication and always have a reference (often kept on the refrigerator or calendar) of class activities.

Remember the activity in Chapter 6 that suggested that you write a letter to parents explaining invented spelling? A letter or newsletter is a great vehicle for informing parents of current thought and practice. Often the only model of education parents have is their own. The primary classroom is very different today from what it was twenty years ago. Parents need to know about current practices—not just what happens but also why. It is challenging to explain complex concepts, such as construction of knowledge, but it is necessary if you really want parents to understand and support your teaching methods. Many teachers plan quarterly parent nights when they address specific topics—the writing process, why we don't use basals anymore, invented spelling—as an additional approach to informing parents. Some schools provide newsletters and parent meetings at the schoolwide level as well, but we think personal communication is much more powerful. Most parents who have helped in the classroom during the school day become a teacher's best allies. Mr. Larson and Mrs. Williams will both tell you that they put a lot of energy into working with parents. Often, it is harder than working with children, but it's a necessary ingredient to success.

We have stated that we don't believe in homework for young children, but we do believe in shared activities for students and their parents. Many of our teachers make it a practice to send a book home weekly for the child to read to the parent or other adult or vice versa. Other "homework" assignments that are meaningful include writing in the home-school journal, investigating and recording information about the home, and writing lists and letters. This week Patrick was asked to find, with the help of his mom, all the things that use energy in his house. He compiled his list himself, and the list was later used in a class discussion. When the class was studying cultures, Patrick interviewed his parents to find out about the ethnicity of his grandparents.

If teachers inform parents and include parents in what they're doing, then parents will become partners, not adversaries, in the educational process. Ongoing communication and support on the teacher's part helps develop authentic partnerships (Rasinski & Padak, 2000). Parent conferences, which we'll discuss in the next chapter, are essential to building personal rapport between teacher and parents. The most important thing parents can do is work with their children. This does not mean doing their homework for them (again, we are not strong advocates of homework for young children anyway). It does mean modeling and supporting literacy and other academic subjects. It means encouraging library use and buying books, reading out loud to children and listening to them read aloud, writing notes and participating in home-school journals, and actually stamping and mailing letters to grandparents. It means regulating television, talking with their children, and paying attention to what they say. It means not criticizing developmental writing, accepting invented spelling, and being patient with slow and stumbling reading.

When teachers inform parents and include parents in what they're doing, they should be able to enlist parents as partners, not adversaries, in the educational process.

Parents are an extremely valuable resource within the school, but many parents are uncomfortable in their child's school. They may remember their own painful experiences, or they may be embarrassed by limited education, poverty, or limited use of English. It is easy but not accurate to assume that when parents don't come to school, they don't value education or they are illiterate. Many parents are not available to come in during school hours.

As a teacher and a member of a school staff, you must make school a welcoming place for parents and community members during the school day and in the evening. Teachers need to be sure they avoid unneccessary parent exclusion, for example, denying parents access to the classroom during or after school hours (Hannon, 1998). Activity nights, cultural events, potlucks, or ball games in the gym or playground are all nonthreatening ways to invite parents into the school building. Translators can help with conferencing and with multilingual editions of school newsletters. English-as-a-second-language (ESL) classes, adult literacy instruction, and study groups and book clubs are valuable to families as a whole, as they empower adults who may otherwise lean heavily on their children for access to the world outside their homes (Morrow, 1995). For those parents who are intimidated by the school, all these small steps help build trust and confidence.

CONCLUSION

We hope you agree with us that nurturing children who have learned to "really read" is an exciting and rich process. It need never be boring because the choices in reading material are boundless. Open-ended response activities allow for individual and group creativity, and reading conferences allow the teacher to keep close contact with each individual reader and his or her needs. In the following chapter, we'll explore how assessment is an integral part of the reading and writing processes in the primary grades.

DISCUSSION QUESTIONS

1. Think about your own reading interests. How did they develop? What experiences have affected your choices of reading materials? How do you decide whether you will read a particular book?
2. Families seem to spend all their free time watching television and no longer read for pleasure. How can we motivate youngsters to do what their parents do not do?
3. Why is response to literature so important? Is it worth valuable reading time to make dioramas or murals, perform skits, or talk to friends? Think of as many ways as you can of how response to literature can be related to writing.

SUGGESTED FOLLOW-UP ACTIVITIES

1. Assist a child in selecting and preparing a story to read aloud to others. Remember that the choice to read aloud must be the child's. The choice of material to read must also be the child's.
2. Observe children as they select books from a library. Note how they choose as they sort through collections. Try to determine by what criteria or on what basis they make their selections.
3. One at a time, engage several children in private discussions about reading. The children should differ in reading abilities and levels. Ask each whether reading is enjoyable and why or why not. Ask each what kinds of reading materials he or she prefers. Ask how they deal with unknown words. Ask how they feel if they can't pronounce some words. Analyze the children's responses to determine the implications for teaching.

4. Begin your exploration of children's literature by compiling a set of books to support a topic of study in a primary classroom. Analyze the books. Which are best to read aloud? Which are appropriate for independent readers? Design a classroom display for your books and share some of them with the class.

5. Learn a story and tell it to a group of young children. Analyze your own delivery and the reactions of your listeners. How does this experience differ from reading aloud?

6. Collect a group of books on a particular topic. Try to include not only books for a wide range of reading levels but also books of different genres.

7. Organize or join a book group and participate in several discussions about books your group reads. What contributes to a good discussion? How is your understanding of a book enhanced by group interaction?

RECOMMENDED FURTHER READING

Clay, M. (1993). *Reading Recovery: A guidebook for teachers in training.* Portsmouth, NH: Heinemann.

Hart-Hewins, L., & Wells, J. (1990). *Real books for reading: Learning to read with children's literature.* Portsmouth, NH: Heinemann.

Harwayne, S. (2000). *Lifetime guarantees: Toward ambitious literacy teaching.* Portsmouth, NH: Heinemann.

Hornsby, D., & Sukarna, D. (1988). *Read on: A conference approach to reading.* Portsmouth, NH: Heinemann.

Huck, C., Hepler, S., & Hickman, J. (2000). *Children's literature in the elementary school.* Fort Worth, TX: Harcourt Brace Jovanovich.

Samway, K. D., Whang, G., & Pippitt, M. (1995). *Buddy reading: Cross age tutoring in a multicultural classroom.* Portsmouth, NH: Heinemann.

8

ASSESSING GROWTH IN LITERACY

Teachers are in a better position to know and learn about an individual's development than outsiders.

R. J. Tierney, 1998

As schools and teachers have become more knowledgeable about comprehensive literacy principles and emergent literacy concepts, teaching methods and materials have changed too. Unfortunately, methods and tools for assessment of instructional outcomes have been slower to change. In response to educational policies and mandates that push assessment, many national organizations, including the National Association for the Education of Young Children, the International Reading Association, the American Educational Research Association, the Council of Chief State School Officers, the Division for Early Childhood of the Council for Exceptional Children, and the National Association of Bilingual Educators, have addressed assessment issues through working groups, position statements, and publications.

Many teachers are faced with state-mandated, standardized tests that are incongruous with their teaching (Altwerger & Strauss, 2002). Others will soon be feeling this pinch. Under the "No Child Left Behind" act, the federal government mandated a single test-based accountability system for all states. This dramatically expands the accountability focus in our country (Elmore, 2002). This is detrimental, as children already face far too much testing. Many educators who strive to involve their students in more authentic reading and writing activities are fearful because this means less time spent preparing children for skills tests. Their common question is, "But what if students don't do well on the test?"

MATCHING ASSESSMENT TO INSTRUCTION

Many teachers have good reason to be fearful, as there are high stakes associated with test scores. In many states, there are serious consequences in terms of student promotion, school funding and management, and even teacher review based on student performance (Altwerger & Strauss, 2002; Kohn, 2000). This is a clear misuse of test data (Haladyna, Haas, & Allison, 1998). In fact, the American Psychological Association's guidelines for test use specifically prohibit basing any consequential judgment about an individual learner on a single test score (Elmore, 2002).

Most tests for assessing reading ability have the same flaws as the outmoded approaches to reading (Clay, 1993a; Tierney, 1998). They emphasize subskills of reading, and they work on these subskills out of the context of real reading or writing. These tests not only lack validity in content but also lack reliability because of the circumstances under which they are administered. For young children, the artificial testing situation totally invalidates the results (Kohn, 2001). For all ages, the results are unreliable because the tests do not provide the continuous text and teacher support that are part of a real reading situation and that assist children in performing at their best.

We want to assess children's best performance. After all, the most important reason for assessing young children is to maximize instruction to help them learn (Leu & Kinzer; 2003; Rasinski & Padak, 2000), but this is not the result when assessment measures are unrelated to classroom practices. In fact, as Tierney

(1998) says, "tests tend to displace teaching and learning activities rather than enhance them" (p. 388). The accountability focus inherent in the standards movement has caused many districts to abandon performance-based assessment in favor of preparing students for tests (Brooks & Brooks, 2003). "Teaching to the test" is a common response when tests are mandated and scores are emphasized. Schools move away from principles of learning, student-centered curriculum, and constructivist teaching practices in their quest for higher test scores. The result is a watered-down curriculum that results in less learning. The focus on high-stakes, test-based accountability has begun to affect teaching approaches (Kohn, 2000; Santman, 2002).

Standardized test scores do not tell the teacher why a child made errors, nor do they give information useful for helping children improve. To guide their teaching, teachers actually rely on data they collect as they teach and observe children's learning processes during their engagement in natural literacy events. Marie Clay (1993a) likens this to coaching a football game, saying, "You do not improve the play of a team by looking at the outcome score. The coach must look closely at how the team is playing the game and help them to change the moves or strategies that produce a better final score" (p. 4). Formal testing processes generally just give the final score.

Nevertheless, the entrenched values related to testing keep school policymakers and the public from accepting more valid approaches. Standardized tests have been revered for their supposed objectivity. However, critical appraisals point out that subjectivity exists in standardized tests via the selection of what to test and the determination of how to test it. Children from minority cultures and those who have limited English proficiency are especially victimized by such subjectivity (Wesson, 2001). Researchers (Kohn, 2002; Wesson, 2001) suggest that standardized tests measure environmental effectiveness, or what is learned outside of school, more than they discriminate school-based learning. Others point out that children's test scores correlate with family income much more than with teaching approaches or student ability (Read, 2001). As the emphasis on the tests increases in schools ranked low, the result is more direct instruction and practice tests (Madaus & O'Dwyer, 1999), widening the gap even further between schools that meet benchmarks and those that don't (often labeled "deficient").

Testing decreases learning by increasing pressure and stress on children and on teachers. This is especially true when test scores are used inappropriately, such as when published scores are used to rank schools (Haladyna et al., 1998). The damage is even greater because most people are uninformed about the meaning of these scores. Many people are horrified to learn that "half the children are below average." We bet you have heard schools criticized for this outcome, but we hope you realize that "average" *means* that half the children will be below and half above. In fact, test questions that are answered correctly by a high percentage of test takers are dropped from the test (Kohn, 2000). Standardized tests would no longer discriminate if the children's score were not distributed in a range. It's a *joke* that all the children are above average in Lake Wobegone!

QUESTIONS TO ASK IN EVALUATING A PROGRAM'S ASSESSMENT PROCEDURES

1. Is the assessment procedure based on the goals and objectives of the specific curriculum used in the program?

2. Are the results of the assessment used to benefit children, i.e., to plan for individual children, improve instruction, identify children's interests and needs, and individualize instruction, rather than label, track, or fail children?

3. Does the assessment procedure address all domains of learning and development—social, emotional, physical, and cognitive—as well as children's feelings and dispositions toward learning?

4. Does assessment provide useful information to teachers to help them do a better job?

5. Does the assessment procedure rely on teachers' regular and periodic observations and record keeping of children's everyday activities and performance so that results reflect children's behavior over time?

6. Does the assessment procedure occur as part of the ongoing life of the classroom rather than in an artificial, contrived context?

7. Is the assessment procedure performance-based, rather than only testing skills in isolation?

8. Does the assessment rely on multiple sources of information about children, such as collections of their work, results of teacher interviews and dialogues, as well as observations?

9. Does the assessment procedure reflect individual, cultural, and linguistic diversity? Is it free of cultural, language, and gender biases?

10. Do children appear comfortable and relaxed during assessment rather than tense or anxious?

11. Does the assessment procedure support parents' confidence in their children and their ability as parents rather than threaten or undermine parents, confidence?

12. Does the assessment examine children's strengths and capabilities rather than just their weaknesses or what they do not know?

13. Is the teacher the primary assessor, and are teachers adequately trained for this role?

14. Does the assessment procedure involve collaboration among teachers, children, administrators, and parents? Is information from parents used in planning instruction and evaluating children's learning? Are parents informed about assessment information?

15. Do children have an opportunity to reflect on and evaluate their own learning?

16. Are children assessed in supportive contexts to determine what they are capable of doing with assistance as well as what they can do independently?

17. Is there a systematic procedure for collecting assessment data that facilitates its use in planning instruction and communicating with parents?

18. Is there a regular procedure for communicating the results of assessment to parents in meaningful language, rather than letter or number grades, that reports children's individual progress?

Source: From "Assessment in Context—Teachers and Children at Work," by T. Hills, 1993 (*Young Children*, 48(5), 24, Copyright © 1993 by the National Association for the Education of Young Children. Reprinted by permission.

Matching Assessment to Young Children

The old system was a tidy one. Teaching was designed to prepare students to do well on certain standardized tests, and good test scores made the teaching look good. Reading-textbook companies focused on skills measured by standardized tests; they aimed at teaching skills and provided testing materials patterned after the standardized tests (Harp, 2000). As more professionals become aware of the mismatch between what creates good readers and the focus on testing isolated skills, they are trying to change it (Laminack & Ray, 2001).

Young children, unsophisticated in the ways of taking tests, are especially disadvantaged by formalized testing. Tests end up testing not reading skills, but children's willingness to pay attention to an uninteresting task (Kamii, 1990). They also test the test-taking skills: filling in bubbles and circling letters properly and carefully as well as sitting still for lengthy periods of time (Kohn, 2001). Many teachers waste days of educational time teaching youngsters how to do these tasks. Despite the efforts of teachers, the resulting scores are totally lacking in reliability. Children may get low scores simply because they weren't in the mood to do what the test required; at another time, the results would be different. This means that standardized tests not only don't measure the things children need to learn but also don't give an accurate picture of what they do try to measure.

For these reasons, the 1998 National Education Goals Panel has recommended against testing young children (Shephard, Kagan, & Wurtz, 1998). The panel's report states that standardized tests are inaccurate for young children and should be delayed until at least the end of third grade. In the past twenty years, a dozen different position statements from seventeen prestigious national professional education associations have acknowledged the mounting evidence that standardized testing often has detrimental and counterproductive effects on children and teachers (Haladyna et al., 1998).

Mrs. Hanna and Mrs. Thomas were among the teachers who dreaded testing days, knowing many children would be in tears. Youngsters felt the pressure as their teachers and parents felt it. Children were admonished to get a good night's sleep, have a good breakfast, and be ready for the big day. The children wanted to do a good job, but when they were confronted with questions that were confusing, the adults they usually relied on wouldn't even explain things. The situation was extremely upsetting to many children. Children with limited English proficiency were doubly disadvantaged by not even understanding the questions. Mrs. Hanna and Mrs. Thomas, like many others, felt morally compromised when they went along with testing policies that they could see were inappropriate for their students. These feelings gave them and other teachers the courage to question school testing policies and to work for change.

When they were still administering the tests, these two teachers found ways to focus on excellence in teaching and learning while preparing the children to take the tests (Buckner, 2002). They consulted sources like *A Teacher's Guide to Standardized Reading Tests: Knowledge Is Power* (Calkins, Montgomery, & Santman, 1998) for ideas on maintaining a constructivist framework while supporting students' test success. At the same time, they followed Alfie Kohn's advice and worked to change their local testing policy (Kohn, 2001). Mrs. Hanna and Mrs. Thomas maintained a clear sense of purpose and focused on their students' needs first as they endured the challenges of working for change (Buly & Rose, 2001). Their struggle against testing paid off for their students. Their district no longer gives standardized tests below third grade, accepting that such tests are not developmentally appropriate for young children.

Those working for assessment practices that are developmentally appropriate for young children have been assisted by the publication of guidelines for the assessment of children ages three through eight published jointly by the National Association for the Education of Young Children and the National Association of Early Childhood Specialists in State Departments of Education (see the box on p. 304).

Question 9 of the guidelines addresses the issue of cultural and linguistic diversity in the match between children and assessment. Ruiz and Enguidanos (1997) have written about the real horror that has resulted from inappropriate testing and resulting placements of children. Though some tests purport to be "culture free," Robert Tierney (1998) asserts that there is no such thing as a culture-free literacy test, and if there were, there shouldn't be. Tierney views literacy as inextricably connected to the individual's cultural background and life experiences

Testing young children means testing their willingness to pay attention to an uninteresting task and their ability to fill in bubbles properly. It tells us little about their literacy development.

and reminds us that teaching is not facilitated by ignoring or removing diversities. Therefore, assessment should pursue a goal of cultural sensitivity by building on each child's unique experiences. As Ruiz and Enguidanos explain, this can be done only through authentic literacy activities.

Matching Assessment to Its Purposes

Decisions about assessment need to be made on the basis of the purposes for assessment. Before you can decide how to measure your students' progress, you need to figure out why you are doing it (Shephard et al., 1998). Are you trying to evaluate your teaching approaches? Are you trying to find out what individual children need to know so that you can teach each child more effectively? Do you want to know how much progress children in your class have made? Do you want to know about progress for individuals or for the group as a whole?

Answers to those questions will guide you in determining what information to collect and in selecting the best approach to collecting it. You need current, detailed, descriptive data about individual children when your assessment purpose is to guide your teaching. You need a picture of children's accomplishments over time when you are documenting progress. If your purpose is to assess your teaching or your program, you need only sample data, and you don't need to gather information on every child.

Assessment decisions are also affected by who will receive the information. Are you needing assessment data to share with others or for your own use? Do you need to discuss the children's progress with their parents? What information and in what forms will be most informative for parents? Do you need information to pass along to the child's next teacher? Are you planning to share your observations with children to involve them in self-evaluation? What kinds of information will be useful for each of these audiences?

QUESTIONS TO ASK IN EVALUATING A PROGRAM'S ASSESSMENT PROCEDURES

1. Is the assessment procedure based on the goals and objectives of the specific curriculum used in the program?

2. Are the results of the assessment used to benefit children, i.e., to plan for individual children, improve instruction, identify children's interests and needs, and individualize instruction, rather than label, track, or fail children?

3. Does the assessment procedure address all domains of learning and development—social, emotional, physical, and cognitive—as well as children's feelings and dispositions toward learning?

4. Does assessment provide useful information to teachers to help them do a better job?

5. Does the assessment procedure rely on teachers' regular and periodic observations and record keeping of children's everyday activities and performance so that results reflect children's behavior over time?

6. Does the assessment procedure occur as part of the ongoing life of the classroom rather than in an artificial, contrived context?

7. Is the assessment procedure performance-based, rather than only testing skills in isolation?

8. Does the assessment rely on multiple sources of information about children, such as collections of their work, results of teacher interviews and dialogues, as well as observations?

9. Does the assessment procedure reflect individual, cultural, and linguistic diversity? Is it free of cultural, language, and gender biases?

10. Do children appear comfortable and relaxed during assessment rather than tense or anxious?

11. Does the assessment procedure support parents' confidence in their children and their ability as parents rather than threaten or undermine parents confidence?

12. Does the assessment examine children's strengths and capabilities rather than just their weaknesses or what they do not know?

13. Is the teacher the primary assessor, and are teachers adequately trained for this role?

14. Does the assessment procedure involve collaboration among teachers, children, administrators, and parents? Is information from parents used in planning instruction and evaluating children's learning? Are parents informed about assessment information?

When you are thinking about communicating with others regarding children's learning, you need to consider whether numerical and statistical data are preferable to descriptive narratives and work samples. In the past, educators and the public have expected numerical comparisons of children despite the grave doubts about the usefulness and relevance of such data. Teachers are now learning to communicate with parents, school administrators, and each other in more meaningful terms. Anecdotal records, reading samples, writing samples, checklists, and a variety of observational evidence are now widely used and enthusiastically received. However, sometimes you do need numbers; then the challenge becomes how to get them to reflect what you know about a child. Problems of accurately quantifying information about a qualitative process are central to the controversies surrounding assessment. Later in this chapter, we will present some suggestions about standardizing and quantifying the direct evidence of a child's learning.

Matching Assessment to Learning Processes

The most essential assessment purpose is to gather information that will assist the teacher in providing optimal instruction for each child. A related goal is to increase the match between what is tested and the best information about what should be taught. Unless assessment is based on what children are learning, it is useless. *Alternative assessment* is a term you may have encountered. It implies that there are assessments that are better than traditional measures (Leu & Kinzer, 2003). Current recommendations for early literacy assessment (for example, Braunger & Lewis, 1997; Cooper & Kiger, 2001; Shephard et al., 1998) emphasize *performance-based assessment*—observing children in the process of learning. Isn't it fairly obvious that we can tell more about how children read by listening to them read than from tests that have little to do with actual reading? Isn't it equally obvious that we can tell more about how they write by analyzing their actual writing over time than we can from seeing their test scores? In addition, assessment should focus on areas of strength to address areas of student need (International Reading Association, 2000).

The term *authentic assessment* has become popular for describing approaches that look at skills and knowledge actually in use (for example, Braunger & Lewis, 1997). Kenneth Goodman takes the idea further and insists that in order to be authentic, assessment tasks must be "real ones that can and do occur in the real world outside of school" (Goodman, Bird, & Goodman, 1992, p. 2). Ruiz and Enguidanos (1997) advocate for the same definition of *authentic*, pointing out that bilingual youngsters perform better with purposeful reading and writing. Such a level of authenticity surely would eliminate tests of subskills unrecognizable as reading or writing. Marie Clay (1993a), originator of the term *emergent literacy*, agrees on the importance of assessing actual reading and writing but cautions that observations of children's literacy behaviors should include "all the behaviors the child produces on the task, including the

Whether you use the term performance assessment, authentic assessment, *or* situated assessment, *the idea is that assessment tasks are the same activities used for developmentally appropriate and comprehensive literacy instruction.*

Performance assessment means assessing reading ability by listening to children read and assessing writing ability through their writing.

comments he makes about what he is doing" (p. 22). Whether you call it alternative assessment, performance-based assessment, or authentic assessment, the idea is that assessment tasks are the same activities used for developmentally appropriate and comprehensive literacy instruction.

Clearly, this type of assessment is most compatible with children's learning processes and best assists them.

Ms. Montoya feels freed by these new recommendations. She feels freed from having to drill students on test items and from teaching them how to take tests. She also feels free to combine teaching and assessment activities and, therefore, has more time for productive learning. The more she learns about children's processes of learning to read and write, the more confidence she has in her own ability to gather relevant data about children's progress in an authentic manner (Ratcliff, 2001–2002).

Mrs. Thomas greatly values information that helps her evaluate how well her teaching procedures are working for each child. She also is keenly aware of the importance of accountability in a first-grade class. However, she appreciates not having to put aside her goals for her students and give unrelated tests in order to get a numerical score for each one. Instead, she documents each child's progress through a series of informal assessment and data-collection processes. Using these approaches, Mrs. Thomas is able to simultaneously gather both formative

The more teachers know about how children learn to read and write, the more confidence teachers have in their own ability to gather relevant data about children's progress.

and summative assessment data. *Formative data* give her information about a child's current instructional needs and help form her teaching for that child. *Summative data* show how far the student has progressed at this point. Both kinds of information are necessary.

ASSESSMENT COMPONENTS

Too often, assessment discussions make no distinction between the collection of data and the methods of recording the data. Many people get confused and end up thinking that observation itself is assessment or that portfolios themselves are assessments. At times, assessment discussions focus on methods of collecting and recording data but leave out the question of what it is that should be assessed. We hope that the following analysis helps you sort this out.

Determining Purpose

We see five components in assessment. The first is determining what it is you want to evaluate. Is it how Chantel's writing has progressed this school year? Or what kinds of help Felicia needs in order to get past memorized reading? Or do you want to know if your literacy program is working for your students in general? Thinking about what or why you are assessing helps you decide what to look for during assessment.

Components of the assessment process:
Determining purpose
Collecting information
Recording data
Organizing
Analyzing

Once you have decided what you are looking for, there are four further components of the assessment process: collecting, recording, organizing, and analyzing data. In most cases, the assessment process is not complete without all these components.

Collecting Information

Let's look first at collecting information. Probably the most common way to collect data is by simply observing children as they read and write. Observation is highly recommended for assessment, but observation is not in itself an assessment approach. Rather, it is a way of collecting data for assessment. You still need to decide your purpose for observing as well as how to record and organize the information in a useful manner. Work samples are another way of collecting information, especially about a child's progress over time. You still need to decide which samples are useful, what to look for as you analyze the samples, and how to interpret that information for others.

Conferences or interviews with children are also data-collection opportunities. These one-on-one meetings utilize interactive conversations for collecting many different kinds of information. They lend themselves exceptionally well to assessment while teaching. As we describe conferences later in this chapter, you will see how teachers use them to simultaneously teach and assess reading and writing skills. Conference settings are also useful for collecting more structured data, such as performance samples.

Tests are yet another method of collecting information. There are formal and informal, standard and nonstandard, norm-referenced and criterion-referenced, and published and teacher-made tests. Tests are just one part of assessment collection, not the entire process, as some believe. Like other methods of data collection, tests must relate to what it is you need to know and why. Test results also require recording, analysis, and organization if they are to be useful to teachers.

Recording

Now let's look at recording assessment data. Keep in mind that recording is the process of putting the information you collect into a form that can be referred to at a later time. Checklists are popular for efficient assessment, but they are only a method of recording information, not an assessment method. You still need to know what you want to record, how you will gather that information, and what it means. The same is true for graphs and charts of progress or accomplishment.

Even collections of work samples require some recording; you at least need the date and the context in which it was produced. Additional comments about whether it was selected by the child or by the teacher and for what reasons are also useful. Photographs as well as audiotapes and videotapes offer some alternative ways to record children's learning, with the capability of recording learning processes rather than just the results. These too require an explanation of the circumstances surrounding their creation and selection as assessment data.

Narrative reports and commentaries about children's processes and behaviors while learning constitute another type of record keeping. These may be short, on-the-spot, anecdotal descriptions or reflective journal entries. The information used for these is collected while observing and interacting with children; like other records, they provide useful guidance only after careful analysis.

Photos like this, as well as videotapes and audiotapes, record children's learning processes rather than just the results.

Detailed records of children's actual reading can be analyzed for information about specific strengths and weaknesses. Teachers use this information as a guide to teaching individual youngsters just the right things at the right time. *Running records* (Clay, 1993b) and *miscue analysis* formats (Goodman, Watson, & Burke, 1987) are well-known standardized guides for this type of recording, and individual teachers frequently devise their own notation systems.

Test scores are also a record of a data-collection process. When teachers grade tests, they are responsible for this recording; commercial tests usually let strangers do the recording. Either way, the teacher needs to analyze the recorded results and put them into perspective with other assessment measures.

Let's not forget children's own record keeping of their progress, which often includes reading logs and may utilize the kinds of personal checklists and reflective questions suggested for children's self-evaluation later in this chapter.

Organizing

A portfolio is a common way to organize data. A portfolio can be used to display the information collected about an individual child's learning. Checklists, running records, reading logs, writing samples, test scores, photographs, audiotapes and videotapes, and anecdotal records all may end up in a child's portfolio. The teacher's task is to select those materials that provide the best picture of a child's current level of development as well as demonstrate the progress a child has made.

Typically, teachers collect and record information constantly and organize it for portfolios periodically. (The impetus to update and organize portfolios usually comes at parent-conference or report-card time.) Portfolio contents provide a basis for parent conferences and progress reports. Most of the portfolio material used during the school year to guide teaching and to communicate with children and their parents is not sent on to the next teacher and does not become part of the child's permanent portfolio. Therefore, teachers must also decide what to include in the permanent portfolio.

Considerations involved in portfolio organization relate to sharing it with parents and other teachers, demonstrating progress over time, and putting different aspects of the child's development into proper perspective. Ease of finding or adding information is also relevant. The analysis components of the portfolio are significant. Not only do individual items require analysis, but a systematic review of all materials in relation to one another is necessary for understanding a child's development.

Portfolio assessment has become a sort of rallying cry for holistic assessment movements. However, portfolios are primarily a means of organizing data and do not in themselves constitute an approach to assessment. You still need to determine what information you need to collect, how to collect it, and how to record it. Portfolios will be discussed in more detail later in the chapter.

Analyzing

"Observing and recording do not, by themselves, constitute assessment. Teachers must reflect on what they have observed and recorded in relation to program goals and objectives for each child" (Hills, 1993, p. 26). We are convinced (as is Ratcliff, 2001–2002) that teachers' reflection on assessment data is the key to improving teaching.

You may think that teachers can't add anything more to their workloads and therefore cannot possibly analyze assessment data. However, despite frequently inhumane workloads, such analysis is already built into narrative progress reports and portfolio procedures. When teachers write reports to parents about children's progress, they are synthesizing all the data they have collected since the last reporting period. Portfolios generally include a rating scale for placing a child on a continuum of literacy levels. Placing youngsters on this scale requires careful analysis of all relevant data. Often such rating is oral rather than written, and we hear teachers conducting fine analytical discussions with parents about the progress shown in children's work samples. Some teachers use frequent writing in their teaching journals to analyze what is happening in their classrooms.

Analysis of data can be informal, as when teachers help parents understand the progress shown in what the child wrote that day.

Analysis can and does happen; the quality of analysis depends on the teacher and also on the school district's allotment of time for such activity. The National Education Goals Panel recommends support for professional development to help teachers understand child development within the curricular areas assessed (Shephard et al., 1998). In order for teachers to make sense of literacy assessment data, they must have a clear idea of what typical literacy development and normal variation look like.

As she analyzes data about a child's progress, Ms. Montoya keeps in mind the various components of assessment and asks herself the following questions:

1. What has the child learned? This question helps focus on the content of assessment and distinguishes it from the processes or activities involved in learning.

2. How do I know? Answering this question requires the reflective analysis that makes assessment data useful.

3. How can I document it? This question seeks the best way to record what she knows about a child's learning. The idea of documenting that information implies that it will be shared with others and that the recording system must communicate effectively.

Three questions for assessment:

1. *What has the child learned?*
2. *How do you know?*
3. *How can you document it?*

She follows up with another question:

4. How can I use this information to assist the child's learning? This question brings her back to the initial purpose of assessment.

Individual Focus

The new approaches to literacy assessment require focus more on individual children than on the total group. This might make some educators fearful of spending too much time on assessment. However, the beauty of these approaches is that for the most part, teaching and assessing happen simultaneously. Therefore, time spent on assessment is not time taken away from teaching.

Mr. Larson finds that the individual nature of his assessment processes gives him helpful information about what each of his second graders considers important to learn and also about personal learning strategies of each. Despite the specificity of narrative descriptions of children's progress, Mr. Larson admits and accepts that he can never know exactly where each child is in every area. This is a comfortable position when children rather than the teacher direct their own learning.

Now that we have dissected literacy assessment processes in an effort to provide better understanding, we will try to put them back together for you in the rest of this chapter. To understand authentic performance-based assessment, it must be viewed in context of the classroom and the instructional process. We begin with some examples of observation and recording.

AUTHENTIC ASSESSMENT IN ACTION

Observation of children's performance serves as the basis of evaluation for most teachers (Cooper & Kiger, 2001). Observation double-checks the teacher's intuitive analysis of a child's needs; observation also can help you decide whether to accept test results as valid or ignore them as inaccurate. Test data can never equal personal knowledge of a child's strengths, motivations, and personality.

Observing

How do you collect assessment data through observation? The process involves getting yourself off center stage and paying attention to what children are doing. This is very difficult for teachers who view all learning as teacher directed. The more independent reading, writing, and exploring are going on, the more free the teacher is to observe. In addition, the more such independent literacy activity occurs, the more there is for the teacher to see. Once you have a child-centered, independent learning environment, you need to talk less and listen more. Most teachers talk way too much in school. Instead of trying to keep kids quiet so they can hear you, try keeping yourself quiet so you can hear children. You will be amazed at how much you will learn.

Effective observing and listening require the ability to step back and look at the big picture in your classroom as well as to zoom your lens in on a specific child. Many teachers collect their best assessment data as they work the room during choice time and independent work times. For example, as children write in their journals, you can often see Mrs. Hanna circulating among her kindergartners and stopping to chat briefly with a few. This allows both for the big picture and for a brief focus on individuals. For a more concentrated focus on individual children, individual weekly conferences are unbeatable.

However, a teacher can "see" only what he or she is prepared to find. For instance, as mentioned in Chapter 1, teachers who don't know about children's pre-alphabetic theories of print do not see the evidence in children's emergent writing. Other teachers who do recognize the forms of writing used by children may simply use that information to label their students. Recording the writing form or the reading level of a child is not enough. We must use our understanding of a child's individual literacy theories to inform our teaching. This understanding is gained through thoughtful analysis of each individual child's strengths. Then we can achieve the primary purpose of assessment—planning our instruction so that it is more relevant to the children and addresses their needs. Johnston (1997) points out that teachers view their classrooms through the filter of their own theory base: Some are watching for children's progress as independent readers and writers, and others are concerned with controlling and organizing children to learn a series of skills. To a large extent, you see what you are looking for.

Taking Notes

Documenting your observations is part of the process. Even though teachers can hold an amazing amount of information in their heads, most teachers find it more reliable to make notes. Ms. Montoya relies heavily on her *anecdotal records* to help her remember details of her multiage-primary children's behaviors. She uses this format to make note of children's behaviors that she considers significant or that she wants to think about further (see Figure 8.1). In order to make it easier to write down observations on the spur of the moment, she keeps a roll of self-sticking address labels in her pocket. She quickly writes her brief observations on these labels while she is busy with youngsters; at the end of the school day, she takes a few minutes to paste these into the appropriate children's folders. If she notices that a few children don't have many such notes in their folder, she realizes she may need to pay more attention to those youngsters. This system encourages paying attention to each student as an individual.

Mr. Larson acknowledges that his perceptions sometimes can be too subjective; they can be affected by personal feelings and extraneous pressures. Because of this, he too keeps an anecdotal file of his specific observations. He uses a card file with a section for each student. Mr. Larson records his second-grade children's behaviors and his own comments here as often as he considers necessary. If Mr. Larson is concerned about a child, he might make a concerted effort to record daily behavior over a period to discover patterns or test his perceptions. For instance, he

Heather read "take a
bath" when it says
"have a bath." The former
sounded right to her. We
looked at the letters. *Oct 3*

Kelsey wants me to tell
her unknown words
instead of helping her to
think about the sentence
and the picture clues. *Oct 3*

Tyler has just become
aware that letters have
sounds. He often comes
to tell me he knows
what a certain letter says:
sometimes he's right. *Oct 3*

Rashidi is unwilling
to take a chance guessing
at words. He only wants
to read something he
knows well.
Oct. 3

FIGURE 8.1

Mrs. Hanna made these notes on self-sticking labels during one literacy period. After school she stuck them into the children's folders.

Many teachers collect their best assessment data as they circulate around the room while children work.

was worrying about Sue recently because she seemed to be asking for help constantly and was unable to work independently. When he kept a tally of her requests, he discovered that the number was decreasing. He then felt reassured.

Ms. Reynolds often observes her preschoolers interacting with literacy materials during dramatic play to find out what they know about functions and uses of written language. She watched them when the dramatic-play area was set up as an airport and noticed who wrote pretend tickets on the ticket forms and who pretended to read the arrival charts and travel brochures. When the children play restaurant, she notices who pretends to write down orders on notepads and who pretends to read the menus. These observations tell her a lot about children's levels of understanding, and she makes anecdotal notes about each child's progress.

When she is observing her multiage-primary students with specific objectives in mind, Ms. Montoya prefers to record her observations on checklists. When she wanted to find out about student recognition of letters, she prepared a checklist showing the names of each new student in her program down the side and each letter across the top. Then she set up an alphabet bingo game, invited the youngsters she wanted to assess to play it, and asked an older child in the program to serve as caller. Ms. Montoya observed the game and was able to record quickly which children had trouble recognizing which letters.

Standardized Recording

Ms. Montoya and her colleagues have been seeking standardized models of checklists and rating scales to extend and validate their own ideas. Though more and more such materials are available, standardization seems a long way off. For example, there are many lists of developmental literacy stages, both published and unpublished. They all have the same idea about literacy's being an emergent process, but they start at different places in a child's development, they categorize development differently, and they use different labels for the stages. The *Developmental Continuum* model from *First Steps* (Reese & Shortland-Jones, 1994) has been well received by teachers, but it is different from the continuum Mrs. Hanna's district has been using for many years (Caudell, 1996), and both are different from the categories listed in Bill Harp's *Handbook of Literacy Assessment and Evaluation* (2000). All these differences make it harder for educators to communicate effectively about student progress.

Similarly, the idea of leveled books is widespread and commonly used to determine a child's reading level. But there is no consistency in how these levels are described or at what level they begin. Some lists are numbered, some use letters, and others are color coded. Fountas and Pinnell (1996) offer an extensive book list leveled from A through R. One school district that used the Fountas and Pinnell list as a resource started at level B and changed the labels to colors. The *Developmental Reading Assessment Resource Guide* (Beaver, 1997), which offers a packet of leveled books with observation guides for each, starts with level A (easier than level 1) and moves up through level 44. Such individualism makes it difficult to communicate between schools and districts.

The field of emergent literacy has spawned some rating scales that have the potential to validate and regularize teachers' observational data. Elizabeth Sulzby created a classification scheme for describing children's emergent reading of favorite storybooks for their forms of emergent writing, and for their forms of reading their own emergent writing. The categories guide teachers in observing and documenting the extent to which a child can orally reproduce a story, the extent to which a child can use written language patterns rather than oral language patterns, and the extent to which a child attends to print rather than to pictures in re-creating a story (Sulzby & Barnhart, 1990). The profile sheets from the *First Steps Reading Developmental Continuum* (Reese & Shortland-Jones, 1994) include many of the same indicators as Sulzby, but they are not organized in the same way, nor do they provide the same level of detail at the emergent levels. At least we seem to be getting a consensus that children's pretend reading and writing are valid literacy activities and worth noting. This offers a guide for evaluating literacy development in the preschool years as well as in kindergarten.

Though the recording system and the categories of literacy behavior are given in Sulzby's plan, the situations for gathering the data depend on children's activities. Self-selected literacy events offer some of the most useful insights into children's literacy development. Therefore, when she sees Jazzmin in the playhouse reading a favorite story to a doll, Ms. Montoya listens to the story. She makes notes for a checklist derived from Sulzby's storybook-reading categories (see Table 8.1). Ms. Montoya notes that Jazzmin's reading sounds like written language even though the words she reads are not exactly those on the page. Her sentences are complete and context free, unlike oral language. Jazzmin still uses picture clues to assist with story sequence, but she has progressed significantly

TABLE 8.1
Sulzby's Classification Scheme for Emergent Reading

Broad Categories	Brief Explanation
☐ Attending to pictures Not forming stories	The child is "reading" by looking at the storybook's pictures. The child's speech is *just* about the picture in view: the child is not "weaving a story."
☐ Attending to pictures Forming oral stories	The child's speech weaves a story across the pages, but the wording and the intonation are like that of someone telling a story.
☐ Attending to pictures Reading and storytelling mixed	The child's speech fluctuates between sounding like a storyteller with oral intonation and sounding like a reader, with reading intonation.
☐ Attending to pictures Forming written stories	The child's speech sounds as if the child is reading, both in the wording and intonation.
☐ Attending to print	The child is exploring the print by such strategies as (1) "refusing to read based on print awareness"; (2) "reading aspectually," using only some aspects of print; (3) "reading with strategies-imbalanced"; and (4) "reading independently" or "conventional reading."

Source: From "The Developing Kindergarten: All Our Children Emerge as Writers and Readers" by E. Sulzby & J. Barnhart. In J. S. McKee (Ed.). The Developing Kindergarten Programs, Children, and Teachers, © 1990, p. 218. Reproduced by permission of Michigan Association of the Education of Young Children. Ann Arbor, Michigan.

since the start of the school year. In September, Jazzmin's reading consisted of telling about the pictures on each page. Using Sulzby's classification, Ms. Montoya can document Jazzmin's emergent storybook-reading progress from the first category to the fourth.

The writing center is a good spot for Ms. Montoya to gather information about her multiage-primary children's emergent-writing progress and current understandings. She wants to watch and listen while children are creating their writing so that she can better interpret the strategies they employ. Not only does she gather data about children's views of composing written language, but she also can find out what they know about letter-sound relationships. She usually has to ask children to read their compositions to her in order to fully understand their intent. This understanding is necessary for analyzing the writing product.

When Ms. Montoya saw that Tuan and Reid were at the science table writing about their jack-o'-lantern's decomposition process, she went over to watch. Each child was keeping a log recording changes in the pumpkin over time. Tuan wrote, "It ss yky," and Reid wrote, "Atc SApsg ckunh." Each boy proudly read his log entry to Ms. Montoya. Tuan's message was "It smells yucky," demonstrating that he is developing his understanding of letter-sound relationships and that he has memorized how to spell *it*. Reid's message was "It smells," showing that he knows that words are made from letters and has a theory about word length. Ms. Montoya recorded the information gained from this observation on another checklist derived from Sulzby's research (Table 8.2). But she doesn't stop there. Mrs. Montoya uses her understanding of a child's current theories to make her teaching more relevant to the child. In this way she can successfully individualize instruction.

Sulzby also offers teachers a classification system to guide observation and recording of children's approaches to rereading what they have written (see Table 8.3). The system covers such issues as whether the child attends to the print during the rereading. Twice-monthly recording of data is recommended for a continuous view of a child's development (Sulzby, Barnhart, & Hieshima, 1989).

Using Sulzby's writing classification (Table 8.2), Ms. Montoya recorded that Reid appeared to be using random letters (although Mrs. Montoya is sure Reid's writing is purposeful) and that Tuan demonstrated intermediate-level invented spelling. Like most writing samples, Tuan's is difficult to classify because it includes conventional spelling along with examples of both syllabic and full invented spelling. Using a checklist with Sulzby's rereading categories (Table 8.3), Ms. Montoya recorded that Reid used a written monologue and that Tuan was rereading at a conventional level.

Though teachers can create their own categories for observation, communication between teachers will be enhanced if they use the same categories with the same criteria. Such common ground is needed if observational data are to be used and disseminated broadly. For instance, if Paul were to move to another city, his new teacher would better understand the records Ms. Montoya sent if both teachers knew the Sulzby categories. Establishing a common vocabulary and approach to observational assessment also will help administrators and school board members understand and view these records as reliable assessment data. As long

TABLE 8.2

Sulzby's Classification Scheme for Forms of Writing

Broad Categories	Brief Explanation
☐ Drawing	Check this form if the child draws one picture for the entire composition.
☐ Scribble/wavy	Scribble is a continuous (or continuous with breaks) form without the definition of letters.
☐ Scribble/letterlike	The child is using different forms within the scribble, and these forms have some of the features of letters.
☐ Letterlike units	The forms may resemble letters, but they appear to be forms the child has created.
☐ Letters: Random	There is no evidence that the child made any letter-sound correspondences.
☐ Letters: Patterns	The child writes with letters that show repeated patterns.
☐ Letters: Name elements	Letters are from the child's first and/or last name.
☐ Copying	Here the child will copy from environmental print in the room.
☐ Invented spelling: Syllabic	The child uses only one letter per syllable (contains phonetic relationships between the sounds in the spoken words and the letters used).
☐ Invented spelling: Intermediate	The invented spelling between *syllabic* and *full.*
☐ Invented spelling: Full	There is a letter for all or almost all of the sounds in the spoken word.
☐ Conventional	The child uses conventional *correct,* or dictionary, spelling.
☐ Other	Mark this box if the child uses a writing system that does not fit the descriptions above.

Source: Adapted from Elizabeth Sulzby, Appendix 2.1: "Forms of Writing and Rereading Example List," in Jana M. Mason (Ed.), Reading and Writing Connections. Copyright © 1989 by Allyn & Bacon. Used with permission of the Center for the Study of Reading, University of Illinois.

as each teacher is presenting different kinds of records, it will be hard for parents, school administrators, and the public to understand them.

However, we are convinced that teachers must not have standardized observation or recording categories forced on them. Teachers must be able to select assessment formats that reflect their teaching approaches and goals. Without this teacher choice, it is possible that standardized observation could create barriers to learning and authentic assessment similar to those created by standardized tests. Tierney (1998) raises the concern that standardization camouflages the subjectivity of assessment, giving a false illusion of objectivity. He reminds us that each student is unique and that any one system of noting progress will represent only a partial view of any child's literacies. With these cautions in mind, we next present further examples of data collection and recording systems that offer possibilities for standardizing the process.

TABLE 8.3

Sulzby's Classification Scheme for Forms of Rereading From Independent Writing

Broad Categories	Brief Explanation
☐ Not observed	In some instances, you will not have heard the child reread.
☐ Refusal	Check this if the child says, "I can't," shakes head repeatedly, etc., after you give numerous encouragements.
☐ "I didn't write."	This response is important enough to indicate separately.
☐ Labeling/describing	Check this response if the child labels items or describes items written or drawn.
☐ Dialogue	Check this if the child will respond only if you ask questions.
☐ Oral monologue	Check this if the child gives an orally told story in the intonation and wording of oral language.
☐ Written monologue	Check this if the child recites a story that is worded like written language and sounds like written language in intonation.
☐ Naming letters	This child makes an important move toward attending to print when she/he "reads" by simply naming the letters she/he has written.
☐ Aspectual/strategic reading	The child is attending to print but not yet reading conventionally.
☐ Conventional	The child is reading from print, conventionally.
☐ Other	Check this when the rereading does not fit the other categories.

Source: From "Forms of Writing and Rereading from Writing: A Preliminary Report" (Technical Report No. 20) by E. Sulzby, J. Barnhart, and J. Hieshima. In J. Mason (Ed.). Reading and Writing Connections, 1989, Newton, MA: Allyn & Bacon. Used with permission of the Center for the Study of Reading, University of Illinois.

ASSESSMENT DURING CONFERENCES

As you've seen in the preceding chapters, individual conferences with children about their reading and writing provide opportunities for assessment of many literacy concepts and skills. Although the primary focus of the conferences is instructional, the performance-based assessment procedures make assessment and instruction complementary parts of the same activity. Sharon Taberski (2000) states, "No predefined scope and sequence of skills can replace . . . watching a child read or listening to her talk about her reading, and then deciding how best to proceed" (p. 36).

Ms. Reynolds and Mrs. Hanna start this process casually in preschool and kindergarten just by answering questions or stopping to talk with individual children about what they are working on. Mrs. Thomas begins scheduling planned, official conference sessions with her first graders as they individually arrive at the "Aha, I can read!" stage. By second and third grade, all children should be able to profit from regular one-on-one sessions to discuss their reading and writing with the teacher.

Ms. Montoya meets in individual conferences with all the students in her multiage-group class of beginning kindergartners through second graders. The content of these meetings varies with the child's level of literacy. At first, however, she works on building trust with the child so that the conference is a comfortable and pleasant experience. Establishing a relationship with a child is an essential part of effective teaching, and it is especially important for one-on-one sessions. Conferences are an excellent time for teachers to practice those listening skills we mentioned earlier in this chapter and those authentic questioning skills we described in Chapter 3.

When children share their reading or writing with her, Ms. Montoya uses a variety of record-keeping systems to keep track of information gathered: checklists of skills, running records, and narrative notes. Conferences provide Ms. Montoya opportunities for individualized performance sampling and record keeping. With emergent readers, a conference can be a time for listening to and analyzing a child's mostly memorized rereading of a book from story time. With beginning readers, Ms. Montoya listens to them read aloud and frequently keeps a running record of correct and incorrect interpretations of the text. She has been trained in recording and analyzing data according to the Reading Recovery system devised by Marie Clay (1985, 1993b) and has adapted that approach to her classroom conferences. With more proficient readers, conferences can be times to help youngsters extend their strategy use and also to discuss the plot of a novel in progress. No matter what a child's level of understanding, Ms. Montoya encourages all her students to write as well as to read and to discuss their writing with her.

At the beginning of the school year, Mr. Larson wanted to find out some baseline information about his second graders' development in literacy. Portfolios were passed to him from the first-grade teacher, but he also had new students coming into his class. Because records did not accompany all the transfer children and their standardized test scores contained information useless for teaching, Mr. Larson depended on both observation and two informal tests that he could easily give during individual reading conferences—the *informal reading inventory* and *primary trait writing analysis*. More information about these follows.

Observing Emergent Readers and Writers

Marie Clay's *running-record* notation system (1985, 1993b) is probably the most standardized documentation system currently used in the primary grades (see Figure 8.2). The system is somewhat similar to notation for a *miscue analysis* (Y. Goodman et al., 1987); however, most teachers find the running record easier to use. A running record is a way of quickly noting exactly what a child says during an individual oral-reading conference. A check is used for each word a child reads

Conferences with children about their reading and writing combine assessment with instruction.

correctly and a dash for those words the child misses. When there is time, the teacher writes the correct word under the dash and the word that was substituted above the dash. A child's self-correction is indicated by the letters *SC*, and rereading for meaning is shown by an arrow going back to the start of the sentence. The running-record form also charts the reading strategies used. This provides information for a detailed analysis of the reading strategies used and not used by an individual child. Teachers need to analyze the miscues and self-corrections to determine how the reader balances use of meaning (semantic), structural (syntactic), and visual (graphophonic) clues (as described in Chapter 4). The focus of the analysis is always on what the child is using as opposed to what the child is lacking. Instructional decisions are made on the basis of patterns that emerge from the analysis of the running record (Leu & Kinzer, 2003). A single instance does not allow generalizations about a reader; sometimes a few running records need to be analyzed together (Salinger, 2002). When used with a leveled book, running records provide information regarding the child's instructional reading level. Unfortunately, many running-record forms highlight the recording of the student's reading level and number of errors, leading users to believe that they are the primary focus of a running record. This is not the case! Teachers find the analyses of a child's use of the three clues rich in useful information about how to guide a young reader and can plan appropriate instruction on the basis of student needs. This information is much more relevant to good teaching than merely knowing a student's level.

Clay (1993a) is also the author of several other widely used performance samples. The most well known is called *Concepts About Print*; it checks such understandings as directionality and sequence of print. The performance sample is

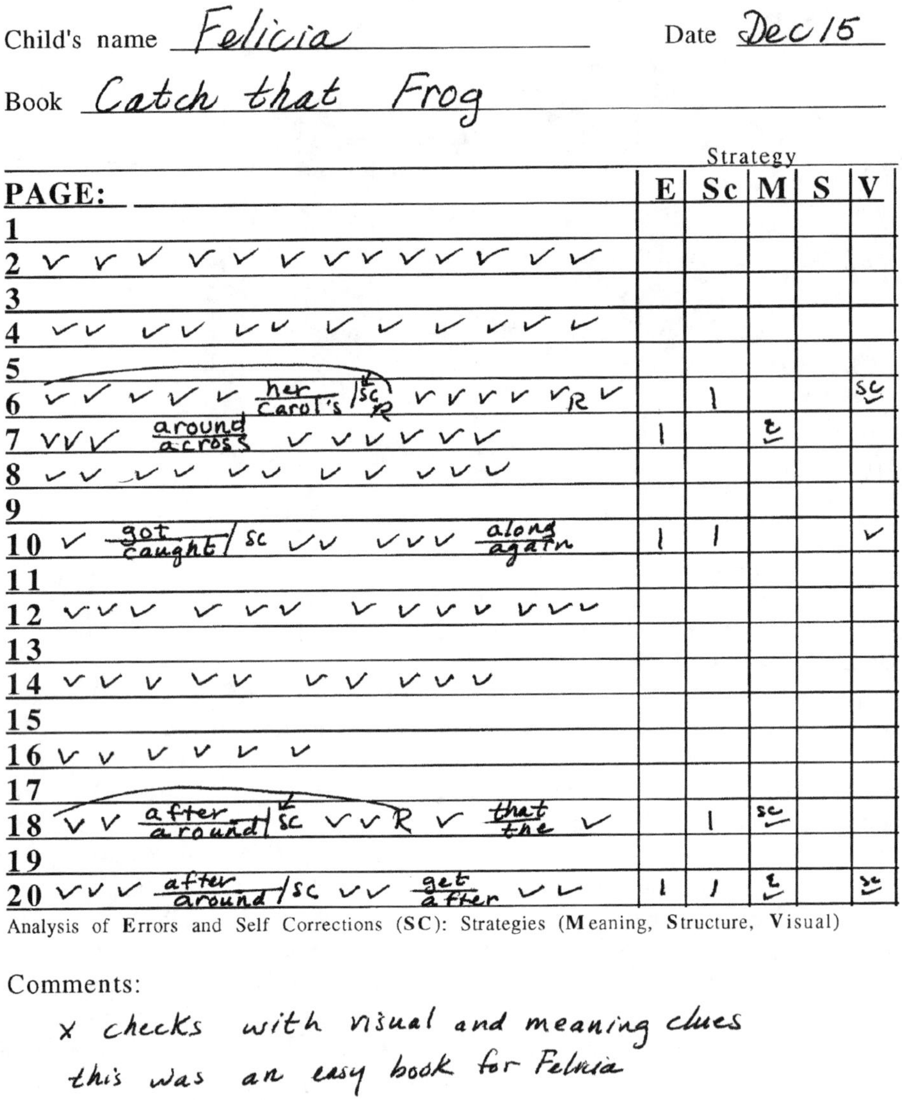

Child's name _Felicia_   Date _Dec 15_

Book _Catch that Frog_

		Strategy				
PAGE:		**E**	**Sc**	**M**	**S**	**V**
1						
2	✓ ✓ ✓ ✓ ✓ ✓ ✓ ✓ ✓ ✓ ✓ ✓ ✓ ✓					
3						
4	✓✓ ✓✓ ✓✓ ✓ ✓ ✓ ✓✓ ✓					
5						
6	✓ ✓ ✓ ✓ ✓ her/Carol's /sc R ✓ ✓ ✓ ✓ ✓R ✓		1			sc
7	✓✓✓ around/across ✓ ✓✓✓✓	1		t		
8	✓✓ ✓✓ ✓✓ ✓✓ ✓✓✓					
9						
10	✓ got/caught /sc ✓✓ ✓✓✓ along/again	1	1			✓
11						
12	✓✓✓ ✓ ✓✓ ✓ ✓✓✓ ✓✓✓					
13						
14	✓✓✓ ✓✓ ✓✓ ✓✓✓					
15						
16	✓✓ ✓✓✓ ✓					
17						
18	✓✓ after/around /sc ✓✓R ✓ that/the ✓		1	sc		
19						
20	✓✓✓ after/around /sc ✓✓ get/after ✓✓	1	1	t		sc

Analysis of Errors and Self Corrections (SC): Strategies (Meaning, Structure, Visual)

Comments:

     x checks with visual and meaning clues

     this was an easy book for Felicia

FIGURE 8.2

A teacher's adaptation of a running record reflecting data collected during an instructional conference.

Source: Adapted from Marie Clay's work.

done with one child at a time and consists of discussing and reading specific small books written by Clay. Clay also offers a rating scale to evaluate children's writing. She recommends looking at several samples collected over a short period in order to get a clearer picture of what a child can do. Another popular assessment process suggested by Clay (1993a) is *Hearing and Recording Sounds in Words*. Using this process, the teacher dictates sentences for the child to write. The writing is scored not according to conventions of spelling but rather according to evidence that the child hears the sounds in the words and can represent those sounds in print. This is another way to analyze a child's phonics-based spelling. Clay suggests three additional assessment processes: one for letter identification, one for reading sight words, and one for writing vocabulary. We're not too excited about these, though, because of concerns about processes that evaluate a child's literacy skills outside the context of authentic reading and writing.

An added feature of these standardized tasks is that Clay has normed them and tested them for reliability and validity. These features allow the observational data resulting from the tasks to be reported in numerical form. Though the numbers don't help you teach better, the raw data you collect to arrive at the numerical figures are still beneficial. Clay is suggesting a way to appease number crunchers and still use observational assessment.

Among other contributions to standardized observational assessment are the *Work Sampling System* (Meisels, 1993, 1995; Meisels, Bickel, Nicholson, Xue, & Atkins-Burnett, 2001) and *Project Construct* (1995). These focus on a broad spectrum of learning and development, including language and literacy. We believe that each offers significant benefits, but each has limitations or drawbacks. One major drawback is that they don't provide in-depth analysis of the processes of learning but only general indicators of progress. Thus, these systems contribute to reporting progress but do not give sufficient details to guide teaching. As Clay (1993a) would say, these systems give us the score at the end of the game but offer little guidance on how to improve play during the game.

Each of these assessment systems is based on a developmentally appropriate view of emerging literacy processes. These views are built into the observations and are explained as part of the assessment materials. An important benefit of adopting these systems would be to focus teacher observation and administrative attention on developmentally appropriate learning processes. These systems recommend observation during authentic learning activities, including spontaneous play. They are all designed for data collection during natural teacher interactions with youngsters, either individually or in groups. Each system includes teacher training in observation and recording procedures.

Phonemic Awareness

Despite the previously mentioned methods of authentic assessment during natural classroom activities, many teachers feel pressure to assess young children's phonemic awareness. You will recall that phonemic awareness is the recognition that individual sounds in words can be manipulated. There are a number of tests of phonemic segmentation available (e.g., Yopp-Singer Test of Phonemic Segmentation; Yopp, 1995). These tests decontextualize language use. When we ask a child to "Tell me the sounds in the word cat" and expect the response /c/, /a/, /t/, it is not an authentic task (especially when it is followed by nineteen similar requests!). Therefore, Mrs. Montoya prefers to assess her students' phonemic awareness in more natural ways, for example, observing who is able to rhyme words. She recognizes that even though the correlation between phonemic awareness and reading success is high, it is not necessary to isolate phonemic awareness and drill children in it (Cunningham, 1999). Mrs. Montoya knows that the children who come to her without phonemic awareness need to develop it. She also knows how it developed in those children who come to her multiage-primary class with it—through home literacy experiences. Her job is to simulate those experiences (e.g., read-aloud, natural language play, rhyming songs) in the classroom. In addition to being natural and authentic, this is an extremely effective way to assess and teach phonemic awareness.

Observing Independent Readers

Because we are interested in assessment for improving instruction (Pellegrino, Chudowski, & Glaser, 2001) as well as for reporting progress, let us return to examples of how teachers observe in order to assist children's learning. Once children have begun to read somewhat independently, effective teaching requires detailed information about the reading strategies used by each child. Mr. Larson even takes notes about how children spend both their reading time and their time for choosing reading material. He keeps track of which children quickly begin reading and which ones seem continually distracted by other things. He notices if a child idly thumbs through books with no apparent purpose in selecting or reading anything. He also considers reading behaviors outside of class to be significant. He wants to know if his students check books out at the school or local library and if they are reading at home.

All this information guides Mr. Larson in selecting the most appropriate strategy to encourage and assist each child's literacy development. He knows that he cannot force a child to want to read or write, but he must figure out how to help each child find personal meaning and satisfaction in those activities. Mrs. Williams also observes her students during silent reading for clues about their reading processes. She watches and makes note of the behaviors using the criteria shown here in Table 8.4.

Information gained from these observations guides Mrs. Williams as she plans activities for her students. Mrs. Williams also has developed a reading-behavior checklist that she distilled from the list of goals shown in Table 8.4.

The informal reading inventory (IRI) is a standardized way to evaluate a child's oral and silent reading of unfamiliar passages at various levels of difficulty. Mr. Larson chooses to use IRIs with children who have become independent readers—they read longer passages and stories, most often silently, fluently and with comprehension. When these children read orally, they may read too much and too rapidly for Mr. Larson to be able to accurately keep a running record. For these children, Mr. Larson can use an IRI to get a picture of each child's reading performance.

TABLE 8.4

Independent Reading Observation Guide

1. Is the child engrossed in the reading?
2. Is the child distracted? If so, by what?
3. How long does the child stay involved?
4. Is involvement time increasing or decreasing?
5. Does the child move his or her lips during silent reading?
6. Does the child ask for assistance?
7. From whom is assistance asked?
8. Does the child ask for help with words only or also with ideas expressed?
9. Are the words that the child can't read difficult to understand in context?
10. Does the child occasionally laugh or otherwise respond while reading silently?
11. How rapidly does the child turn pages?
    So slowly as to indicate subvocalizing?
    So rapidly as to indicate skimming?
    So irregularly as to imply carefully reading selected portions?

With an IRI, oral reading of unfamiliar passages gives indications of a child's reading strategies. Answering questions about a silent-reading passage demonstrates general levels of reading comprehension. Mr. Larson learned to give and interpret IRIs by studying and applying several different published forms, such as the Classroom Reading Inventory (Silvaroli & Wheelock, 2001) and the Qualitative Reading Inventory-3 (Leslie & Caldwell, 2001). Over the years, he found that each of these tests varied in its reading passages and instructions but that the underlying principles and problems of each were the same.

An informal reading inventory is given individually. A child reads passages of increasing difficulty until the material is clearly too difficult. The teacher records and analyzes the deviations from text that a child makes while reading unfamiliar passages aloud. Comprehension is evaluated through the child's answers to questions about other unfamiliar passages that the child reads silently. The teacher then uses the data to make decisions about the child's reading abilities.

The teacher can analyze the words a child miscalled during oral reading with a process called *miscue analysis,* which was developed by Yetta Goodman and Carolyn Burke in *Reading Miscue Inventory Manual: Procedure for Diagnosis and Evaluation* (1972). Teachers can categorize a child's errors according to whether the misreadings sound or look like the original words (graphophonemic clues), whether the substitutions make sense in the text (semantic clues), and whether the changes make sense grammatically (syntactic clues). This is similar to the analysis of errors done as part of a running record.

Mr. Larson finds that informal reading inventories and miscue analysis are very useful diagnostic processes. They help him track the child's thinking and give him some idea why errors are occurring. This is more useful information than merely knowing that the child made a mistake. It allows Mr. Larson to maximize his instruction to meet his students' needs.

Mr. Larson no longer uses published informal reading inventories. Many of them have passages that have no relationship to his students' experience and are too short to show any patterns in the child's miscues. Others rely on inadequate questions. According to some researchers (e.g., Leu & Kinzer, 2003), up to half the main idea questions may be inappropriate because the passages don't have a unified focus. Mr. Larson just chooses material from books he has in the room—books that have text for emergent, beginning, and fluent readers. Mr. Larson makes sure the materials he chooses have content that is familiar to his students. Today it is Ron's turn, and Mr. Larson has chosen passages about baseball that he thinks Ron will find easy, challenging, and difficult. After Ron silently reads a selection, Mr. Larson asks him questions about it because he wants to find out whether Ron understands that passage well enough to organize ideas, make inferences, evaluate critically, and apply ideas to other situations.

After experiencing success at one level, Ron is able to face more difficult challenges. Mr. Larson tells him the next reading selections are pretty hard and that he just wants to see if Ron can do them. This preparation prevents Ron from feeling like a failure if he isn't successful with all the material. When Ron's responses indicate that he hasn't understood all that he has read, Mr. Larson asks Ron to read the passage aloud so that he can identify the cause of the confusion.

As Ron reads aloud, Mr. Larson records his reading performance on a copy of the same passage (see Figure 8.3). Mr. Larson doesn't worry when Ron miscalls a word that makes sense in the story. When Ron confuses the words *Miss* and *Mrs.* and reads *didn't* for *don't*, he is so intent on making meaning from the selection that this minor miscue makes no impact on the message of the passages. Later, however, when he misreads *inside* for *instead* and *reasons* for *raisins*, Mr. Larson makes a note that Ron is not paying attention to meaning and contextual clues.

The informal reading inventory gives Mr. Larson more valuable information than any standardized test. He knows not only the approximate level of reading difficulty at which Ron can read independently but also that sometimes Ron over-relies on phonics. Mr. Larson will use these results as baseline information describing Ron's reading ability at the beginning of second grade.

By making a careful record of Ron's oral reading, Mr. Larson can evaluate Ron's reading growth over the school year ahead. He can have Ron reread the same text later in the year and again record miscue information. Ron most likely will show improvement, which Mr. Larson can clearly document. If Ron does not show improvement, Mr. Larson will have good cause for concern.

Observing Independent Writers

Having kids write is one of Mr. Larson's primary goals. When he observes children writing, he has an additional set of specific goals in mind. He looks for children's progress toward the aims shown in Table 8.5. Mr. Larson is convinced that if children can attain the first two goals, they will be successful in reaching the others. When a child shows little progress in writing, Mr. Larson first looks for problems with the child's progress toward the first and second goals—finding satisfaction in writing and recognizing a variety of purposes for writing.

After school, we told
h (above "told")

Mrs. TP (handwritten above "Miss Kellar")

Miss Kellar about the soccer practice

as we ate a snack.

didn't (handwritten above "don't")

"I don't play very well," I began.

Tommy (handwritten above "Thomas")

Thomas added,

inside (handwritten above "instead")

"He kicked me instead of the ball."

h (handwritten above "Thomas")

"I am really sorry about that," I told Thomas.

more reasons (handwritten above "raisins")

Miss Kellar gave me some raisins.
∧

h = hesitate
t p = teacher pronounce

"I used to play soccer. Maybe I could

help you practice," she said.

FIGURE 8.3
Mr. Larson's transcript of Ron's reading shows that Ron fluently read and understood this passage despite several miscues.

TABLE 8.5
Writing Goals

1. Find satisfaction in writing.
2. Recognize a variety of purposes for writing.
3. Select their own topics for writing.
4. Increase fluency and time spent writing.
5. Communicate thoughts, feelings, and information.
6. Expand vocabulary and use of varied sentence patterns.
7. Take into account their audience.
8. Develop their own style.
9. Build plot and characters into story writing.
10. Develop an ability to express themselves poetically.
11. Begin to use writing-process strategies.

Writing goals for ___Caleb___   Teacher ___Larson___   Grade _2_

	September	November	January	March	May
Enjoys writing		✓			
Sees purpose		✓			
Chooses topics		✓			
Fluency					
Time spent	5 min	20			
Communicates: Thoughts		✓			
Feelings					
Information	✓	✓			
Vocabulary		+			
Sentence patterns					
Sense of audience					
Personal style					
Sense of story					
Poetic sense					
Writing process					

FIGURE 8.4
Mr. Larson developed this check sheet from his list of writing goals.

Mr. Larson and Mrs. Williams have written hundreds of note cards and filled dozens of notebooks with anecdotal records of their students' actions, triumphs, and difficulties. They have found that they can make more sense of their information if they summarize it in some form of check sheet. This year, Mr. Larson experimented with a check sheet, shown in Figure 8.4, that he put together from his goals for children's writing development. He knows that children do not develop writing strategies in a specific sequence, so he is not concerned with the seemingly haphazard growth Caleb has shown between September and December. Mr. Larson will continue to use this check sheet to summarize his observations throughout the year. It is important to note that many of Mr. Larsons's observations are of Caleb's writing process, not just his products. Further information comes from discussions between Caleb and Mr. Larson during reading and writing conferences. Caleb's mother is interested in Mr. Larson's check sheet because it reflects the changes she has noticed in the papers Caleb brings home.

Goals in a comprehensive literacy program:

To enjoy reading and writing

To frequently choose to read and write

To read with increasing depth of understanding

To write with increasing fluency, accuracy, and style

Using the Writing Process   Grade _2_   Teacher _Summers_

Molly can	Oct	Nov	Dec	Jan	Feb	Mar	Apr	May
Write independently	✓	✓	✓					
Keep papers in a folder	✓	✓	✓					
Keep a log of writing	begins	✓	✓					
Make a plan								
Write a draft	✓	✓	✓					
Work in a response group			✓					
Share own writing		✓	✓					
Respond to others			✓					
Request a conference	✓	✓	✓					
Make revisions Add								
Delete								
Change								
Copyread								
Publish and Share	✓	✓	✓					
Evaluate self			✓					

FIGURE 8.5

A check sheet such as this helps both teacher and child be aware of progress made in the writing process.

In teaching her third graders to use the writing process, Mrs. Williams finds that a progress sheet (see Figure 8.5) is useful to both her and the children in demonstrating how youngsters learn to use various parts of the formal writing process. In conferences, Mrs. Williams is careful to remind children that revision and editing are necessary only for a few selected writings. When children decide to polish a paper, the check sheet is useful in reminding them of the steps they might follow.

Mr. Larson and Mrs. Williams are both wary of checklists that seem to dictate what a child is supposed to learn; they choose to make their own lists on the basis of what they see happening in their own classrooms. However, they are aware that no teacher could document all the strategies a child uses or all the goals a child reaches. There are just too many, and besides, these teachers are not interested in breaking down reading and writing into tiny steps as reading and language programs did in the past.

TABLE 8.6
Ideas for Assessing Writing

Observe and Gather Data
Teacher
    Watches children writing daily
    Conferences weekly with each student
    Collects writing samples
Children
    Seek responses from teacher and peers
    Collect writing samples

Keep Records
Teacher
    Uses a notebook or file to keep notes on conferences
    Assembles portfolios for all children
    Utilizes checklists and writing samples to document development
Children
    Keep daily logs of writing
    Use a writing folder to hold fastwrites and drafts

Analyze and Organize
Teacher
    Organizes portfolio materials to document growth
    Occasionally analyzes writing pieces in depth
    Summarizes development, maintaining a positive attitude
Children
    Participate in the evaluation process
    Set own goals
    Participate in response groups and conferences

Determined not to get sidetracked by details such as how many phonics rules children know, Mrs. Williams keeps a clear idea of the general literacy goals for her students as she assesses their progress. These long-range goals are generally accepted by all educators, but in the past they often got lost in the crunch of test scores.

Some teachers keep a sample of each child's writing early in the school year as a comparison for papers written later in the school year. Mr. Larson is careful to have the children read these stories aloud to him if he can't understand their writing and then keeps these translations in with the baseline papers in the children's portfolios. Later in the year, he or his aide will dictate this transcription to the child, who rewrites the story as he or she hears it. Then the original and dictated versions of the story are compared. It is easy for Mr. Larson to point out growth in mechanics and spelling. Mr. Larson, along with the children and parents, is amazed at the progress these comparisons show. Table 8.6 summarizes the main ideas to keep in mind about assessing children's writing. Notice how many involve process, product, or both.

Mrs. Williams uses a more complex form of holistic writing assessment with her third graders. Drawing on an assessment procedure called *primary trait analysis* (Spandel, 1996), she believes that all writing, even that of professional authors, can be analyzed by looking at six aspects of the writing (Jarmer, Kozol, Nelson, & Salsberry, 2000). These aspects, or traits, are ideas, organization, voice, word choice, fluency, and conventions (see Table 8.7). For more on the Six-Trait Writing Model, see the Northwest Regional Educational Laboratory Web site at *http://www.nwrel.org/eval/writing*). In terms of young independent writers, let's look at what each of these traits means. The trait *ideas* has to do with the content of the writing—is there a clear message or a story that makes sense? *Organization* refers to ordering that makes sense. For young writers, a major organizational feature to be learned is that a piece has a beginning, a middle, and an end. *Voice* means the personality of the writer shows in the piece. We expect that each child has his or her own voice, just as each has his or her own personality. Skilled writers can even take on someone else's voice. *Word choice*, or vocabulary, refers to the writer's selection of appropriate, strong words that convey meaning specifically. *Fluency* means the writer shows a feeling for the flow of language—sentences flow and are varied from one another. Finally, the term *conventions* means the writer's ability to use grammar, mechanics, and spelling to convey meaning. Have you noticed that the list of traits starts with *ideas* and ends with *conventions*? This demonstrates Mrs. Williams's belief that ideas and what the writer has to say are most important; conventions only support and make a message clearer (see Figure 8.6).

Mrs. Williams uses these primary writing traits mainly for instruction because she believes that assessment and instruction take place concurrently. During guided writing, she teaches and coaches her children in improving each of the six traits of their writing and constantly assessing their own progress. Children learn to evaluate their own progress and to pinpoint which trait they are focusing on.

At least twice a year, Mrs. Williams does a formal assessment of each child's writing for the child's permanent portfolio. She asks each child to choose a paper he or she is proud of for assessment. In December, Devin chooses a paper on *Scary Stories* by R. C. Welch that he has formatted into a letter to his class book club. Mrs. Williams is delighted in Devin's choice, as it is his most developed paper to date (Figure 8.7).

Together with the third- and fourth-grade teachers in the building, Mrs. Williams has created a rating form to assess the six traits of writing (Figure 8.8). The teachers have translated the characteristics of the six traits into descriptive sentences that children can understand. As you can see, this form is written in the first person so that children can rate their own writing. For Devin's first time around, however, Mrs. Williams rates Devin's paper on each trait, using the 1-to-5 numerical scale. (Some teachers refrain from using numerals and instead use a series of checks and pluses or an array of sad to smiling faces.) Mrs. Williams's goal is to provide a standardized rating system that Devin can use to see his own progress in writing. In addition, this system can easily be used to compare progress during

TABLE 8.7

Six-Trait Writing Rubric: By placing ideas first and conventions last, this list of primary traits places highest value on the writer's message.

Ideas
- What is the message?
- Does it make a point? Does it tell a story?
- Details, details, details

Organization
- Beginning and ending
- Like things go together
- Balance on the page
- Order makes sense

Voice
- Personality!
- Pizzazz!
- Flavor, charm, liveliness
- New, different, full of adventurous spirit

Word Choice
- Using words correctly
- Trying something new
- Verbs!
- Flair, personal phrasing

Fluency
- Sentences hang together
- Sentence sense
- Variety
- Rhythm and flow
- An ear for language patterns

Conventions
- Left-to-right orientation
- Up-to-down orientation
- Letters facing in the right direction
- Spaces between words—and between lines
- Distinguishing between lowercase and capitals
- Playing with punctuation (correctly placed or not)
- Knowing names of some conventions
- Copying environmental print
- Having readable spelling as a goal

Source: Seeing with New Eyes, by V. Spandel, 1996, Portland, OR: Northwest Regional Educational Laboratory.

Score each trait as emerging, developing, or proficient.

Clark's Story:

My Volcanic Driem

By Clark

"For My Mommy and Daddy and Sistr"

Once upon a time I was playing in my yard and a volcano ertptid and I ran from the lava I was scared. The volcano was scary. And my freds had to run to. We ran to my drivway my mommy and daddy wr wosh the car. the end

Ideas: Clark is proficient with ideas. He creates a text and images the reader can easily interpret without help. He creates a text and images with identifiable main ideas. Clark reads work with ease and elaboration and adds significant detail to enrich and expand the text and pictures. Knowing him as a writer, he also meets two of the other qualities of a proficient early beginner writer: he writes on a range of topics, and he writes for a variety of purposes.

Organization: Clark is proficient with organization as well. He uses a title or other indicator of beginning and creates a visually pleasing layout of his text with pictures. He begins his text at the top of the page and fills the remaining page space with his illustrations. His title is top and center, and his "the end" is centered on the last page. His pictures are clearly related to the text on each page, and he uses "the end" to indicate the closing of his story.

Voice: Clark is proficient with the trait of voice. He writes for an audience as well as for himself and creates a text and drawings that are his own. He shows emotion as he and his friend run from the lava, right to Mom and Dad, and catches the reader's attention.

Word Choice: Clark is proficient with word choice as he uses a range of simple words, writes simple words (some of which are from the word wall), and uses simple conjunctions.

Sentence Fluency: Clark is a developing writer in the area of sentence fluency. He shows understanding that multiple words are needed to form a sentence and writes at least one readable sentence. I do not yet consider him proficient because of incomplete sentences, and he does not use questions.

Conventions: Clark is on his way to being a proficient writer. He writes legibly with most letters formed correctly. He spells numerous simple words correctly but has received help from a classroom visitor for many of the words in his story. He has also received help in starting to add periods to the end of the sentences, as they have not appeared in any other of Clark's writing. He is comfortable using invented spelling. Clark does not yet consistently leave spaces between his words, and he does not yet proficiently discern between upper- and lowercase letters.

FIGURE 8.6

Example of six-trait rubric evaluation from Mrs. Girard.

scary stories

Dear Boys and Girls

I'm reading Scary stories, by R.C. Welch It has 122 Pages, The genre is horror fiction, It takes place in 1995, I chose to read this book because it was scary so I thought I should read it, I also like Comedy fiction books.

Briefly this book is about horror, One of the stories is called "Nightmare" it is about this one Kid who loves horror and he always has nightmares about this monster who could hide in shadows, And one night he sees the monster, he ran into his parents room, he backed up and felt something familiar and then you'll have to read the book to find out. Another story I liked was "Crying Wolf." It was about a girl and a boy, So one day the boy was at her house making something She saw something out the corner of her eye, She was so scared she talked to her friend about it all the time, He thinks she is seeing things but she isn't and one night you'll have to read the book to find out, This book's themes are, horror and adventure I'd give this book a 8 because it is a little scary but I think it's good for 1st graders and above because it's a little scary,

Your friend
Devin

FIGURE 8.7
Devin's paper.

	Rating of 1	Rating of 2	Rating of 3	Rating of 4	Rating of 5
Ideas and content: *I know allot about my topic. *I show what is happening. *I included interesting tidbits. *I made sure my topic was small enough to handle *I could easily tell what the point of my writing was.	*good showing writing*				*5*
Organization *My beginning gets the readers attention *Every detail adds a little more to my story *All my details are in the right place. Everything fits like a puzzle. *I ended at a good spot and didn't drag on for too long.	*Your writing had a clear plan.*			*4.5*	
Voice *I have put my personal stamp on this writing. *Readers can tell I am talking to them. *I write with confidence and sincerity. *I am not afraid to say what I think. *No one else sounds like me.		*Be proud of your creative gifts!*			*5*
Word Choice *My words seem just right. *My words are colorful, snappy, vital, brisk, and fresh. *My words are not fuzzy or vague. *Some of my words and phrases are unforgettable.		*3*		*4*	
Sentence Fluency *I have long stretchy sentences short snappy sentences Different types of beginnings a writing that flows no excess baggage				*4*	
Conventions *I have used these things correctly capitals punctuation Spelling paragraphs grammar/usage	*Please use cursive*		*3* *Watch for paragraph breaks*		

Writing assessment for *Jenn*

Title of the piece *Scary Stories*

25/30

FIGURE 8.8
Primary trait analysis.

children's time in the school. A similar process is used on the statewide writing assessment done in later grades.

PORTFOLIOS

What do you do with all this information you collect? That's where the need for organization and analysis comes in. As we said earlier in this chapter, portfolios are an excellent organizational tool. Perhaps you know what a portfolio is, but if you don't, you might compare it to an artist's portfolio that demonstrates the artist's talents. A student's portfolio generally is a large folder containing selected assessment documents and examples of the child's work.

Perhaps comparing a portfolio to a baby book will be more meaningful to you. If you have children, you probably have done what we have—kept baby books that recorded significant events in your children's lives. We recorded the eruption of teeth, first words, visits to the doctor, and first steps. When our babies grew into toddlers, we began to collect papers with scribbles they'd made with crayons and to jot down favorite books and playthings. Looking through these treasures clearly shows our children's development, and we marvel at how our children have grown and changed.

Teachers who use holistic teaching approaches are now keeping similar records of their students' growth for similar reasons. They find that by collecting

August

October

August: Kuutuuq's writing is scribbling, showing that she has no idea about letters or any mechanics of writing.

October: She knows that writing is linear, left to right. She writes with letters, but uses random letters to write *rainbow*, showing lack of alphabetic principle.

FIGURE 8.9
Materials in her portfolio document Kuutuuq's writing progress.

and organizing a set of materials over a school year, they easily can document growth in literacy as well as other areas of the curriculum. All the primary teachers at Joey and Amy's school worked together to develop a portfolio system that helps them, their students, and their students' parents marvel at the children's growth. The major difference between private collections of mementos and school portfolios is the systematic selection and analysis of portfolio contents. Portfolios are not just for your own use; they must communicate important information to parents and to the child's future teachers (Cohen & Wiener, 2003).

All the primary teachers at Mrs. Hanna's school keep a portfolio on every child and find it a valuable testament to growth (see Figure 8.9). Teachers, parents, and children can use the materials in a portfolio to document progress (Courtney & Abodeeb, 2001). At the end of a school year, parents can take much of the material home, but enough will be retained in the portfolios to inform the next teachers. Those children who are lucky enough to complete all their primary grades here will leave third grade with portfolios that clearly show their growth in literacy over a four-year span. Many teachers in the upper grades continue the portfolios when the students reach their classrooms.

Though portfolios are not themselves an assessment, they are an organizational tool that can help make best use of the multiple pieces of information pertaining to each child's progress. Different school districts organize language arts

March

March: She writes, "My mom says Sh Sh Sh Sh Sh to me." She uses memorized forms of common words and some invented spelling, which shows her knowledge of phonics. Notice she also knows about editing.

April

April: Kuutuuq writes, "I'm getting a bloodied nose." Her writing includes letters to represent most of the sounds heard. She has also noticed the use of an apostrophe in *I'm*.

FIGURE 8.9

Continued

portfolios differently, but most of them include a rating scale that provides a summary of the child's progress (Barrentine, 1999). The conclusions reflected in the rating scale are supported by the rest of the portfolio's contents—narrative observations, samples of writing and responses to literature, examples of books read, audiotapes of oral reading, test results, teacher-made checklists, and student records of reading and writing. We believe that individual teachers need the freedom to select portfolio entries that are meaningful to them and to their students. Otherwise, portfolios can become nearly as impersonal and unrelated to the classroom as standardized tests.

Joey's folder from second grade includes a fastwrite he did the first day of school as well as a polished report with several drafts stapled to it. Joey's list of favorite books is in there too as well as a photograph of his chart about chickens. Mr. Larson included a writing-behavior checklist that he designed and that has entries for four months. Just like a baby book, this portfolio contains information on special events in Joey's development. Joey's writing sample documents the first time he carried the writing process through all its stages. Joey's book list shows that he has begun to read nonfiction as well as fiction stories. The writing-behavior checklist indicates when Joey began to try to write poems, and it also shows his progress in transitional spelling and use of mechanics conventions. Mr. Larson wrote narrative reports explaining all this—one at midyear and one at the end of the year. In addition, in Joey's school district the portfolios include a letter of reflection written by the student at the end of each grade. In his letter, Joey explains the importance of items in the portfolio and discusses how he feels about himself as a learner.

Portfolios are described as respectful of the learner. They compare the child's current progress to his or her own previous ability rather than comparing children with one another (Leu & Kinzer, 2003). Portfolios also provide for teacher-student collaboration in assessment. Creating portfolios is something the teacher does *with* the students rather than to them. In addition, the very process of keeping work samples in a portfolio suggests that the children's work has value and is important (Farr & Tone, 1998; Harp, 2000). Children can take ownership of their portfolios too—Joey enjoys selecting material to add to his. When Joey seems especially proud of something he's done, Mr. Larson invites him to compare it with earlier work. Joey beamed with pride when he submitted his first poem and when he noticed that he had learned to write in paragraphs.

Mr. Larson finds that portfolios are easy to share with Joey's parents. During conferences, parents see exactly what their children have accomplished without having to undertake the task of trying to interpret seemingly meaningless test scores. Seeing evidence of Joey's work and having the teacher's written and oral explanations tell Joey's parents so much more than grades on a report card.

Mrs. Hanna has been recording and storing much of her portfolio data on her computer. This solves some of the storage problems and is efficient for generating reports from her records. For instance, when her checklists are done on spreadsheets, she can merge checklist material from different students to give comparison data when needed. After typing her anecdotal notes into the computer, she can later electronically copy parts of those records for narrative sum-

Portfolios help parents see exactly what their children have accomplished.

maries. Her school will get a scanner soon, which will allow her to copy photos and artwork as part of the computer record. Mrs. Hanna looks forward to that but has heard that such graphics quickly fill up computer memory. The site-based management team at her school is discussing whether to invest in CD-ROM technology to supplement computer storage capabilities.

She has been using portfolios for several years, and it is clear to Mrs. Hanna that they offer an excellent method of demonstrating a child's development regardless of whether she stores the information on a computer or in a box under her desk. Portfolios documenting literacy development have been so successful that her school district now encourages their use for all areas of the curriculum.

SELF-EVALUATION FOR CHILDREN AND TEACHERS

Self-reflection is valuable in both learning and teaching (Cooper & Kiger, 2001). If you wish children to become autonomous, self-motivated learners, you must encourage their reflection on their learning (Johnston, 1997). As an autonomous, self-motivated teacher, you will feel more confident and better able to articulate your teaching approaches as a result of your own self-reflection (Risko, Roskos, & Vukelich, 2002).

Children's Self-Evaluation

Children have a responsibility to keep records as part of their self-directed learning and as part of their role in self-evaluation. For example, the cumulative files of sample writings clearly show children how far they have come since the beginning of the school year. Mr. Larson provides a file-cabinet drawer where each child can file writing samples in his or her own folder. Most of his students take pride and pleasure in selecting new samples and reviewing old ones. When selecting pieces for possible inclusion in their portfolios, children are encouraged to reflect on and answer questions such as these:

> Why did you choose this piece?
>
> What does this work show about you as a learner?
>
> What should the reader know in order to appreciate it?

Mr. Larson listens carefully as students select pieces for their portfolios. He knows that their oral conversations about their work are often much richer than their written responses to these questions (Cohen & Wiener, 2003).

Journal-writing samples, with dated entries, are themselves records of children's progress as writers. Youngsters also can use their journals to note relevant information, such as the name of a book just finished or a reaction to a book. Children also can use their journals to record other reading-and-writing-related activities, such as reading a story to a kindergarten child, making up a skit and sharing it with the class, completing a mural project about a book, or writing a poem for Mom's birthday. Records kept by both student and teacher are an important guide during teacher-pupil conferences and for parent conferences.

Guide to self-evaluation of writing:

Am I writing more now than I was before?

Do I like most of what I write?

What have I written besides stories?

Can other people understand what I write?

Mrs. Williams encourages her students to keep daily logs of their reading and writing activities at the front of their journals. In this way, both she and the students have a record of how they used their time each day. She also encourages them to keep a list of possible writing topics and books they would like to read. As a guide to self-evaluation of writing, Mr. Larson has developed a set of questions for children to ask themselves. His students can read these questions from a chart in the conference area.

Mrs. Hanna asks her kindergartners to respond orally to similar questions. Their answers tell her a lot about what they think. For instance, when asked if he is writing more now, Jason enthusiastically answers yes. When asked what kind of writing he likes to do, he responds, "Draw pictures," and explains that he didn't used to know how to draw but now he does. Clearly, Jason has not yet distinguished between drawing and writing.

Many teachers also encourage their students to keep records of the books they have read. On Mr. Larson's record sheet, shown in Figure 8.10, Mary "graded" the books she read or that were read to her. Mary keeps this record sheet in her own language arts folder. Notice that this record sheet can also be used for personal writing.

Reading and Writing Log

Name _Mary_

Super	★	★	★	★
Good	★	★	★	
Fair	★	★		
Poor	★			

School _Eagle River_

Date	Title and Writer	R/W	Comments: . Why I read/wrote it . Why I like/dislike it . Other comments	Rating
	once e apon a time with mary kateih Ashley			★★ ★
	on cat Mountain		it's My favrit	★★ ★★
	Little women			★★ ★★
	Pocahontas		it's grat!	★★ ★★
	kirsten learns a lesson		it's sad.	★★ ★
	happy birthday kirsten		it's giveing	★★ ★★
	Josefina's Surprise		it's sad.	★★★ ★

Teacher's Notes:

Mary—I see you and your mom like history!

FIGURE 8.10

Personal record sheets help children monitor their own accomplishments.

Mr. Larson never makes charts for the whole classroom that compare numbers of books read by students. Like Mrs. Williams, he knows this would promote unnecessary comparison among the children. He prefers that students keep their own records of their reading. When Carlos first began "really reading," Mr. Larson helped him make a chart to keep track of the minutes he read each day at school. Carlos was so impressed with the time he could concentrate that he also kept track of the minutes he read at home and compared it to the minutes he watched television.

The culmination of student self-evaluation and record keeping comes at parent conference time. Mr. Larson and Mrs. Williams have student-led parent conferences. This means that the child is in charge when the parents come to school to find out about their child's progress. Each child carefully prepares for the parent conference through discussions with the teacher and through teacher-child collaboration on updating the portfolio.

Juan is very proud and serious when his parents arrive for their conference. He has carefully organized his portfolio materials and has a clear idea of his accomplishments as well as the areas where he needs to work or learn more. Because his parents are more comfortable speaking Spanish than speaking English, he conducts the conference in Spanish.

Mr. Larson is in the room and available to respond to questions, but he does not sit down with the children and their parents. At first, he tried to have student-led conferences while he was sitting right beside the child, but that resulted in the child and the parents talking to him instead of to one another. He has learned the wisdom of having several simultaneous parent conferences. This allows him to be accessible but not to hover and makes the conferences truly student led. Now Mr. Larson schedules four or five parent conferences for up to a full hour at the same time instead of four fifteen-minute conferences per hour. Parents' response to this system has generally been very favorable.

Evaluating Your Program and Your Teaching

Whatever your students' strengths and weaknesses, you will want to continuously evaluate your program and your teaching. An ongoing journal can help you record and process day-to-day events. Systematically reflecting on our own practice is an important step in modifying practice (Anders, Hoffman, & Duffy, 2000). The end of the school year calls for an in-depth look at what really happened to the children in your care—what they accomplished on their way to becoming responsible, contributing citizens.

You will want to analyze your efforts in helping them move toward confidence in their own thinking, in their ability to identify a problem, and in their approaches to solving it. How much more responsibility are they taking for their own actions, for their learning, for initiating useful suggestions and activities, and for providing needed assistance to others? How much more clearly and effectively can they talk to others, write for useful purposes, and write for their own satisfaction? How far have they progressed toward becoming lifelong readers?

Teacher self-evaluation includes asking yourself: "How much more am I able to listen to what children really mean?" "How much more confidence have I developed in children's ability and desire to learn?" and "How often do I ask questions that challenge children to think?"

Input on these and other questions may include comments from parents, any school personnel, and children themselves. The answers to these questions will vary with each individual. A teacher needs to consider each issue for each child to get a complete picture.

For you, other questions arise. Ask yourself, "How much more able am I to listen to children, to what they really mean?" "How much more confidence have I developed in children's abilities to learn, to think, to be self-directed, and to be responsible?" "How much more often do I raise challenging questions rather than make instructional statements?" "How effectively have I been able to integrate the language arts, thus saving time and making learning more productive?" "How much more capably have I used language skills as a useful tool in the total school curriculum?"

In some school districts, this type of self-assessment has led to a "teacher researcher" movement that encourages dialogue among teachers. This classroom research and teacher dialogue facilitate self-analysis and ultimately result in better teaching.

CONCLUSION

Though there isn't agreement on the format, most recommendations for emergent-literacy assessment support the value of recording observations of common classroom activity periods. Early childhood and emergent literacy experts agree that children's abilities are indicated more accurately by their performances in familiar situations than their performances in artificial testing situations. Children's behaviors during literacy events, such as story time, guided reading, independent reading, writing, and choice time, tell teachers most of what they need to know about individual children's levels of understanding. Individually focused conferences offer further opportunities for observing, recording, and analyzing a child's learning process and progress. Several published observation and recording systems offer models for standardizing and quantifying observational data.

Portfolios provide a way to keep track of a child's accomplishments by organizing all relevant data. When portfolios are carefully planned and skillfully used, the children, teachers, and parents feel a sense of accomplishment. The analysis of information in a portfolio can give teachers useful feedback about a child's learning progress and problems and about the effectiveness of the curriculum.

DISCUSSION QUESTIONS

1. Discuss the pros and cons of teacher-made versus standardized forms of collecting, recording, and communicating information about a child's progress.
2. A parent complains at a parent-teacher conference about being shown a portfolio rather than a graded report card. How would you respond if you were that teacher?

SUGGESTED FOLLOW-UP ACTIVITIES

1. Use a published informal reading inventory to assess the general reading abilities of several children who are fairly conventional readers. When you feel comfortable with this, assemble and administer your own IRI, using passages you select yourself from texts or trade books.
2. Try doing a running record. Analyze errors a child has made during oral reading according to the strategies used. If desired, consult Marie Clay's book *An Observation Survey of Early Literacy Achievement* (1993a) for further information on running records.
3. Observe children reading silently. Note behavior and expressions that indicate comprehension and attitude toward the material.

4. Assist a teacher in assembling a reading or writing portfolio. If possible, sit in on a parent conference when the portfolio is used.

5. Observe a second or third grader's writing behavior and then fill in a copy of Mr. Larson's checklist of writing development (see Figure 8.4) with your data. Or observe a child's ability to use the writing process and fill in a copy of Mrs. Williams's progress sheet (see Figure 8.5) with your data. Or design your own checklist of writing development.

6. Use the six-trait writing rubric (Table 8.7) to analyze an independent writer's piece of writing.

7. With a preschooler or kindergartner, try out the checklists using the Sulzby categories reprinted in this chapter (Tables 8.1, 8.2, and 8.3) to guide and document your observations of the child's emerging literacy. Analyze this experience for convenience and accuracy of information.

RECOMMENDED FURTHER READING

Barrentine, S. J. (1999). *Reading assessment: Principles and practices for elementary teachers: A collection of articles from* The Reading Teacher. Newark, DE: International Reading Association.

Clay, M. (1993). *An observation survey of early literacy achievement.* Portsmouth, NH: Heinemann.

Ford, M. P. (2001). What to do about jabbering parrots: Lessons learned while advocating for best practices. *Language Arts, 79*(1), 53–60.

Kohn, A. (2001). Fighting the tests: Turning frustration into action. *Young Children, 56*(2); 20–24.

Kohn, A. (2002). Poor teaching for poor kids. *Language Arts, 79*(3), 251–255.

Morrow, L. M. (2001). *Literacy development in the early years* (4th ed.). Boston: Allyn & Bacon.

Ratcliff, N. J. (2001–2002). Using authentic assessment to document the emerging literacy skills of young children. *Childhood Education, 78*(2), 66–69.

Ruiz, N. T., & Enguidanos, T. (1997). Authenticity and advocacy in assessment: Bilingual students in special education. *Primary Voices K–6, 5*(3), 35–43.

Shephard, L., Kagan, S. L., & Wurtz, E. (Eds.). (1998). *Principles and recommendations for early childhood assessments.* Washington, DC: National Education Goals Panel.

Spandel, V. (1996). *Seeing with new eyes.* Portland, OR: Northwest Regional Educational Laboratory.

West, K. R. (1998). Noticing and responding to learners: Literacy evaluation and instruction in the primary grades. *The Reading Teacher, 51*(7), 550–559.

Wesson, K. A. (2001). The Volvo effect: Questioning standardized tests. *Young Children, 56*(2), 16–18.

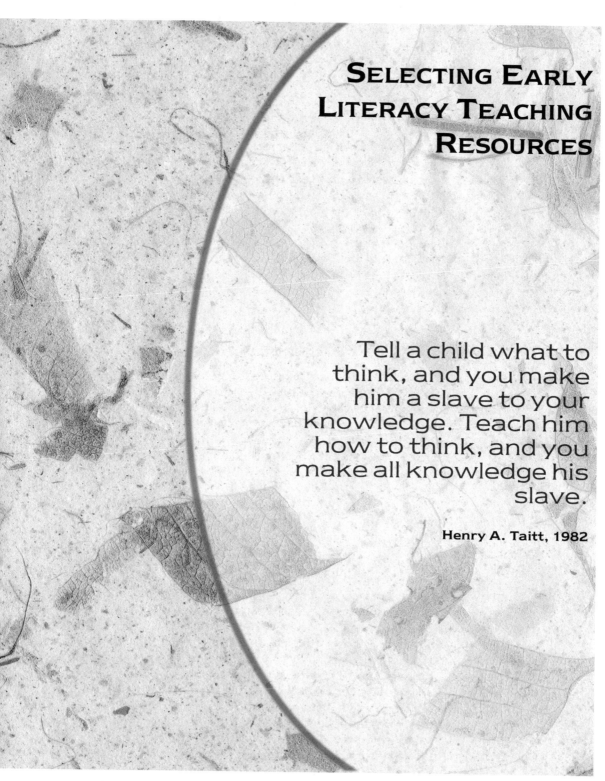

SELECTING EARLY LITERACY TEACHING RESOURCES

Tell a child what to think, and you make him a slave to your knowledge. Teach him how to think, and you make all knowledge his slave.

Henry A. Taitt, 1982

In this chapter, we're going to look at materials for young readers. We'll start with libraries and the types of trade books most relevant for beginning readers. Then we'll analyze commercial reading programs and end with a discussion of some technology products and services. We offer this overview with the recommendation that teachers select their materials from many sources and not limit their choices to one program or publishing company.

Whereas once there was a clear distinction between library books and textbooks for teaching reading, now textbook companies sell library books and also publish books for teaching reading that are more similar to library books than to textbooks. Most teachers now offer their students many small books rather than collections of stories in a single text. Many teachers use library books in place of textbooks, and many teachers encourage students to use textbooks as if they were library books. The lines are definitely blurred; therefore, the distinctions we make in this analysis are somewhat artificial. Nevertheless, we hope they serve some purpose in helping you consider the variety of literacy materials available in schools today.

CHOOSING TRADE BOOKS

We can divide the types of books found in schools that support a literature program into two basic categories: textbooks and trade books. Remember that textbooks are sold as sets of materials and that their basic purpose is to instruct. Trade books, on the other hand, generally are purchased and used individually. Parents and the public know trade books mainly as library books. In this section, we'll look at how library books are made available in school and classroom libraries. We'll also briefly introduce the types of trade books that are essential to a literacy program for young children.

The School Library

Making the library a focal point of the curriculum has been a gradual process at Mr. Larson's school. He remembers when Mrs. Sanders, the school librarian, not only had to run the library but also had to select and order all the books, teach library skills, and do read-aloud programs by herself. Back in those days, the children went to the library during the teachers' planning time, so that even if he went to the library with his class, Mr. Larson had very little time to talk with the librarian. When the school district adopted the literature-based reading program, a group of teachers and librarians pressed the school board to provide additional support for the school libraries. As a result, the schools now have library aides who assist with ordering, checkout, and shelving routines; cataloging; and new-book processing. The teachers' planning time was reorganized so that the teachers could work more effectively with the librarian and be with the children during library time. Funds that were formerly used for workbooks and other consumable textbook materials were diverted to books for the library. Since the change to reading more library books than basal texts, the library has had to expand, and the adjacent classroom was remodeled to accommodate more shelving, an audiovisual area, and worktables for children. Now the library is an inviting place, always open, always busy, and always filled with plenty of reading materials. This is the focal point for the school's literature program. All the teachers consider Mrs. Sanders a teacher first as well as a resource person and their school librarian.

When a class comes to use the library, Mrs. Sanders and the teacher have had adequate planning time together to prepare the lesson. Mr. Larson now feels that he and Mrs. Sanders's team teach much of the second-grade literature program, and he is relieved to have such an accessible resource person. Mrs. Sanders always reads or tells a story when each class comes in, and she was the one who convinced Mr. Larson to learn to tell stories himself.

Every class in the school visits once a week for formal library instruction, and Mrs. Sanders also has an open-door policy for individual children who show that they can use the library responsibly. Children love having a workplace besides their classrooms for special projects. This library is far from that old stereotype of the quiet, dusty place where noise was admonished. Instead, the library has become a focal point of the school (Carletti, Girard, & Willing, 1991; Giorgis & Peterson, 1996).

Mrs. Sanders also sees the library as the heart of support for the overall curriculum of the school. She asks teachers to request books or topics that they need to complement their studies. Mrs. Sanders sees herself as a reading teacher and as a school leader in the development of the literature-based curriculum. She believes that a well-stocked library is absolutely necessary for a constructivist holistic literacy program, and she constantly lobbies for better funding and support. Luckily, her principal is supportive and diverts a large portion of the school's materials' budget her way.

Mr. Larson and his colleagues remember trying to set up an independent reading program before the school library was expanded and remodeled. It was difficult at best—a true literature-based independent reading program has to be supported by lots of available books in an environment that invites children.

Children's Literature That Supports Emergent and Beginning Readers

When you think of library books for young readers, do you remember the bins or shelves of picture books in the library? Do you think of Dr. Seuss or Mike Mulligan and his steam shovel? These classic images of trade books are still accurate, but they make up only a fraction of the books that are available today for emergent and beginning readers.

Thousands of trade books are published every year. Among these are expensive hardcover, illustrated storybooks that truly are works of art; inexpensive paperbacks that are meant to be consumed after a few uses; and everything in between. We cannot give you a course on children's literature here but instead will discuss several types of books that are essential to a constructivist literacy program for young children. We recommend *Children's Literature in the Elementary School* (Huck; Hepler; Hickman; & Kiefer, 2001) for a comprehensive look at the field of children's literature.

An open and inviting school library filled with plenty of good literature is the focal point of children's literacy development.

"Baby Books"

Today's children literally can cut their teeth on children's books. Books for babies, of course, are not designed for them to read but simply for them to become familiar with books. Bright, familiar pictures in simple formats capture the interest of very young children, and heavy, nontoxic cardboard, soft plastic, and strong cloth characterize books that hold together even after repeated "tastings." Books for babies obviously are designed primarily for home or child care use, not for school settings. They have an important effect on later schooling, however, in that they familiarize the youngest children with books. Children who have experienced such materials will understand that books carry meaningful and enjoyable messages inside. They also will become familiar with some beginning book-handling knowledge—how to turn pages, directionality, and making choices. In addition, many trade books are now offered in board book formats. A child who comes to preschool will find familiar trade books and even big books, such as Audrey Wood's *The Napping House* (1984). We recommend a visit to a children's bookstore to look at the baby section if you haven't already done so. We think you'll be charmed by the works of Eric Hill,

Jan Ormerod, Helen Oxenbury, Jose Aruego, John Burningham, and scores of others. Incidentally, the local reading association that Mrs. Thomas and other teachers belong to has an ongoing service project in their community. Each baby born in the local hospital is presented with a bag containing a baby book and literature for the parents on introducing books to their baby.

Picture Books

Short, large-format books with both illustrations and text are probably the most familiar of the books for young children. The range of types of picture books is wide, and we will discuss here the types that Ms. Reynolds, Mrs. Thomas, Mrs. Sanders, and their colleagues choose for young children.

Alphabet Books

You probably think of alphabet books when you think of young children. Alphabet books are a part of a larger class of picture books: concept books. These books teach simple concepts, such as colors, numbers, shapes, and the ABCs. As you know, we are not advocates of letter-of-the-week alphabet programs, but we do recognize that children can learn something about letters from alphabet books.

The best alphabet books contain illustrations that relate clearly to each letter of the alphabet, text that makes sense, and sometimes even a story line. We particularly like alphabet books that invite continued inquiry, such as *On Market Street* (Lobel, 1981), which shows market vendors, each hawking items related to a different letter, and *A Caribou Alphabet* (Owens, 1988), which gives both scientific and cultural information about caribou in rhyming, narrative format. *Alphabet City* (Johnson, 1995) allows children to be detectives as they find letter shapes in photographs of natural objects. Alphabet books such as these allow children to construct their knowledge about letters within a fascinating context.

Concept books abound that deal with numbers, shapes, colors, time, size, and any number of abstractions. We especially like the work of Ruth Heller, who tackles concepts from "animals that lay eggs" (*Chicken's Aren't the Only Ones*, 1981) to camouflage (*How to Hide an Octopus*, 1992) to parts of speech (*Merry-Go-Round*, 1990). You will be amazed at how her clever words and bold, graphic pictures bring abstract ideas to life.

Wordless Picture Books

These unique books have little or no text. They are often humorous, with piquant illustrations. They can be as simple as Helen Oxenbury's *Good Night, Good Morning* (1982), which shows, in eight simple pictures, a child's nighttime routine, or Raymond Briggs's *The Snowman* (1978), a soft tale of a snowman who is invited into a little boy's life. On the other hand, some wordless books are extremely sophisticated, such as *Good Dog Carl* (Day, 1988). In this book and its sequels, Carl, a large, black dog with more-than-doglike intelligence, cares for a baby while the mother is out. Their improbable adventures in familiar settings, which range from swimming in the fish tank to riding down the laundry chute, delight both children and adults. In *Tuesday*, by David Wiesner (1991), frogs leave their lily pads and wreak havoc on small-town life. Wordless books give children power to "read" on their own and demand that children interact with the story. Today's wordless books are less frequently aimed at preschoolers, with sophisticated stories and humor attractive to elementary-school-aged children. They also are powerful tools to use in school for oral language development.

Everybody Books

Many picture books are not meant for children to read to themselves! This may surprise you until you compare the text and the concepts presented in picture books with the reading abilities of young children. We now call these books "everybody books" because adults can read them aloud, emergent readers can listen to them, and more proficient readers may enjoy them on their own. Generally, the text presents the story or information without regard to beginning reading ability. As a result, the language is often eloquent and the stories are complex. Consider a favorite of ours, *Miss Rumphius* (Cooney, 1982), which traces the life of an unmarried librarian who travels the world trying to live up to her grandfather's advice to "make the world a more beautiful place." In the end, she returns home and sprinkles the countryside with lupine seeds, leaving her legacy behind her. In *Sweet Clara and the Freedom Quilt* (Hopkinson, 1993), a young girl sews the map of the Underground Railroad into a quilt that she leaves behind when she escapes to her freedom. Such picture storybooks are sophisticated in story, illustrated with works of art, and rich and beautiful in language. Increasingly, historical fiction, folklore, biography, and information are being found in the picture book format. *Golem* (Wisniewski, 1996) retells an ancient and terrifying legend of a man-made giant who saves the Jews of Prague; *Baseball Saved Us* (Mochizuki, 1993) takes place in an internment camp. *This Place Is Wet* (Cobb, 1989) is one of a series about climates. *Meet the Orchestra* (Hayes, 1991) introduces the instruments and the wild animals that play them (Who might play the string bass? A walrus, of course!). *The Divide* (Bedard, 1997) tells the story of a young Willa Cather as she moves with her family to Nebraska. Lucky for those of us who often read aloud to our students or our own children, these books are so good that they are a joy to read over and over again.

Predictable Books

As you browse through the everybody book or picture book sections in Mrs. Sanders's library, you will also find picture books that young children can read themselves. Predictable books make heavy use of pictures as clues to the story as well as predictable story patterns, questions, cumulative sequences, and children's songs and rhymes. *Have You Seen My Cat?* by Eric Carle (1987) has only two sentences—the title and the answer, "This is not my cat"—but carries a complete story line through pictures that show a child looking for his lost cat not only at home and in the neighborhood but also in the jungle, the mountains, and the zoo. Eric

A wide variety and great number of fiction and nonfiction books are now available for children to choose from.

Carle's *From Head to Toe* (1997) also offers success for emergent readers with his trademark dramatic illustrations moving the story along. In *Five Little Monkeys Jumping on the Bed* (Christelow, 1989), a predictable pattern and silly illustrations lead the young readers through a mama's tribulations in getting her little ones to bed:

> Then . . . five little monkeys jumped on the bed!
> One fell off and bumped his head.
> The mama called the doctor. The doctor said,
> "No more monkeys jumping on the bed!"
> So four little monkeys . . . jumped on the bed.

Can you tell what will happen next? Can you imagine the fun an emergent reader has with a book like this? Can you see how text like this will aid a youngster in constructing ideas about reading, about the story, and even about phonics?

Because of demand for this type of book from schools, hundreds, if not thousands, of predictable "instant reader" books are now available. Several publishing companies specialize in small, attractive books that have few words and use patterns and pictures to indicate what those few words are. Also, because many schools are demanding leveled books, most of these companies indicate the level of each book in at least one system of leveling (as discussed in Chapter 8). Most also give a word count for the book as another criterion for selection. Are these real books, or are they instructional materials? Perhaps it depends on how they are used.

Easy-to-Read Books

Many easy-to-read books have also been published for the reading-instruction market. Traditionally, we think of books with controlled vocabulary, large print, and short sentences when we think of easy-to-read books. The characters in the best of these, such as Dr. Seuss's *The Cat in the Hat* (Seuss, 1957), Arnold Lobel's *Frog and Toad Are Friends* (1970) and *Frog and Toad Together* (1972), Else Minarik's *Little Bear* (1957), and Russell Hoban's Frances series (1960–1980) have stood the test of time despite sometimes contrived and unusual language. The worst of the easy-to-read books, fortunately, have largely been replaced in school and classroom libraries with paperback books designed especially for beginning readers.

When you visit a children's bookstore or library, look for books from the following series: Parents Magazine Read-Aloud Originals, Scholastic Hello Reading Books, Bank Street Ready-to-Read Books, Random House Picturebook Readers, Dial Easy-to-Read Books, Children's Press New True Books, and Dell Yearling Books. You will find a wide variety of fiction, nonfiction, and folktales, with beginning reading levels, good illustrations, and captivating stories and topics. Teachers receive many catalogs for beginning reading materials from publishers such as Wright Group and Rigby. These catalogs list books according to whatever categories teachers are currently looking for. They will not only level books and count words for you but they will also identify books for shared reading, for guided reading, and for independent reading.

Mrs. Thomas doesn't let publishers tell her how to use books and isn't so interested in what level a book is; her concern is what will attract her first-grade students. She says that if a student is "passionate" about a book, that child will learn to read it regardless of the level. Her students enjoy the stories and artwork in such quality books as those by Eric Carle and by Caldecott Medal–winning author and illustrator Lois Ehlert. Another example of a popular book is *Three by the Sea* by Edward Marshall (1981). In this book, each of three first graders tells a story while they're all digesting their lunches before they can go swimming. The stories are humorous and short and use normal language patterns—perfect for a young reader to read aloud. Mrs. Sanders, Mrs. Thomas, and Mr. Larson fill their libraries with such books. They are inexpensive, popular, and, though possibly not all fine literature, surely good books for youngsters beginning to "really read." For more information on sources and a list of predictable and easy-to-read books, we recommend *Matching Books to Readers: Using Leveled Books in Guided Reading, K–3* (Fountas & Pinnell, 1999). In addition, journals such as *The Reading Teacher* and *The New Advocate* publish monthly reviews of notable books for young readers.

Big Books

We have mentioned in previous chapters that many fine children's picture books are published in large format. These are marketed both as trade books and as textbooks. They are available in fiction and nonfiction. It is important to consider the layout of a big book. Some stories are not designed for big book form. And others are poorly designed big books. For example, the print size is too small to make them useful for a group shared reading. If you've not seen a big book, be sure to locate one in a primary classroom. You may be surprised that they are *really* big. Most teachers purchase an easel or use the chalk tray to hold these books and use a pointer to enhance group reading. Young children also enjoy the large format, whether in groups or reading on their own.

Chapter and Information Books

By the time children are in second or third grade, their tastes usually have graduated to books shelved in the library as juvenile fiction and nonfiction. They may begin their chapter-book reading with something their teacher has read aloud to them—maybe *Charlotte's Web* (White, 1952) or a *Ramona* book by Beverly Cleary (1968, 1977). Teachers of the upper primary and middle grades must continue the practice of reading aloud to their classes every day not only to share wonderful stories and beautiful language with the whole group but also to introduce young readers to authors, topics, and genres that they will enjoy in the future.

With so many kinds of books and so many choices, it is essential that every teacher build a classroom library that serves as an addition to the resources of the school and public libraries. Children's literacy development is highly correlated to access to books (Neuman & Celano, 2001). In the following section, we'll look at how Mr. Larson tackled that task.

Building a Classroom Library

It takes a lot of books to meet the needs of young readers. Providing fifteen hundred books per classroom (Moustafa, 1997) has been recommended as a powerful way to improve reading instruction. "That would cost too much!" complain many people. Yet the immense quantity of money spent on sets of reading textbooks, workbooks, work sheets, teachers' guides, and supplementary materials goes unquestioned.

Some teachers create their own inexpensive reading material. Ms. Montoya and other teachers in her district wrote little books that can be photocopied and taken home as "keepers" (see Figure 9.1). These teachers wanted to increase the books available at home as well as at school.

Mr. Larson wants a wide variety of books in his classroom and is always on the lookout for books that will interest various children in his class. In fact, one of the first things he does each school year is to find what his students like by giving them an interest inventory to fill out. He keeps these inventories (Figure 9.2) at the front of the children's folders to help remind him of their likes and dislikes. The inventories help Mr. Larson suggest books or writing topics.

Any environment that fosters independent reading of literature must be rich with books. Mr. Larson has worked hard to collect an adequate number of books to make up his classroom library. The year he started his library, he aimed for five to eight books per child. Since then, he has amassed hundreds of books and has a group of parents and friends who continue to help him gather books.

Many fine children's books are published as Big Books as well as in regular formats.

Mr. Larson and several of his students' parents are always on the lookout for children's books at garage sales, secondhand stores, and library sales. This year at the school carnival, the librarian had a booth selling old books she had weeded from her collection. Mr. Larson bought about twenty-five books at fifty cents apiece, including old but serviceable copies of *Stone Soup* (M. Brown, 1947), *Harry the Dirty Dog* (Zion, 1956), and *Curious George* (Rey, 1941). Later, Linda's mother spent a morning sorting through the books, discarding those with missing pages and taping and recovering the remaining books.

The bottom shelf of the classroom library is devoted to serial books such as Encyclopedia Brown, The Magic Treehouse, and Nancy Drew. These belonged to Mr. Larson's neighbor's son and daughter when they were in elementary school.

Potlatch

Written by
Vivian Montoya

Illustrated by
Nancy Davidson

We have the totem.

We have the blanket.

We have the fish.

 When reading "It's a Keeper" books with your child:
• make sure the experience is fun;
• don't make your child struggle
(if the book is too hard, read it to the child
or read it together);
• focus on reading the whole book,
not on isolated words; and
• praise your child for his or her efforts.

Reread these books many times. It is through rereading, that children:
• really understand the meaning of the book;
• enjoy the books over and over;
• have the chance to read fluently;
• learn many words over time;
• become familiar with the words and language patterns; and
• solve new words within a story that is meaningful and familiar.

We have the basket.

FIGURE 9.1

These are some pages from a "keeper" book. These books are written and illustrated by teachers and printed by photocopy. Inexpensive production allows children to take them home for keeps.

Name _____

Interest Inventory

Check the 5 things you like best:

__ snowshoeing	__ movie stars	__ airplanes
__ skiing	__ singers	__ cooking
__ sledding	__ drawing	__ animals
__ ice skating	__ jokes	__ dinosaurs
__ roller skating	__ hiking	__ plants
__ soccer	__ ballet	__ birds
__ football	__ dolls	__ cameras
__ hockey	__ stars	__ singing
__ basketball	__ space	__ puzzles
__ baseball	__ video games	__ pioneers
__ swimming	__ computers	__ fishing
__ running	__ TV	__ painting
__ karate	__ radio	__ pets

What was the best book you've ever read?

If you could buy a book, what would you buy?

What book would you like to read?

FIGURE 9.2
An interest inventory gives teachers a general idea of their students' interests.

These are very popular with second graders because of their predictable characters and plots. Mr. Larson even asks former students when they visit him if they have any donations for his library.

Mr. Larson subscribes to *Booklinks* and considers the cost well worth it. The bimonthly publication includes expert reviews of new books that he might purchase and also offers articles that help him use books more effectively in his teaching. The Trumpet Book Club and Scholastic are inexpensive sources of books, and Mr. Larson encourages the children in his class to order paperbacks from the monthly catalogs. For every so many books the children buy, Mr. Larson is able to order free books. He has used this system to obtain sets of especially good books that groups of children might enjoy reading together. This year, he received six copies each of *Frog and Toad Are Friends (Lobel 1970)*, *Amelia Bedelia* (Parish, 1963),*Charlotte's Web* (White, 1952), *Hailstones and Halibut Bones* (O'Neill, 1961), and *Dr. DeSoto* (Steig, 1982). Seth has requested *Runaway Ralph* (Cleary, 1970) to be the next set Mr. Larson orders. Mr. Larson is aware that these book clubs place great stock in materials that aren't literature: computer games, stickers, and series books. Although he can't prevent families from spending their money on such items, he makes it a point to talk up the literature he recommends—"book talk."

Mr. Larson finds that many children want to read the kinds of books sold in the grocery store. These books may not be high-quality literature, but the short books printed on inexpensive paper, sticker books, Garfield books, and comic books provide a source of reading entertainment and are acceptable as a type of reading. Mr. Larson knows that his job is to help children expand their reading tastes beyond such books. Many youngsters are fascinated by reference books and encyclopedias. The *Guinness Book of World Records* (McWhirter, 1999) is a standard favorite and is published each year. *The World Almanac for Kids* (Levey, 1999) is in constant use in Mr. Larson's class. The Golden Book encyclopedias (Parker, 1969) have entries written at a level most primary-grade children can understand. Some children are interested in using dictionaries; one that seems to be useful for second graders is the *Clear and Simple Thesaurus Dictionary* (Wittles, 1996). A stack of nature guides, including Roger Tory Peterson's *Field Guide to the Birds* (1998), is used constantly.

Another shelf in the class library holds books the children have written themselves: One is about Carolina's trip to Mexico, and another includes stories about the class's trip to the zoo. Right now a group is working on a book about the hatching of the chicks. These books, beautifully bound, decorated, and laminated, are very popular with second graders. At the end of the school year, a few of the best will be donated to the school library, and the rest will go home with individual children.

Because Mr. Larson has focused on inexpensive, homemade, or free reading materials, he still has some money in his book budget for trade books. However, the field of children's literature is overwhelming to him, and he often has difficulty choosing what to buy. So he has narrowed his choices to two types of books for his collection. First, he buys new books that are especially popular with second graders. He can rely on ideas from the "Young Readers' Choice" list that is published each October in *The Reading Teacher*, the journal of the International Reading Association for elementary teachers. He buys about fifteen books a year from this list. For nonfiction books, Mr. Larson focuses on his personal interest in the outdoors and chooses books about camping, nature, weather, and survival. Several other teachers in the building have pet topics: Mr. McCormick likes books about art, Mrs. Williams buys winter-sports books, and Ms. Butters has a large collection of books about whales.

When Mr. Larson's class expressed interest in learning more about whales, he knew Ms. Butters would lend them her collection of whale books.

When Mr. Larson stopped using sets of basal readers, he couldn't imagine just throwing away books that had some good literature in them. So he kept a few copies of each of the various levels of books from several reading series and shelved them with the storybooks. He also didn't want to give up the plays, poems, and choral readings that were so popular with the second graders, so he marked materials he wanted to save and asked Linda's mother to cut them out from the discarded basals with a razor blade. She then bound the pages in a spiral binder, and Mr. Larson invited children to illustrate the cardboard covers after they had read, discussed, and written about the poems or plays. There are now dozens of sets of these materials, and small groups of children love to use them to read plays or to give choral readings or readers' theater presentations.

Rich classroom libraries like these allow every child to have plenty of fiction as well as nonfiction materials to choose from during reading time. The classroom library often is most useful when a child wants to find something to read right away or needs to look something up quickly. The library nook also serves as a comfortable, relaxed, and quiet place where you can almost always find someone reading contentedly.

Libraries as a source of reading material can dramatically improve the teaching and learning of reading; however, using library books instead of basal readers sometimes is only a superficial change. Some teachers are so programmed from years with basal texts and teachers' guides that when they give them up in favor of library books, they use the library books just as they used the basal readers. They beat the literature to death with the multitude of questions, lessons, and assignments they have always used. They are "basalizing the literature" without the help of a teachers' guide.

ANOTHER TYPE OF RESOURCE

School volunteers offer another type of resource for helping children become readers. Many caring adults have responded to the America Reads initiative, spending time each week reading with children. Service organizations, such as the Kiwanis Club, encourage this volunteerism as well. In some communities, Big Brothers and Big Sisters programs coordinate their volunteers to provide reading assistance in the schools. But a large number of volunteers are individuals who offer assistance on their own.

Many schools tap the expertise and time of retired citizens for volunteer grandparents programs. A cry of "Grandpa!" goes up as Mrs. Thomas's first graders see a favorite volunteer enter the room for reading time. Children's affection, as well as their reading progress, offers rich rewards for time given to schools. Retired people frequently live far from their own grandchildren but are able to give time and attention to surrogate grandchildren. Mrs. Thomas relies on "Grandpa" to help her provide the one-on-one assistance required by most beginning readers.

Volunteer grandparents programs are one way to provide individual assistance to beginning or struggling readers.

In Ms. Montoya's school, diverse sources of volunteers are coordinated by reading specialists and incorporated into special programs for struggling readers. The large reading resource room is full of children and adults reading together, as are an adjacent multipurpose area and walkways. Volunteer grandparents, Kiwanis Club members, and other volunteers work side by side with the school reading specialists to provide individual attention for reading instruction. In this school, with large numbers of children in ESL (English as a second language) and LEP (limited English proficiency) programs, half the students need special help with reading every day—and they get it.

Volunteers can be an enormous resource for schools hoping to improve their effectiveness in a time of budget restraints (Brown, 1998). Tapping this resource on a large scale is a fairly recent social phenomenon.

RESOURCE GUIDES AND LITERATURE UNITS

Resource guides and literature units offer sources of inspiration to teachers as they plan a curriculum around children's literature. Not surprisingly, the quality of such publications varies greatly, as does the level of literacy understanding demonstrated in them. They can be critiqued using most of the same criteria we set out for analyzing reading programs in the following section.

We have been impressed with the *First Steps* materials developed in Australia (Education Department of Western Australia, 1994) and distributed in the United States by Heinemann publishers. Rather than a detailed script for what the teacher is to say, *First Steps* materials, such as the *Reading Resource Book* (Education Department of Western Australia, 1997b), offer general guidelines to the teacher. This respect for the teacher's ability to implement a plan is similar to that shown in another Australian import, *Bookshelf Stage 1: Teacher's Resource Book* (Bolton, Green, Pollack, Scarfee, & Snowball, 1986). *Bookshelf* works from the premise that "literacy develops naturally through meaningful, functional use" (p. 4). Long explanations of why this approach is better than others are not needed in a country that is used to doing it this way. Both resource series utilize oral language learning as the model for written language learning. They also celebrate approximations of intent rather than expecting beginners to use conventional forms of literacy. In addition, *First Steps* offers a booklet called *Parents as Partners* (Education Department of Western Australia (1997a) to help teachers explain how children become literate.

Respect for both teachers and children permeates these guides. Besides respecting children as individuals in the skill acquisition process, they also respect children's choices for reading and writing topics. Children are empowered with ownership as they choose their own reading and write their own ideas.

Even the terminology demonstrates a different attitude; instead of saying "have" children do something, *Bookshelf* suggests that teachers "invite" or "encourage" children. There is no sacred sequence of books to be covered, and there is no one way to introduce an activity or read a story. *First Steps* assumes that teachers "will adapt and change procedures according to the children's needs, their own level of comfort, their school organization and the availability of resources" (p. 15). It is assumed that teachers are competent and do not need a script to follow. This empowers teachers rather than controls them.

Mrs. Thomas has been guided for several years by another import from Australia. *Reading in Junior Classes* (New Zealand Ministry of Education, 1987) was designed as a handbook for the New Zealand Ready to Read series but has information applicable to helping children learn to read with any books. This guide starts by laying out the theory base:

The best reading programs respect children's individual learning processes and also their individual choices of reading and writing topics.

Reading programmes should be child centered.

Reading for meaning is paramount.

Reading must always be rewarding.

Children learn to read by reading.

Children learn best on books that have meaning and are rewarding.

The best approach to teaching reading is a combination of approaches.

The best cure for reading failure is good first teaching.

The foundations of literacy are laid in the early years. (p. 9)

The constructivist principle of learning by making "mistakes" is also emphasized in the New Zealand guide. In keeping with this principle and with a child-centered focus, it starts with the assumption that children must first learn that print carries a message. Too much other reading material starts with letters and sounds, reflecting the assumption that children have somehow already acquired the alphabetic principle and phonemic awareness.

Some teachers are using the book *Guided Reading* (Fountas & Pinnell, 1996) as a resource guide. This comprehensive book offers an extensive list of leveled books plus instructions for guided reading lessons. It also contains an overview of how the rest of a reading program might be organized, including all the aspects of reading and writing to, with, and by students outlined in the preceding chapters of this text. The companion text, *Matching Books to Readers: Using Leveled Books in Guided Reading, K–3* (Fountas & Pinnell, 1999), includes an extensive list of texts that have been leveled. The authors have created an equivalence chart to compare their list to others. They listed many pieces of literature as opposed to a specialized set of small books published strictly as leveled texts. And the on-line database *http://www.leveledbooks.com* provides quick access to trade book titles for emergent readers. This broadens the array of choices children have for guided as well as independent reading. Children do not need to be limited to reading at a specific level, but it is helpful to expand the number of leveled books in the classroom for diagnostic and assessment purposes.

We hope that many teachers are using *Once Upon a Time . . . An Encyclopedia for Successfully Using Literature With Young Children* (Hurst, 1990). This resource book presents hundreds of worthwhile children's books and organizes them by author, by theme, and by subject. Each book is accompanied by a list of related literature and a short list of relevant activities for children. We think this offers just enough help for the teacher and just enough extension activities for youngsters. There is still room for teacher initiative and still time left for reading. A set of *Literature-Based Thematic Units* by the same author (Hurst, 1992) offers the same set of advantages. Many books designed to help teachers plan literature activities try too hard to be helpful and end up offering enough ideas to beat to death any piece of literature. Many also reach too far in their efforts to come up with activities across the curriculum; a great number of the activities are not worth doing and do not enhance children's understandings in any way. Teachers need to carefully pick and choose among ideas offered from any source.

With the current emphasis on reading comprehension strategies, many teachers have turned to *Strategies That Work* (Harvey & Goudvis, 2000) for guidance. Expanding on the influential work of *Mosaic of Thought* (Keene & Zimmermann, 1997), this text outlines the comprehension strategies identified as effective after extensive research (listed previously in Chapter 7). The first section of the text explains how readers create meaning as they read. The latter part outlines the instructional plan: model the strategy use (to), guide readers as they use it (with), and provide opportunities for practice (by). The text has an extensive reference list for literature that lends itself to these steps.

ANALYZING READING PROGRAMS

We constantly see advertisements for hugely expensive reading-instruction programs that ensure success for all children. Many new or improved reading programs guarantee success if you follow their "recipes." With all these claims, how does the teacher or curriculum committee decide which approach to choose?

To make this decision more confusing, all programs have the same goal—for children to become proficient readers. Also, most make statements about the importance of helping children to succeed and to enjoy reading. Most offer attractive and colorful formats for children and time saving, packaged teaching aids for teachers. In practice, the large textbook companies, with their array of readers, workbooks, drill sheets, flash cards, record-keeping forms, and tests, have long dictated how reading is taught in the United States. U.S. society has put its trust in publishing companies instead of in teachers, which explains why Australian and New Zealand teachers have to help American teachers learn to take charge of their classrooms.

A look into classrooms suggests that many teachers have rebelled against the old basal, cookbook approach to teaching. Many are selecting their own eclectic mix of reading materials and children's literature. The small books from the New Zealand–based Wright Group found their way into most classrooms for young children in the 1980s, and their popularity significantly influenced U.S. publishers. Now many publishers, such as Rigby, Richard C. Owen, and Creative Teaching Press, offer small fiction and nonfiction books for emergent and beginning readers. During the 1990s, most school districts quit purchasing the hugely expensive packaged reading programs from the major publishers and opted instead to allow teachers to purchase little instant readers and library books. However, in many districts and classrooms, the focus has become leveled books rather than the quality of the literature.

The move toward authentic literature for reading instruction drastically altered reading textbooks. Instead of offering basal readers, major publishers of reading programs began to offer literature anthologies, big books, little books, journals, and trade books. As a result of the widespread move to literature-based approaches, most materials are now advertised as being literature based. These claims are made with varying degrees of accuracy.

Recently, the publishing companies responded quickly to the back-to-basics swing of the pendulum, gladly offering expensive skills workbooks, work sheets, computer programs, charts, posters, videotapes, audiotapes, puppets, flash cards, and anything else schools will buy. Although they have not completely abandoned their literature focus or the use of leveled texts, many publishing companies now advertise the "direct, explicit, systematic and sequential phonics instruction" incorporated into their programs, such as Open Court Reading (McGraw-Hill; 2002). With the U.S. government (No Child Left Behind) and other policymakers demanding "evidence based reading instruction," publishers have begun to tout their materials' compliance with scientific research. The definition of scientific research and evidence-based reading instruction is highly controversial. However, that does not prevent publishers from making claims in order to sell textbooks.

Open Court Reading (McGraw-Hill, 2002) claims that it is the only reading program that provides an educational philosophy based on scientific research and forty years of practical experience. In April 2002, McGraw-Hill put out a press release extolling the "impressive improvement in reading performance," the "raised test scores," and the "marked jumps in . . . students' literacy skills" attributable to Open Court reading instruction (*http://www.mheducation.com*, 2002).

On closer analysis of the reading scores of the California schools named in the press release, it is apparent that the statistical analysis compared scores by teachers. Instead of comparing one group of children's scores from year to year, two different groups were compared. The problem is that there are many reasons

Many publishers offer small fiction and nonfiction books for emergent and beginning readers.

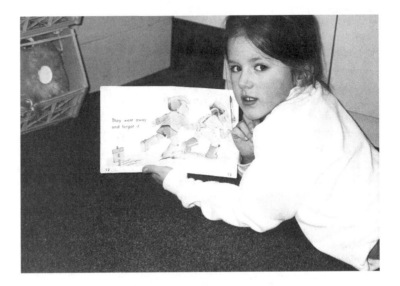

the third-grade scores might improve from one year to the next. A true comparison needs to compare a group's third-grade scores with their scores the following year, when they are in fourth grade. This sort of analysis would compare the same children from one year to the next. In fact, when the children were followed, none of the scores went up, and some of them went down (Moustafa, 2002). This is an excellent example of why we advocate careful analysis of any reading program being considered for use with young children.

Because the conflicting advertising claims are so confusing, we recommend a systematic analysis of reading programs. Start with what you believe to be the basic principles of sound reading instruction and build your program using those criteria. Just as consumers must be cautious about advertising of any product, we caution against just accepting *any* publisher's claims for *their* program. The material often doesn't live up to its stated aspirations, so you need to check for yourself. For your analysis, we recommend the reading-instruction principles explained in this text and have created a checklist to record your findings (see Table 9.1). This provides you with a tool to assist you in making your own informed decisions about materials. This checklist will outlast any specific recommendations we could make about particular materials. The position statement of the International Reading Association (2002) on evidence-based reading instruction concludes with a recommendation that teachers ask whether the materials and practices they are considering are a good match for their own students and educational contexts. Our checklist provides a useful tool for analysis.

Allow Construction of Knowledge

Following the organization of this book, we begin our analysis with criteria explained previously. When complex understandings are involved, are children allowed to construct their knowledge in personally meaningful ways? We recognize the existence

TABLE 9.1

Checklist for Analyzing Reading Programs

Does the reading program do the following?

- Allow construction of knowledge
- Encourage oral language
- Utilize high-quality literature
- Encourage purposeful writing
- Authentically integrate the curriculum
- Respect teachers

- Utilize play and experiences
- Incorporate story time
- Include nonfiction reading
- Teach skills in context
- Utilize performance-based assessment
- Respect all children

of social and conventional knowledge that can be told to children but make a distinction between that kind of information and the intricate web of relationships involved in logical-mathematical kinds of knowledge. As explained previously, the names of letters are social knowledge, but the relationship between letters and meaningful communication through print must be individually constructed.

Creating such relationships is a thoughtful, reflective process requiring unpressured time for thought and experimentation. Teachers' guides that prescribe a rapid-fire series of questions with specific right answers are antithetical to thoughtful reflection. Open-ended questions to provoke thought without expectations for specific or immediate answers are the kind of questions that encourage construction of knowledge. The "answers" may come months later and will be different for each learner. Most questions and discussion topics suggested in teachers' guides focus on immediate answers.

Instead of providing work sheets, developmentally appropriate programs for emergent readers offer materials that encourage writing messages and lists during pretend play.

The time needed for thought and experimentation is rarely built into any program. In fact, mainstream U.S. culture rarely allows for reflective processes and makes it difficult to justify taking time for those processes in school. Quick, superficial reactions with immediately observable products generally are valued over deeper thought involving sustained focus. Work sheets and teacher-centered lessons too often get in the way of real learning, and reading programs still suggest multitudes of nonreading and nonwriting busywork. Though the practice of having each child read aloud in turn (round-robin reading) is no longer recommended, teachers' guides still assume that youngsters are reading with a group under the teacher's supervision. This approach requires that everyone move along at the same pace and discourages personal thought processes. In contrast, reading a self-selected book alone or with a good friend offers opportunity for self-paced processing of the reading experience. Children are free to raise their own questions and discuss their own interpretations of text. Most programs acknowledge that this type of reading is useful but treat it more as something to do if there is time than as an essential learning activity.

Utilize Play and Experiences

In Chapter 2, we explained the role of play and experiences in emergent literacy. Play is routinely ignored in reading programs. One exception was the Scott Foresman *Celebrate Reading* (1997) kindergarten program authored by Sulzby and Morrow. It did explain the importance of play and showed how to arrange classroom learning centers to accommodate it. But the program schedule showed it happening only once a week and then only in extended-day kindergartens. However, play was cleverly incorporated into the program through materials that substitute for work sheets. These include a form for making out a shopping list while playing store, a form for taking pretend phone messages while playing house, and a secret-code message form for pretend superheroes. Some reading programs seem to misunderstand play and consider the dramatic-play center as a place for putting on plays. We thought that activity books might be related to play, but they mostly focus on paper-and-pencil or cut-and-paste "activities." Frequently, activity books are just fancy workbooks.

Experiences get a little more attention, especially as they relate to integrating the curriculum. Collecting and observing plants or bugs for science-related topics can enhance understanding of what is read, provide ideas for writing, and increase understanding of the objects being studied. This is an example of useful and authentic curriculum integration. On the other hand, making caterpillars out of neckties stuffed with old pantyhose (add eyes and antennae) isn't likely to increase any kind of understanding. Meaningful, in-depth connections are more important than broad, loosely conceived links. Teachers need to exercise professional judgment in choosing from the many ideas now offered for extending literature into theme units.

READING MATERIALS IN THE TERRARIUM

"These are reading materials tool" exclaims Mrs. Thomas as she shows off the large bumpy toad and the tiny frog hiding in her classroom terrarium. Observing these creatures has inspired her students to read books from her collection of books about toads and frogs. Youngsters are poring over books such as *The Complete Frog: A Guide for the Very Young Naturalist* (Lacey, 1989) and *Frog* (Chinery, 1991).

At group time, Mrs. Thomas shares the big book *Tadpole Diary* (Drew, 1992), about a classroom watching tadpoles change into frogs. This generates much discussion, including the question, "Do frogs breathe under water?" Mrs. Thomas says that she doesn't know but that she is sure the answer can be found in some of the books they have. As children disperse to independent reading, several plan to research that question. Sure enough! Pretty soon someone finds the answer and shares it with the class. They have discovered the value of reading for information.

While the class is busy with self-selected books. Mrs. Thomas sits on the floor with two boys who want to read the book *Frogs* (MacLulich, 1996b). The high-quality photographs help the boys gain meaning as they try to make sense of the print. Mrs. Thomas helps them follow the print by pointing to each word as she reads it. When she comes to the often-repeated word *frog*, she stops and encourages them to read it. She does the same with a few other words she thinks they can figure out, such as *swim*. With only two children, interactive reading comes naturally: "What's *marsh*?" asks Shane after Mrs. Thomas reads that word. This is a shared reading activity conducted spontaneously in response to children's interest. The interest started with the frog and toad in the terrarium.

Encourage Oral Language

We discussed the relationship of oral and written language development in Chapter 3 and emphasized that children need opportunities to talk. Heinemann's First Steps series includes an *Oral Language Resource Book* (1998) that is useful. Talking is encouraged in most reading programs through a multitude of discussions and story reenactments. Children are asked to orally predict events and also to retell the plots in stories they encounter. They also are requested to share their favorite parts and to comment on the illustrations. However, most programs' teachers' guides encourage child talk in structured and teacher-directed situations, forgetting about authentic peer exchange of viewpoints. Collaborative groups offer the potential for more informal discussions, but the teacher is usually directed to assign specific and limiting roles, such as recorder and reporter, to group members. Such structure has a place, but so does unstructured conversation.

Recommendations for interpretive oral reading can enhance oral language development. Certainly, preparing a reading selection to share with others is an improvement over round-robin reading. There are many other ways to use oral reading. In *Good-Bye Round Robin Reading* (1998), Michael Opitz and Timothy Rasinski outline twenty-five other oral-reading strategies. One alternative, interpretive oral reading, offers a reason for reading aloud and an opportunity to practice for a successful performance. Songs, poems, and rhyming games suggested as extensions of reading also assist general language development. There are useful options to select from, but teachers may need to adapt suggestions so that children are free to direct their own involvement in the activities. Most teachers' guides still assume a teacher-centered rather than a child-centered classroom.

Incorporate Story Time

The importance of story time apparently is recognized widely. Most programs recommend books for teachers to read to children and usually sell them either separately or in read-aloud anthologies as part of the program. This saves teachers making trips to the library. Although it is convenient for teachers not to have to search for books on their own, we worry that many wonderful books are overlooked when teachers have no reason to go to the library. Also, we dislike read-aloud anthologies for the same reason we dislike anthologies of stories for children to read themselves: They dictate a selection of stories and sequence of reading unrelated to reader interest.

Some programs acknowledge the link between emergent reading and story time. Their teachers' guides suggest introducing a reading selection to children by having the teacher read it to them first. Often the teacher reads a big book version of a story with youngsters and makes little book versions available for emergent reading subsequently. As youngsters ponder the print in these books and relate it to the story their teacher read, they construct their understandings of written language. Too often this is not the regular routine. Most series do not include big book versions of all their literature.

Utilize High-Quality Literature

The big change in reading materials for youngsters today is that there are a lot of good books for them to read. Because schools have been buying more children's books, more have been written. Of course, textbook publishers are concerned about their share of the market. Most publishing companies now offer anthologies of respected children's literature instead of the "made-for-reading-group" material you probably had to read as a child.

When anthology selections are faithful to the original, they are a big improvement over old basal-reader stories. The latest editions advertise that their literature selections are no longer adapted, but you need to compare with the originals to be sure. Until recently, the old monster "controlled vocabulary" reared its ugly head in reader anthologies, "adapting" good literature into predigested, tasteless, boring pap. The problem was worst in books for the youngest readers; when editors assume that children know nothing about reading, they give them reading that is nothing. Rather than change the words, newer adaptations tend to cut out illustrations. This approach may lower publishers' costs, but it sacrifices meaning. The illustrations provide much of the meaning for early readers, so much is lost in the editions in which illustrations are omitted.

Illustrations are part of the predictability that emergent readers rely on to decipher books. For the most part, new reading materials recognize that predictable stories are required for beginners. The publishers now accept that controlled vocabulary actually makes reading more difficult because it creates unnatural language. Thus, most new beginning-reading materials are filled with lively pattern stories and old-favorite tales and rhymes, giving youngsters the various kinds of predictability we described in Chapter 4.

Predictability is the basis for the instant readers now common in kindergarten and first-grade classrooms. These little books rely heavily on picture clues to help youngsters figure out the words; some consist primarily of captions for the pictures. A combination of a repeated word pattern and picture clues allows a beginning reader to experience instant success. As we said previously, predictable books from the Wright Group have been helping young readers get started since the early 1980s, and textbook companies now offer similar kinds of books. We are not suggesting that these are great literature, but they clearly offer children a great sense of achievement. With creative use of illustration, some of them manage to convey a meaningful story or significant information despite limited text. Like other kinds of books, they vary in quality. With some practice, many teachers become adept at leveling texts on their own. This way, they can use "real" literature as leveled books. Rog and Burton (2001–2002) describe one system developed to support emergent literacy. Daily exposure to high-quality literature and models of rich language can also occur daily via read-aloud or shared reading.

It is much easier to find high-quality literature for experienced readers because they are able to read "real" books. Reading anthologies for older children offer wider choices, and publishers now are attempting to be true to the original books. The importance of the way the text is arranged on the page and how the illustrations interface with the text appears to be better recognized. We also like how some anthologies feature certain authors; they not only highlight other stories by the same author but also give information about the person and the process of creating the story. When youngsters realize that the authors they read are real people like themselves, they are more likely to see themselves as writers.

Having said that the contents of most literature anthologies are generally good, we need to repeat our concerns about anthologies themselves. The anthology approach is not compatible with a view of each child as a unique person with individual interests and motivations. We acknowledge the usefulness of having several copies of a story to encourage interaction and cooperation among those who are interested in reading the same thing at the same time, but we believe that five or six

Predictability of text and picture clues allow beginning readers to experience instant success.

copies of the original book suffice. Some reading programs do offer books with this packaging, and we prefer the flexibility of separate books over anthologies.

Another concern about anthologies is the small number of stories in them and the amount of time spent on those few stories. Readers need quantity as well as quality—quantities of books to choose from and quantities of time to read. If teachers view the anthology selections as the bulk of what children need to read, there won't be much reading happening. In the McGraw-Hill (2000) literature anthology, every story in the student volumes is followed by a page each of questions, story activities, study skills, and test power. The teacher's edition has an additional page for "selection assessment."

Often, the teachers' guides that accompany the literature anthologies further diminish the focus on actual reading. The guides are crammed with pages and pages of questions, skills lessons, related information, writing assignments, and extension activities. We counted the number of pages of such suggestions for one story and discovered that there were thirty pages of extensions and skills lessons plus a video—the story "Who Hid It?" (Gomi, 1996) is ten sentences long! Do you see why we are worried about reading getting shortchanged? When you hear people talk about "basalizing the literature," such overkill on nonreading activity is the sort of thing they are referring to.

The teachers' guides say that the anthologies are intended as just the start of reading and not the total program (McGraw-Hill, 2000; Scott, Foresman, 2000). A small number of trade books are sold with most programs to supplement the anthologies, and some teachers' guides include coverage of those additional books too, which again results in more teaching and less reading. Children need not only high-quality literature but also high-quality time to spend with it. The publishers' vision of reading time still seems to be a group of children reading assigned selections together in front of a teacher rather than individual children spending relaxed time alone with a book. With this vision, trade books are not only "taught" rather than read but also apparently assigned rather than selected by the reader. Clearly, teachers using such programs need to exercise professional judgment rather than merely follow directions.

Include Nonfiction Reading

Of course, literature is only one type of reading material. It is important for children to learn to read for pleasure *and* for information. Reading for information involves reading in content areas, such as science, social studies, and math. Most publishers market some nonfiction selections. For instance, Wright Group and Rigby are among the publishers offering wonderful examples of nonfiction texts. They all offer nonfiction in addition to the fiction selections in their series of leveled texts. These publishers allow you to design your own customized text sets. This enables teachers to create a library of leveled texts. Sundance Publishing has a new series that includes Nonfiction Science Explorers. Each uses wonderful photographs to present facts. This use of incredibly beautiful detailed photographs in an individual small book format typifies our favorites.

The photos greatly extend the information in the limited text for beginning readers. A favorite of many young children is *Bats* (MacLulich, 1996a), which offers close-up photos of several kinds of bats. *Bats* is published by Scholastic, which also offers sets of such books for emergent readers as part of a science resource center. Some publishers offer these texts in big book format so that they can be used for shared reading.

Reading for information is not limited only to books but extends to many other sources as well, including newspapers, magazines, and pamphlets as well as

Reading for information involves reading in the content areas, such as science, social studies, and math.

the Internet. Familiarity with all these sources is part of becoming literate. Though many reading programs include factual sources along with fiction in the lists of books on topics related to anthology stories, magazines, newspapers, pamphlets, and other materials not sold by the publisher seem to be ignored. It is up to the teacher to include a full selection of reading materials.

Encourage Authentic and Purposeful Writing

As explained in Chapters 5 and 6, current views of literacy emphasize the interrelatedness of reading and writing, which makes it imperative that children write in conjunction with reading. Publishers of reading programs are very aware of this mandate. Teachers' manuals include information about the importance of writing and about emergent-writing processes. Programs that have authors and consultants who are emergent-writing experts, such as Elizabeth Sulzby or William Teale, present the most current and accurate explanations.

Students' journals for children's writing generally are part of the reading-program package, and most of the newest activity books also encourage narrative writing. Notice that we make a distinction between "narrative writing" and filling in the blanks. Some materials confuse these two and offer youngsters only a chance to copy a word onto a blank line in a sentence. Most programs offer materials for both real writing and for skills drills masquerading as writing. It is up to the teachers and the schools to choose what to purchase.

We realize that publishers cater to the market, but we were shocked at the mislabeling of a skills book put out by McGraw-Hill. This *Writers Workshop* (1993) book represents the worst of the old workbooks: It consists of drills for copying letters, penmanship practice, spelling drills, and unscrambling sentences—all separate from actual writing. We can't imagine why it is called *Writers Workshop* because it violates every principle of an actual writers' workshop. A much better investment would be *Writing Workshop: The Essential Guide* (2001), a practical guide to the workshop approach for writing instruction.

Other programs are not much different. A check of "writing workshop" pages from Silver Burdett Ginn (1997) shows, among other things, an illustration for children to write about. That doesn't sound too bad? Well, the writing is to be one sentence on each of the four lines provided, and three kinds of sentences are to be included: telling, asking, and exclaiming. There's not much room for individual expression, is there?

The best of the journals offer plenty of blank pages with creative ideas for writing topics (see Figure 9.3). The worst consist mainly of directions for copying the right word onto the correct blank. In the middle are those that seem to offer children freedom to write—as long as they incorporate a given list of vocabulary or spelling words in their stories. Even the best journals are a poor substitute for blank paper, yet they cost considerably more. Besides the cost, the problem with the better journals is that the blank pages are not *entirely* blank: they have a title to indicate what the child is to write about, and they are usually framed or decorated to make an important-looking finished product. These may sound like nice touches until you think about some principles for writing.

One principle is related to personal interest. Being given the title plus the teacher's directions ignores the child's own interests as a topic. What if Felena doesn't want to write about that topic and has another idea? Another principle has to do with the multiple drafts involved in the writing process. What if Felena makes a mistake as she writes or changes her mind about how to write something? Then the beautifully framed page is ruined, and Felena feels like a failure. A polished writing product fit for such a fancy page always requires more than one draft, yet the teacher's manual simply says to assign that page, with no mention of rough drafts. Thus, the writing process is circumvented, and children lose the opportunity to learn spelling and punctuation rules in a meaningful context. Though blank paper is preferable, no one pays much for it. Publishers sell what they can make money from—whether it is what young writers need or not. Thus, we get a product that on the surface seems responsive to current research yet misses the essence.

Name molgen

Write about your deep-sea dive.

i C s t r Fc h.
i CAWA L.
i c Pe PL.

FIGURE 9.3

The best of the commercial journals offer plenty of empty pages with ideas for writing topics. Morgan wrote, "I see a starfish. I see a whale. I see people."

Source: From Celebrate Reading! Kindergarten, Activity/Home-School Connection Sheets. Copyright © 1993 Scott Foresman and Company. Reprinted by permission.

Not only is the writing process frequently misinterpreted in reading materials, but understanding and respect for emergent writing are varied. The Houghton Mifflin kindergarten journal gives a clear message that kindergartners can't write. This journal invites youngsters to draw pictures or copy letters; sometimes they can fill in one word. In contrast, the Scott, Foresman kindergarten journal encourages actual writing and guides teachers to remind children that they can write "the kindergarten way."

Obviously, teachers need to be knowledgeable about how children learn to read and write in order to select the best from the huge array of both good and bad materials. For instance, a Literacy Activity Book (Houghton Mifflin, 1999) accompanying a first-grade anthology includes several pages titled "Reading-Writing

Though scratch paper best provides for pressure-free exploration of print and multiple drafts needed for writing development, publishing companies want to sell fancy writing booklets.

Workshop," but few actually encourage writing. Some of these pages require children to copy words printed on the page, and some are for spelling practice. Only about 5 percent of the 220-page workbook invites children to write their own ideas, and these opportunities usually prescribe the topic and its organization. Nevertheless, we are impressed with a three-page section called "The Writing Process" and wish that more of this type of material were included. Instead of offering a framed page for a finished product, this section guides children through five steps for writing: prewriting, drafting, revising, proofreading, and publishing. Another useful page in this workbook helps children think about the beginning, middle, and end of a story as they write.

Remember, publishing companies exist solely to make a profit; therefore, educators must exercise professional judgment in how best to spend education dollars. In addition, individual preferences of the children need to be considered; teachers can share writing ideas with youngsters and allow them to decide which sound interesting. There are many fine ideas offered, but they become undesirable if forced on unwilling writers.

Teach Skills in Context

Virtually all the reading programs offer materials that explain why skills should not be taught out of context, and yet virtually all offer materials for doing so. Those respected reading experts hired by the major publishers write valuable descriptions of how to teach necessary skills as part of the reading and writing process and give admirable justifications for abandoning isolated skills drills; however, materials for skills drills are still part of the program and available to those who want them. Publishers' sales representatives apologize for the discrepancies and explain that many teachers won't buy a program unless it has all the familiar workbooks for phonics, handwriting, punctuation, and spelling.

Although programs continue to provide separate skills materials, most teachers' guides do also attempt to help teachers demonstrate reading strategies as part of actual reading. The focus is more on meaning and fluency than on "barking at print." There are frequent directions for helping youngsters use multiple clues when faced with an unknown word. Sometimes the strategy lessons are done effectively, but often they interrupt the story too much. When practice books offer pages and pages of work on various skills following a story and literature anthologies have multiple pages of skills for each piece, it seems that the purpose for learning skills has been lost, as the skills work overwhelms the actual reading. We're not against teaching skills, but isn't this a bit much?

Because such systems are set up for group instruction, it is inevitable that this instruction will not be a good match for the needs of all—and perhaps not for the needs of any. Still, isolated skills practice is commonly offered by reading-program publishers. Workbooks and work sheets typically ask children to copy words and letters into the correct blanks according to specific graphophonemic patterns or else direct them merely to circle the word or letter indicated. In case the workbook pages aren't enough, publishers add packets of black-line masters to be photocopied and given to students for intensive phonics drill. There are colorful charts and "letter cards" (flash cards) for additional phonics drills. These all look like the same materials that have turned off students' brains for decades. Yet this is comfortingly familiar material to many. As a result, teachers who have learned more effective methods of teaching reading and writing skills often find themselves on the defensive. Parents as well as teachers who don't understand the new approaches criticize the lack of separate, visible drill sheets. Many parents hear the advertisements for the Hooked on Phonics program (Parker, 1993) and think they need to spend their own money to ensure that their children get this background. Because the idea of learning reading and writing skills while reading and writing is new to most parents, schools or individual teachers find that explanatory presentations at parents' night meetings are helpful. For example, a demonstration of interactive writing can illustrate how phonics can be addressed in a meaningful, authentic way. Once they understand and observe the new approaches, parents generally become strong advocates and begin to demand that their children continue with the more balanced literature-based approaches. This puts pressure on principals, who then put pressure on teachers to get new training. Obviously, some teachers are not pleased about this; fortunately, others are excited about ways to reach more children.

Teachers and textbook publishers clearly are in transition. Publishing companies are trying to cater to both those demanding literature-based materials with skills in context and those wanting the isolated skills drills. In almost every school you will find teachers on both sides of the controversy. Many teachers gradually are making changes in their classrooms as they work out their own transitions; others are leaders in helping colleagues understand and implement emergent-literacy instruction that keeps the focus on meaning while teaching skills. Some teachers are eager to try new ideas, and others are resisting them with all their might. How does a reading program fit all these different teachers?

Utilize Performance-Based Assessment

Next, we look at how assessment is treated in reading programs. We see that publishers of reading materials know the latest research and recommendations. Most offer excellent explanations of performance-based assessment but offer materials for both the old and the new assessment approaches. Typically, publishers refer to these as "formal" and "informal" assessment. When these are in separate packages, the knowledgeable educator easily can choose to purchase only the desirable materials. When a contradictory mix of approaches is combined into one assessment document, it is difficult for *any* teacher to sift through for the preferred materials.

This dual approach is reflected in most current reading programs. Scott Foresman Reading (2000) provides extensive guidance in creating portfolios to document children's progress and offers forms to record observational data. However, the company also offers several sets of "formal" assessment materials, focusing mainly on phonemic awareness, phonics, and other skills. Houghton Mifflin (1999) encourages teachers to use a wide variety of its assessment

Once they understand and observe new teaching approaches, parents generally become strong advocates and begin to demand that their children continue to have holistic language teaching.

materials and guidelines. These range from multiple-choice tests to notes in the teacher's manual that tell teachers when there are opportunities for assessing children's work during instruction (clearly assuming that teachers don't know). Whatever type of assessment you want to do, the publishers will sell you materials for doing it.

Scott Foresman's distinguished group of reading experts provide a wonderful overview of assessment in the Assessment Handbook in *Reading* (Scott, Foresman, 2000). Robert Tierney says, "I think it's very important not to separate assessment from teaching and learning, and that's where assessment goes beyond feedback." Richard Allington offers this view of performance-based assessment: "Authentic assessment simply involves new ways of looking at children as they proceed through the day, doing the kinds of things that children typically do." But then look inside the program, and you will find typical multiple-choice assessment items on familiar-looking work sheets.

However, this same assessment handbook also provides a useful overview of holistic scoring of children's writing, and the kindergarten materials show the Sulzby categories for emergent reading and writing checklists that we referred to in Chapter 8. In addition, Scott Foresman's material shows teachers how to take running records, to record miscues, and to administer an Informal Reading Inventory. Program materials also explain the value of children's self-assessment, anecdotal records, observation, and portfolios. They even provide forms to facilitate all this.

Obviously, there is much valuable assistance for performance-based assessment in the new reading-program materials. Teachers have to be very careful in selecting what they use, however.

Integrate Curriculum

Efforts to integrate the curriculum are very evident in the new reading materials we have seen. It is typical for teachers' guides to list extension activities for each area of the curriculum for each story. The result is some very artificial integration when every story has to lead to science, math, health and safety, social studies, art, and music activities.

You will see an amazing number of suggested art or craft activities accompanying each story. Children constantly are asked to draw their favorite character or a picture of a similar event in their own lives. We see value in this when the drawing assignment is self-selected or accompanied by an opportunity to write; drawing tends to help youngsters think about what they want to write and serves a planning, or prewrite, function. However, most young children can't draw realistic or recognizable figures and may be intimidated by workbook pages with framed spaces awaiting drawings on specified topics.

The crafts activities are endless and often incredibly silly and worthless. As with the caterpillars made of old ties and pantyhose, teachers must ask, "What are children *learning* from this activity?" Too often, we found that these craft ideas perpetuated the school tradition of substituting paper activities for the real ones. Do youngsters really learn science from making construction-paper replicas of things they read about? Another problem with the recommended craft ideas is that they aren't the children's ideas. If youngsters have free access to a variety of craft materials and freedom to create in response to their experiences with literature or with real bugs, babies, bunnies, and so on, the children themselves will invent personally meaningful craft activities.

Songs and poems frequently accompany reading selections. These often are used for repeated shared readings and help youngsters extend their sight-word vocabulary as they memorize the verses. Creating new versions of songs and poems also is suggested often and generally is described as a group activity, although it could be done by children individually or in pairs. Such approaches to authorship can help children learn about writing. Recommendations for writing new versions of pattern stories or new endings for other stories can serve the same purpose for developing writers. But, once again, the value can be destroyed for the child who isn't interested in that particular activity. To ensure that children will benefit from activities, teachers need to make suggestions rather than assignments. Giving children options and letting them choose their own approaches will provide the personal meaning and involvement essential to learning.

We also mentioned token forays into content areas. Too often, a vaguely related item of information or activity will be added in and called curriculum integration. Counting plastic teddy bears after reading a book about bears is not integrating math and literature; it is tokenism. Making a graph of who likes what kind of bear (or ice cream and so on) does not integrate curriculum either—we consider these examples of correlated curriculum. We make a distinction between correlated curriculum and authentically integrated curriculum. Authentic integration demands that children use the activities to add to their understanding of a topic. For instance, figuring out how high a bear can reach in order to plan safe food storage while camping would

Authentic curriculum integration involves literacy with various content areas as children add to their understanding of a topic.

provide math measurement problem-solving practice and also enhance understanding of bears. This understanding would help children bring more meaning to future reading about bears. Planting seeds and recording their growth may extend children's understanding of such stories as *Pumpkin Pumpkin* (Titherington, 1986). Houghton Mifflin's *Invitations to Literacy* (1999) suggests many such actual science investigations instead of construction-paper science projects.

Project approaches to curriculum planning assist authentic integration by focusing on what children want to learn about a topic (Katz & Chard, 1989). Various content areas are included in the process of gathering relevant information for the project. This is a natural integration and quite different from artificially adding activities from different content areas for the purpose of integration. The Scott Foresman kindergarten units suggest authentic integration across the curriculum as well. For instance, the Creeping Crawling Creatures unit suggests that children keep track of the insects they see each day by recording their observations on the class insect graph (see Figure 9.4); later, they will discuss which insects were seen

Name _____

Insect Graph

Make a • when you see an insect.

	Mon.	Tues.	Wed.	Thurs.	Fri.	Total
ant						
bee						
mosquito						
butterfly						
fly						

FIGURE 9.4

This insect graph shows that a work sheet can be part of a relevant and thoughtful learning experience rather than a meaningless task, which is all too common with work sheets.

Source: From Celebrate Reading! Kindergarten, Activity/Home-School Connection Sheets. Copyright © 1993 Scott Foresman and Company. Reprinted by permission.

most and least frequently. Other suggestions include observing an ant colony and a spider spinning a web, with follow-up discussions and activities. Many excellent fiction and nonfiction books are recommended as part of the unit. Unfortunately, the Scott, Foresman kindergarten units are not typical examples of approaches to curriculum integration.

Respect All Children

When we ask whether teaching materials respect all children, we are looking at respect for various kinds of differences. For instance, are children who learn more slowly still treated as people who are capable of learning and who want to learn? Additionally, are children from all cultures and with language backgrounds other than English fully included in the learning process?

Children who experience reading difficulty traditionally have been deprived of important reading experiences. Those who most need exposure to high-quality books and who most need to experience joy in reading are the least likely to get either in a traditional reading program. Often, children who have trouble reading are given more work in the resource booklets and fewer chances to read. The very students who should be reading one good story after another are doing one work sheet after another instead. Those who are doing well in reading are allowed to enjoy the additional literature selections. The *Report Card on Basal Readers* (Goodman, Shannon, Freeman, & Murphy, 1988) calls this phenomenon "The poor get poorer" (p. 93).

Newer reading materials make some progress in changing this picture. The Scholastic teachers' guide skills pages feature boxed tips for assisting second-language learners and tips on providing extra help for those who need it. Many

Children who experience reading difficulty are the ones who most need exposure to high-quality books and who most need to experience joy in reading; however, they are the ones least likely to get either in a traditional reading program.

publishers offer tips on modifying instruction so that everyone can experience the same literature at the same time. This demonstrates some movement in allowing all children access to good literature but makes the unfounded assumption that everyone would want to read the same thing at the same time. Further, the recommendations seem based on an ability-group model, though a model in which all groups read the same thing in different ways. Close examination suggests that the group that requires more help seems to spend more time talking about reading and less time actually reading than the others. It looks as though they are likely to be cut off from higher-level thinking too. The questions for children reading below grade level tend to involve literal recall of the story; in contrast, the questions for those reading above grade level encourage critical thinking. Teachers are told that some children might not be ready to benefit from a discussion of previewing and predicting before reading.

One crucial difference between traditional reading programs and child-centered approaches is ability grouping. In a child-centered program, children choose their own reading partners or become part of a group based on common interest in a topic or a book. Shared reading is done in heterogeneous groups so that hesitant readers can benefit from the models of their more confident peers. When you do away with ability groups, you help poor readers learn more quickly and keep them from being labeled "dumb." This is acknowledged in what publishing companies say in the reading materials but is not carried through to their teaching recommendations.

Sometimes politically correct terms are used to describe the same old approaches. Silver Burdett Ginn (1997) uses the label "flexible grouping" when describing adaptations for different levels of readers, yet the approaches the company suggests clearly do not lend themselves to flexibility. There are no suggestions for grouping in ways other than by the generic idea of ability. The multitude of different reasons for lesser ability is not addressed except for some variations aimed at children learning English as a second language.

Apart from the fact that many children who end up in the "low" reading group are those from cultures and languages that differ from those of the school, new reading materials do attempt to address multicultural and bilingual issues. All present stories about children of various colors and from many different lands. Most publishers offer tips with each story to assist ESL (English as a second language) students. They provide practice in context and language models for children who have trouble pronouncing certain sounds. They also utilize tape recordings of stories and songs that allow youngsters to hear unlimited repetitions in Standard English. Children who are working at learning English do seem to gravitate to tapes of familiar songs and stories.

Respecting children includes giving them some decision-making opportunities. We see children thrive as learners when they are allowed personal responsibility for their learning. This responsibility includes having a say in what they read and what they want to achieve. It also includes self-evaluation of their progress. Most reading materials we looked at included some opportunity for student involvement in the assessment progress but little chance to set personal goals and not enough choices in general. The Wright Group materials, in contrast, recommend that students decide

CHAPTER 9

what they want to achieve, under the guidance of the teacher. The Wright Group approach emphasizes the importance of giving children as much responsibility for planning and running their learning projects as possible.

Respect Teachers

The Wright Group approach not only appears to respect children as learners but also respects teachers' ability to teach. The Wright Group teachers' guides give one detailed example of conducting an effective shared reading session and then assume teachers can figure out how to conduct similar sessions with other stories. Rather than several dozen pages of directions to guide the teacher through each story, the Wright Group offers only two pages of related-activity extension ideas per story. This is consistent with our previous observations about materials originating in New Zealand and Australia.

Children thrive as learners when they are allowed personal responsibility for their learning, including self-evaluation of their progress.

It is clear that textbooks are changing, but they themselves are antithetical to the constructivist vision of teaching and learning. Effective learning is a "result of the learner's own activity" (Ferreiro & Teberosky, 1982, p. 15), and effective teaching "responds to what the child is trying to do" (F. Smith, 1976, p. 298). This means that children must be free to direct their own learning and that teachers must be free to respond to children's efforts. This cannot happen when textbook companies dictate what children are to read and to think. It cannot happen as long as teachers are reduced to "scripted technicians" in following the teachers' manuals (K. Goodman et al., 1988).

Teachers' freedom to exercise their professional judgment is also threatened by those who would legislate teaching practices. James V. Hoffman, International Reading Association board member, expressed this concern: "Teachers are no longer being asked to make instructional decisions. They are being asked to implement a program, transmit a curriculum, and train students. Responsibility for decision making has been lifted from the teacher to a level lodged somewhere in an expanding educational bureaucracy that is unresponsive to the reality of the individual teacher and individual learner" (International Reading Association, 1998, p. 6).

The good news is that some teachers are taking control. They are picking and choosing among their options and creating rich, meaningful learning environments for their students. They are using pieces from various reading programs, selecting from literature programs, and trying ideas from resource books. As a result, not only are children enjoying learning more, but the teachers are enjoying teaching more.

INCORPORATING TECHNOLOGY

Today's teachers grew up with television. Today's children are growing up with computers as well. An estimated one-third of all U.S. homes now have computers, and they are used by children as well as adults. Children whose families can afford computers now are playing computer games, using educational software, and surfing the Internet at home as well as at school. It may not be long before a home without a computer will be as rare as a home without a television. There are no longer questions about whether to use computers with children; what is most important is how computers are used with children (Haugland, 2000). These learning materials also must be evaluated and used with care.

Using CD-ROMs, the new multimedia platforms integrate computer technology with audio input, videotapes, and graphics. Technology creates ever increasing media possibilities. Many reading programs offer a computer package, and many computer companies offer reading programs. Hardware, software, and Internet sites are rapidly being developed to appeal to young children, their parents, and their teachers. These are all being included in the latest editions of every reading program. The education market is obviously attractive to the technology industry.

Computer Software

Hundreds of new software titles are added to the market each year (McNair, Kirova-Petrova, & Bhargava, 2001). Teachers and parents are bombarded with advertisements for increasingly sophisticated types of computer software and hardware that manufacturers guarantee will enhance children's learning. The dilemma for decisions about educational technology is the same as for any other kind of instructional materials. Teachers need well-defined theories about appropriate instruction and must evaluate materials using criteria on the basis of those theories. We find that the same criteria we use for selecting written materials can be used to evaluate media materials. Therefore, we recommend adapting the checklist we used for critiquing reading programs and applying it to selecting computer software for the language arts. There are other useful sources of evaluation criteria: The position statement on technology and young children from the National Association for the Education of Young Children (1996b) implies criteria based on developmentally appropriate practice; the Haugland/Shade scale (Haugland & Wright, 1997) is based on Piagetian theory and developmentally appropriate practice, as is the Developmental Software Scale (Haugland, 1999 Available on-line at *http://www.children* and *http://www.computers.com*); and the *High/ Scope Buyer's Guide to Children's Software* (Hohmann, Carmody, & McCabe-Branz, 1995) is based on the view of children as active learners who should be in control of the computer environment.

After reviewing 750 programs being marketed for young children, Haugland and Wright (1997) concluded that most such software is not developmentally appropriate. Of course, the advertisements say they are all wonderful. As with other kinds of instructional materials, you cannot merely rely on publishers' descriptions—you must examine software programs yourself. Practical experience has been identified as a critical component of teacher training in technology use (Haugland, 2000). Leu and Kinzer (2003) have developed a list of twenty-two questions for evaluating reading and writing instructional software. Ms. Montoya complains that the advertisements always sound so wonderful, but some programs wind up being terrible when she actually tries them. She finds that even award-winning programs aren't necessarily winners on her terms; the awards may have been for the program's technological merit and have nothing to do with its educational value. Once again, it boils down to the criteria used to make judgments.

If you want children to construct their own understanding of reading and writing, you will not select programs that just replicate workbook formats. Too many instructional computer "games" are merely animated work sheets. Notice that the "interactive" aspects advertised for most programs often are limited to the child's giving an answer and the machine's indicating if it is the correct one. If you are committed to teaching skills in actual reading and writing contexts, you will not select programs that focus on isolated skills drills. If you want children to engage in purposeful writing, you will not select programs that dictate writing topics or merely allow them to fill in the blanks.

Computer software has been steadily improving, and it is possible to find a few excellent programs that support and extend children's explorations of reading and writing. *Wiggleworks* by Scholastic New Media reads stories to children, allows word processing, and says aloud whatever the child writes (a talking word processor); it also offers a simple drawing program. The talking word processor even "reads" phonics-based spelling, encouraging children to write even though they may not yet be conventional spellers. This program allows children to be in control instead of merely responding.

Storybook Weaver DELUXE (MECC) also offers children control. It is an example of a writing tool that enhances word processing with options to include graphics, music, and other sound effects. If hardware allows, children can even use color in the illustrations they create for their writing. There are many good word processing and drawing programs, including *Kid Works Deluxe* (Davidson & Associates), *Make-A-Book* (Teacher Support Software), and *Once Upon a Time—Journey Through Nature* (Compu-Teach). Any word processing program, with or without fancy frills, is an asset for writing. Word processing encourages risk taking with writing because it is easy to fix mistakes; word processing also takes the pain out of revising, editing, and polishing a finished product. In addition, finding a letter on a keyboard is easier for some beginning writers than forming a letter correctly with a pencil. There is a program that is especially useful for the prewriting, brainstorming portion of the writer's workshop.

Kidspiration (Inspiration Software) is a visual learning tool designed for children from preschool age up. Using two complementary views, Picture and Writing, children can create webs, maps, and other visual diagrams and then connect and expand those visual representations with words. An audio feature enables children to hear the words they write or record their own words.

Kid Pix Deluxe 3 (Broderbund), designed for children as young as preschool age, allows them to draw in color with a variety of "brushes," as in the

CHAPTER 9

Macintosh paint program. It also offers a variety of pictures as choices to zap onto the screen for telling or illustrating a story. Using the alphabet letter option, children can even label or name their creations. Six-year-old Patrick demonstrated the program capabilities by combining several functions into one project. He selected pictures of palm trees and an airplane, put them on the screen, and began his oral narrative about a trip to Hawaii. Then he "painted" in a big mountain, which he said was an active volcano. Patrick illustrated the volcanic eruption with a paintbrush stroke that resembled clouds of smoke and soon covered the whole screen. An action narrative such as this can provide an effective prewrite experience and enhance language development (see Figure 9.5).

The Living Books series (Broderbund) is an example of how multimedia technology attempts to enhance storybook reading by adding animation, voices, music, and sound effects. These "talking book" (McKenna, Young, & Gatliff, 2001) programs are built around children's literature and use the original illustrations, making them much more worth reading than some computer story-reading offerings. In addition, though the introduction and menus are always in English, they offer Spanish and some Japanese versions of the stories to assist second-language learners. However, the Haugland/Slade rating scale indicates that the interactive nature of the software is too limited and doesn't make good use of the computer's capabilities (Haugland & Wright, 1997). Mrs. Hanna notices that children end up spending more time with point-and-click activities than

FIGURE 9.5

Since the volcanic eruption obliterated his Hawaii trip illustration, Patrick made this picture about dinosaurs to show what he can do with the *Kid Pix* program.

with reading. She tends to agree with the idea that "bringing the book to life on CD-ROM most often means killing the text" (Kraft, 1998, p. 337) by making the sound and animation more important than the reading.

Teachers and parents must beware of software that electronically extends poor educational practices. They "must look beyond the compelling graphics, intriguing sound, and technical wizardry to the core-values and beliefs about writing and about children that are housed in the software environment" (Sharp, 1993, p. 7). What teachers know about teaching and learning must determine the role of computers in the classroom. Computers themselves are neither good nor bad; they either add to or detract from the educational experience, depending on how they are used.

The Internet

The Internet is redefining literacy (International Reading Association, 2002; Leu & Kinzer, 2000). Being literate in the twenty-first century means navigating through many information sources and discriminating between sources of information. The Internet provides students and teachers with improved access to people and information (International Society for Technology in Education Standards Projects, 2002). The Internet provides many learning opportunities that include information gathering, research, virtual field trips; global communication; publishing; and interactive sites (Gerzog & Haugland, 1999). Whether we like it or not, computers cannot be ignored. Computer use fits with established views of information literacy: Gaining information through the Internet constitutes a purposeful reason to read, communicating via electronic mail or on-line discussion groups constitutes a purposeful reason to write. However, the dynamic interactive nature of on-line communication offers a dimension to writing that is different from using a word processing program. It also offers a dimension to reading that is different from static material on a page. Such interaction offers exciting motivation for reading and writing.

The interactive aspect also facilitates peer exchange of viewpoints, which we earlier described as essential for construction of knowledge. As students share their interpretations of information and events and compare their interpretations with those of others, they create meaning on a much higher level than without such interaction. Electronic communication can enhance face-to-face peer dialogue and extend dialogue far beyond the classroom, thus assisting teachers' efforts to stimulate critical thinking in a learner-centered environment.

If the goal is to stimulate children's thought rather than memorization of teacher-given information, seeking information via the Internet can be a big help. Search engines are designed to find information on the Internet. Ask Jeeves for Kids (*http://www.ajkids.com*) and Yahooligans (*http://www.yahooligans.com*) are specifically designed to find information for children. Whereas youngsters are unlikely to question the accuracy of the teacher's input, they can be taught to seek out diverse opinions and to question everything they see on the Internet. This will be excellent practice for the real world of advertising as well as for academic thought.

As literacy educators, preparing children for their future is our central role (Leu, 2002). According to some researchers (Leu, 2002; Leu & Kinzer, 1999), it is difficult for individuals to be experts in all the new technologies for reading and writing. For this reason, it is important to know how to acquire and use information from others. The Internet is a useful tool for professional development. Joining a mailing list or listserv allows you to get responses from a large number of people. There are also many Web sites devoted to education. The best way to become familiar and comfortable with them is to explore them. A useful starting point is The Literacy Web (*http://www.literacy.uconn.edu*). In Don Leu's words, "The Literacy Web is an extensive collection of the very best resources on the Internet to support teachers with limited time." For assistance in selecting Web sites, try The Haugland/Gerzog Developmental Scale for Web Sites (Gerzog & Haugland, 1999). The authors also have a Web site where they feature monthly selections (*http://www.childrenand computers.com*: click on Web Site Evaluations) (Gerzog & Haugland, 1999). Some sites they recommend are dedicated to publishing the works of children. They are Education by Design (*http://www.edbydesign.com/kidsact.html*), Kids Space (*http://www.kids-space.org*), Kidpub (*http://www.kidpub.org/kidpub*), and Poetry Pals (*http://www.geocities.com/EnchantedForest/5165/index1.html*) (Gerzog & Haugland, 1999; Haugland, Bailey, & Ruiz, 2002).

Television

Like computers, television is good or bad, depending on how it is used. Poor choices of programs, too much television, or too many videos appear harmful (Healy, 1990); however, television has much to offer if used wisely. Of course, there are many valuable informational programs and videos and some high-quality movies. For instance, *Reading Rainbow* is a television program that actually seems to promote reading; it features a variety of quality books for children and models interactive reading processes (Wood & Duke, 1997). There are two key Web sites associated with this popular series. Both offer descriptions and suggested activities (*http://www.canlearn.com/READING/rr-alt.html* and *http://www.gpn.unl.edu/rainbow*).

Even poor television programming can be put to advantage. For instance, children can participate in discussions that evaluate violence in cartoons or honesty in advertising. They can become more thoughtful consumers and critics of media and more skillful writers as they create their own commercials, newscasts, and even soap operas. Parents have more influence than teachers on children's television viewing; teachers can only suggest that television viewing be monitored and that it not be used as a baby-sitter. Obviously, when children are watching television, they are not reading, and too often they are not thinking either. Those losses affect their lifelong learning potential.

CONCLUSION

We strongly recommend authentic literature and purposeful writing for literacy instruction. Though many instructional materials advertise that they are literature based, we encourage you to evaluate this claim for yourself. Though many programs claim to encourage writing, we suggest that you examine what they mean by "writing."

If educators select computer software or commercially prepared reading and writing materials on the basis of their best understanding about how children learn and about what is worth teaching, then using these materials is both educationally sound and efficient. However, if educators choose materials on the basis of whether the format is attractive, how easy the materials are to implement, or how well the materials align with standardized tests, then educators are making decisions based on nonprofessional criteria.

A sound, research-based theoretical stance must guide judgment in selecting language arts education approaches and materials. Educators first must have a clear idea of what literacy is and how students develop reading and writing competence, then find materials that fit that understanding. Materials should not determine the teaching approach; the approach must determine the materials.

DISCUSSION QUESTIONS

1. Compare your analysis of a reading program with evaluations of other programs done by your colleagues or classmates.
2. What criteria would you change or add to the reading-program analysis offered in this chapter?

SUGGESTED FOLLOW-UP ACTIVITIES

1. Observe a reading program from a major publishing company in action. Use the criteria presented in this chapter for analyzing reading programs to critique what you observe.
2. Interview a teacher about the use of officially adopted texts. Does this teacher feel obligated to use them? Does he or she use them as directed? If not, how does he or she adapt or extend the materials?
3. Observe children using computer-based learning materials and/or try some computer educational software yourself. Evaluate the material in terms of the criteria for analyzing reading programs discussed in this chapter or one of the other rating scales listed.

4. Visit a school library or media center. Interview the librarian and focus on his or her role in the school's language arts program. Be sure to look around the library and decide whether it invites children to come in and to use it.

RECOMMENDED FURTHER READING

Haugland, S. W. (2000, March). *Computers and young children*. ERIC Digest.

Haugland, S. W., & Wright, J. L. (1997). *Young children and technology: A world of discovery*. Boston: Allyn & Bacon.

Huck, C., Hepler, S., & Hickman, J. (2000). *Children's literature in the elementary school*. Boston: McGraw-Hill.

Hurst, C. O. (1990). *Once upon a time . . . An encyclopedia for successfully using literature with young children*. Allen, TX: DLM Publishing.

National Association for the Education of Young Children. (1996). NAEYC position statement: Technology and young children—Ages three through eight. Washington, DC: Author.

REFERENCES

BOOKS AND PERIODICALS

Abbott, S., & Grose, C. (1998). "I know English so many, Mrs. Abbot": Reciprocal discoveries in a linguistically diverse classroom. *Language Arts, 75*(3), 175–184.

Allington, R. L. (1993). Michael doesn't go down the hall anymore. *The Reading Teacher, 46*(7), 602–604.

Allington, R. L. (Ed.). (1998). *Teaching struggling readers.* Newark, DE: International Reading Association.

Allington, R. L., & Baker, K. (1999). Best practices in literacy instruction for children with special needs. In L. B. Gambrell, L. M. Morrow, S. B. Neuman, & M. Pressley (Eds.), *Best practices in literacy instruction* (pp. 292–310). New York: Guilford.

Allington, R. L., & Walmsley, S. (Eds.). (1995). *No quick fix: Rethinking literacy programs in America's elementary schools.* New York: Teachers College Press.

Altwerger, B., Diehl-Faxon, J., & Dockstader-Anderson, K. (1985). Read-aloud events as meaning construction. *Language Arts, 62*(5), 476–484.

Altwerger, B., & Strauss, S. L. (2002). The business behind testing. *Language Arts, 79*(3), 256–262.

American Educational Research Association. 2000. *Position statement on high stakes testing.* Washington, DC: Author. [Online]. Available: http://www.aera.net

Anders, P. L., Hoffman, J. V., & Duffy, G. G. (2000). Teaching teachers to teach reading: Paradigm shifts, persistent problems, and challenges. In M. L. Kamil, P. B. Mosenthal, P. D. Pearson, & R. Barr (Eds.), *Handbook of reading research* (Vol. 3, pp. 719–742). Mahwah, NJ: Erlbaum.

Armington, D. (1997). *The living classroom.* Washington, DC: National Association for the Education of Young Children.

Arnqvist, A. (2000). Linguistic games as a way to introduce reading and writing in preschool groups. *Childhood Education, 76*(6), 365–367.

Au, K. H. (1997). Literacy for all students: Ten steps toward making a difference. *The Reading Teacher, 51*(3), 186–194.

August, D., & Hakuta, K. (Eds.). (1997). *Improving schooling for language-minority children: A research agenda.* Washington, DC: National Academy Press.

Baghban, M. (1984). *Our daughter learns to read and write: A case study from birth to three.* Newark, DE: International Reading Association.

Bagley, D. M., & Klass, P. H. (1997). Comparison of the quality of preschoolers' play in housekeeping and thematic sociodramatic play centers. *Journal of Research in Childhood Education, 12*(1), 71–77.

Bakley, S. (1998). On teasing, taunting, and "I can do it by myself." *Young Children, 53*(2), 42.

Barnitz, J. G. (1997). Linguistic perspectives in literacy education: Emerging awareness of linguistic diversity for literacy instruction. *The Reading Teacher, 51*(3), 264–266.

Barnitz, J. G. (1998). Linguistic perspectives in literacy education: Revising grammar instruction for authentic composing and comprehending. *The Reading Teacher, 51*(7), 608–611.

Barrentine, S. J. (1996). Engaging with reading through interactive read-alouds. *The Reading Teacher, 50*(1), 36–43.

Barrentine, S. J. (1999). *Reading assessment: Principles and practices for elementary teachers.* Newark, DE: International Reading Association.

Beaver, J. (1997). *Developmental reading assessment resource guide.* Glenview, IL: Celebration Press.

Bergin, C. (2001). The parent-child relationship during beginning reading. *Journal of Literacy Research, 33*(4), 681–706.

Berk, L. E., & Winsler, A. (1995). *Scaffolding children's learning: Vygotsky and early childhood education.* Washington, DC: National Association for the Education of Young Children.

Berliner, D. C., & Biddle, B. J. (1995). *The manufactured crisis.* New York: Addison-Wesley.

Bialystock, E. (1997). Effects of bilingualism and biliteracy on children's emerging concepts of print. *Developmental Psychology, 33*(3), 429–440.

Blasi, M. J., & Priestley, L. (1998). A child with severe hearing loss joins our learning community. *Young Children, 53*(2), 44–49.

Block, C. C. (1999). Comprehension: Crafting understanding. In L. B. Gambrell, L. M. Morrow, S. B. Neuman, & M. Pressley (Eds.), *Best practices in literacy instruction* (pp. 98–118). New York: Guilford.

Braunger, J., & Lewis, J. P. (1997). *Building a knowledge base in reading.* Portland, OR: Northwest Regional Educational Laboratory; Urbana, IL: National Council of Teachers of English; Newark, DE: International Reading Association.

Bredekamp, S., & Copple, C. (Eds.). (1997). *Developmentally appropriate practice in early childhood programs.* Washington, DC: National Association for the Education of Young Children.

Bredekamp, S., & Rosegrant, T. (Eds.). (1995). *Reaching potentials* (Vol. 2). Washington, DC: National Association for the Education of Young Children.

Bromley, K. (1999). Key components of sound writing instruction. In L. B. Gambrell, L. M. Morrow, A. B. Neuman, & M. Pressley (Eds.), *Best practices in literacy instruction* (pp. 152–174). New York: Guilford.

Brooks, M. G., & Brooks, J. G. (2003). The courage to be constructivist. In J. W. Noll (Ed.), *Taking sides: Clashing views on controversial educational issues* (pp. 159–167). Guilford, CT: McGraw-Hill/Dushkin.

Brown, D. J. (1998). *Schools with heart: Voluntarism and public education.* Boulder, CO: Westview.

Bruneau, B. (1997). The literacy pyramid organization of reading/writing activities in a whole language classroom. *The Reading Teacher, 51*(2), 158–160.

Buckner, A. (2002). Teaching in a world focused on testing. *Language Arts, 79*(3), 212–215.

Buly, M. R., & Rose, R. R. (2001). Mandates, expectations and change. *Primary Voices K–6, 9*(3), 3–6.

Burns, S., Snow, C., & Griffin, P. (1998). *Preventing reading difficulties in young children.* Washington, DC: National Academy Press.

Casbon, J., Schirmer, B. R., & Twiss, L. L. (1997). Diverse learners in the classroom. *The Reading Teacher, 50, 7,* 602–604.

Calkins, L. M. (1994). *The art of teaching writing.* Portsmouth, NH: Heinemann.

Calkins, L. M. (2000). *How's it going? A practical guide to conferring with student writers.* Portsmouth, NH: Heinemann.

Calkins, L. M. (2001). *The art of teaching reading*. New York: Longman.

Calkins, L. M., Montgomery, K., & Santman, D. (1998). *A teacher's guide to standardized reading tests: Knowledge is power*. Portsmouth, NH: Heinemann.

Cambourne, B. (1988). *The whole story: Natural learning and the acquisition of literacy in the classroom*. Auckland, New Zealand: Ashton Scholastic.

Carger, C. L. (1993). Louie comes to life: Pretend reading with second language emergent readers. *Language Arts, 79*(7), 542–547.

Carletti, S., Girard, S., & Willing, K. (1991). *The library classroom connection*. Portsmouth, NH: Heinemann.

Casbon, J., Schirmer, B. R., & Twiss, L. L. (1997). Diverse learners in the classroom. *The Reading Teacher, 50*(7), 602–604.

Caswell, L. J., & Duke, N. K. (1998). Non-narrative as a catalyst for literacy development. *Language Arts, 75*(2), 108–117.

Caudell, L. S. (1996). Voyage of discovery: An Alaska odyssey for effective portfolio assessment. In, *Assessment in action*. Portland, OR: Northwest Regional Educational Laboratory.

Cazden, C. B. (1988). *Classroom discourse: The language of teaching and learning*. Portsmouth, NH: Heinemann.

Christie, J. F., & Wardle, F. (1992). How much time is needed for play? *Young Children, 47*(3), 28–33.

Claire, N. (1995). Mainstream classroom teachers and ESL students. *TESOL Quarterly, 29*, 189–196.

Clay, M. M. (1966). *Emergent reading behavior*. Unpublished doctoral dissertation, University of Auckland, New Zealand.

Clay, M. M. (1975). *What did I write?* Auckland: Heinemann.

Clay, M. M. (1985). *The early detection of reading difficulties*. Portsmouth, NH: Heinemann.

Clay, M. M. (1993a). *An observation survey of early literacy achievement*. Portsmouth, NH: Heinemann.

Clay, M. M. (1993b). *Reading Recovery: A guidebook for teachers in training*. Portsmouth, NH: Heinemann.

Clay, M. M. (2001). *Change over time in children's literacy development*. Portsmouth, NH: Heinemann.

Clymer, T. (1996). The utility of phonic generalizations in the primary grades. *The Reading Teacher, 50*(3), 182–187.

Cohen, J. H., & Wiener, R. B. (2003). *Literacy portfolios: Improving assessment, teaching, and learning*. Upper Saddle River, NJ: Merrill/Prentice Hall.

Colasent, R., & Griffith, P. L. (1998). Autism and literacy: Looking into the classroom with rabbit stories. *The Reading Teacher, 51*(5), 414–420.

Cole, A. D. (1998). Beginner-oriented texts in literature-based classrooms: The segue for a few struggling readers. *The Reading Teacher, 51*(6), 488–501.

Cooper, J. D., & Kiger, N. D. (2001). *Literacy assessment: Helping teachers plan instruction*. New York: Houghton Mifflin.

Cooper, J. L., & Dever, M. T. (2001). Sociodramatic play as a vehicle for curriculum integration in first grade. *Young Children, 56*(3), 58–63.

Courtney, A. M., & Adodeeb, T. L. (2001). *Journey of discovery: Building a classroom community through diagnostic-reflective portfolios*. Newark, DE: International Reading Association.

Cuevas, J. (1997). *Educating limited-English proficient students: A review of the research on school programs and classroom practices*. San Francisco: WestEd.

Cunningham, J. W. (1999). How can we achieve best practices in literacy instruction? In L. B. Gambrell, L. M. Morrow, S. B. Neuman, & M. Pressley (Eds.), *Best practices in literacy instruction* (pp. 34–48). New York: Guilford.

Cunningham, P., Hall, D., & Defee, M. (1998). Nonability-grouped, multilevel instruction: Eight years later. *The Reading Teacher, 51*(8), 652–664.

Cutting, B., & Milligan, J. (1991). Learning to read in New Zealand. In C. Kamii, M. Manning, & G. Manning (Eds.), *Early literacy: A constructivist foundation for whole language* (pp. 83–89). Washington, DC: National Education Association.

Dahl, K. L., & Scharer, P. L. (2000). Phonics teaching and learning in whole language classrooms: New evidence from research. *The Reading Teacher, 53*(7), 584–594.

Dahl, K., Scharer, P., Lawson, L., & Grogan, P. (1999). Phonics instruction and student achievement in whole language first-grade classrooms. *Reading Research Quarterly, 34,* 312–341.

D'Angelo-Bromley, K. (1996). *Webbing with literature.* Boston: Allyn & Bacon.

Daniels, H., & Bizar, M. (1998). *Methods that matter: Six structures for best practice classrooms.* York, ME: Stenhouse.

De Gaetano, Y., Williams, L. R., & Volk, D. (1998). *Kaleidoscope: A multicultural approach for the primary school classroom.* Upper Saddle River, NJ: Merrill/Prentice Hall.

DeVries, R. (2001). Transforming the "play-oriented curriculum" and work in constructivist early education. In A. Goncu & E. Klein (Eds.), *Children in play, story, and school* (pp. 72–106). New York: Guilford.

Dixon-Krauss, L. (1996). *Vygotsky in the classroom.* White Plains, NY: Longman.

Dolch, E. W. (1945). *A manual for remedial reading.* Champaign, IL: Garrard.

Durkin, D. (1980). *Teaching young children to read.* Boston: Allyn & Bacon.

Dyson, A. H. (1990). Weaving possibilities: Rethinking metaphors for early literacy development. *The Reading Teacher, 44*(3), 202–213.

Dyson, A. H. (1997). *Writing superheroes: Contemporary childhood, popular culture, and classroom literacy.* New York: Teachers College Press.

Education Department of Western Australia. (1994). *First Steps.* Portsmouth, NH: Heinemann.

Education Department of Western Australia. (1998). *Oral language resource book.* Portsmouth, NH: Heinemann.

Education Department of Western Australia. (1997a). *Parents as partners.* Portsmouth, NH: Heinemann.

Education Department of Western Australia. (1997b). *Reading resource book.* Portsmouth, NH: Heinemann.

Edwards, L. H. (1994). Kid's eye view of reading: Kindergartners talk about learning how to read. *Childhood Education, 70*(3), 137–141.

Egawa, K. (1990). Harnessing the power of language: First graders' literature engagement with Owl Moon. *Language Arts, 67,* 6, 582–588.

El-Hindi, A. E. (1998). Beyond classroom boundaries: Constructivist teaching with the Internet. *The Reading Teacher, 51*(8), 694–700.

Elmore, R. F. (2002). Testing trap. *Harvard Magazine, 105*(1), 29–35.

Elster, C. A. (1994). I guess they do listen: Young children's emergent readings after adult read-alouds. *Young Children, 49*(3), 27–31.

Falk-Ross, F. (1997). Developing metacommunicative awareness in children with language difficulties: Challenging the typical pull-out system. *Language Arts, 74*(3), 206–216.

Farr, R., & Tone, B. (1998). *Portfolio and performance assessment: Helping students evaluate their progress as readers and writers.* Belmont, CA: Wadsworth.

Feeney, S., & Kipnis, K. (1990). *Code of ethical conduct: Guidelines for responsible behavior in early childhood education.* Washington, DC: National Association for the Education of Young Children.

Feeney, S., & Moravcek, E. (1994). *Discovering me and my world.* Circle Pines, MN: American Guidance Service.

Ferreiro, E. (1978). The interplay between information and assimilation in beginning literacy. In W. H. Teale & E. Sulzby, (Eds.), *Emergent literacy: Writing and reading* (pp. 15–49). Norwood, NJ: Ablex.

Ferreiro, E. (1978). What is written in a written sentence? A developmental answer. *Journal of Education, 160*(4), 25–29.

Ferreiro, E. (1990). Literacy development: Psychogenesis. In Y. Goodman (Ed.), *How children construct literacy* (pp. 12–25). Newark, DE: International Reading Association.

Ferreiro, E. (1991). Literacy acquisition. In C. Kamii, M. Manning, & G. Manning (Eds.), *Early literacy: A constructivist foundation for whole language* (pp. 31–56). Washington, DC: National Education Association.

Ferreiro, E., & Teberosky, A. (1982). *Literacy before schooling*. Exeter, NH: Heinemann.

Fields, M. (1998). *Your child learns to read and write*. Olney, MD: Association for Childhood Education International.

Fields, M. V., & Hillstead, D. V. (1995). Learning to write during pretend play. Paper presented at the annual conference of the National Association for the Education of Young Children, Washington, DC.

Fields, M. V., & Hillstead, D. (2001). *Learning centers that build early reading and writing skills*. New York: Scholastic.

Fillmore, L. W. (2000). Loss of family languages: Should educators be concerned? *Theory Into Practice, 39*(4), 203–210.

Fisher, B. (1998). *Joyful learning*. Portsmouth, NH: Heinemann.

Fitzgerald, J. (2000). How will bilingual/ESL programs in literacy change in the next millennium? *Reading Research Quarterly, 35*(4), 520–521.

Fletcher, R. (1999). Teaching the craft of writing. *Primary Voices K–6, 7*(4), 41–43.

Fletcher, R., & Portalupi, J. (1998). *Craft lessons: Teaching writing K–8*. York, ME: Stenhouse.

Fletcher, R., & Portalupi, J. (2001). *Writing workshop: The essential guide*. Portsmouth, NH: Heinemann.

Fountas, I. C., & Pinnell, G. S. (1996). *Guided reading*. Portsmouth, NH: Heinemann.

Fountas, I. C., & Pinnell, G. S. (1998). *Word matters*. Portsmouth, NH: Heinemann.

Fountas, I. C., & Pinnell, G. S. (1999). *Matching books to readers: Using leveled books in guided reading, K–3*. Portsmouth, NH: Heinemann.

Frank, C. R. (2001). What new things those words can do for you: A focus on one writing project teacher and writing instruction. *Journal of Literacy Research, 33*(3), 467–506.

Frank, M. (1979). *If you're trying to teach kids how to write, you've gotta have this book!* Nashville, TN: Incentive Publications.

Franklin, E. (1988). Reading and writing stories: Children creating meaning. *The Reading Teacher, 42*(3), 184–190.

Fraser, J., & Skolnick, D. (1994). *On their way: Celebrating second graders as they read and write*. Portsmouth, NH: Heinemann.

Fresch, J. J., & Wheaton, A. (1997). Sort, search, and discover: Spelling in the child-centered classroom. *The Reading Teacher, 51*(1), 20–31.

Fry, E. (1998). *Phonics patterns: Onset and rhyme word lists*. Laguna Beach, CA: Laguna Beach Educational Books.

Fry, E. B., Kress, J. E., Fountoukidis, D. L., & Polk, J. K. (1993). *The reading teachers' book of lists* (3rd ed.). Upper Saddle River, NJ: Merrill/Prentice Hall.

Gallas, K. (1997). Story time as a magical act open only to the initiated: What some children don't know about power and may not find out. *Language Arts, 74*(4), 248–254.

Gallas, K., Anteon-Oldenburg, M., Ballenger, C., Beseler, C., Griffin, S., Papperheimer, R., & Swaim, J. (1996). Focus on research: Talking the talk and walking the walk: Researching oral language in the classroom. *Language Arts, 73*(8), 608–617.

Gallas, K., & Smagorinsky, P. (2002). Approaching texts in school. *The Reading Teacher, 56*(1), 54–61.

Gambrell, L. B., & Mazzoni, S. A. (1999). Principles of best practice: Finding the common ground. In L. B. Gambrell, L. M. Morrow, S. B. Neuman, & M. Pressley (Eds.), *Best practices in literacy instruction* (pp. 11–21). New York: Guilford.

Ganske, K. (2000). *Word journeys*. New York: Guilford.

Gardner, H. (1991). *The unschooled mind: How children think and how schools should teach*. New York: Basic.

Gaskins, I. W. (1998). There's more to teaching at-risk and delayed readers than good reading instruction. *The Reading Teacher, 51*(7), 534–547.

Genishi, C. (2002). Young English learners: Resourceful in the classroom. *Young Children*, 57(4), 66-72.

Gerzog, E. H., & Haugland, S. W. (1999). Web sites provide unique learning opportunities for young children. *Early Childhood Education Journal*, 27(2), 109-114.

Gillet, J. W., & Beverly, L. (2001). *Directing the writing workshop: An elementary teacher's handbook*. New York: Guilford.

Giorgis, C., & Peterson, B. (1996). Teachers and librarians collaborate to create a community of learners. *Language Arts*, 73(7), 477-482.

Girling-Butcher, W., Phillips, G., & Clay, M. (1991). Emerging readers and writers: Fostering independent learning. *The Reading Teacher*, 44, 9, 694-697.

Glazer, S. M. (1998). *Phonics, spelling, and word study: A sensible approach*. Norwood, MA: Christopher Gordon.

Goebel, B. (1996). Honoring Native cultures: Reflections and responsibilities. *Primary Voices*, 4(3), 3-10.

Goldenburg, C. (2002). Making schools work for low-income families in the 21st century. In S. B. Neuman & D. K. Dickinson (Eds.), *Handbook of early literacy research* (pp. 211-231). New York: Guilford.

Goldhaber, J., Lipson, M., Sortino, S., & Daniels, P. (1996-1997). Books in the sand box? Markers in the blocks? Expanding the child's world of literacy. *Childhood Education*, 73(2), 88-91.

Goodman, K., Shannon, P., Freeman, Y., & Murphy, S. (1988). *Report card on basal readers*. Katonah, NY: Richard C. Owen.

Goodman, K. S. (1996). *On reading*. Portsmouth, NH: Heinemann.

Goodman, K. S. (Ed.). (1998). *In defense of good teaching*. York, ME: Stenhouse.

Goodman, K. S., Bird, L. M., & Goodman, Y. M. (1992). *The whole language catalogue: Supplement on authentic assessment*. Chicago: SRA, Macmillan/McGraw-Hill.

Goodman, Y. (1985). Kid watching: Observing children in the classroom. In A. Jaeger & M. Smith-Burke (Eds.), *Observing the language learner*. Newark, DE: International Reading Association.

Goodman, Y. M. (1986). Children coming to know literacy. In W. Teale & E. Sulzby (Eds.), *Emergent literacy: Writing and reading* (pp. 1-14). Norwood, NJ: Ablex.

Goodman, Y. M., & Burke, C. L. (1972). *Reading miscue inventory manual: Procedure for diagnosis and evaluation*. New York: Macmillan.

Goodman, Y. M., Watson, D. J., & Burke, C. L. (1987). *Reading miscue inventory: Alternative procedures*. Katonah, NY: Richard C. Owen.

Graham, S. (1993-1994). Are slanted manuscript alphabets superior to the traditional manuscript alphabet? *Childhood Education*, 70(2), 91-96.

Graves, D. (1994). *A fresh look at writing*. Portsmouth, NH: Heinemann.

Green, C. R. (1998). This is my name. *Childhood Education*, 74(4), 226-231.

Greenberg, P. (1998). Some thoughts about phonics, feelings, Don Quixote, diversity, and democracy: Teaching young children to read, write and spell. *Young Children*, 53(4), 72-83.

Griffith, P. L., & Leavell, J. A. (1995-1996). There isn't much to say about spelling . . . or is there? *Childhood Education*, 72(2), 84-90.

Gross, A., & Ortiz, W. L. (1994). Using children's literature to facilitate inclusion in kindergarten and the primary grades. *Young Children*, 49(3), 32-35.

Groth, L. A., & Darling, L. D. (2001). Playing "inside" stories. In A. Goncu & E. L. Klein (Eds.), *Children in play, story, and school* (pp. 220-240). New York: Guilford.

Gunning, T. G. (1998). *Best books for beginning readers*. Boston: Allyn & Bacon.

Haladyna, T., Haas, N., & Allison, J. (1998). Continuing tensions in standardized testing. *Childhood Education*, 74(5), 262-273.

Hakuta, K., & Garcia, E. (1989). Bilingualism and education. *American Psychologist*, 44, 2, 374-379.

Halliday, M. A. K. (1982). Three aspects of children's language development: Learning language, learning through language, learning about language. In Y. Goodman, M. Haussler, & D. Strickland (Eds.), *Oral and written language development research: Impact on the schools*. Urbana, IL: National Council of Teachers of English.

Hannon, P. (1998). How can we foster children's early literacy development through parent involvement? In S. B. Neuman & K. A. Roskos (Eds.), *Children achieving: Best practices in early literacy* (pp. 121–143). Newark, DE: International Reading Association.

Harp, B. (2000). *Handbook of literacy assessment and evaluation*. Norwood, MA: Christopher Gordon.

Harvey, S. (2002). Nonfiction inquiry: Using real reading and writing to explore the world. *Language Arts, 80*(1), 12–22.

Harvey, S., & Goudvis, A. (2000). *Strategies that work*. York, ME: Stenhouse.

Harwayne, S. (2000). *Lifetime guarantees: Toward ambitious literacy teaching*. Portsmouth, NH: Heinemann.

Haugland, S. W. (1999). Developmental software scale. Cape Girardeau, MO: K.I.D.S. & Computers, Inc.

Haugland, S. W. (2000). Outstanding developmental software for 2000. *Early Childhood Education Journal, 28*(2), 117–124.

Haugland, S. W., Bailey, M. D., & Ruiz, E. A. (2002). The outstanding developmental software and web sites for 2001. *Early Childhood Education Journal, 29*(3), 191–200.

Haugland, S. W., & Wright, J. L. (1997). *Young children and technology: A world of discovery*. Boston: Allyn & Bacon.

Haussler, & Strickland, D. (Eds.). (1982). *Oral and written language development research: Impact on the schools*. Urbana, IL: National Council of Teachers of English.

Heald-Taylor, B. G. (1998). Three paradigms of spelling instruction in grades 3 to 6. *The Reading Teacher, 51*(5), 404–413.

Healy, J. M. (1990). *Endangered minds*. New York: Touchstone.

Heller, M. F. (1999). *Reading-writing connections: From theory to practice* (2nd ed.). Mahwah, NJ: Erlbaum.

Hendrick, J. (1996). *The whole child* (5th ed.). Upper Saddle River, NJ: Merrill/Prentice Hall.

Hill, S. (2001). Theoretical tools for talk. In P. G. Smith (Ed.), *Talking classrooms: Shaping children's learning through oral language instruction* (pp. 14–26). Newark, DE: International Reading Association.

Hillal Gill, C., & Scharer, P. L. (1996). Why do they get it on Friday and misspell it on Monday? Teachers inquiring about their students as spellers. *Language Arts, 73*(2), 89–96.

Hills, T. W. (1993). Assessment in context—Teachers and children at work. *Young Children, 48*(5), 20–28.

Hohmann, C., Carmody, B., & McCabe-Branz, C. (1995). *High / Scope buyer's guide to children's software*. Ypsilanti, MI: High/Scope Press.

Holdaway, D. (1979). *The foundations of literacy*. New York: Ashton Scholastic.

Holdaway, D. (1991). Shared book experience: Teaching reading using favorite books. In C. Kamii, M. Manning, & G. Manning (Eds.), *Early literacy: A constructivist foundation for whole language* (pp. 91–110). Washington, DC: National Education Association.

Hornsby, D., & Sukarna, D. (1988). *Read on: A conference approach to reading*. Portsmouth, NH: Heinemann.

Hoyt, L. (1992). Many ways of knowing: Using drama, oral interactions, and the visual arts to enhance reading comprehension. *The Reading Teacher, 45*(8), 580–584.

Hubbard, R. A. (1996). *Workshop of the possible: Nurturing children's creative development*. York, ME: Stenhouse.

Huck, C. (1996). *Children's literature in the elementary school*. New York: Wm C Brown and McGraw-Hill.

Huck, C., Hepler, S., Hickman, J., & Kiefer, B. Z. (2001). *Children's literature in the elementary school*. Boston: McGraw-Hill.

Hymes, J. L. (1965, March). Being taught to read. *Grade Teacher, 82,* 88–92.

Hymes, J. L. (1981). *Teaching the child under six.* Upper Saddle River, NJ: Merrill/Prentice Hall.

International Reading Association. (1998). IRA leaders testify before reading panel. *Reading Today, 16*(1), 1, 6.

International Reading Association. (2002). *What is evidence-based reading instruction? A position statement of the International Reading Association.* Newark, DE: Author.

International Reading Association and National Association for the Education of Young Children. (1998). Learning to read and write: Developmentally appropriate practices for young children. A joint position statement of the International Reading Association and National Association for the Education of Young Children. *Young Children, 53*(4), 30–46.

International Society for Technology in Education Standards Projects. (2002). [Online]. Available: http://www.iste.org/standards

Invernizzi, M. A., Abouzeid, M. P., & Bloodgood, J. W. (1997). Integrated word study: Spelling, grammar, and meaning in the language arts classroom. *Language Arts, 74*(3), 193–200.

IRA Position Statement. (2000). *Making a difference means making it different: Honoring children's rights to excellent reading instruction.* Newark, DE: International Reading Association.

Jarmer, D., Kozol, M., Nelson, S., & Salsberry, T. (2000). Six-trait writing model improves scores at Jennie Wilson Elementary. *Journal of School Improvement, 1*(2), 1–5.

Johnson, D. D. (2001). *Vocabulary in the elementary and middle school.* Boston: Allyn & Bacon.

Johnston, P. H. (1997). *Knowing literacy: Constructive literacy assessment.* York, ME: Stenhouse.

Kameenui, E. J. (1998). Diverse learners and the tyranny of time: Don't fix blame; fix the leaky roof. In R. L. Allington (Ed.), *Teaching struggling readers* (pp. 4–8). Newark, DE: International Reading Association.

Kamii, C. (1985). Leading primary education toward excellence: Beyond worksheets and drill. *Young Children, 40*(6), 3–9.

Kamii, C. (1990). *Achievement testing in the early grades: The games grownups play.* Washington, DC: National Association for the Education of Young Children.

Kamii, C. (1991). What is constructivism? In C. Kamii, M. Manning, & G. Manning (Eds.), *Early literacy: A constructivist foundation for whole language* (pp. 17–30). Washington, DC: National Education Association.

Kamii, C., & DeVries, R. (1993). *Physical knowledge in preschool education: Implications of Piaget's theory.* New York: Teachers College Press.

Kamii, C., Long, R., Manning, M., & Manning, G. (1990). Spelling in kindergarten: A constructivist analysis comparing Spanish-speaking and English-speaking children. *Journal of Research in Childhood Education, 4*(2), 91–97.

Kamii, C., & Randazzo, M. (1985). Social interaction and invented spelling. *Language Arts, 62*(2), 124–133.

Karweit, N., & Wasik, B. A. (1996). The effects of story reading programs on literacy and language development of disadvantaged preschoolers. *Journal of Education for Students Placed at Risk, 1*(4), 319–348.

Katz, L. G., & Chard, S. C. (1989). *Engaging children's minds: The project approach.* Norwood, NJ: Ablex.

Keene, E., & Zimmerman, S. (1997). *Mosaic of thought: Teaching comprehension in a reader's workshop.* Portsmouth, NH: Heinemann.

Koeller, S., & Mitchell, P. (1996–1997). From Ben's story to your story: Encouraging young writers, authentic voices, and learning engagement. *The Reading Teacher, 50*(4), 328–336.

Kohn, A. (2000). *The case against standardized testing: Raising the scores, ruining the schools.* Portsmouth, NH: Heinemann.

Kohn, A. (2001). Fighting the tests: Turning frustration into action. *Young Children, 56*(2), 20–24.

Kohn, A. (2002). Poor teaching for poor kids. *Language Arts, 79*(3), 251–255.

Kraft, E. (1998). Killing the text, digitally. *The Reading Teacher, 51*(4), 337.

Krashen, S. (1992). *Fundamentals of language education.* Torrance, CA: Laredo.

Labbo, L. D. (1996). A semiotic analysis of young children's symbol making in a classroom computer center. *Reading Research Quarterly, 31,* 356–385.

Laminack, L. L., & Ray, K. W. (2001). Message from the editors. *Primary Voices, 9*(3), 1–2.

Lancia, P. J. (1997). Literary borrowing: The effects of literature on children's writing. *The Reading Teacher, 50*(6), 470–475.

Landsmann, L. T. (1990). Literacy development and pedagogical implications: Evidence from the Hebrew system of writing. In Y. Goodman (Ed.), *How children construct literacy* (pp. 26–44). Newark, DE: International Reading Association.

Learning First Alliance. (1998). Every child reading: An action plan of the Learning First Alliance. *American Educator, 22*(1 & 2), 52–63.

Lee, D., & Allen, R. V. (1963). *Learning to read through experience.* Upper Saddle River, NJ: Merrill/Prentice Hall.

Leslie, L., & Caldwell, J. (2001). *Qualitative reading inventory—3.* Boston: Allyn & Bacon.

Leu, D. J. (2002). Internet workshop: Making time for literacy. *The Reading Teacher, 55*(5), 466–472.

Leu, D. J., & Kinzer, C. K. (1999). *Effective literacy instruction, K–8.* Upper Saddle River, NJ: Prentice Hall.

Leu, D. J., & Kinzer, C. K. (2000). The convergence of literacy instruction with networked technologies for information, communication, and education. *Reading Research Quarterly, 35*(1); 108–127.

Leu, D. J., & Kinzer, C. K. (2003). *Effective literacy instruction, K–8.* Upper Saddle River, NJ: Merrill/Prentice Hall.

Madaus, G., & O'Dwyer, L. M. (1999). A short history of performance assessment: Lessons learned. *Phi Delta Kappan, 80*(9); 688–695.

Mallett, M. (1999). *Young researchers: Informational reading and writing in the early and primary years.* New York: Routledge.

Manning, M., Manning, G., Long, R., & Kamii, C. (1993). Preschoolers' conjectures about segments of a written sentence. *Journal of Research in Childhood Education, 8*(1), 5–11.

Manning, M., Manning, G., Long, R., & Kamii, C. (1995). Development of kindergartners' ideas about what is written in a written sentence. *Journal of Research in Childhood Education, 10*(1), 29–36.

Marinelli, S. (1996). Integrated spelling in the classroom. *Primary Voices, 4*(4), 11–13.

Mason, J. (1989). *Reading & writing connections.* Needham Heights, MA: Allyn & Bacon.

May, F. B. (1994). *Reading as communication: An interactive approach* (4th ed.). Upper Saddle River, NJ: Merrill/Prentice Hall.

McCarrier, A., Pinnell, G. S., & Fountas, I. C. (2000). *Interactive writing: How language and literacy come together, K–2.* Portsmouth, NH: Heinemann.

McCracken, J. (1993). *Valuing diversity in the primary years.* Washington, DC: National Association for the Education of Young Children.

McDevitt, T. M., & Ormrod, J. E. (2002). *Child development and education.* Upper Saddle River, NJ: Merrill/Prentice Hall.

McGill-Franzen, A. (2002). Policy and instruction: What is the relationship? In M. L. Kamil, P. B. Mosenthal, P. D. Pearson, & R. Barr (Eds.), *Handbook of reading research* (Vol. 3, pp. 889–908). Mahwah, NJ: Erlbaum.

McKenna, M. C., Young, T., & Gatliff, J. (2001, December). *Creating and using talking documents with struggling second grade readers.* Paper presented at the National Reading Conference annual meeting, Scottsdale, AZ.

McNair, S., Kirova-Petrova, A., & Bhargava, A. (2001). Computers and young children in the classroom: Strategies for minimizing gender bias. *Early Childhood Education Journal, 29*(1); 51–55.

McQuillan, J. (1998). *The literacy crisis: False claims, real solutions.* Portsmouth, NH: Heinemann.

Meier, D. R. (2000). *Scribble, scrabble learning to read and write: Success with diverse teachers, children, and families.* New York: Teachers College Press.

Meisels, S. J. (1993). Remaking classroom assessment with the work sampling system. *Young Children, 48*(5), 34–40.

Meisels, S. J. (1995). *Performance assessment in early childhood education: The work sampling system.* Urbana, IL: ERIC Clearinghouse on Elementary and Early Childhood Education. (ERIC Document Reproduction Service ED 382 407).

Meisels, S. J., Bickel, D. D., Nicholson, J., Xue, Y., & Atkins-Burnett, S. (2001). Trusting teachers' judgments: A validity study of a curriculum-embedded performance assessment in kindergarten to grade 3. *American Educational Research Journal, 38*(1); 73–95.

Moore, L. M. (1998). Learning language and some initial literacy skills through social interactions. *Young Children, 53*(2), 72–75.

Morrow, L. M. (1993). *Literacy development in the early years.* Boston: Allyn & Bacon.

Morrow, L. M. (1995). *Family literacy: Connections in schools and communities.* Newark, DE: International Reading Association.

Morrow, L. M. (2001). *Literacy development in the early years: Helping children read and write.* Boston: Allyn & Bacon.

Morrow, L. M., & Gambrell, L. B. (2000). Literature-based reading instruction. In M. L. Kamil, P. B. Mosenthal, P. D. Pearson, & R. Barr (Eds.), *Handbook of reading research* (Vol. 3, pp. 563–586). Mahwah, NJ: Erlbaum.

Morrow, L. M., Strickland, D. S., & Woo, D. G. (1998). *Literacy instruction in half- and whole-day kindergarten.* Newark, DE: International Reading Association.

Moss, B., Leone, S., & Dipillo, M. L. (1997). Exploring the literature of fact: Linking reading and writing through information trade books. *Language Arts, 74*(6), 418–427.

Moustafa, M. (1997). *Beyond traditional phonics.* Portsmouth, NH: Heinemann.

Moustafa, M. (2002). *Literacy for all Re: Open Court documents reading achievements.* NRCEMAIL listserv.

National Association for the Education of Young Children. (1988, March). NAEYC position statement on standardized testing of young children 3 through 8 years of age. *Young Children, 42,* 42–47.

National Association for the Education of Young Children. (1996a). NAEYC position statement: Responding to linguistic and cultural diversity—Recommendations for effective early childhood education. *Young Children, 51*(1), 4–12.

National Association for the Education of Young Children. (1996b). *NAEYC position statement: Technology and young children—Ages three through eight.* Washington, DC: Author.

National Association for the Education of Young Children and the National Association of Early Childhood Specialists in State Departments of Education. (1991). Guidelines for appropriate curriculum content and assessment in programs serving children ages 3 through 8. *Young Children, 41*(3), 47–52.

National Research Council (1999). *Starting out right: A guide to promoting success.* Washington, DC: National Academy Press.

Neuman, S. B. (1999). Books make a difference: A study of access to literacy. *Reading Research Quarterly, 34,* 286–312.

Neuman, S. B., & Celano, D. (2001). Access to print in low-income and middle-income communities: An ecological study of four neighborhoods. *Reading Research Quarterly, 36*(1), 8–26.

Neuman, S. B., Copple, C., & Bredekamp, S. (2000). *Learning to read and write: Developmentally appropriate practices for young children.* Washington, DC: National Association for the Education of Young Children.

Neuman, S. B., & Roskos, K. (1992). Literacy objects as cultural tools: Effects on children's literacy behaviors in play. *Reading Research Quarterly, 27,* 202–225.

Neuman, S., & Roskos, K. (1997). Literacy knowledge in practice: Contexts of participation for young writers and readers. *Reading Research Quarterly, 32*(1), 10–32.

New Zealand Ministry of Education. (1985). *Reading in junior classes.* Wellington, New Zealand: Learning Media Limited.

O'Flahavan, J., & Blassberg, R. (1992). Toward an embedded model of spelling instruction for emergent literates. *Language Arts, 69*(6), 409–417.

Oken-Wright, P. (1998). Transition to writing: Drawing as a scaffold for emergent writers. *Young Children, 53*(2), 76–81.

Opitz, M. (1997). *Flexible grouping in reading: Practical ways to help all students become better readers.* New York: Scholastic.

Opitz, M. (1998). Text sets: One way to flex your grouping—In first grade, too! *The Reading Teacher, 51*(7), 622–623.

Opitz, M. F., & Rasinski, T. V. (1998). *Good-bye round robin reading.* Portsmouth, NH: Heinemann.

Otto, B. (2002). *Language development in early childhood.* Upper Saddle River, NJ: Merrill/Prentice Hall.

Owens, R. F., Hester, J. L., & Teale, W. H. (2002). Where do you want to go today? Inquiry-based learning and technology integration. *The Reading Teacher, 55*(7), 616–625.

Parker, D. H. (1993). *Hooked on phonics.* Orange, CA: Gateway Educational Products.

Pellegrini, A. D. (1991). A critique of the concept of at risk as applied to emergent literacy. *Language Arts, 68*(5): 380–385.

Pellegrino, J. W., Chudowsky, N., & Glaser, R. (Eds.). (2001). *Knowing what students know: The science and design of educational assessment.* Washington, DC: National Academy Press.

Peterson, R., & Eeds, M. (1999). *Grand conversations: Literature groups in action.* New York: Scholastic.

Piaget, J. (1962). *Plays, dreams, and imitation.* New York: Norton.

Piaget, J. (1973). *To understand is to invent.* New York: Viking.

Piaget, J. (1985). *The equilibration of cognitive structures.* Chicago: University of Chicago Press.

Piaget, J., & Inhelder, B. (1969). *The psychology of the child.* New York: Basic.

Pica, R. (1997). Beyond physical development: Why young children need to move. *Young Children, 52*(6), 4-11.

Picket, L. (1998). Literacy learning during block play. *Journal of Research in Childhood Education, 12*(2), 225–230.

Pikulski, J. (1996). IRA board questions definition of "learning disabilities." *Reading Today, 14*(1), 15.

Pikulski, J. (1997). IRA and "learning disabilities": An update. *Reading Today, 15*(3), 34.

Pontecorvo, C., & Zucchermaglio, C. (1990). A passage to literacy: Learning in a social context. In Y. Goodman (Ed.), *How children construct literacy* (pp. 59–98). Newark, DE: International Reading Association.

Poplin, M. (1988). Holistic/constructivist principles of teaching/learning process: Implications for the field of learning disabilities. *Journal of Learning Disabilities, 21*, 401–416.

Portalupi, J. (1999). Learning to write: Honoring both process and product. *Primary Voices K–6, 7*(4); 2–6.

Pressley, M. (1998). *Reading instruction that works: The case for balanced teaching.* New York: Guilford.

Pressley, M. (1999). Self-regulated comprehension processing and its development through instruction. In L. B. Gambrell, L. M. Morrow, S. B. Neuman, & M. Pressley (Eds.), *Best practices in literacy instruction* (pp. 90–97). New York: Guilford.

Pressley, M. (2000). What should comprehension instruction be the instruction of? (pp. 545–562). In M. L. Kamil, P. B. Mosenthal, P. D. Pearson, & R. Barr (Eds.), *Handbook of reading research* (Vol. 3, pp. 545–562). Mahwah, NJ: Erlbaum.

Raban, B. (2001). Talking to think, learn, and teach (pp. 27–41). In P. G. Smith (Ed.), *Talking classrooms: Shaping children's learning through oral language instruction* (pp. 27–41). Newark, DE: International Reading Association.

Ramirez, G., & Ramirez, J. L. (1994). *Multiethnic children's literature.* Albany, NY: Delmar.

Ramos, F., & Krashen, S. (1998). The impact of one trip to the public library: Making books available may be the best incentive for reading. *The Reading Teacher, 51*(7), 614.

Rasinski, T., & Padak, N. (2000). *Effective reading strategies: Teaching children who find reading difficult.* Upper Saddle River, NJ: Merrill.

Ratcliff, N. J. (2001–2002). Using authentic assessment to document the emerging literacy skills of young children. *Childhood Education,* 78(2), 66–69.

Read, S. (2001, June). Perspectives on assessment in early childhood: The teacher's perspective. *Early Education / Child Development AERA SIG Newsletter,* 3.

Reese, D., & Shortland-Jones, B. (1994). *Reading developmental continuum.* Portsmouth, NH: Heinemann.

Reutzel, D. R. (1999). Organizing literacy instruction: Effective grouping strategies and organizational plans. In L. B. Gambrell, L. M. Morrow, S. B. Neuman, & M. Pressley (Eds.), *Best practices in literacy instruction* (pp. 292–310). New York: Guilford.

Richgels, D. J. (2002). Invented spelling, phonemic awareness, and reading and writing instruction. In S. B. Neuman & D. K. Dickinson (Eds.), *Handbook of early literacy research* (pp. 142–158). New York: Guilford.

Risko, V. J., Roskos, K., & Vukelich, C. (2002). Prospective teachers reflection: Strategies, qualities, and perceptions in learning to teach reading. *Reading Research and Instruction,* 41(2), 149–176.

Ritchie, J. S., & Wilson, D. E. (1993). Dual apprenticeships: Subverting and supporting critical teaching. *English Education, 25*(2), 67–83.

Robinson, C. C., Larsen, J. M., & Haupt, J. H. (1995). Picture book reading at home: A comparison of Head Start and middle-class preschoolers. *Early Education and Development, 6*(3), 241–252.

Robinson, C. C., Larsen, J. M., & Haupt, J. H. (1996). The influence of selecting and taking picture books home on the at-home reading behaviors of kindergarten children. *Reading Research and Instruction, 35,* 249–259.

Rog, L. J., & Burton, W. (2001-2002). Matching texts and readers: Leveling early reading materials for assessment and instruction. *The Reading Teacher, 55*(4), 348–356.

Roller, C. M. (1996). *Variability not disability.* Newark, DE: International Reading Association.

Roskos, K., & Christie, J. F. (Eds.). (2000). *Research from multiple perspectives.* Mahwah, NJ: Erlbaum.

Roskos, K., & Christie, J. (2001). On not pushing too hard: A few cautionary remarks about linking literacy and play. *Young Children, 56*(3), 64-66.

Roskos, K., & Neuman, S. B. (2002). Environment and its influences for early literacy teaching and learning. In S. B. Neuman & B. K. Dickinson (Eds.), *Handbook of early literacy research* (pp. 281–294). New York: Guilford.

Routman, R. (1996). *Literacy at the crossroads.* Portsmouth, NH: Heinemann.

Routman, R. (2000). *Conversations: Strategies for teaching, learning, and evaluating.* Portsmouth, NH: Heinemann.

Routman, R., & Butler, A. (1995). Why talk about phonics? *School Talk, 1*(2), 22–24.

Rowe, D. W. (1999). The literate potentials of book-related dramatic play. *Reading Research Quarterly, 33,* 10–35.

Rowe, D. W. (2000). Bringing books to life: The role of book-related dramatic play in young children's literacy learning. In K. A. Roskos & J. F. Christie (Eds.), *Play and literacy in early childhood: Research from multiple perspectives* (pp. 3–27). Mahwah, NJ: Erlbaum.

Ruiz, N. T., & Enguidanos, T. (1997). Authenticity and advocacy in assessment: Bilingual students in special education. *Primary Voices K–6, 5*(3), 35–43.

Rust, F. (1997, June). Seminar discussion at the conference of the National Association for the Education of Young Children, Seattle.

Sacks, C. H., & Mergendoller, J. R. (1997). The relationship between teachers' theoretical orientation toward reading and student outcomes in kindergarten children with different initial reading abilities. *American Educational Research Journal, 34*(4), 721–739.

Salinger, T. (2002). Assessing the literacy of young children: The case for multiple forms of evidence. In S. B. Neuman & D. K. Dickinson (Eds.), *Handbook of early literacy research* (pp. 390–418). New York: Guilford.

Samuels, S. J. (1997). The method of repeated readings. *The Reading Teacher, 50*(5), 376–381.

Santman, D. (2002). Teaching to the test? Test preparation in the reading workshop. *Language Arts, 79,* (3) 203–211.

Schickedanz, J. A. (1999). *Much more than the ABC's: The early stages of reading and writing.* Washington, DC: National Association for the Education of Young Children.

Schifini, A. (1996). Discussion in multilingual, multi-cultural classrooms. In L. Gambrell & J. F. Almasi (Eds.), *Lively discussions* (pp. 37–53). Newark, DE: International Reading Association.

Sharp, J. (1993). Selecting or designing software to support children's writing. *The Whole Idea, 4*(1), 6–7.

Sheldon, K. (1996). Can I play too? Adapting common classroom activities for young children with limited motor abilities. *Early Childhood Education Journal, 24*(2), 115–120.

Shephard, L., Kagan, S. L., & Wurtz, E. (Eds.). (1998). *Principles and recommendations for early childhood assessments.* Washington, DC: National Education Goals Panel.

Siegrist, F., & Sinclair, H. (1991). Principles of spelling found in the first two grades. In C. Kamii, M. Manning, & G. Manning (Eds.), *Early literacy: A constructivist foundation for whole language* (pp. 57–68). Washington, DC: National Education Association.

Silvaroli, N. J., & Wheelock, W. H. (2001). *Classroom reading inventory.* New York: McGraw-Hill.

Sinclair, H. (1996). Personal communication regarding pretend play.

Sipe, L. R. (2001). Invention, convention, and intervention: Invented spelling and the teacher's role. *The Reading Teacher, 55*(3), 264–273.

Slapin, B., & Seale, D. (1992). *Through Indian eyes.* Philadelphia: New Society Publishers.

Smith, C. (1989). Emergent literacy—An environmental concept. *The Reading Teacher, 42*(7), 528.

Smith, F. (1976). Learning to read by reading. *Language Arts, 53*(3), 297–299, 322.

Smith, F. (1983, May). Reading like a writer. *Language Arts, 60,* 558–567.

Smith, F. (1987). *Reading without nonsense.* New York: Teachers College Press.

Smith, F. (1994). *Understanding reading.* Hillsdale, NJ: Erlbaum.

Snow, C. (1991). The theoretical basis for relationships between language and literacy in development. *Journal of Research in Childhood Education, 6,* 5–10.

Snow, C., Burns, M. S., & Griffin, P. (1998). *Preventing reading difficulties in young children.* Washington, DC: National Academy Press.

Snow, C., Tabors, P., Nicholson, P., & Kurland, B. (1995). SHELL: Oral language and literacy skills in kindergarten and first-grade children. *Journal of Research in Childhood Education, 10,* 37–48.

Soriano-Nagurski, L. (1998). And the walls came tumbling down: Including children who are differently abled in typical early childhood educational settings. *Young Children, 53*(2), 40–41.

Soundy, C. S. (1993). Let the story begin! *Childhood Education, 69*(3), 146–149.

Soundy, C. S., & Stout, N. L. (2002). Fostering emotional and language needs of young learners. *Young Children, 57*(2), 20–24.

Spandel, V. (1996). *Seeing with new eyes.* Portland, OR: Northwest Regional Educational Laboratory.

Spear-Swerling, L., & Sternberg, R. J. (1996). *Off track: When poor readers become "learning disabled."* Boulder, CO: Westview.

Stokes, S. J. (1997). Curriculum for Native American students: Using Native American values. *The Reading Teacher, 50*(7), 576–584.

Strickland, D. (1994). Educating African American learners at risk: Finding a better way. *Language Arts, 71*(5), 328–336.

Strickland, D. (1998). *Teaching phonics today: A primer for educators.* Newark, DE: International Reading Association.

Sulzby, E. (1985). Children's emergent reading of favorite storybooks: A developmental study. *Reading Research Quarterly, 20*(4), 458–481.

Sulzby, E. (1986). Writing and reading: Signs of oral and written language organization in the young child. In W. Teale & E. Sulzby (Eds.), *Emergent literacy: Writing and reading* (pp. 50–89). Norwood, NJ: Ablex.

Sulzby, E., & Barnhart, J. (1990). The developing kindergarten: All our children emerge as writers and readers. In J. S. McKee (Ed.), *The developing kindergarten programs, children, and teachers* (p. 218). Ann Arbor: Michigan Association of the Education of Young Children.

Sulzby, E., Barnhart, J., & Hieshima, J. (1989). Forms of writing and rereading from writing: A preliminary report. In J. Mason (Ed.), *Reading and writing connections* (pp. 31–63). Needham Heights, MA: Allyn & Bacon.

Swan, A. M. (1993). Helping children who stutter: What teachers need to know. *Childhood Education, 69*(3), 138–141.

Tabors, P., & Snow, C. (1994). English as a second language in preschool programs. In F. Genessee (Ed.), *Educating second language children: The whole child, the whole curriculum, the whole community* (pp. 103–125). New York: Cambridge University Press.

Taberski, S. (2000). *On solid ground: Strategies for teaching reading K–3.* Portsmouth, NH: Heinemann.

Tabors, P. O. (1997). *One child, two languages.* Baltimore: Paul H. Brookes.

Taylor, B. M., Hanson, B. E., Justice Sewanson, K., & Watts, S. (1997). Helping struggling readers: Linking small group intervention with cross-age tutoring. *The Reading Teacher, 51*(3), 196–206.

Teale, W. H. (1988). Developmentally appropriate assessment of reading and writing in the early childhood classroom. *The Elementary School Journal, 89,* 2, 173–183.

Teale, W., & Sulzby, E. (1989). Emergent literacy. New perspectives. In D. Strickland & L. Morrow (Eds.), *Emerging literacy: Young children learn to read and write* (pp. 1–15). Newark, DE: International Reading Association.

Teale, W. H. (1988). Developmentally appropriate assessment of reading and writing in the early childhood classroom. *Elementary School Journal, 89*(2), 173–183.

Teberosky, A. (1990). The language young children write: Reflections on a learning situation. In Y. M. Goodman (Ed.), *How children construct literacy: Piagetian perspectives* (pp. 45–58). Newark, DE: International Reading Association.

Temple, C., Martinez, M., Yokota, J., & Naylor, A. (1998). *Children's books in children's hands.* Boston: Allyn & Bacon.

Temple, C. A., Nathan, R. G., Temple, F., & Burris, N. A. (1993). *The beginnings of writing.* Boston: Allyn & Bacon.

Thaler, M. (1990). *Fantastic phonics riddles.* Cleveland: OH: Modern Curriculum Press.

Thomas, W. P., & Collier, V. T. (1997, December). *School effectiveness for language minority students* (NCBE Resource Collection Series No. 9). Washington, DC: George Washington University.

Tierney, R. J. (1998). Literacy assessment reform: Shifting beliefs, principled possibilities, and emerging practices. *The Reading Teacher, 51*(5), 374–390.

Tompkins, G. E. (2003). *Literacy for the 21st century* (3rd ed.). Upper Saddle River, NJ: Merrill/ Prentice Hall.

Townshend, J. S., & Fu, D. (1998). A Chinese boy's joyful initiation into American literacy. *Language Arts, 75*(3), 193–201.

Truax, R. R., & Kretschmer, R. R. (1993). Finding new voices in the process of meeting the needs of all children. *Language Arts, 70*(7), 592–601.

Vacca, R., & Vacca, J. (1999). *Content area reading.* New York: HarperCollins.

Vacca, J. L., Vacca, R. T., & Gove, M. K. (1995). *Reading and learning to read.* New York: HarperCollins.

Veatch, J. (1968). *How to teach reading with children's books* (2nd ed.). New York: Citation.

Vygotsky, L. A. (1978). *Mind in society: The development of higher psychological processes* (M. Cole et al., Trans. & Ed.). Cambridge, MA: Harvard University Press.

Wade, S. E., & Moje, E. B. (2000). The role of text in classroom learning. In M. L. Kamil, P. B. Mosenthal, P. D. Pearson, & R. Barr (Eds.), *Handbook of reading research* (Vol. 3, pp. 609–628). Mahwah, NJ: Erlbaum.

Wagstaff, J. M. (1998). Building practical knowledge of letter-sound correspondences: A beginner's word wall and beyond. *The Reading Teacher, 51*(4), 298–304.

Walker-Dalhouse, D. (1993). Beginning reading and the African American child at risk. *Young Children, 49*(1), 24–28.

Weaver, C. (1996). *Teaching grammar in context.* Portsmouth, NH: Heinemann.

Wells, G. (1986). *The meaning makers: Children learning language and using language to learn.* Portsmouth, NH: Heinemann.

Wesson, K. A. (2001). The Volvo effect: Questioning standardized tests. *Young Children, 56*(2), 16–18.

Whitehurst, G. J., & Lonigan, C. J. (1998). Child development and emergent literacy. *Child Development, 68,* 848–872.

Whitehurst, G. J., & Lonigan, C. J. (2002). Emergent literacy: Development from prereaders to readers. In S. B. Neuman & D. K. Dickinson (Eds.), *Handbook of early literacy research* (pp. 3–10). New York: Guilford.

Whitin, P., & Whitin, D. J. (1997). *Inquiry at the window: Pursuing the wonders of learners.* Portsmouth, NH: Heinemann.

Wiencek, J., & O'Flahavan, J. F. (1994). From teacher-led to peer discussions about literature: Suggestions for making the shift. *Language Arts, 71*(7), 488–498.

Wilde, S. (1990). A proposal for a new spelling curriculum. *Elementary School Journal, 90*(3), 275–289.

Wilde, S. (1992). *You kan red this! Spelling and punctuation for whole language classrooms, K–6.* Portsmouth, NH: Heinemann.

Wilde, S. (1997). *What's a schwa sound anyway? A holistic guide to phonetics, phonics, and spelling.* Portsmouth, NH: Heinemann.

Wilson, C. (1996). Exploring the United States with Native American literature. *Primary Voices, 4*(3), 19–25.

Winter, S. M. (1997). "SMART" planning for inclusion. *Childhood Education, 73*(4), 98–104.

Wong Fillmore, L. (1991). When learning a second language means losing the first. *Early Childhood Research Quarterly, 6*(3), 323–346.

Wood, J. M., & Duke, N. K. (1997). Inside "Reading Rainbow": A spectrum of strategies for promoting literacy. *Language Arts, 74*(2), 95–106.

Yaden, D. B., Rowe, D. W., & MacGillivray, L. (2000). Emergent literacy: A matter (polyphony) of perspectives. In M. L. Kamil, P. B. Mosenthal, P. D. Pearson, & R. Barr (Eds.) *Handbook of reading research,* Vol. 5, pp 425–454. Mahwah, NJ: Lawrence Erlbaum Associates.

Yopp, H. K. (1992, May). Developing phonemic awareness in young children. *The Reading Teacher, 45*(9), 696–703.

Yopp, H. K. (1995). A test for assessing phonemic awareness in young children. *The Reading Teacher, 49*(1), 20–28.

Yopp, H. K., & Yopp, R. H. (2000). Supporting phonemic awareness development in the classroom. *The Reading Teacher, 54*(2), 130–143.

CHILDREN'S BOOKS

Aardema, V. (1975). *Why mosquitoes buzz in people's ears.* New York: Dial.

Alexander, M. (1982). *Maggie's moon.* New York: Dial.

Allard, H. (1974). *The stupids step out.* Boston: Houghton Mifflin.

Appelt, K. (2000). *Oh my baby, little one.* Harcourt.

Arnold, T. (1987). *No jumping on the bed!* New York: Dial.

Barlin, A., & Kalev, N. (1989). *Hello toes: Movement games for children.* Pennington, NJ: Dance Horizons Book, Princeton Book Co.

Bedard, M. (1997). *The divide.* New York: Doubleday.

Blood, C., & Link, M. (1976). *The goat in the rug.* New York: Aladdin.

Briggs, R. (1978). *The snowman.* New York: Random House.

Brown, M. (1945). *The important book.* New York: Harper.

Brown, M. (1947). *Stone soup.* New York: Scribner's.

Brown, R. (1981). *A dark, dark tale.* New York: Dial.

Burch, R. (1980). *Ida Early comes over the mountain.* New York: Avon.

Carle, E. (1974). *The very hungry caterpillar*. New York: Scholastic.

Carle, E. (1984). *The very busy spider*. New York: Philomel Books.

Carle, E. (1987). *Have you seen my cat?* New York: Scholastic.

Carle, E. (1997). *From head to toe*. New York: Scholastic.

Chinery, M. (1991). *Frog*. Mahwah, NJ: Troll Associates.

Christelow, E. (1989). *Five little monkeys jumping on the bed*. New York: Clarion.

Cleary, B. (1968). *Ramona the pest*. New York: Morrow.

Cleary, B. (1970). *Runaway Ralph*. New York: Morrow.

Cleary, B. (1977). *Ramona and her father*. New York: Morrow.

Cobb, V. (1989). *This place is wet* (B. Lavalle, Illus.). New York: Walker.

Cohen, M. (1977). *When will I read?* New York: Greenwillow.

Cole, J. (1997). *The magic schoolbus and the electric field trip* (B. Degen, Illus.). New York: Scholastic.

Cooney, B. (1982). *Miss Rumphius*. New York: Viking.

Cowley, J. (1990). *Mrs. Wishy-Washy*. San Diego: Wright Group.

Damon, E. (1995). *A kaleidoscope of kids*. New York: Dial Books for Young Readers.

Day, A. (1988). *Good dog Carl*. San Diego: Green Tiger Press.

DePaola, T. (1975). *Strega Nona: An old tale*. Upper Saddle River, NJ: Prentice Hall.

DePaola, T. (1985). *Watch out for the chicken feet in your soup*. New York: Aladdin Library.

Dixon, A. (1998). *Trick or treat*. New York: Scholastic.

Dixon, F. (1985). *The Hardy Boys: The great airport mystery*. New York: Grosset & Dunlap.

Drew, D. (1992). *Tadpole diary*. Barrington, IL: Rigby Education.

Dwyer, M. (1997). *Coyote in love*. Anchorage, AK: Alaska Northwest.

Emberly, B. (1968). *Drummer Hoff*. Upper Saddle River, NJ: Prentice Hall.

Feeney, S., & Fielding, A. (1989). *From sand to sea*. Honolulu: University of Hawaii Press.

Fowler, S. G. (1992). *Fog*. New York: Greenwillow.

Goble, P. (1983). *Star boy*. Scarsdale, NY: Bradbury.

Gomi, T. (1996). Who hid it? In *Literacy Place*. New York: Scholastic.

Gross, R. B. (1979). *Los músicos de brema*. New York: Scholastic.

Hamanaka, S. (1994). *All the colors of the earth*. New York: Morrow Junior Books.

Hayes, A. (1991). *Meet the orchestra*. San Diego: Harcourt Brace.

Heller, R. (1981). *Chickens aren't the only ones*. New York: Grosset & Dunlap.

Heller, R. (1990). *Merry-go-round*. New York: Grosset & Dunlap.

Heller, R. (1992). *How to hide an octopus*. New York: Platt & Munk.

Hest, A. (1995). *In the rain with Baby Duck*. Scott, Foresman.

Hopkinson, D. (1993). *Sweet Clara and the freedom quilt*. New York: Knopf.

Hudson, C. W. (1990). *Bright eyes, brown skin*. Orange, NJ: Just Us Books.

Hyland, H. (1999). *The wreck of the Ethie*. Peachtree.

Janovitz, M. (1996). *Bowl patrol!* New York: North-South Books.

Johnson, S. (1995). *Alphabet city*. New York: Viking.

Jonas, A. (1984). *The quilt*. New York: Greenwillow.

Joosse, B. M. (1991). *Mama, do you love me?* San Francisco: Chronicle.

Keats, E. J. (1962). *The snowy day*. New York: Viking.

Keats, E. J. (1982). *Clementina's cactus*. New York: Viking.

Kellogg, S. (1973). *The island of the Skog*. New York: Dial.

Knudson, K. (1992). *Muddigush*. New York: Macmillan.

Lacey, E. A. (1989). *The complete frog: A guide for the very young naturalist*. New York: Lothrop, Lee, & Shepard Books.

Lasky, K., & Knight, M. (1993). *Searching for Laura Ingalls*. New York: Aladdin.

Lawson, R. (1944). *Rabbit hill*. New York: Viking.

Leedy, L. (1994). *Fraction action*. New York: Holiday.

Lenski, L. (1946). *The little fire engine*. New York: Henry Z. Walck.

Levey, J. S. (Ed.). (1999). *The world almanac for kids*. Mahwah, NJ: K-III References Corp.

Lobel, A. (1970). *Frog and toad are friends*. New York: Harper.

Lobel, A. (1972). *Frog and toad together*. New York: Harper & Row.

Lobel, A. (1981). *On Market Street*. New York: Greenwillow.

Loomis, C. (1996). *Rush hour*. Boston: Houghton Mifflin.

MacLachan, P. (1985). *Sarah, plain and tall*. New York: Harper & Row.

MacLulich, C. (1996a). *Bats*. New York: Scholastic.

MacLulich, C. (1996b). *Frogs*. New York: Scholastic.

Marshall, E. (1981). *Three by the sea*. New York: D. C. Heath.

Marshall, J. (1997). *George and Martha: The complete stories of two best friends*. Boston: Houghton Mifflin.

Martin, B., Jr. (1983). *Brown bear, brown bear, what do you see?* New York: Holt, Rinehart and Winston.

Martin, B., & Archambault, J. (1989). *Here are my hands*. New York: Scholastic.

Martinson, D. (1975). *Real wild rice*. Duluth, MN: Anishinabe Reading Materials.

Mazer, A. (1991). *The salamander room*. New York: Knopf.

McCloskey, R. (1948). *Blueberries for Sal*. New York: Viking.

Medearis, A. S. (1997). *Rum-a-tum-tum*. New York: Holiday House.

Minarik, E. H. (1957). *Little bear*. New York: Harper & Row.

Miska, M. (1971). *Annie and the old one*. Boston: Little, Brown.

Mochizuki, K. (1993). *Baseball saved us*. New York: Lee & Low.

Munsch, R., & Kusugak, M. (1988). *A promise is a promise*. Toronto: Annick Press.

Murphy, J. (1993). *Humpity-bump!* Glenview, IL: Scott, Foresman.

O'Neill, M. (1961). *Hailstones and halibut bones*. New York: Doubleday.

Ormerod, J. (1981). *Sunshine*. New York: Lothrop, Lee & Shepard Books.

Ormerod, J. (1982). *Moonlight*. New York: Lothrop, Lee & Shepard Books.

Owens, M. B. (1988). *A caribou alphabet*. Brunswick, ME: Dog Ear Press.

Oxenbury, H. (1982). *Good night, good morning*. New York: Dial.

Parents Magazine read-aloud originals. New York: Bantam.

Parish, P. (1963). *Amelia Bedelia*. New York: Harper & Row.

Patterson, F. (1985). *Koko's kitten*. New York: Scholastic.

Potter, B. (1902). *Peter Rabbit*. London: Warne.

Prelutsky, J. (1976). *Nightmares: Poems to trouble your sleep*. New York: Greenwillow.

Rattigan, J. K. (1993). *Dumpling soup*. Boston: Little, Brown.

Rey, H. A. (1941). *Curious George*. Boston: Houghton Mifflin.

Rey, H. A. (1952). *Curious George rides a bike*. Boston: Houghton Mifflin.

Root, P. (2001). *Rattletrap car*. Candlewick.

Rohman, E. (1994). *Time flies*. New York: Crown.

Royston, A. (1991). *What's inside my body?* New York: Doring Kindersley.

Scieszka, J. (1995). *Math curse*. New York: Viking.

Seuss, Dr. (Geisel, T. S.). (1957). *The cat in the hat*. New York: Random House.

Seuss, Dr. (1996). *A hatful of Seuss*. New York: Random House.

Shahan, S. (1997). *The changing caterpillar*. Katonah, NY: Richard C. Owen.

Simmons, J. (1998). *Come along, Daisy!* Little, Brown.

Simont, M. (2001). *The stray dog*. HarperCollins Juvenile Books.

Spier, P. (1961). *The fox went out on a chilly night*. Garden City, NY: Doubleday.

Spier, P. (1977). *Noah's ark*. Garden City, NY: Doubleday.

Stamm, C. (1990). *Three strong women: A tall tale from Japan*. New York: Viking.

Steig, W. (1982). *Doctor DeSoto*. New York: Farrar, Straus & Giroux.

Steiner, B. (1988). *Whale brother*. New York: Walker & Company.

Steptoe, J. (1984). *The story of Jumping Mouse: A Native American legend*. New York: Lothrop, Lee & Shepard.

Stevenson, J. (1972). *The bear who had no place to go*. New York: Harper & Row.

Titherington, J. (1986). *Pumpkin pumpkin*. New York: Greenwillow.

Viorst, J. (1972). *Alexander and the terrible, horrible, no good, very bad day*. New York: Atheneum.

Viorst, J. (1974). *Rosie and Michael*. New York: Antheneum.

Walsh, J. P. (1992). *When Grandma came*. New York: Penguin.

Watanabe, S. (1980). *What a good lunch!* New York: N. Collins.

Waterton, B. (1978). *A salmon for Simon*. Hartford, CT: Connecticut Printers.

Wells, R. (1997). *Bunny cakes*. Dial Books for Young Readers.

Wheeler, C. (1982). *Marmalade's snowy day*. New York: Knopf.

White, E. B. (1952). *Charlotte's web*. New York: Harper & Row.

Wiesner, D. (1991). *Tuesday*. New York: Clarion.

Wilder, L. I. (1953). *Little house on the prairie*. New York: Harper & Row.

Wiseman, B. (1978). *Morris has a cold*. New York: Dodd Mead.

Wisniewski, D. (1996). *Golem*. New York: Clarion.

Wolf, S. (1992). *Peter's truck*. Morton Grove, IL: Whitman.

Wood, A. (1984). *The napping house*. New York: Harcourt Brace.

Wood, A. (1985). *King Bidgood's in the bathtub*. San Diego: Harcourt Brace Jovanovich.

Yashima, T. (1955). *Crow boy*. New York: Viking.

Zion, G. (1956). *Harry the dirty dog*. New York: Harper & Row.

CHILDREN'S BOOK SERIES

Parents Magazine read-aloud originals. New York and Milwaukee: Parents Magazine Press.

Bank Street ready-to-read books. New York: Bantam.

Children's Press new true books. Chicago: Children's Press.

Choose your own adventure series. New York: Bantam.

Dell yearling books. New York: Dell.

Dial easy-to-read books. New York: Dial Books for Young Children.

Farley, W. *The black stallion*. New York: Random House. (Sixteen more books in set)

Hoban, R. Frances series. New York: Harper & Row.

Keene, C. Nancy Drew series. Wanderer Books, Pocket Books, Grosset & Dunlap.

Osborne, M. P. The Magic Treehouse series. New York: Random House.

Random House picturebook readers. New York: Random House.

Sobol, D. J. Encyclopedia Brown series (1963–1999). Madison, WI: Demco Media.

READING PROGRAMS

Houghton Mifflin. (1999). *Invitations to literacy.* Boston.

A new view. (1993). New York: McGraw-Hill.

Bolton, F., Green, R., Pollack, J., Scarfee, B., & Snowball, D. (1986). *Bookshelf stage 1: Teacher's resource book.* New York: Multimedia International (U.K.) Ltd.

Bookworm. (1991). Boston: Houghton Mifflin.

Celebrate reading. (1997). Glenview, IL: Scott, Foresman.

McGraw-Hill Literature Anthology. (2000). New York: McGraw-Hill.

Open Court Reading. (2002). McGraw-Hill.

Scholastic. (1996). *Literacy place.* New York.

Scott Foresman. (2000). *Reading.*

Scott Foresman. (1993). *Celebrate reading, professional handbook.* Glenview, IL: Scott, Foresman.

Silver Burdett Ginn. (1997). *Literature works.* Needham Heights, MA.

Sundance Kid's Corner Science Explorers books. Littleton, MA: Sundance Publishing.

Teachers' Guides

Hurst, C. O. (1990). *Once upon a time . . . An encyclopedia for successfully using literature with young children.* Allen, TX: DLM Publishing.

Hurst, C. O. (1992). *Literature-based thematic units.* Allen, TX: DLM Publishing.

Project Construct National Center. (1995). *Constructivism in education.* Columbia: Missouri Department of Elementary and Secondary Education.

The Wright Group. (1990). *The story box.* Bothell, WA.

COMPUTER SOFTWARE FOR KIDS

Apple early language connections. Cupertino, CA: Apple Computer.

Broderbund's Living Books. (1991). *Grandma and me.* Broderbund Software, Inc.

Broderbund's Living Books. (1992). *Arthur's teacher trouble.* Broderbund Software, Inc.

Broderbund's Living Books. (1993). New kid on the block. Broderbund Software, Inc.

Broderbund's Living Books. (1993). Tortoise and hare. Broderbund Software, Inc.

Broderbund's Living Books. (1994). Little monster. Broderbund Software, Inc.

Broderbund's Living Books. (1994). The ruff's bone. Broderbund Software, Inc.

Broderbund's Living Books. (1995). Dr. Seuss's ABC. Broderbund Software, Inc.

Kidspiration. (2001). Inspiration Software, Inc.

Kid pix deluxe 3. (1998). Broderbund Software, Inc.

Kid Works Deluxe. (1995). Torrance, CA: Davidson & Associates.

Larimer, N., & Hermann, M. A. Mickey's Magic Reader. Cupertino, CA: Apple Computer, Inc.

Literature Enrichment Activities for Paperbacks. (1984). Amelia Bedelia. Sundance Publishers & Distributors.

Make-A-Book. (1993). Gainesville, FL: Teacher Support Software.

Millie's math house, Edmark. 800-426-0856.

Once Upon a Time—Journey Through Nature. (1994). New Haven, CT: Compu-Teach.

Storybook Weaver DELUXE. (1994). Minneapolis: MECC.

The media experience. (1991). Boston: Houghton Mifflin.

The playroom, Broderbund, 800-521-6263.

Wiggleworks Story Pack 2. (1995). New York: Scholastic New Media.

CHILDREN'S MAGAZINES

Highlights for Children, Inc. *Highlights for Children.* Columbus, OH.

National Wildlife Federation. *Ranger Rick.* Washington, DC.

Instructional Reading Materials

Clay, M. M. (1972). *Sand—The concepts about print test.* Auckland, New Zealand: Heinemann.

Clay, M. M. (1979). *Stones—The concepts about print test.* Auckland, New Zealand: Heinemann.

Rigby Education. (1984). *Mrs. Wishy Washy.* San Diego: Wright Group.

Scholastic hello reading books. New York: Scholastic.

REFERENCE MATERIALS

McWhirter, N. (1999). *Guinness book of world records.* New York: Sterling.

Parker, B. M. (1969). *Golden Book Encyclopedia.* Chicago: Goldencraft.

Peterson, R. T. (1998). *Field guide to the birds.* Boston: Houghton Mifflin.

Wittles, H. (1996). *Clear and simple thesaurus dictionary.* New York: Grosset & Dunlap.

Magazines for Adults

Booklinks. Aurora, IL: American Library Association.

The New Advocate. Boston: Christopher-Gordon.

INDEX